Alfred Hermann Fried

Brill's Specials in Modern History

Series Editor

Aristotle Kallis (*Keele University*)

VOLUME 5

The titles published in this series are listed at *brill.com/smh*

Alfred Hermann Fried. Photograph by Scherl/Süddeutsche Zeitung

Alfred Hermann Fried

Peace Activist and Nobel Prize Laureate

By

Petra Schönemann-Behrens

Translated by

Edward T. Larkin and Thomas B. Ahrens

BRILL

LEIDEN | BOSTON

Cover illustration: linocut of Alfred Hermann Fried by the contemporary artist Klaus Schiesewitz of Bremen, Germany (2021).

Library of Congress Cataloging-in-Publication Data

Names: Schönemann-Behrens, Petra, 1962- author.
Title: Alfred Hermann Fried : peace activist and Nobel Prize Laureate / by
   Petra Schönemann-Behrens ; translated by Edward T. Larkin and Thomas B.
   Ahrens.
Other titles: Alfred H. Fried. English
Description: Leiden ; Boston : Brill, 2022. | Series: Brill's specials in
   modern history, 2468-578X ; volume 5 | Includes bibliographical
   references and index.
Identifiers: LCCN 2021046461 (print) | LCCN 2021046462 (ebook) | ISBN
   9789004470156 (hardback) | ISBN 9789004470378 (ebook)
Subjects: LCSH: Fried, Alfred H. (Alfred Hermann), 1864–1921. | Peace
   movements–Europe–History. | Pacifists–Austria–Biography. | Nobel
   Prize winners–Austria–Biography.
Classification: LCC JZ5540.2.F74 S3613 2022 (print) | LCC JZ5540.2.F74
   (ebook) | DDC 327.1/72092 [B]–dc23/eng/20211020
LC record available at https://lccn.loc.gov/2021046461
LC ebook record available at https://lccn.loc.gov/2021046462

Typeface for the Latin, Greek, and Cyrillic scripts: "Brill". See and download: brill.com/brill-typeface.

ISSN 2468-578X
ISBN 978-90-04-47015-6 (hardback)
ISBN 978-90-04-47037-8 (e-book)

Copyright 2022 by Petra Schönemann-Behrens. Published by Koninklijke Brill NV, Leiden, The Netherlands. Koninklijke Brill NV incorporates the imprints Brill, Brill Nijhoff, Brill Hotei, Brill Schöningh, Brill Fink, Brill mentis, Vandenhoeck & Ruprecht, Böhlau Verlag and V&R Unipress.
Koninklijke Brill NV reserves the right to protect this publication against unauthorized use. Requests for re-use and/or translations must be addressed to Koninklijke Brill NV via brill.com or copyright.com.

This book is printed on acid-free paper and produced in a sustainable manner.

Contents

Foreword IX
Preface X
Acknowledgments XIV

1 **Childhood and Youth** 1
   1 The Early Years 1
   2 Apprenticeship with a Bookseller and Fried's First Experiences of Pacifism 9

2 **The Berlin Years 1884–1903** 21
   1 From Apprentice Bookseller to Publisher 21
   2 Alfred H. Fried and Company 26
   3 The Path to the Peace Movement 31
   4 Experiments 57
      4.1 *Fried's Hygienic Trash Collection and Removal Apparatus* 60
      4.2 *The Self-Dating Envelope* 60
      4.3 *An Election Atlas* 61
      4.4 *Supplemental Encyclopedia* 61
   5 The Conference at The Hague 1899 66
      5.1 *The Founding of the Friedens-Warte in 1899* 81
   6 Consolidation Attempts around 1900 84
      6.1 *Esperanto* 90
   7 Flight from Berlin (1903) 96

3 **The Vienna Years, 1903–1915** 103
   1 A Reluctant Return Home 103
   2 Fried, von Suttner, and the Austrian Peace Society 111
   3 Work as a Journalist to 1907 119
   4 Impulses from The Hague 126
   5 *The Foundations of Revolutionary Pacifism*, 1908 132
   6 Integration and Recognition 140
   7 The Association of International Understanding 148
   8 Nobel Peace Prize in 1911 and Honorary Doctorate in 1913 158
   9 Before the Great War 171

4 **In Swiss Exile 1914/15–1919**   185
   1   The Move to Berne   185
   2   1916: In the Crossfire of the Critics   195
   3   Swiss Exile from 1917 to the End of the War   203
   4   After the War – the Final Months in Switzerland   210

5 **Everywhere a Foreigner**   222
   1   Back to Vienna, via Munich   222
   2   Final Works and Plans   229
   3   Obituaries and Testimonials   236

6 **Survivors and Successors**   243
   1   Therese Fried   243
   2   Fried and German Pacifism after 1921   250

7 *Die Friedens-Warte*   255
   1   The First Years 1899–1904   255
   2   Consolidation Phase 1904–1909   261
   3   Period of Growth, 1910–1914   264
   4   War Censorship and the Path into Exile   268
   5   *Die Friedens-Warte* in Swiss Exile   272
   6   The *Friedens-Warte* after the War, 1918–1919   275
   7   The Conflict over Succession, 1921–1924   278
   8   The *Friedens-Warte* under Hans Wehberg, 1924–1962   282
   9   A New Beginning in 1974   286

   Epilogue   287
   Appendix 1: To My Beloved Wife   294
   Appendix 2: Program of Revolutionary Pacifism, 1908   297
   Bibliography   299
   Index   317

Foreword

The Austrians Bertha von Suttner and Alfred H. Fried were leading figures in the European and international peace movement in the decades preceding the First World War. Their great merits were recognized with the award of the Nobel Peace Prize in 1905 and 1911, respectively. Fried was von Suttner's closest collaborator who had been inspired by her, just as she had inspired her friend Alfred Nobel to leave a legacy for 'champions of peace'.

While there are many biographies of the Baroness (several in English, or English translation), until recently, there were none of Fried, not even in German. The best one, by Petra Schönemann-Behrens, was published in 2011, coinciding with the 100th anniversary of his Nobel prize. I am delighted that, ten years later, it is now appearing in an English translation. Like so many peace activists of the period, Fried was an Esperantist but he would concede that today English is the undisputed world language. For the first time, readers around the world will be able to learn of the fascinating life of a true pioneer – the founder of peace journalism, author of the first peace encyclopedia, editor of the world's best peace periodical, and much else.

Professors Edward Larkin and Thomas B. Ahrens are to be congratulated for their translation of this excellent biography. Theirs has been a labor of love – as was so much of the tireless efforts of von Suttner and Fried themselves. Fried died in May 1921; events to commemorate the centenary of his passing in 2021 were either cancelled or held virtually because of the pandemic. It is therefore all the more pleasing that this solid biography is appearing at this time. It should find many readers and will greatly contribute to make its subject much better known and appreciated around the world. Fried's central message – that the world needs to be better organized, based on a just international legal order, and that armed peace is no peace – has not lost any of its relevance in a world where survival is gravely threatened by nuclear deterrence.

Dr. Peter van den Dungen
Bertha von Suttner Peace Institute, The Hague
July 2021

Preface

The idea for this book arose in 1984 when I was writing my master's thesis on the novel *Die Waffen nieder!* by Bertha von Suttner. As I did background research on von Suttner's life and her influence, I kept finding references to the name of Alfred Hermann Fried, who at one point was portrayed as her secretary and occasionally as an equal or even fellow leader in the campaign for peace. But he was also sometimes viewed as her counterpart.

Although I did not do any further research for a couple of years, I followed the book market in the expectation that Bertha von Suttner's great popularity as well as the issues relating to the policies of peace that suffused the 1980s would sooner or later lead to an exhaustive biography of Alfred Fried. However, my expectations were not fulfilled. In addition to the biographies that already existed on Georg Friedrich Nicolai,[1] Ludwig Quidde,[2] and Baron d'Estournelles de Constant,[3] there were new works on Bertha von Suttner,[4] Otto Umfrid[5] and Count Kessler,[6] but research on Fried remained nonexistent. In 1987, the only works on Fried that I came across were the older essays by Hans Wehberg,[7] the unfortunately worthless, biographical work of Doris Dauber,[8] and a short biographical sketch by Dieter Riesenberger in the volume *Wider den Krieg*[9] (Against War). A year later a short biography of Fried by Wolfgang

---

1 Wolf Zuelzer, *Der Fall Nicolai* (Frankfurt a. M., 1981).
2 Utz-Friedebert Taube, *Ludwig Quidde. Ein Beitrag zur Geschichte des demokratischen Gedankens in Deutschland* (Kallmünz, 1963).
3 Adolf Wild, Baron d'Estournelles de Constant (1852–1924). *Das Wirken eines Friedensnobelpreisträgers für die deutsch-französische Verständigung und europäische Einigung* (Hamburg, 1973).
4 Brigitte Hamann, *Bertha von Suttner. Ein Leben für den Frieden* (Munich, 1986). And later Harald Steffahn, *Bertha von Suttner* (Reinbek bei Hamburg, 1998).
5 Christoph Mauch / Tobias Brenner, *Für eine Welt ohne Krieg. Otto Umfrid und die Anfänge der Friedensbewegung*. With a foreword by Walter Jens (Schönaich, 1987).
6 Peter Grupp, *Harry Graf Kessler 1868–1937. Eine Biographie* (Munich, 1995).
7 Hans Wehberg, "Alfred H. Fried," in *Die Führer der deutschen Friedensbewegung (1890 bis 1923)*, ed. Hans Wehberg (Leipzig, 1924).
8 Doris Dauber, *Alfred Hermann Fried und sein Pazifismus* (Diss., Leipzig, 1924).
9 Dieter Riesenberger, "Alfred Hermann Fried (1864–1921). Die Überwindung des Krieges durch zwischenstaatliche Organisation," in *Wider den Krieg. Große Pazifisten von Immanuel Kant bis Heinrich Böll*, eds. Christiane Rajewsky, Dieter Riesenberger (Munich, 1987), 54ff.

Stenke[10] appeared in the Nobel Prize edition of Michael Neumann. But after that there was nothing more.[11]

Fried still belonged to the "diappeared people," "to the unsatisfactory stick figures or disembodied spirits" as Sandi E. Cooper referred to them in her book *Patriotic Pacifism* in 1991.[12] To change this situation, I began my own research project in 1999 and five years later submitted my results in the form of a historical-biographical dissertation at the University of Bremen.

Why Alfred H. Fried deserves special attention may be explained first by the fact that there is hardly a book about German pacifism of the imperial era that does not quote from his works and second that any engagement with the intentions and aims of pacifism in these decades always necessitates an engagement with Fried's theories. The fact that he was apparently acknowledged as a leading pacifist in German-speaking countries and yet never held a leading position in the German Peace Society (Deutsche Friedensgesellschaft) makes the question of Fried's personality and his career all the more interesting.

This book will chronicle the life of Alfred H. Fried from his familial roots in Hungary's liberal Jewish bourgeoisie, his first experiences in school and his subsequent education, the period of futile attempts to establish himself as a publisher and journalist in Berlin, his gradual, successful professional establishment in Vienna, his prominent yet vulnerable position in Swiss exile, and his death in post-war Vienna.

Fried, the eldest son of an impoverished Jewish family, was an academic failure at the *Gymnasium* (College Preparatory School); he was industrious and ambitious, but at the same time he was also very spirited and not very adaptable. Only shortly before the First World War, at well over 40 years of age, did he achieve the social advancement that he sought. But the outbreak of the war destroyed all hopes and forced him to emigrate to Switzerland. When he died in the Rudolf Hospital in Vienna after the war, he was destitute and both physically and emotionally homeless; he seemed to have worked in vain as the world grew further distant from his ideas of peace than ever before. There were a few people who preserved his memory even in the turbulent Weimar period, but

---

10   Wolfgang Stenke, "Alfred Hermann Fried – ein Pazifist der Tat," in *Der Friedens-Nobelpreis von 1901 bis heute*, ed. Michael Neumann, vol. 2, *Der Friedens-Nobelpreis von 1905 bis 1916* (Zug, 1988), 168–179.

11   Two years after I completed my dissertation, which was published online through the University of Bremen, another biography of Fried was published: Walter Göhring, *Verdrängt und vergessen. Friedensnobelpreisträger Alfred Hermann Fried* (Vienna, 2006).

12   Sandi E. Cooper, *Patriotic Pacifism. Waging War on War in Europe 1815–1914* (New York/Oxford, 1991), 9.

his ideas seemed to have lost all relevance at least from the time of the Second World War and the beginning of the Cold War in the 1950s.

Today, however, a different picture is emerging, one that brings to life many of Fried's insights that his contemporaries mocked and thought unattainable. The economic and, indeed, political integration of Europe, which has been accompanied by a reduction and revaluation of armies, very much approximates Fried's ideas about the development of Europe. Likewise, the scientific conception of the idea of peace that he advanced has not only become a reality in the development of international law, but, since the 1970s, it has also influenced research on peace and conflict resolution as well as on historical research on peace, both of which can claim Fried as one of their progenitors.[13]

Fried may set an example for us today. He advocated for peace journalism and he sought to have peace societies establish and disseminate clearly defined concepts and positions.

But not least of all, it is the unconditionality with which he also voiced his opinion, even in times of war, against a world "in the green fog"[14] that connects him to the long chain of freedom fighters from the 1848 revolution to the resistance fighters under National Socialism to the individuals and groups persecuted in recent decades for their "different opinions." When Sandi Cooper writes, "To be a pacifist in the political culture of Wilhelminian Germany was akin to professing communism in Cold War America," one recalls the resurgent discrimination against peace forums and groups in the 1980s in Germany. It is precisely in this context that Fried should (and will) remain a possible role model for our contemporaries.

Even a hundred years later, many of the discussions that the pacifists of that era participated in have not lost their relevance. The question of the "correct" kind of response and of the possible deployment of the German military is just as controversial now as 1) the long desired improvements within the United Nations, 2) the structure of the European constitution, and 3) the extent to which the proposition of absolute nonviolence should be generally binding on pacifists.[15]

---

13 This opinion is also shared by Friedrich Karl-Scheer who urges that one should take another look at the accusation of "methodological syncretism" (which had been leveled at Fried) in light of the modern, interdisciplinary, and goal-oriented scholarship on peace. Cf. his *Die deutsche Friedensgesellschaft (1892–1933)*, 2nd, improved ed. (Frankfurt a. M., 1983), 133ff.

14 This expression, which may have originated with Orson Welles, was used repeatedly by Fried in his diaries to characterize the war-time atmosphere that confounded the thinking and behavior of the population. Cf. *Kriegs-Tagebuch*, I, 217 and IV, 213.

15 Cf., among others, the article "Streit in der Friedensbewegung: Frieden schaffen mit Waffen?" *ZivilCourage* 1, (February, 2004): 4ff.

The recent events in the Middle East have especially shown the importance both of continuing these discussions and of the necessity to search for truly effective notions of peace; but, above all, they have shown the need for effective means to create conditions that are conducive to peace. What Fried wrote in his war diary on July 28, 1915 still applies today: "A look into the past shows us such terrible and delusional things that we have no choice but to turn our gaze to the future to find consolation. The future then may [...] provide us with the kind of understanding that we have thus far failed to apply to the affairs of the world."[16]

Petra Schönemann-Behrens
September 2011

16   Fried, *Kriegs-Tagebuch* I, 471.

Acknowledgments

At this point, I would like to once again thank all those who provided me with assistance from 1999-2004 as I was doing research for this book in archives and libraries, in particular, Bernadine Pejovic (Völkerbundarchiv - League of Nations Archive - Geneva), Gregor Pickro (Bundesarchiv - Federal Archive - Koblenz), Anne C. Kjeling (Nobelarchiv - Nobel Archive - Oslo) and Peter Grupp (Politisches Archiv des Auswärtigen Amtes - The Political Archive of the Foreign Office).

I especially want to thank my dissertation advisor, Karl Holl, and Dieter Senghaas, who facilitated contact with the Berghof Foundation without whose generous subsidies I would not have been able to travel to many important archives.

Two people are primarily responsible for the publication of this book: Peter van den Dungen, who enthusiastically and repeatedly urged me to look for a publisher and who ultimately was personally involved in the search; and Anne Rüffer, who accepted the manuscript and whose great care and encouragement ensured that the dissertation was appropriately revised into a book-length biography.

CHAPTER 1

Childhood and Youth

1   The Early Years

On April 17, 1896, Berta Fried wrote to her son, Alfred, who was living in Berlin at the time: "One cannot deny that Hungarian blood flows through your veins."[1] In fact, both of Fried's parents came from Hungary: his father, Samuel Fried, was born in 1833 in the part of Hungary known as Szigetvár, and he most likely came to Vienna and assisted business clients in legal matters (Geschäftsagent) before he married. Fried's mother, Berta Engel, was born into a liberal, artistically-minded Jewish merchant family in Budapest in 1842. Her brother Moritz would later found the successful newspaper *Wiener Salonblatt*, and another brother, Sigismund, eventually became the ballet master in Schöppenstedt near Brunswick, Germany.

For several years following the death of their parents, Berta's younger sister, Katharina (Kathinka), lived in Vienna with her brother Moritz. While she was training to become a singer, she met the poet Ludwig Albert Ganghofer[2] at Vienna's Burgtheater; they were married in 1882.[3] In a biography of Ludwig Ganghofer that was presented to him on his fiftieth birthday, the poet Vincenz Chiavacci, a friend of the couple, described Berta's sister "as a small, agile figure. A pair of cheerful eyes – just the type of a well-formed Viennese woman – laughed from the round, flourishing face, beneath blond braids."[4] It was probably not an oversight that the poet forgot to mention Katharina's Hungarian heritage, as well as her Jewish background.[5]

---

1   Berta Fried to Fried, April 17, 1896. Nachlass Fried, Box 30.
2   Dr. Ludwig Albert Ganghofer, (1855–1920). A regional author who is still read today: *Der Herrgottschnitzer von Ammergau*, 1880; *Der Klosterjäger*, 1892; *Das Schweigen im Walde*, 1899. On Ganghofer, see *Ludwig Ganghofer 1855–1920: Ein Symposium über Leben und Werk,* ed. Egon Guggemos (Kaufbeurer Geschichtsblätter, Sonderheft 8, 1896).
3   The wedding took place on May 7, 1882 in the Augustinerkirche in Vienna.
4   Vincenz Chiavacci, *Ludwdig Ganghofer. Ein Bild seines Lebens und Schaffens* (Stuttgart, 1905), 63.
5   There is no reference to a relationship between Alfred Hermann Fried and Ganghofer in the latter's autobiography *Lebenslauf eines Optimisten*, 3 vol, 1909–1911 (Munich, 1966) nor in biographies about him. Katharina Engel is only described as a "real Viennese girl;" there is no mention of the fact that she was a Hungarian Jew. Only the complete repression of this fact makes it possible for recent Ganghofer research to acknowledge his apparently less than well-developed antisemitism. See, for example, Thomas Kraft, "Ludwig Ganghofer – Politische Dimensionen eines Bestsellerautors," in Guggemos, *Ganghofer*, 39ff.

© PETRA SCHÖNEMANN-BEHRENS, 2022 | DOI:10.1163/9789004470378_002

After they were married in Budapest in 1863, Samuel and Berta Fried moved to Vienna, accompanied by the Engel family. They lived at 4 Radetzkystraße in the third district (Landstraße). At this time, Samuel dealt in straw and felt hats and presumably had a pretty good income. Their first child was born on November 11, 1864: Alfred Hermann. Berta was only 23 years old, and her husband was 31. Berta gave birth to eight more children after Alfred, but for several years he remained the only son: after the births of Gisela (1865), Pauline (1867), Charlotte (1869) and Betti (1871), Alfred got his first brother in Otto Emil (1873), who was followed by two other brothers Carl Theodor (1876) and David Leopold (1879). The last child, Sidonie, was born in 1880, on the 47th birthday of Fried's father.[6]

Throughout his life, Alfred Hermann Fried remained close to his family; as the oldest child, he had to help provide for the family from an early age. Several of his siblings took ill or died prematurely: Alfred's sister Gisela, who was not quite a year younger than he, fell victim to meningitis at 18 months. At age seven Charlotte succumbed to an illness that the death registry of the Jewish community in Vienna characterized as "the gangrenous croup." His sister Betti died in 1885 at the age of 14 of a congenital heart defect, the symptoms of which had caused the family great concern even in the years before her death.[7]

Two of Fried's brothers were also not healthy: Carl, who had a congenital heart defect, like his sister Betti, would be weak and sickly; he remained dependent on the family for help and support until his death in 1904 at 28 years old. Leopold suffered from epilepsy, and he too was initially unable to live independently of the family. Otto, the second-oldest son, quickly turned out to be the black sheep of the family. Even before he turned 20, he was arrested a number of times for theft and embezzlement and was given a harsh prison sentence. Long before his father's death in 1900, Alfred became the principal family member with whom the Fried children could discuss their concerns, particularly his two younger brothers, but the other family members as well.

Alfred spent his early years in the Landstraße district. Little is known about his life at this time; apart from his own posthumously published memoir of his youth (*Jugenderinnerung*),[8] there is an unpublished recollection by Siegfried

---

6 Just as the spelling varies between Moriz and Moritz (and Gisela and Gisella), so too do the documents show variation between Sidonie and Sidonia. She herself signed her letters as Toni.
7 Most of the dates are taken from the birth and death registers located in the religious community in Vienna. They are supplemented by the extant registration forms as well as written documentation provided by Ms. Weiss, the head of the registration office of the Jewish religious community.
8 Alfred H. Fried, *Jugenderinnerungen* (Berlin 1925). *Der Völkerfriede. Beihefte zur Friedens-Warte*, no. 1.

CHILDHOOD AND YOUTH

Frankl, Fried's childhood friend and rival.[9] The author of this current biography of Fried was able to discover a privately owned, earlier version of Fried's memoir. In many respects it is more detailed than the published version.[10] It forms a part of the autobiography that Fried had planned and begun in 1920; it was to be published under the title *Dreißig Jahre Pazifismus* (Thirty Years of Pacifism) and would describe his life from the perspective of a pacifist. In his memoir Fried depicts how he had played "Prussian and Frenchman"[11] with his playmates during the Franco-Prussian War. But he also explains that the events of the war were not enthusiastically embraced in his parental home: "As a result of the conversations of the adults and the pictures in the magazines, the events of the war penetrated my childlike soul. I could tell from my parents' horror that something terrible must have occurred that day when they talked in my presence about what they had heard or read; [...] this first impression may well have been decisive for my subsequent thinking and sensibilities."[12]

The actual roots of his later turn toward pacifism may well lie in the liberal, humanistic education he received in his parents' home. His mother, Berta Fried-Engel, was raised in a liberal, Jewish middle-class home in Budapest where the principal family interests lay in the artistic-literary realm and in the aversion to any form of militarism. Not much is known about the family and outlook of Samuel Fried,[13] but his views were likely not too different from those of his wife. In any case, Berta might have exerted greater influence on the children than her husband, at least in the first years of their marriage, as he was focused on improving the family's social and economic situation. A hat seller, he was, according to later indications, rarely at home. When his business failed, the broken and introverted man was no longer in a position to provide for his family; only through Berta's indefatigable energy and her brother Moritz's financial assistance was the family able to keep itself afloat.

Early on, however, Fried's father had seemed successful. In the fall of 1870 the family moved out of the apartment in Radetzkystrasse to Hirschengasse 45 in the Viennese district Ober-Döbling,[14] a suburb of large villas. Alfred, who was now required to attend school, was sent to a private school in Döbling that

---

9   Paul Franken (actually Siegfried Frankl), "Altes und Neues vom 'Friedens-Fried,'" Zum zehnten Todestag von Alfred H. Fried" (Berlin, 1931). Manuscript in Nachlass Fried, Box 92.
10 Typewritten manuscript with a handwritten title "Biographische Skizze Alfred H. Fried," around 1918. Privately held by Trude Simonsohn, now in Nachlass Fried.
11 Fried, *Jugenderinnerungen*, 5.
12 Fried, *Jugenderinnerungen*, 6.
13 There are virtually no documents referring to the lineage of Fried's father in the Nachlass.
14 Fried specifies the fall of 1871 in his *Jugenderinnerungen*. But the correct date is likely the fall of 1870, as noted in the biographical sketch, since the birth registry of his sister Betti in April 1871 lists Hirschengasse 45 as the place of birth.

was connected to a boarding school. He also had a private tutor who taught him about the history of the battle of Troy, the heroic deeds of Achilles, and the wanderings of Odysseus.[15] For the young Alfred, the significance of his time in Döbling can be seen in a letter to his third wife Therese: "I spent my childhood in Döbling, perhaps the most beautiful years of my life. The first floor in the house at the corner of Schegargasse and Hirschengasse is where I dreamed the golden dreams of childhood."[16] But the idyllic life did not last long. In the fall of 1873, Alfred and his three young sisters, along with his father and their very pregnant mother, had to leave the apartment and find new quarters in Leopoldstadt. He later noted: "I was nine years old when my parents moved to the city, and I completed the last year of elementary school there."[17] It is a statement that does not quite presage what this move would mean for the Frieds.

Up to this point and indeed beyond, the story of the Fried family was typical of Jewish life in Vienna: they did as well as ". . . nearly all the Jewish residents in the Austrian capital, the immigrants or the children of immigrants who had been drawn to this city, after the Austrian government had lifted the traditional settlement restrictions for Jews during the revolution of 1848."[18]

The immigration took place in three waves.[19] The first wave, which complemented the immigration of those Jews who came to Vienna from Bohemia and Moravia as a result of the imperial Tolerance Patent (1781), consisted of Czech Jews arriving in the 1850s and 1860s. This wave was quickly surpassed by a second large wave from Hungary; a third came from Galicia. The Engel family, as well as Berta and Samuel Fried, were part of the second wave. Nearly a quarter of the Jews living in Vienna originally came from Hungary, most of them were from Budapest, which its detractors labeled "Judapest" because of the extraordinarily high number of Jews living there (25%).

The majority of Jews offered a similar reason for their move to Vienna: as the capital of the Dual Monarchy and as a supranational, cosmopolitan center of the Habsburg Empire, Vienna presented them with the best chance for professional and social advancement. But there was still another reason: in addition to its role as the Imperial City, Vienna was also considered, even after 1866, a thoroughly German city, "the last bastion of German culture in southern Central Europe."[20] Besides the economic reason, there were also cultural and

---

15 Fried, *Jugenderinnerungen*, 7.
16 Fried to Therese Frankl, March 10, 1903, Nachlass Fried, Box 92.
17 Fried, "Biographische Skizze," 1.
18 Marsha L. Rozenblit, *Die Juden Wiens 1867-1914. Assimlation und Identität* (Vienna, Cologne, Graz, 1988), 20.
19 In reference to this and to what follows, see Rozenblit, *Juden Wiens*, 20ff.
20 Steven Beller, *Wien und die Juden 1867–1938* (Vienna, Cologne, Weimar, 1993), 181.

CHILDHOOD AND YOUTH 5

ideological reasons to move to Vienna. And at first the hopes of many immigrants for a better and freer life in the metropolis seemed to be realized.

In 1867, three years after Alfred's birth, the internal reforms that were carried out as part of the Austro-Hungarian Compromise brought full equality to the Jews. In one stroke, the liberal government removed all the existing restrictions on political and basic civil rights as well as on professional opportunities. It thereby created not only the possibility of assimilation, but it actually encouraged the Jews to do so, which in fact was hardly necessary particularly for the emancipated Hungarian Jews. Even into the 1890s the Jewish immigrants associated Vienna with a feeling of freedom and liberalism; they worked predominantly in and for the German-Liberal Party, "even after the Liberals abandoned them and many Austrians had already turned to anti-Semitism."[21]

For the most part, the immigrants who came to Vienna moved into areas of the city where many Jews were already living, most notably to the districts of Leopoldstadt, the Alsergrund, and the Inner City. But national heritage or social standing was not the primary reason for the choice of residence.[22] Interestingly, the Frieds deviated from this path. At first, they lived in the Landstraße district, a district of the municipal middle class, which bordered on Leopoldstadt and the Inner City and in which Jews were underrepresented. Even fewer Jews lived in Ober-Döbling, the suburb of villas in the northwestern part of the city, where primarily important city officials, doctors, and industrialists resided.

The choice of these districts suggests that the Frieds were motivated more by concerns of social class than by the desire to have Jewish neighbors. And, indeed, there is nothing in Fried's papers, nor in his writings, that suggests that the family embraced the Jewish faith or had a desire for contact with the Jewish religious community. Later Fried wrote that he "had experienced nothing of the Jewish faith" in his education.[23]

Mixed marriages were very common in the Engel family. Both Moritz and Katharina Engel married Catholics and raised their children primarily in the Catholic tradition,[24] which gives a first indication of the extent to which complete assimilation was desired. And Alfred's own siblings, with the exception of his youngest sister Sidonie, married partners of different faiths, or claimed

---

21   Rozenblit, *Juden Wiens*, 42f.
22   Ibid, 84ff.
23   Fried to Otto Umfrid, May 24, 1909, Nachlass Fried, Box 84.
24   Only one of Moritz Engel's four children, a daughter, was raised in the Jewish faith. All four children in the Ganghofer family were raised as Catholics.

to be non-religious, or even converted to Christianity, as Pauline did.[25] In 1909, Fried was then not wrong to claim that Christianity "was epidemic" in his family.[26]

The years of relative prosperity for the family coincided with the general upturn of the Austrian economy after 1867. The Austro-Hungarian Compromise and the tenets of liberalism led to a clear improvement in the economic situation. In the run-up to the World Exhibition in Vienna (1873) there was a significant increase in the founding of new companies in many branches of the economy, since authorizations for the establishment of public holding companies were issued quite liberally. In broad sections of the Viennese population a real speculation fever set in.

On May 1, 1873, after two years of intense preparations, the Viennese World's Fair opened its doors in the Prater. It was an event that can be viewed as a pinnacle in the history of the Imperial City as well as the cause of a serious crisis. Companies and speculators had been working with more or less unsecured loans; when the Kredit-Anstalt cancelled short-term loans in April 1873, many had to declare bankruptcy, and the result was a collapse of the share prices. May 9, 1873 was "Black Friday" on the exchange, only eight days after the opening of the World's Fair. The economic catastrophe resulted in a large number of bankruptcies, but it also severely impacted countless people from various classes who had been involved in speculation on the exchange and who had taken out loans. Whole fortunes were lost and investors were plunged into misery – perhaps even the Fried family.

In the long run, it was the political aspect of the crisis that was to be among the worst effects of the crisis for the Jews. The catastrophe was intensified by the outbreak of the cholera epidemic and the resultant absence of the expected crowds, which further weakened liberalism in Austria and was the cause of the constant growth of anti-semitic sentiment in Vienna.

We cannot know with certainty whether Samuel Fried was among those who suffered as a result of his unsuccessful speculation on the stock market in 1873 or whether he lost his job in the course of a business failure. But by fall of that year, the financial situation of the Fried family had deteriorated so dramatically that they had to abandon their apartment in Ober-Döbling, even though Berta was quite pregnant at the time. The family was at first able to move temporarily to Leopoldstadt, where they may have lived with relatives.

---

25 The children of this marriage were also baptized as Catholics. Only the youngest daughter, Sidonie Fried, had a Jewish husband, Alfred Simonsohn; she raised her children in the Jewish religion.
26 Fried to Otto Umfrid, May 24, 1909, Nachlass Fried, Box 84.

CHILDHOOD AND YOUTH

There, in Lichtenauergasse 5, is where Otto Emil was born on December 2, 1873. Later the Frieds moved back to the Landstraße district, to Löwengasse 2,[27] where they lived for several years before returning to Leopoldstadt in 1880. Alfred completed his schooling in Leopoldstadt at the Weintraub school, an elementary school attended primarily by Jewish children. In the fall of 1875 he transferred to the *Gymnasium* in the nearby Sperlgasse.

The significance of an academic education, particularly for Jewish families, has been well documented. Attending a *Gymnasium* was considered the most important means to break through class and social barriers, and so aspiring Jewish immigrants tried to send one of their sons to a *Gymnasium*.[28] While at some *Gymnasien* it was possible to have the annual school tuition waived, it is important to remember that only a very small segment of the population attended a *Gymnasium* (in 1881 it was 0.6% of the total population in Vienna, but among the Jews it was 2.2%). In spite of the increased potential to enhance social mobility through education, the vast majority of those attending the *Gymnasium* came from the upper class. Just the additional costs, such as proper clothing, represented a serious hurdle for poorer families. The decision to send Alfred to a *Gymnasium*, in spite of the family's worsened financial situation, was probably not an easy one for his parents und suggests the high level of achievement expected of him. After his father lost his job – in subsequent years he was rarely able to find work – the oldest son would now be given (and take advantage of) a chance to get ahead.

Students at the *Gymnasium*, typically from age 10 to 18, had usually first attended an elementary school (*Volksschule*) for four years. The curriculum at humanistic *Gymnasien*, which had been supervised and administered by the state since 1869, included the study of classics, including Latin, German language and literature, and, from the third grade on, Greek. Mathematics and the natural sciences were secondary subjects.[29] Alfred showed great interest in literature, but the ancient languages gave him some trouble. In general, his interests did not always conform to what was included in the curriculum. In spite of his obvious intelligence, he soon had great difficulty at school: "At 10, I attended the *Gymnasium*. But I was a poor student, since I was always an autodidact. I was not lazy. My problem was that I was always ahead of the curriculum or

---

27 Here is where Carl and Leopold Fried were born according to the birth registries of the Jewish community in Vienna of 1876 and 1877.
28 According to Rozenblit, the percentage of Jewish children attending the *Gymnasium* (university preparatory high school) was three times higher than its percentage in the total population. Cf. Rozenblit, *Juden Wiens*, 110f.
29 Cf. Rozenblit, *Juden Wiens*, 108.

learned things that had not been part of the curriculum. And so it happened that I neglected what was taught, because I did not find it interesting."[30]

Fried was an avid reader and, at 11 years of age, taught himself stenography outside of school. At 12, he bought his first book, *Leyer und Schwert* (Lyre and Sword), a "delightful collection of military poems, published by Reclam."[31] Since he was not getting an allowance, for several days he went without his "morning snack" (*Jausensemmel*). When the Turkish-Serbian War broke out in the same year (1876), Alfred began reading the newspaper: "Once again I sacrificed my morning snack to surreptitiously buy the newspaper for two *Kreuzer*. At home I was not allowed to read the paper. But since the morning paper cost four *Kreuzer*, I had to content myself with the evening paper, and so I could only follow a portion of the events."[32]

In February 1877, at the age of seven, Alfred's little sister, Charlotte, died; it was a death that Alfred, her big brother, took years to get over. Three years later he observed: "Today marks the third anniversary of the death of my blessed little sister Lotti. With a heavy heart I thought of the hour when the poor girl, alone and without any relatives nearby, passed away amid great suffering. No gentle mother's eye stood watch, no father at her bedside; alone and abandoned by all her relatives, her parents, her siblings, her loyal playmates in happier times, she succumbed in her battle with death."[33]

The extent to which the death of his sister influenced Alfred's performance at school is unknown. The fact is, however, that he had to repeat the second year at the *Gymnasium* because of his poor performance.[34] And when in his third year he had difficulty with Greek,[35] he decided to leave the *Gymnasium*: "I was supposed to attend the university, but since I did so poorly at school, my parents were quite happy when I told them that I wanted to become a bookseller and had already secured a position as an apprentice in a bookstore."[36]

---

30   Fried, "Biographische Skizze," 3.
31   Fried, *Jugenderinnerungen*, 8.
32   Ibid, 10.
33   See the handwritten diary of Alfred H. Fried, entry February 23, 1880. Nachlass Fried, Box 13, file 259.
34   The documents are located in the basement of the Sigmund-Freud-Gymnasium in Vienna today. According to the documents, Fried was a student at the school during the school year 1875–1876; he was matriculated there until January 20, 1879. He had to repeat the second grade.
35   Fried, diary. April 9, 1880: "As I looked through the schoolbooks, I found that a teacher had written a list of vocabulary items to accompany *Schenkels Übungsbuch*, which were intended to enable the students to look up the Greek words more easily. If I had known that, maybe I would not have left school…"
36   Fried, "Biographische Skizze," 3.

CHILDHOOD AND YOUTH

On January 20, 1879, his parents withdrew him from the *Gymnasium*, and so the sure path to "higher education" and to social advancement ended in failure for him. Fried gave still another reason for his decision: "I had an immense love of books, which I could not satisfy in my parents' home, and so I imagined that if I worked in a bookstore I would have the opportunity to read and study all day. Besides that, a friend of mine had also quit the *Gymnasium* and taken a position in a bookstore. That, too, was a great allure for me."[37]

The friend in question was likely Siegfried Frankl who would repeatedly play a role in Alfred's life. Siegfried Frankl, born in Oedenburg, Hungary, in 1861, had come to Vienna in 1866 with his family; in 1877, two years earlier than Fried, he left the *Gymnasium* to become a bookseller at a publishing house.[38]

2 Apprenticeship with a Bookseller and Fried's First Experiences of Pacifism

One year after he left the *Gymnasium* to start his apprenticeship, Fried began his handwritten diary (February 1, 1880 to May 25, 1880). It includes a short postscript of March 1–13, 1882.[39] Never published, this particular snapshot can give us a subjective, authentic picture of the internal and external conditions that the fifteen-year-old had to confront.[40]

As is often the case, this diary also marked a period of radical change: a teenager's desperate search for the right path in life. But at the same time it highlights a familiar situation: "February 1: Today I received one Gulden, my salary, and after I gave it to my mother, I demanded it back. I didn't get it, which caused a bit of scene, but which then worked out all right."[41] Only rarely was Fried able to keep even a small portion of his salary. He often had to ask his boss for an advance of a week or two so that his mother could pay an overdue bill: "April 9: Today I asked for an advance of six Gulden for three weeks because Mama needs five Gulden tomorrow for the wetnurse."

The reason that even this meager amount from Fried's apprenticeship was needed is simple: Samuel Fried did not have a job. His constant attempts to

---

37 Ibid, 3.
38 Cf. the biographical sketch of Siegfried Frankl in Richard Wrede, Hans von Reinsfeld (eds.), *Das geistige Berlin*, vol. 1 (Berlin, 1897), 111.
39 Nachlass Fried, Box 13, file 259.
40 A copy of my typed transcription of the handwritten diary, which is quite difficult to read, can be found in Geneva today.
41 The following quotes were edited to ensure correct spelling. I have inserted appropriate months, which were missing in the original, in parentheses.

earn some money through part-time work were only rarely successful. Hardly a week went by without an entry in the diary like this: "February 3: My parents' situation is bad, there is hardly any money in the house."

Sometimes the family was helped out by Uncle Moritz, Berta's successful and highly respected brother, the editor and owner of the *Wiener Salonblatt*, an Austrian newspaper: "February 4: The situation with my parents has improved a bit since Uncle Moritz gave us a small amount of money and some wine, but the interest is due soon and our misery is growing; not an evening goes by that we don't lack something. Papa has had a worried look on his face for some time now; he never smiles, which just about breaks my heart."

On February 9, the Frieds were about to lose their apartment. Once again Uncle Moritz intervened. He paid the rent that was due and was able to arrange for the family to stay in the apartment until May. But in the long run, even this support was inadequate. Around Pentecost the situation worsened: "May 19: My parents are in awful shape. This evening we didn't even have bread, let alone a meal. The woman who does the wash could not be paid. Papa came home at nine o'clock. Around nine o'clock Mama sent me to the pawnshop with a bundle of clothes, but it was closed. Miserable, miserable, miserable is our existence. Day and night, I keep trying to think of a way to improve our situation."

Poverty and the search for a way out occupied much of the young man's thoughts. Again and again, he wondered how he could make the situation better, which was difficult given his small salary as an apprentice bookseller. The prospect of becoming a famous poet sounded better to him, so he sent his poems to the journal *Deutschen Dichterfreund*,[42] but not one of them was ever published. What the boy apparently did not know is that the journal had already ceased publication in February 1880. At this time he was also preoccupied with plans to write a drama about General York; this too was intended to help him "climb out of this morass."[43] For a short time, he considered asking Uncle Moritz to help him start a publishing house that would feature calendars and journals for young people. He would be the editor-in-chief. But he did not dare express this idea "[...] since I don't want my parents to feel the pain of seeing me quit something again and then consider me a good-for-nothing. I have no other choice but to pull myself together and create a dynamic literary work."[44]

---

42 *Deutscher Dichter-Freund, Journal zur Belehrung und Unterhaltung* (Bückeburg, Minden 1878-1880).
43 Fried, diary February 11, 1880.
44 Fried, diary February 26, 1880.

Secretly, he began to collect his literary efforts and wrote a letter to the well-known Viennese poet Ludwig Anzengruber, a representative of liberalism, who had become famous through his naturalistic, anticlerical peasant dramas and comedies.[45] He hoped that Anzengruber's opinion would lead to a breakthrough. The writing proceeded slowly, since he usually had to work late, and since he continued to pursue his self-education: he studied Latin almost every day and stenography as well, but he was constantly dissatisfied that he could not do more: "February 21: I want to learn, to study, I have to, I must find a way out of this quagmire of ignorance and dilettantism."

Since exhaustion and weariness repeatedly thwarted his ambitious plans, he concluded that working at the bookstore was finally the greatest impediment to his further education. He wanted nothing more than to leave the bookstore in order to fully concentrate on his education and on his career as a poet: "March 2: I am spending my time filled with inner conflict. During the day, when I am in the store and I'm caught up in the bustling activity and time speeds by, I constantly think that I have to become something. – When I go home in the evening and take a look at my books, and when I realize how badly I would like to know everything, how I have to understand it all in order to satisfy my inner urge, and when I see how impossible it is to learn it now, how I am drawn to my bed, that's when I think that I can't stay in the bookstore, that I have to leave, I just have to, so that I can continue my education. Yes, I believe, it is my destiny to be strung between two horses and to be torn apart by them. This inner struggle will tear me to pieces unless something unforeseen intervenes, unless some savior appears on the scene." A similar entry can be found a week later: "March 10: Desperation, grief, misery, worries, pains, oh, everything, yes everything is coming together now. The beautiful days of emergent spring, which only serve to make the shackles of my store even more unbearable, conspire against my soul, and at home I also have to look on as hardship raises its head. Papa came back from his trip today because he was not able to do any business. Once again he is without work. When I saw his aggrieved face and his loving, endearing expression, I felt a pain, that I was going to slight him, who does so much for us, if I left the store."

To make matters worse, Fried's little sister Betti took ill at this time. "She has arthritis, pleurisy, and fluid around her heart; the whole family is in a terrible mood."[46] But once he had purchased some suitable paper, he was able to write

---

45 Ludwig Anzengruber (1839–1889) was a book dealer, actor, clerk with the Viennese police, and freelance writer as of 1871. In the Austrian culture war, he stood on the side of the liberals.
46 Fried, diary March 26, 1880.

a letter to Anzengruber, a letter, "on which he places all of my hopes."[47] Since his own handwriting is not that good, he has a friend write the letter for him. The text of the letter is preserved under the date March 28: "My dear Sir, if I dare to trouble you with this letter, so please excuse this bold step and do not ascribe it to presumption or vanity. It is inner doubt about my own self that causes me, to choose you, dear Sir, as my judge, to hear the judgment from your mouth [. . .]"

Fried signed the letter using the pseudonym "Alfred Armin" and requested that the answer be sent "*poste restante* to Alfred Armin at the main post office" so that his parents would not know of his plans. He waited impatiently for an answer, but it did not arrive. A few days later, he wrote in resignation: "April 3: In the meantime Easter has passed, both the Catholic and the Jewish one. [. . .] I have not received an answer from Anzengruber. Now that eight days have passed since I wrote the letter, I have given up all hope."

In spite of this deep disappointment, the boy did not in fact give up hope so quickly. If Anzengruber would not respond, then perhaps another poet might. The choice fell to the liberal Viennese writer and secretary of the Jewish Community Ludwig August Frankl.[48] This second letter was written within the week but was not sent until a few days later because he had no money for the postage. The famous poet answered promptly. What he actually wrote can only be inferred from an article, written from memory, that Siegfried Frankl authored in 1931 on the tenth anniversary of Fried's death. Frankl quoted the poet as saying: "It is really quite embarrassing to tell you – and you insisted on knowing the truth – that from the examples that I have reviewed I don't see any talent, not to mention the fact that you are still struggling with language and form."[49] Even if the authenticity of this quote can no longer be verified, such a judgment is more than probable, for the letter apparently shocked Fried: "April 14: I received an answer from Frankl today in which he denies me any talent – I am deeply discouraged."

Alfred did not consider doubting the judgment of the old man. On the contrary, he totally reoriented himself. Two days later he wrote of his new plans for the future: "April 16: Yes, Frankl's letter caused me great distress. A new plan is taking shape in me: I will turn to a more practical activity and will dedicate

---

47 Fried, diary March 28, 1880.
48 Ludwig August Ritter von Frankl-Hochwart (1810–1894) was a doctor and liberal writer in Vienna. He was also the secretary of the Jewish religious community and a professor of aesthetics.
49 Frankl, *Friedens-Fried*. The letter, as well as the documents that Frankl cites, is not located in the Nachlass in Geneva. Nothing is known of what happened to Frankl after 1931.

myself, heart and soul, to the book trade. To establish a secure and worry-free existence, I will limit my studies to only what is absolutely necessary, and then once I have achieved such an existence, I will dedicate myself to the pursuit of scientific knowledge, as a secondary source of income, give up my interest in poetry, and devote myself solely and completely to the systematic pursuit of scientific knowledge. Perhaps this plan will take root in me, perhaps."

The plan did in fact take root. Although he continued to read a lot, there is no indication that he tried to write literary works. On May 23, he even noted that he had sold all of his books, except those pertaining to his pursuit of knowledge. The family's ongoing difficult financial situation would not allow for any more experiments. At Pentecost, the Fried family, with its seven children, had to move: "This week we moved to a new apartment. Untere Donaustraße 47, Floor 3, door 17. We have an apartment with two rooms, one small room and an antechamber, a kitchen, a splendid view of the Danube, the railway, the Franzensbrücke and the Aspernbrücke."[50]

As before, whenever possible, Alfred had to continue to ask for an advance on his salary. Every Kreuzer was needed. And his mother preferred to turn to him with her worries. The boy reacted with typical indignation when he learned from his sister about some money that the family had recently received as a gift: "I heard from Pauline that Mama received a money order of forty Gulden from Pest yesterday. While I am happy about that, I feel slighted that Mama did not say anything to me about it, even as she often tells me of the more unpleasant things."[51] Since his father's continued search for work had been unsuccessful, it was up to Alfred to be the main support of the family, a status that, within the family, probably gave him some sense of importance and recognition, but at the same time did not leave him much time for himself.[52] A short story that Fried wrote as a young man sheds some light on this period. Entitled "Frostiger Lenz" (Frosty Spring) and located in his papers, it describes an episode in the life of a boy who, in order to feed his family of eight, has to work as an apprentice six days a week on the lowest rung of the ladder in a general store where he is bullied by other employees and mocked by his previous fellow classmates. "And freezing the whole day. – Salvation only comes belatedly. The last one home for the meager bread that he shares with six siblings. Everything tastes good to him, even if the bread is dry, but sometimes there isn't even dry bread, then hunger is joined by misery, the misery brought about by horrific

---

50   Fried, diary May 16, 1880.
51   Fried, diary May 9, 1880.
52   "Frostiger Lenz," in Nachlass Fried, Box 8, file 94. This is a typewritten manuscript with handwritten corrections, undated.

conditions." The boy gets paid every Saturday, but immediately he gives his wages up at home. "This is something that is decided beforehand; never does even a little bit of the money fall his way, the one who fought to get it. But, still, it brings him some joy that in the evening he can place the fruits of his hard labor into such devoted hands and brighten the saddened faces if only for a short time." But on this Saturday the boy wants to secretly purchase a birthday gift for his mother with his money. Since he has to work so late, many of the shops are already closed. After much wandering about, he can only find a small figurine in a porcelain shop: "Blushing and with beaming eyes, he steps into the living room. In the light of the gas lamp, a table with a red tablecloth and the unused utensils lay neatly arranged on the table. – His parents and the six siblings were seated around the table. All were quiet. He knew this silence of sorrow. – His mother stared pensively into space. – His father held his head in his hands. The children know what is going on and dare not even whisper." Impatiently and angrily his parents bark at him to give them his money, and they are appalled when he admits that he no longer has it. "We don't have any money for dinner and are hungry as we wait for you and the money […] you wretched child, tell me, what did you do with it!" Finally, and tearfully, the boy shows them the porcelain figurine, and the criticism stops, although they all have to go to bed hungry.

In spite of the continuing financial difficulties and the lack of living space in which the nine-member family lived, Berta and Samuel Fried were caring parents who paid special attention to the "proper" behavior of their children and ensured that they didn't run wild. While his sister Pauline, who was three years younger than Alfred, thought that their parents were solely responsible for the poverty they experienced in their youth, Leopold, fifteen years younger, attributed his own failure in Berlin to the fact that their parents sheltered them too much. "Systematically, our will and our sense of self were broken. Mama and Papa expended all the love and care they had on us, but all of my schoolmates, who were allowed to go to the Prater alone without supervision, who were allowed to go to listen to music at the Burgtheater and to go to the parades, all these 'scoundrels' became 'individuals', became people, and what about me? - Broken in spirit, body and soul."[53] But Alfred, throughout his whole life, showed his parents deference and respect, precisely for the way they conducted themselves in those unfortunate years. What he especially experienced with his mother and what he admired about her would also become one of his own most salient features: a deep-rooted optimism, a combative spirit, and a never-say-die attitude, even in the most desperate situations.

---

53   Leopold (Poldi) Fried to Fried, February 3, 1904. Nachlass Fried, Box 31.

As early as 1880, Alfred was fascinated by people who placed intellectual interests above material well-being and dedicated their lives to a cause; he met one such person in the bookstore in February 1880: "Today a gentleman came into the store and bought a copy of *Meyers Lexikon*. He said that he had been working on a scholarly project for 24 years; it was to be a work that contradicted Humboldt's cosmos and was to present an ethical and physical *Weltanschauung*. He will spend one more year on the introduction of the work. – Poor devil! From what I could tell from his comments, he had certainly done battle with hardship and misery during his lifetime. He has become an old man as he wrote the book. What will the contemporary world owe you, and what about posterity, and what do you get out of it if posterity should one day honor you and pay you tribute."[54]

In spite of this harsh criticism, the man makes a lasting impression on the boy: "The man who has been working on his scholarly project for 24 years picked up his copy of *Meyers Lexikon* today. The poor guy. He is a baron, a nobleman who has fallen on hard times. Snow-white hair at his temples. Everyone in our shop mocks and disparages him. I'm the only one who has compassion, empathy, and great respect for him. He wrote his signature in each of the volumes of the *Lexikon*. I lent him my pencil to do it, so that I could keep the pencil as a reminder that this man, whom I really esteem, once wrote with it."[55]

This entry indicates quite clearly the direction in which Fried's thinking would later move. He did not admire the well-known generals, the famous men of power, or the successful businessmen like his uncle Moritz Engel, whose audience with the Crown Prince merited a single sentence from him.[56] His admiration was directed toward "intellectual" individuals, the "noble people" who were working to advance the moral and cultural progress of humanity. And so it almost sounds like an early rejection of materialism when Fried places the sentences "Fight for victory and acquire what you can. Then despair and die." – alongside Mephistopheles' words that serve as a motto to his diary.

In his memoir Fried quoted a stenographic note, which he claimed to be from at least 1880, as the first record of his pacifism. There one reads: "In ancient times the glory of a people lay in the power of weapons, where physical force exceeded intellectual power. And the weapons of our ancestors were their hands, their own physical powers. Nowadays, when culture rules, when international law prevails, nowadays, when killing occurs during fierce

---

54   Fried, diary February 25, 1880.
55   Fried, diary March 8, 1880.
56   Fried, diary March 28, 1880. "Uncle Moritz had an audience with the Crown Prince, and the Crown Prince himself gave him a picture of his bride."

fighting, when rancor prevails on the battlefield, when outside of the battlefield international law makes a brother of one's enemy, nowadays the glory of a nation no longer lies in military victory but in the arts and in sciences."[57] (For what is a nation that can murder effectively? It is not its own strength that does the murdering, but rather the strength of their murderous machines and the power of technological science). These sentiments fit very nicely with the image that the diary draws of Fried, and they are presumably authentic. To be sure, they are not at all original, for statements such as these were part and parcel of the normal repertoire of liberal progressive thinking, which was also cultivated in the Fried household.

One other experience might have played an even greater and more significant role in the development of pacifist thinking at this time: "One Sunday afternoon I went to the museum, without any expectations, to see a collection of paintings that had been much discussed in the newspapers. Paintings of the Russo-Turkish War by Vasily Vereshchagin[58] were on display. This visit gave my life a decisive turn. The exhibition taught me to hate war. I became fully conscious of the horror and the wretchedness of war. Even today, four decades later, I still feel the disgust that flared up in me when I saw the paintings."[59]

Although this story at first sounds like a well-conceived legend, on closer look it is indeed probable that this museum visit did take place and that the paintings did have an effect on the sensitive teenager. Entitled "Paintings and Drawings by V. Vereshchagin," the exhibition displayed 113 works of art and ethnographic objects, among them 21 "paintings of the Russo-Turkish theater of war." The exhibition caused quite a sensation in Vienna and, in the end, set an attendance record with 94,892 visitors.[60] In his memoir Fried described individual paintings in detail and related the impression that they made on him: "Here was a pyramid made of dead skulls with a raven standing nearby; it was labeled 'Apotheosis of War.' There a field covered with greenish-yellow corpses, which a Pope blessed business-like and cool, assisted by a petty officer who

---

57   Fried, *Jugenderinnerungen*, 12.
58   Vasily Vasilyevich Vereshchagin, born in 1842 at Cherepovets, near Novgorod, was a painter and graphic artist. He took part in the Russian battles in Central Asia as an officer and as a painter. In particular, his paintings of the Russo-Turkish War have become famous. Vereshchagin died on April 13, 1904 when the *Petropavlovsk*, the battleship he was on as he was sketching war scenes, hit a Japanese mine while returning to Port Arthur. Cf. Nicole Gysemberg in Miodrag Jelesijevic, *Apotheose des Krieges. Leben und Werk des russischen Malers Wassili Wereschagin* (Hamburg: Kämpfer, 2001).
59   Fried, *Jugenderinnerungen*, 12.
60   Written information provided by Dr. Wladimir Aichelburg, archivist at the Künstlerhausarchiv, Vienna, on June 25, 2001.

looked on indifferently. Then, the frozen sentry with the inscription 'All Quiet at the Shipka Pass.' And finally the picture that triggered my greatest anger: Alexander II sitting in a comfortable fauteuil, behind him a brilliant entourage, all with field glasses and binoculars, all of them far removed from the fighting, watching the course of the battle at Plevna. Down below, the death and suffering of thousands, up above the ruler and his lords, monitoring the whole thing as if it were merely an interesting spectacle. The thought occurred to me that while, for the masses, war brings untold sacrifice with respect to their lives, their health and their possessions, for the higher-ups of this world war is merely a kind of parlor game [...]."[61]

Fried describes the impact of this afternoon in rather drastic terms: "When I left the exhibition, all of the atavistic inclinations that had appeared in my youth and had been furthered by an unscrupulous public education fell from me. For some time my thinking had already begun to dissolve this artificially effected mental slime. The perspective of reality that a philanthropic artist had shared with me completed the cleansing process all at once. I now could see clearly: On that memorable day, I left the museum holding a deep conviction that at the time had no name. I had become a pacifist."[62] In hindsight, this claim is probably somewhat exaggerated, for in the next few years Fried showed no signs of a distinctly pacifistic ethos. "During that time my pacifism remained latent. It was at best evident in my political thinking as I moved to the left and developed an interest in liberalism and democracy with strong opposition to anything conservative and nationalistic."[63] Fried explained that there was a gap between his pacifist "thinking and feeling" and pacifist action – "his efforts to put into reality the idea that he had come to embrace"[64] – because there were no nearby like-minded others, but especially because the "Storm-and-Stress years, which filled my life at the time, did not allow the path from thinking to acting to be found."[65]

After his painstaking efforts in 1880 to continue his training as a book dealer, he now committed himself to the task with great energy. At the end of 1882 Alfred Fried completed his training with the bookseller Bergman & Altmann in Vienna, apparently with good grades, and began to apply for positions in the German Reich. He wanted to get away from Vienna, away from the city that had only shown him its dark side. Even as late as 1903, shortly before he was to

---

61   Fried, *Jugenderinnerungen*, 12.
62   Fried, *Jugenderinnerungen*, 13.
63   Fried, "Biographische Skizze," 4.
64   Fried, *Jugenderinnerungen*, 13.
65   Ibid, 13.

return to Vienna, not quite of his own volition, he wrote to Therese Frankl: "If one doesn't see this miserable city under good circumstances, then it is simply unbearable."[66] And elsewhere he wrote, even more clearly: "So, you are going to Löwenstraße? I would so much like to visit the old haunts of my youth with you there! Unfortunately, they don't bring up many good memories. For me, Vienna represents a whole host of misery and anxieties."[67]

Now, after concluding his training, he had his first opportunity to leave the city. His primary choice was of course the capital of the German empire, Berlin, where his friend Siegfried already had a position. In January 1883 Siegfried wrote to him that he couldn't think of anything better than to be able to "work together and enjoy each other's company in the coming summer" in Berlin, and he would do everything in his power to help Alfred find a position.[68] To increase the probability of their success, he gave Fried some tips: "By all means send me your resume so that I have something of yours in hand. One thing that you have not been able to overcome – much to my dismay, you are still not very good at orthography. – And your style also leaves something to be desired. Furthermore, I don't like the irregularity of your handwriting. One can write poorly, but at the same time it can still be business-like and manly."[69] But in spite of all his efforts, Fried did not find a position in Berlin in the next couple of months. He did, however, have more luck in Hamburg: on October 1, 1883 he began his first job with the bookseller Moritz Glogau.

For this young man, who was now almost nineteen, it was an opportunity to put some distance between himself and his family. He was also not particularly pleased that his mother had asked her brother Sigismund Engel, who was working as a ballet master in Brunswick at the time, to keep an eye on him. In his very first letter to Alfred upon his arrival in Hamburg, Uncle Sigismund made clear that he wanted to be kept informed about everything in great detail: "Tell me in your next letter how much money you are earning with Glogau and how you have arranged your life there. When do you close the store in the evening? Where do you eat dinner? How do you do your laundry? How are you managing your money? Do you have enough so that you don't need an advance this month? Because that would give a very bad impression; on the other hand, it is not typical in Germany to ask for an advance. So, a precise

---

66   Fried to Therese Frankl, March 3, 1903. Nachlass Fried, Box 92.
67   Fried to Therese Frankl, March 28, 1903. Nachlass Fried, Box 92.
68   Cf. Siegfried Frankl to Fried, January 16, 1883. Nachlass Fried, Box 12b, file 249.
69   Ibid.

report about everything."[70] At the same time, he directed the boy not to write home about his problems and concerns, since the family would just "get anxious and despondent." Alfred was to always inform him first.

Alfred's return letters are no longer extant, but the uncle's near-weekly admonitions and complaints suggest that the young Alfred only sent short reports to Schöppenstedt and reserved the more informative letters for others. He remained in frequent contact with his old friends Siegfried and Max. He also stayed in touch with a younger colleague from the Viennese bookstore, Viktor Bloch, who kept him well informed of the cultural developments in Vienna as well as of the events and changes at Bergmann & Altmann: "Since your departure, things have been rather quiet in the shop," he wrote to Fried in October, "and there is seldom any trouble with the old man."[71] At the same time, however, he complained – and he was not the only one – about Fried's "indecipherable hieroglyphics," which a few years later would lead to Fried's exclusive use of a typewriter to compose letters. Later he would frequently make carbon copies, which can still be found in his documents today.

Fried reports to the astonished Viktor that in Hamburg he often went to the theater and wrote articles about the plays he saw. Viktor asked him for copies of his reviews and he seemed truly impressed: "Your article in *Salonblatt* really surprised me. I would not have thought you capable of such writing; you who were never very interested in the theater. I read the name at the end of the piece several times just to assure myself that you were indeed the author."[72] In point of fact, this is not the first piece that Fried wrote for a journal. Even while he was an apprentice, he wrote book reviews for his uncle's *Wiener Salonblatt*.

In November, acknowledging Fried's superior linguistic skills, Viktor asked his friend to help him with his own applications, in particular in the composition of a classified ad. In the same letter, he also showed his affection for Fried: "It would of course be best for me to find a position in Hamburg; I very much desire to be with you again and to be able to have heart to heart talks."[73]

But Fried was drawn to Siegfried in Berlin. By January 1884 at the latest he applied for positions with booksellers in the capital. And he was not modest in the selection of positions to which he applied, as the few extant rejection letters indicate. For example, the publisher Prager in Berlin wrote: "It is my experience that the position you seek requires experience and circumspection

---

70 Sigismund Engel to Fried, October 9, 1883. Nachlass Fried, Box 13, file 251.
71 Viktor Bloch to Fried, October 22, 1883. Nachlass Fried, Box 13, file 251.
72 Viktor Bloch to Fried, December 10, 1883. Nachlass Fried, Box 13, file 251.
73 Viktor Bloch to Fried, 22 October 1883, Nachlass Fried, Box 13, file 251.

which, for all your talents, you do not seem to possess according to the documents you submitted. These qualities, to the extent that we require them, can only be acquired over time."[74] But just two lines later one reads: "It would be a pleasure if, after you have had the chance to see a bit more of the world, I might have the opportunity to return to this correspondence and to show you that I have really been impressed by your letter."

In spite of several rejections Fried's tenacity was rewarded this time. In March 1884 he succeeded in finding a position in Berlin.

---

74   This and the following citation are taken from the Buchhandlung Prager to Fried, February 16, 1884, Nachlass Fried, Box 13, file 251.

CHAPTER 2

The Berlin Years 1884–1903

1   From Apprentice Bookseller to Publisher

Berlin, the capital of the new German Reich, was a young, modern city, full of excitement and of opportunities for social mobility, a real magnet for people who had ambition, people like Fried. In contrast to Vienna, where a strict separation of social classes still existed, there was a large number of *nouveau riche* social climbers in Berlin (in addition to the nearly one percent of its aristocratic residents) who undermined the social barriers and contributed to the myth of "unlimited possibilities," even if, vis-á-vis America, it was only on a small scale. Industrialists like Siemens and Borsig as well as the owners of large department stores like Wertheim and Tietz lived and worked in Berlin; so too did the great contemporary newspaper publishers, Mosse, Scherl and Ullstein, who flooded the city several times a day with a variety of newspapers ranging from the conservative to the liberal to the socialist and thus served the needs of all levels of readership. The new millionaires in Berlin were mostly newcomers from the lower or middle classes, since "the need to 'get ahead' had spread across all levels of Berlin society at that time."[1]

Although Jews in Berlin had received full legal equality as a result of the law passed by the North German Confederation in 1869 (just two years after the Jews in Vienna had acquired the same right), their social integration into the emerging bourgeoisie progressed much more quickly than it had in the Habsburg monarchy.[2] Even at the beginning of the 19th century, the municipal ordinance put into place by Karl Freiherr von Stein in 1808 had granted citizenship to the Prussian Jews and included active and passive suffrage; one year later David Friedländer was elected to the city council of Berlin. In 1811, the introduction of freedom of trade abolished the requirement to become a member of a guild and opened the craft trades to Jews who had hitherto been barred from them. And finally, in 1812, Jews were officially declared "residents and Prussian citizens." Government positions as well as teaching positions,

---

1 Eberhard Roters, "Emporgekommen," in *Berlin um 1900*. Exhibition of the Berlin Gallery in connection with the Akademie der Künste during the Berlin festival weeks, 1984, 49.
2 Of relevance to this and what follows, see, among others, Inka Bertz, "Juden in Berlin," in *Jüdisches Städtebild Berlin,* ed. Gert Mattenklott (Frankfurt am Main, 1997), 15f.

however, remained closed to them, and this continued to be the practice even after 1869 when it was no longer legal.

The opportunities for living well and finding good employment led to a rapid increase in the Jewish population. Around 1890, 79,000 Jews lived in Berlin, thus making up five percent of the population; the vast majority of them worked in commerce, either in medium-sized businesses or as employees. They ran small grocery stores, market stalls, or dry goods stores (Schnittwarengeschäfte) outside the city center. As was the case everywhere, Jewish university graduates preferred to work in their own practices as doctors or lawyers, or as freelance writers and journalists; sometimes they entered the field of industrial research as scientists. In particular, the expanding media landscape in Berlin offered a broad range of options to many intellectually-minded Jews: "Jewish critics, gallery owners, publishers, editors, theater directors and film directors – Alfred Kerr, Paul Cassirer, Samuel Fischer, Moritz Heimann, Otto Brahm and Max Reinhardt – all shaped the urban culture of Berlin."[3]

But Berlin was not only an early haven of Jewish emancipation, it was also the city where in 1879 the term "antisemitism" was coined. The continuing economic crisis following "Black Friday" in 1873 had also weakened liberalism in Berlin, and with it the ideas of the Enlightenment. In contrast to Vienna, however, antisemitism in Berlin was championed in particular by the elite leadership, the professors, and the influential Protestant clergy. Among the best-known antisemitic propagandists were the journalist Wilhelm Marr,[4] the court preacher Adolf Stöcker,[5] and the historian Heinrich von Treitschke,[6] who, taken collectively, represented the racial, religious and national expressions of antisemitism. Besides their impact on both the educated bourgeoisie and the petite bourgeoisie, who were indeed receptive to such ideas, they also exerted

---

3   Ibid, 19f.
4   From 1862 on, Wilhelm Marr (1819–1904) wrote antisemitic articles and attained some fame with his essay "Der Sieg des Judentums über das Germanentum," which expressed his racially motivated antisemitism. In the same year, he founded the "Antisemite League" (Antisemitenliga), which proposed that all Jews be sent to Palestine and which coined the notion of "antisemitism."
5   Adolf Stöcker (1835–1909), a preacher in the cathedral and at the court in Berlin, was a representative of the German-Conservative Party for many years. In 1880, he founded the "Berlin Movement" (Berliner Bewegung) which was intended to bring all of the antisemitic groups into one organization. After several failed attempts to influence the working class through antisemitic propaganda, Stöcker turned his attention to the lower middle class and to students.
6   Heinrich von Treitschke (1834–1896) was well known for the phrase "The Jews are our misfortune" in the Preußische Jahrbücher. It precipitated the controversy about antisemitism in Berlin.

considerable influence on the universities. In 1880, a petition that called for the abolition of emancipation was signed by nearly half of Berlin's students.

For a young Viennese bookstore apprentice, Berlin offered excellent career opportunities, but it also held the danger of social isolation, especially for someone like Fried, who was neither rooted in the Jewish community nor a member of the numerous Jewish associations that had been formed to counter the increasing social exclusion. Whether the young Fried was aware of these dangers seems rather doubtful. At least in the early years, his hope for swift economic and social integration might well have outweighed all possible doubts.

Initially, the young bookstore clerk worked in the commission and export division of M. Neufeld in southwestern Berlin and rented a nearby room. Later, he took a position with Neufeld & Mehring, a publisher and seller of rare books, on Wilhelmstraße.[7]

At least one member of the family was not happy about Fried's move to Berlin: Alfred's sister Pauline tirelessly tried to persuade her older brother to return to Vienna. Her characterizations of the family situation grew ever more drastic: "No, Alfred, you would not possibly like living in a foreign country if you knew of our present situation; 17 times this month, it was 11 o'clock and Mama still did not know where she would get lunch for us all. On such days, Papa leaves in the morning and comes back for lunch, then he goes off again without saying a word and returns so late in the evening that the children are already asleep. It must be difficult for him to come home in the evening with empty pockets and so many mouths to feed."[8] Pauline wrote that on other days it was her own meager income or gifts from Uncle Moritz that ensured the family's nutritional welfare in the short run. It was only Alfred, she claimed, who was able to substantially help the family by taking a job in Vienna and giving part of his income to the family. "How much easier would life be for Mama if you were here."[9] With ever more urgency, Pauline wrote in the next letter of her parents' increasingly frequent quarrels, mostly about a few *Kreuzer*: "After such dramatic scenes, which are not uncommon, Mama always sighs, and when she sighs, she simply says: 'Oh God, if only I had not let Alfred go off, if only he knew what he was doing to me.'"[10]

But Fried did not return just yet. Instead, in addition to his work, he was also busy with the publication of his own first work, a collection of quotations,

---

7   References to the names and places can be found in the correspondence with Siegfried Frankl, Nachlass Fried, Box 12b, file 249.
8   Pauline Fried to Fried, undated (1884), Nachlass Fried, Box 13, file 251.
9   Ibid.
10 Pauline Fried to Fried, April 30, 1884. Nachlass Fried, Box 13, file 251.

based on the well-known large selection by Georg Büchmann,[11] which he called *Der kleine Büchmann* (The Little Büchmann).[12] "The readers for whom the book is intended will find what they are looking for, and it is intended for all social classes who do not want to get involved with philological studies. I have not written this book for scholars; disappointed, they will surely put my work aside."[13] Even his first book was aimed at a broad readership, at the "little man," who had literary or academic interests but was not educated, and who did not have the money or the time to spend on particular topics – a person like the young publisher himself. The concept was apparently successful because in the same year a second edition was published.

The family was also impressed by his debut. Even his very religious uncle, Salomon Fried from Fünfkirchen in Hungary, with whom the family had had no contact for many years, got in touch with Alfred to congratulate him:

"In the history of the creation it is said [Hebraic insertion], when God created man, he made him in the image of God, that is, he instilled in him reason with all its faculties and capabilities, but that is not what made him human, for that only gave him the potential to become human, because those who have been created only become human if they create themselves anew, educate themselves, and bring their talents to completion. And that, my dear nephew, is what I see in you; you endeavor to educate yourself to become a perfected human being."[14] This was praise that the young Fried was happy to hear, this was what he was striving for: to create a self, to climb out of an oppressive social environment and become an educated, respectable, successful and finally a 'perfected' human being. The family's approval may have encouraged him on his chosen path. Barely a year and a half later, in February 1888, Fried published a collection of German quotations,[15] and in the autumn of the same year, the next volume, *Lexikon fremdsprachlicher Zitate* (Dictionary of Foreign-language Citations), appeared.[16]

---

11 Georg Büchmann, *Geflügelte Worte. Der Zitatenschatz des deutschen Volkes*, 1st edition, 1864 (Munich, 2002). The fifth edition appeared in 1869, and the thirteenth in 1882. At the time of the publication of Fried's work, the "Büchmann" was already a well-known expression.

12 *Der kleine Büchmann. Eine Sammlung der landläufigsten Zitate und berühmtesten Ausssprüche deutscher, lateinischer, französischer, englischer und italienischer Sprache*, ed. Alfred Hermann Fried, 2nd edition, Leipzig, no date given, 1886.

13 Fried, *Der kleine Büchmann*, see the introduction to the first and second edition.

14 Salomon Fried to Fried, January 6, 1887. Nachlass Fried, Box 12b.

15 *Lexikon deutscher Zitate*, ed. Alfred Hermann Fried (Leipzig, no date given [1888]). Universal-Bibliothek, Nr. 2461–2463.

16 *Lexikon fremdsprachlicher Zitate*, ed. Alfred Hermann Fried (Leipzig, no date given [1888]).

But first the young bookseller returned to Vienna for a short time, albeit involuntarily. On January 15, 1887, three years after he had first been summoned for his military physical examination in Hamburg,[17] Fried began his military service in Vienna as an infantryman in the 44th Infantry Regiment in Obersievering. Interestingly enough, he remained silent about this period of his life, which later surely would have produced examples of the horrors of blind obedience. But all that one can read is: "In 1887 I completed my military service in Vienna, which was fortunately short."[18]

In fact, it is hard to imagine that the months that this "latent pacifist" served in the military did not leave behind a trace. The recurring battle in the 1890s between Fried and the authorities, which was fought over his participation or non-participation in the prescribed exercises,[19] suggests that not everything went so smoothly. In this short reference, written in his memoir toward the end of his life, one might detect the need of the well-known pacifist, who was often excoriated during the First World War, to avoid any doubt about his patriotism and sense of duty. Nevertheless, critical remarks about the military can be found elsewhere: "The appearance of the soldiers as involuntary marionettes, who were struck and cursed at, such that often the soldier turned red with anger and shame, unable to defend himself, filled me with rage and the wish to be able to help somehow."[20]

Fried finds harsher words for the "war bondage" in the journal *Friedens-Warte*; the coercion to serve in the military was "the worst, the most scandalous, the most shameful slavery that ever existed. This institution, which denied the individual control over his body, the most disgusting subjugation of his soul, the reduction of a man to a totally submissive and selfless animal, is a disgrace to all humanity."[21]

Even while he was still serving in the military in Sievering, he launched his first publishing project. The *Verlag des Allgemeinen deutschen Hochschulkalenders* (General German College Calendar), published in Vienna in July 1887, was dedicated exclusively to the advertising and distribution of the *Allgemeiner deutscher Hochschulkalender* (General German College Calendar) that was published by Dr. R. Kulka "with the endorsement of and support of the k. k. Ministerium für Kultus und Unterricht (Royal Imperial Ministry for Education

---

17   Cf. the summons issued to Fried by the imperial and royal Austrian-Hungarian embassy in Hamburg, dated January 10, 1884. Nachlass Fried, Box 14, file 267.
18   Fried, *Jugenderinnerungen*, 13.
19   Nachlass Fried, Box 25 file 358. Thus a lengthy exchange arose concerning an enlistment order of thirteen days to be served in Vienna, which Fried did not want to serve.
20   Fried, *Jugenderinnerungen*, 6.
21   *Friedens-Warte* 21, no. 1 (January 1919): 26.

and Teaching). Fried sent book order cards to potential buyers and at the end of August even received a special three-month military passport, which enabled him to travel from Vienna to Berlin. The identification card[22] has no photo, but it does contain a personal description:

build	of medium height
face	elongated
hair	brown
eyes	gray
mouth and nose	proportioned
distinguishing traits	none

2   Alfred H. Fried and Company

After his return to Berlin, Fried established the Alfred H. Fried Verlag on November 25, 1887.[23] One of the first books to be published, in April 1888, was *Buch berühmter Duelle* (Book of Famous Duels). In addition to book-order cards and posters, Fried also used another advertising medium: he offered newspapers and magazines a multi-page feature article entitled "Das Duell im modernen Rechtsstaat" (The Duel in the Modern Constitutional State) that they could print at no cost "with the understanding that they also print the ad for *Buch berühmter Duelle* by Dr. Adolph Kohut."[24] In the same year four more works appeared, which Fried advertised aggressively. In addition, from the Oppenheim Publishing House in Berlin, he acquired *Geschichte der jüdischen Literatur in 18 Lieferungen* (History of the Jewish Literature in 18 Installments) by Dr. Gustav Karpeles.

The destitute Fried later explained in a letter to his creditors where he got the money: "In the spring of 1888, I established a publishing house with Mr. Jacques Gnadenfeld, then an apprentice in banking. [...] I brought my knowledge and experience as well as my wealth of ideas and entrepreneurial spirit to the business. Mr. Gnadenfeld was to share equally in the earnings. Mr. Gnadenfeld's father, Mr. Leopold Gnadenfeld, was opposed to his son's participation in the endeavor, but in May 1888, when our successes were already apparent, he

---

22   The personal property of Trude Simonsohn, now in the Fried Nachlass.
23   Alfred H. Fried Verlag, Berlin N.W. 7, Unter den Linden 59a, 2nd Floor. Cf. *Gesamt-Verlags-Katalog des Deutschen Buchhandels, 14. Ergänzungsband*, part one (Münster, no date given), 867ff. *Adressbuch des Deutschen Buchhandels*, Leipzig, Vol. 51 (1889) and vol. 54 (1892).
24   Cf. Fried's newspaper ads. Nachlass Fried, Box 14, file 271.

extended a line of credit of 3,000 marks to the new company. On the strength of this credit, we continued our work, and I take pride in the fact that, based on my good ideas, almost all of which were successful, we achieved sales–with the small amount of capital–that I don't think anyone else will soon achieve."[25]

In point of fact, Jacques Gnadenfeld, an apprentice at the bank Daniel & Frankenstein, and son of the manufacturer Leopold Gnadenfeld from Breslau, joined the company as a silent partner in the spring of 1888. However, the money that the banker had borrowed from various friends was soon no longer enough to cover the expenses of the small publishing house. So Fried urged Gnadenfeld to ask his wealthy father for a blank loan. Leopold Gnadenfeld, however, signed off on a loan of 3,000 marks with the condition that Jacques immediately become an official partner.[26] On October 1, 1888, Fried announced to the book trade world that his former silent partner "[...] is now an official shareholder in my publishing firm and that we will continue the same course jointly, under the name Alfred H. Fried & Co., once the registration with the commercial court has been completed."[27] Fried, who had characterized himself as a lonely person,[28] was in fact more of a solitary person who was prone to violent temperamental outbursts.[29] Moreover, Jacques Gnadenfeld's letters document early on that Fried evidently did not have too high an opinion of his partner.[30]

At first, everything seemed to go well. In 1889 more than 20 books were published amounting to a total of over 60 volumes. It was clear even in these first years that Fried was not afraid to broach hot topics. This brought him into contact with Richard Grelling in 1889, with whom he would later work to found the German Peace Society. In the collection of commemorative writings published on the occasion of Fried's death in 1922, Richard Grelling[31] mentioned

---

25 Nachlass Fried, Box 14, file 271: double-sided printed flyer, 1891.
26 The move of the publishing house to Neustädter Kirchstraße 15 in Berlin NW 7 goes hand in hand with the partial ownership by Gnadenfeld.
27 Cf. Nachlass Fried, Box 14, file 271.
28 Cf. Fried, "Biographische Skizze," 3. "In my youth I was by and large a solitary figure, which was also the case later in life."
29 "I admit that you have an unhappy disposition, something that we all inherited." Fried to Pauline Wyon-Fried, November 30, 1908. Nachlass Fried, Box 31.
30 "Be assured, dear Alfred, that, as far as I'm concerned, everything is being done and will be done to promote our business. Regrettably, I must agree with your comments on my knowledge of literature because there is much that I do not know that an educated person must know." Jacques Gnadenfeld to Fried, January 7, 1888. Nachlass Fried, Box 14, file 271.
31 On Richard Grelling, see Helmut Donat, "Richard Grelling," in Helmut Donat, Karl Holl (eds.), *Die Friedensbewegung. Organizierter Pazifismus in Deutschland, Österreich und in der Schweiz* (Düsseldorf, 1983), 162f.

his first encounter with Fried: "I suppose I'm the only one who had a relationship with Fried when he was not yet Fried the peacemaker, – nomen, omen – but a simple publisher, owner of the firm Alfred H. Fried & Co., when he had pacifist leanings but was not yet a pacifist by profession. One of my speeches to the Fortschrittlicher Verein Waldeck entitled "Kaiser Friedrichs Tagebuch und der Prozess Geffcken" (Kaiser Friedrich's Diary and the Geffcken Trial) had aroused considerable interest by virtue of its harsh criticism of an investigation of treason, initiated by Bismarck, against the former close friend of Emperor Friedrich III, namely the well-known professor of international law Friedrich Heinrich Geffcken. [...] It was both widely known at that time that one should not accuse Bismarck of anything, just as it is dangerous in Germany today to make an accusation against Wilhelm and his crowd for the World War. But that did not stop me or the young publisher Fried [...] from confronting the storm. And so – as the first product of our public political cooperation –my lecture, under the above title, appeared with a bright red cover in 1889 in the publishing house of Alfred H. Fried & Co."[32]

There were no objections to the publication. Fried even came into contact with Bismarck himself a year later and published a popular edition of his *Gesammelte Werke* (Collected Works).[33] Fried realized a profit from the sale of the books. He later stated: "We had revenues of 58,000 marks in the first year and 68,000 marks in the second year. Our net earnings in the first year were 11,000, in the second year 17,000 [...] marks."[34]

The signs were all positive for the young publishers — especially for Fried, who besides the founding of a successful publishing company and the publication of two books of quotations with the publisher Reclam seemed to have hit the jackpot in his private life. During a visit to Breslau (Wroclaw, Poland today) in 1888, he met the family of his business partner. Leopold Gnadenfeld owned a factory that manufactured woolen and cotton-knitted stockings and socks; he was a well-known and wealthy citizen of Breslau. The twenty-four-year-old Fried fell in love with Gnadenfeld's second-oldest daughter, Gertrud, who was just 19 years old at the time. The wedding took place in Wroclaw on February 7, 1889. But Gertrud brought "only the home furnishings" into the marriage, as Fried later stated. Perhaps because of his disappointment over this frugal dowry, but perhaps also because Fried did not appreciate the work of the more mercantile-minded Jacques, there was increasing friction between the two:

---

32   Goldscheid, *Gedenkblätter*, 31f.
33   Bruno Walden, ed. *Fürst Bismarcks gesammelte Werke. Briefe, Reden und Aktenstücke. Erste Volksausgabe* vol. 2: *Politische Reden* (Berlin, undated).
34   Cf. Fried, "Flugblatt," 1891.

"Mr. Gnadenfeld participated in my success and profits, but did nothing else for me, nothing at all; at most he performed a few mechanical tasks, things that a simple assistant does for 100 marks a month. But he did understand that if a supplier demands a price of 90 Pfennig, you should then offer and be able to secure the deal for 85 Pfennig."

Fried continued to regard the publishing company solely as his own creation, and in January 1890 he tried to cut ties with his partner and with the Gnadenfeld family by claiming an increased cost of living due to the marriage. The Gnadenfelds were ready to compromise and increase Fried's share of the profits. Nevertheless, only one year later he insisted on a separation. On February 1, 1891, Fried announced through a newspaper advertisement to the book trade that from now on he was the sole owner of Alfred H. Fried & Co: "Today, after an amicable agreement, my former partner Mr. Jacques Gnadenfeld is leaving the publishing company that the two of us managed together under the name Alfred H. Fried & Co. The company will retain its name, and I will be the sole manager."[35]

But it was not quite as easy as Fried imagined. Jacques Gnadenfeld and his father fought back and forced Fried to divide the company: both partners were to take on a proportional share of the liabilities. "I agreed, although it tore my heart apart to see my own intellectual progeny and the fruits of my work spirited away from me."[36] But that was not the end of it. Jacques Gnadenfeld, his brother-in-law, and Sally Simon, a new partner, demanded a guarantee that Fried would pay the assumed liabilities. Fried's frightfully naive hope that his father-in-law would once again jump into the breach was misplaced. Even an initially eager partner may break off a deal shortly before the conclusion of the contract. Thus Fried found himself compelled to issue an appeal to his creditors in the spring of 1891: "[...] and to ask you, through your united action, to enable me to carry on the business which I have founded and created by myself out of nothing. The analyses of certified public accountants as well as those of our own business associates demonstrate that a continuation of our business will not result in the slightest loss to you." He evidently managed to persuade the creditors that he could continue successfully.

Gnadenfeld retained primarily the classical authors, while Fried offered works by less well-known writers such as Hans Land[37] and Heinrich Zschokke;[38]

---

35   Newspaper clipping of an ad of February 18, 1891. Nachlass Fried, Box 14, file 271.
36   For this and the following quotation, see Fried, "Flugblatt," 1891.
37   Hans Land, *Amor Thyrannus. Drama* (1889), *Die am Wege sterben* (1889), *Stiefkinder der Gesellschaft* (1889).
38   Heinrich Zschokke, *Ausgewählte Werke*, 5 vols., 1889.

he also published on topics that were more modern and often controversial, such as a series on hygiene in which various authors dealt with the relationship between hygiene and chastity, the honeymoon, intellectual work, and food.[39] And he continued on this path for a while. Among the 27 works that were published or reissued in 1891, four volumes were authored by the women's rights activist Gisela von Streitberg,[40] five volumes were devoted to hygienic issues, and a new series combined works of erotic literature under the title *Sammlung Fried* (Fried Collection). Since the publication of this series would later lead to criticism of Fried when he was a member of the board of the German Peace Society, it is worth noting now some additional titles: 1) Restif de la Bretonne, *Die Liebe mit 45 Jahren. Intime Memoiren* (Love at 45. Intimate Memoirs), 2/3) Paul Mantegazza, *Die Hygiene der Liebe* (The Hygiene of Love), 4) Arthur Schopenhauer, *Zur Metaphysik der Geschlechterliebe* (On the Metaphysics of Gender Relations) 5/6) Paul Mantegazza, *Die Physiologie der Liebe* (The Physiology of Love), 7) Paul Mantegazza, *Die Physiologie des Genusses* (The Physiology of Pleasure), 8: J. S. Mill, *Die Hörigkeit der Frau* (The Subjection of Women). It is hard to argue that these books were pornographic literature, but in the puritanical times of the empire they were certainly controversial.

Despite these largely relevant and sometimes controversial topics, Fried seems to have taken on the commercially weaker part of the publishing program; while Gnadenfeld quickly did increasingly better and the publishing house continued to grow until 1935, Fried remained heavily in debt. And things did not fundamentally change when he altered his publishing program to include political and lexical works in 1892. But this latter change did have consequences, because as soon as Fried's new program came out in autumn 1891, Gnadenfeld, who had exclusive rights to encyclopedias and classical works, accused Fried of plagiarism and of a breach of contract.

The two opponents carried out their quarrel publicly, sending posters and multi-page circulars to the booksellers, and they all too often hit far below the belt. Fried finally put an end to the shenanigans in November 1891, on his birthday: "Enough! I hereby declare that I will no longer enter into further hostilities with Jacques Gnadenfeld, Adolf Hein, and Sally Simon, but will simply suffer the shenanigans of my brothers-in-law in silence and thus spare the book trade

---

39   Dr. Carl von Gelsen, *Die Hygiene der Flitterwochen*, 1888 (5th edition, 1892); Dr. Th. G. Kornig, *Die Hygiene der Keuschheit*, 1890 (2nd edition, 1891); Dr. E. F. Rain, *Die Hygiene der Nahrungsmittel*, 1890; Dr. Otto Dornblüth, *Die Hygiene der geistigen Arbeit*, 1890.

40   G. v. Streitberg, Vol. 1: *Die Erziehung der Töchter. Grausamkeiten im Familien- und gesell. Leben*, Vol. 2: *Die verehelichten und ehelosen Frauen*, Vol. 3: *Die falsche Moral im Leben des Weibes*, Vol. 4: *Die Enterbten, Gefallenen, Verlorenen. Ein Beitrag zur Kulturgeschichte des Weibes*.

exposure to any further unpleasant public correspondence until the court has rendered a decision. Any further attack will find its way into the wastepaper basket, and I ask every right-thinking colleague to pay proper tribute to this nonsensical activity. Berlin, November 11, 1891. Yours sincerely, Alfred H. Fried."[41]

In the end, Fried won this battle, and in the summer of 1892 Gnadenfeld had to revoke his accusation of plagiarism.[42] However, the damage to Fried's reputation in the circle of booksellers was almost irreparable.

It is at this time of unrest and material insecurity that Fried first encountered the peace movement.

3 The Path to the Peace Movement

"It might have been on November 1 or 2, 1891,"[43] wrote Fried, "and I sat in the Café Kaiserhof in Berlin and read to my astonishment and with great interest that Baroness Bertha von Suttner was the President of an Austrian Peace Society in Vienna and that she would leave for Rome in the next few days to attend the Peace Congress there as a delegate. [...] So, in Vienna there was a society that was committed to opposing war; there were still people who, like me, regarded war as a something evil. Were there such people in other countries who could come together at an international congress? This came over me like a revelation. I heard a voice in me exclaim, I belong to these people, my life's task is to participate in their work! That very same day, I wrote to Bertha von Suttner, who was then living at Harmannsdorf Castle in Lower Austria [...] and expressed my firm desire to work with her on the great endeavor she was undertaking. I suggested to her that I publish a monthly magazine to disseminate the idea of peace in Germany and Austria."[44]

Bertha von Suttner answered immediately and indicated her interest in his proposal. For Fried "the most important signpost in my career. [...] From that day on, I was integrated into the machinery of the peace movement, and from then on, I never stopped working for peace. [...] I remember exactly the hour when it came over me, like a higher power, and I told myself, here is something

---

41 Nachlass Fried, Box 14, file 272.
42 It is not known how the courts ruled; a newspaper notice of June 15, 1892 is appended to Adolph Hein's plagiarized circular published by Gnadenfeld-Verlag. It can be found in the Nachlass. According to the notice, he "hereby fully rescinds the content of the circular in accord with an agreement."
43 In his "Biographische Skizze," Fried writes the date as April 4. See his "Biographische Skizze," 4.
44 For this and what follows, see Fried, *Jugenderinnerungen*, 16f.

that you can use to create a fulfilling life and to make your life meaningful. Unsatisfied with my job, filled with a yearning for higher things, I suddenly saw a goal that was worth working and fighting for."

This confession is to be taken quite literally. Although he worked nonstop, the publishing business did not fare as well as he had hoped. Above all, the young man did not get what he desired: social prestige. What was clear in the fifteen-year-old's diary, namely, the driving desire to "rise up out of the mud," did not only refer to his material situation, but also to his position in society. This would remain for Fried a life-long motivating force of his actions. So it is not surprising that he was thrilled with the prospect of fighting for a good, ethical cause, along with the support of those whose names resonated with the public. The enormous success of Suttner's book *Die Waffen nieder!*[45] (Lay Down Your Arms) had not escaped the notice of the young publisher: "The tenor of this book seemed to touch a nerve in society; its impact on the times was so clearly felt. Lengthy articles about the book appeared in the newspapers, there were lectures about it, and in the Austrian Reichsrat the Minister of Finance referred to the book in a military debate and recommended that the deputies devote a few hours to the reading of the novel."[46] Fried imagined that a journal that followed the popular book would quite likely also be successful, especially if there were a financially powerful publisher behind it. The general atmosphere seemed favorable. The founding of the Austrian Peace Movement gave reason to hope for the successful founding of a German Peace Society, and thus a large number of subscribers to the new journal.

Negotiations began as soon as Bertha von Suttner returned from Rome. It quickly became clear that one condition could not be met: a publisher who was in a strong financial position. While Fried considered the author herself to be well-off, so too the Baroness believed Fried to be a successful, independent businessman. For example, she asked for a reasonable fee for the publication of the magazine: "You figured on 3,000 marks for paper and printing costs. You'll have to add 2,400 marks for editors and authors. It is not right that they work for nothing."[47] For Fried, this demand was too great. Burdened by substantial debt, he was not even able to pay a small fee of 50 marks a month, which was the sum that he finally agreed on with Bertha von Suttner.[48] Although both

---

45   Bertha von Suttner, *Die Waffen nieder! Eine Lebensgeschichte* (Dresden, 1889). The book went through 14 editions by 1896.
46   Fried, *Jugenderinnerungen*, 19.
47   Bertha von Suttner to Fried, December 22, 1891. Nachlass Fried, Box 25. Cf. Hamann, *Bertha von Suttner. Ein Leben für den Frieden* (Munich/Zurich, 1991), 168 (Note 51, p. 525).
48   Ibid, 168ff.

quickly realized that they would not get any financial support from each other, they nevertheless continued and hoped to receive the required funds through a fixed number of subscribers.

Just as Fried did not let himself be discouraged by Suttner's unexpected financial situation, so too did she seem to accept his social background and his current situation She observed: "It is precisely because you are still so young, that we can place our hopes in your passion and energy – and that you are a *self* soon to appear as *made*. Growth – that is the basis of all greatness and strength; the greatness that falls from heaven (by birth or wealth) often stops growing and sometimes diminishes."[49]

In the second half of January 1892, Fried published the first issue of the journal. It was, as he had hoped, a success, at least with respect to prestige: "We received congratulations from all quarters. It was regarded everywhere as a special event, the publication of a journal dedicated to the notion of peace in the midst of a militarized Berlin, and what's more it appeared under the title *Die Waffen nieder*, a polemic that was more than ever anachronistic. Larger German newspapers published the ad and occasionally even longer reviews. Even abroad, the journal was welcomed. Sympathetic comments appeared in newspapers in Paris and London."[50]

However, the high expectations did not come to fruition. The number of subscribers remained too low, likely because a German Peace Society could not be founded as quickly as had been expected. In January 1892, Bertha von Suttner wrote to Fried: "I am embarrassed by the number of subscribers. We both seem to have been too sanguine [...] everyone is so indifferent and cautious [...] I'm not worried about finding superb contributors – just about the quantity of subscriptions: it's hard to achieve."[51] In February, as a precautionary measure, Fried had only 370 copies printed, but these too were not sold.[52] "In all, there were two hundred subscribers who supported the endeavor,"[53] he observed. That's not enough to get the journal out of the red; when the situation did not improve in the following months, Fried handed it over to the E. Pierson publishing house in Dresden in the spring of 1893, which, as he wrote, "could easily handle the deficit.[54]

---

49   Bertha von Suttner to Fried, undated [January 1892], quoted in Hamman, *Bertha von Suttner*, 169.
50   Fried, *Jugenderinnerungen*, 22.
51   Bertha von Suttner to Fried, January 2, 1892, quoted in Hamman, *Bertha von Suttner*, 169.
52   Ibid.
53   Fried, *Jugenderinnerungen*, 22.
54   Ibid, 23.

This was a bitter disappointment for Bertha von Suttner as well. On the occasion of her 50th birthday on June 9, 1893, Fried wrote a very rueful letter: "My Dear Madam Baroness! Wearing penitential vestments and bearing ashes on his forehead, a quiet guest is approaching today's festivities to offer his modest congratulations. The old tragedy of wanting too much and being too little capable of achieving it has rendered the man speechless and contemplative . . ."[55] He noted that he had thought long and hard about whether he might be allowed to congratulate her, but he nevertheless did want to embrace the memory of the most beautiful episode of his life, "the short span of time that put my work in the service of a great person," and that he would continue to be "your faithful squire." But the uneasy feelings between the two did not last long, and Fried soon became a regular contributor to the magazine, which, as Karl Ferdinand Reichel observed, "was not insignificant for its content, since he wrote in a concise journalistic style and had success as an advertiser."[56]

Fried was now fully committed to the founding of a German Peace Society since his most fundamental idea, i.e., that the new journal should become a focal point of the emerging movement, absolutely included the founding of a German peace society. "The hugely successful creation of the Austrian Peace Society was to be a model."[57]

In the winter of 1890–91, Bertha von Suttner had a chance meeting in Venice with the painter and writer Felix Moscheles,[58] who was also a founding member of and active collaborator in the "International Arbitration and Peace Association" in Great Britain and Ireland. Moscheles had recently read her novel *Die Waffen nieder!* and, like many other contemporaries, considered it autobiographical. As such, he imagined his first meeting with Bertha von Suttner would be with a "poor widow" who was living proof of the cruelties of the war. He was thus very surprised when he learned that the story was pure fiction. Nevertheless, he immediately took the opportunity to convince the well-known author of the necessity of a peace society in Austria.[59] Ultimately with success. On September 3, 1891, Bertha von Suttner published a notice in the liberal Viennese daily newspaper *Neue Freie Presse*, in which she reported about the upcoming World Peace Congress in Rome, about the activities of

---

55   Fried to Bertha von Suttner, June 9, 1893. Nachlass Bertha von Suttner, Box 19. The following quotations are taken from this letter.
56   Karl Ferdinand Reichel, *Die pazifistische Presse* (Würzburg, 1938), 4.
57   Fried, *Jugenderinnerungen*, 24.
58   On Felix Moscheles (1833–1917), see J. O. Baylen in Josephson, *Biographical Dictionary*, 669ff.
59   For more on this meeting, see Bertha von Suttner, *Memoiren* (Stuttgart/Leipzig, 1909), 190ff.

foreign peace societies, and finally about support for the establishment of a peace association in Austria.[60] Surprisingly, the resonance was quite great.

Bertha von Suttner later spoke of the hundreds of supportive letters from all parts of Austria that she had received. She then invited the residents of Vienna to a meeting to form a provisional committee. The first meeting took place on September 29. Those assembled proclaimed themselves as the new national branch of the London Association, and they once again turned to the public on October 18 to present their goals, emphasizing in particular the completely apolitical, purely humanitarian character of society, and to invite the public to an inaugural meeting. A preliminary committee drew ten people,[61] of whom Bertha von Suttner was the only woman and P. K. Rosegger the only person who was not an aristocrat. Just a few days later, with official approval, the Austrian Peace Society (Österreichische Friedensgesellschaft) was formed and six representatives were sent to Rome. Due to individual donations the society's finances were in such good shape at this time that travel subsidies could be awarded.

It took less than two months to establish an association in Austria, one that not only included lustrous names, but also had a full treasury and 2000 members right from the beginning.[62] A tempting example for Berlin. It seemed as if one only needed an initial spark – a speech, an article, a visit by a well-known pacifist followed by a few big names – and one would quickly be able to form a peace society in Berlin. But unlike in Austria, the last wars, especially those fought by the Prussians of the German Reich, had turned out extremely favorable. France had been pushed back, and the German nation had been formed according to Prussia's wishes. The military enjoyed an excellent reputation, and its breath swept through all parts of society – especially in the young imperial capital of Berlin. In addition, at the end of the Three Emperors Year in 1888, a monarch had come to power, in the person of William II, who left no doubt that he intended to further expand his own power and that of his state.[63]

---

60 For more on this topic and the following discussion, see Suttner, *Memorien*, 204ff.
61 B. Ritter von Carneri, Privy Secretary Carl Coronini, Count Rudolf Hoyos, Baron Richard von Krafft-Ebing (professor), Reichstag deputy Baron von Pirquet, P. K. Rosegger, Dr. Carl Ritter von Scherzer, Baron A. G. von Suttner, Baroness Bertha von Suttner-Kinsky, Prince Alfred Wrede. Cf. Suttner, *Memoiren*, 210.
62 The initial successes were quickly followed by greater sobriety. The accounting reports of the Austrian Peace Society show a stagnation in the number of members from 1892 to 1893 and shrinking financial resources. Cf. Josef Bauer, "Die österreichische Friedensbewegung," Diss. Vienna, 1949, 45f.
63 On Wilhelm II, see Gerd Fesser, "Kaiser Wilhelm II. und der Wilhelminismus," in Karl Holl, Hans Kloft, Gerd Fesser, *Caligula – Wilhelm II. und der Cäsarenwahnsinn* (Bremen, 2001), 117ff.

After Bismarck's fall in 1890, Count Leo Caprivi became chancellor. As chancellor, he wanted domestically to enhance social equity. Through his policies, he sought to integrate both the center and the left liberals but at the same time strengthen the military through increased armament procurements. After he had already expanded the army in the summer of 1890, he demanded in November 1892 a further increase of 80,000 men.[64] Despite the rejection of this bill by the liberals and by the Center Party in the Reichstag,[65] the parliamentary debates in the run-up to the bill had a rather negative impact on the intended establishment of a peace society. Moreover, the base in the Reich on which the peace movement was able to build was shrinking.[66]

The first peace association in the area of what was later to be the German Reich had been founded in Königsberg in September 1850 by the preacher of the Free Evangelical Church Julius Rupp and the physician Robert Motherby following an international peace congress held in Frankfurt in August. Despite its brief existence it still had 140 members. However, the association was banned and then disbanded by the police in May 1851 as the political reaction heated up. At the end of the sixties and in the middle of the seventies, the journalist Eduard Loewenthal made two attempts, first in Dresden and then in Berlin, to found associations with pacifist goals. These, too, did not last long. The wars to unify the empire, which under Prussian leadership sought to establish the widely desired German nation-state through "blood and iron," were a poor breeding ground for pacifist ideas.

It was not until ten years later that the Englishman Hodgson Pratt, Chairman of the International Arbitration and Peace Institute in London, succeeded in establishing a few new local peace associations through two recruitment trips across Germany in the summer and autumn of 1885. In Berlin only the formation of a preparatory committee came into existence, under the direction Rudolf Virchow, a physician and free-thinking Reichstag deputy. But peace associations were indeed founded in Darmstadt, Stuttgart, and Frankfurt.

---

64 See, among others, Dieter Riesenberger, *Geschichte der Friedensbewegung in Deutschland. Von den Anfängen bis 1933* (Göttingen, 1985), 59f. On the policy of rearming the army in the German Reich, see Stig Förster, "Alter und neuer Miltarismus im Kaiserreich," in Jost Dülfer/Karl Holl (eds.), *Bereit zum Krieg. Kriegsmentalität im wilhelminischen Deutschland 1890–1914*, 122ff, and in particular 125.

65 This was a rejection that led to the dissolution of the Reichstag on May 6, 1893 and to the split of the German Radical Party (Deutsch-Freisinnige Partei), also known as German Free-minded Party, which further weakened social liberalism (Linksliberalismus) and thus also the foundation of the peace movement.

66 On the following notions, see Scheer, *Deutsche Friedensgesellschaft*, 24ff. Cf. also Dr. Alexander Dietz, *Franz Wirth und der Frankfurter Friedensverein* (Frankfurt a. M., 1911), 18ff.

Around 1892, however, of these three, only the Frankfurt branch still existed; after disagreements with Pratt on the Alsace-Lorraine question, the other two disbanded within two years. The seventy-one member Frankfurt peace association, which had been under surveillance by the police and was led by the 66-year-old patent attorney Franz Wirth, was the only one on which Fried and Bertha von Suttner could base their attempt to found a peace society.

Fried and von Suttner were optimistic about founding the new journal, and they also believed that a German peace society could be easily established. When Bertha von Suttner received an invitation from the association "Berliner Presse" to give a lecture in March, they decided to take advantage of the seemingly good opportunity. Fried had sign-up sheets labeled "Vorbereitendes Komitee zur Gründung einer deutschen Friedensgesellschaft (Preparatory Committee for the Founding of a German Peace Society), where people could register if they wished to participate. However, it was only the banquet, which was held in Bertha von Suttner's honor, that was able to attract an organizing committee consisting of members who were well-known for their political and intellectual contributions. The committee included first and foremost the vice president of the Reichstag Dr. Karl Baumbach, but also members of parliament such as Theodor Barth, M.D., Dr. Max Hirsch, Friedrich Spielhagen, and Prince Heinrich zu Schönaich-Carolath,[67] as well as writers such as Fritz Mauthner, Wilhelm Bölsche, Hans Land, and Dr. Arthur Levysohn, the editor-in-chief of the *Berliner Tageblatt*. Fried made the administrative arrangements and printed both the advertising materials and the admission tickets, which his publishing house sold for 6 marks.

The lecture and the banquet, which, according to Fried, were attended by over 250 people,[68] were a success, but more for the well-known author and as a social event rather than as a pacifist event. Von Suttner's visit hardly contributed to the founding of a peace society. Nevertheless, according to Fried, the gathering was not without effect: "After the approbation and tribute given to the Austrian spokeswoman in the capital of the Reich, it did not seem quite so embarrassing to support the idea of pacifism."

The national press was also apparently following the event with some concern. At least, the satirical article that Fried cites suggests this: "The lady, who has decided to strangle the god of war with an apron, is coming to Berlin in the middle of this month, and her worshippers consider this event to be worthy of a banquet celebration. This is the festival that is scheduled for March 18 in

---

67 The participating deputies of the Reichstag were members of the "Deutsches parlamentarisches Komitee für Schiedsgericht und Frieden."
68 Cf. Fried, *Jugenderinnerungen*, 27ff. The following quotes are also taken from this source.

the English House. Members of the invitation committee include not only the vice president of the Reichstag and several members of parliament, but also a number of well-known local writers and journalists, all of whom join in the peaceful battle cry: "'Lay down your arms, take up your pens!' Whoever wants to eat for world peace, must pay 6 marks; tickets are of course only available at Fried's. After the dinner, the world peace pipe will be smoked. Some of the members of the committee are said to have decided to drink war out of existence; they allegedly will stay up all night drinking champagne. Meanwhile, the ladies intend to carry out an experiment: to resolve the difficult peace question, they will dance all the lieutenants to death, thus preventing an unintended war due to a lack of available lieutenants."

For the young Fried and his friend Hans Land, Bertha von Suttner's stay in Berlin was their first personal encounter with her — and at first a bitter disappointment: "Today I really no longer know what the disappointment was. Bertha von Suttner was around 49 years old at the time. We young men could have hardly imagined an erotic experience. Was it the clumsiness of the conversation, perhaps the inanity of the topic. In short, we enthusiasts suffered terribly, and after we had poured out our hearts for a long time, we tramped home laden with *weltschmerz* at four o'clock in the morning."

In the course of the visit, however, the relationship improved and became more and more cordial: "[...] on the way to the train station Bertha von Suttner took a twig of a lily of the valley from her bouquet and stuck it in my buttonhole. A tribute and a thank you." This little gesture meant a lot to Fried; he put the twig under the glass of her picture, and it would remain there for the rest of his life. On March 26, he wrote to the Suttners: "Your presence here was an important stage in my life. Through your presence my heart's impetuosity was transformed into the knowledge that I will put my life in the service of the cause that you represent in such sublime and magnificent fashion. Take me into the ranks of your army and let me strive under your wings for the greatest of all goals. I want to thank you through my deeds."[69]

But even in the following months Fried was unable to create a German peace society. The liberal-minded parliamentarians on whom he placed his hopes were hesitant, not only because of the current debate over the Caprivian militia, but also because they did not want to combine the new peace society with one of their own founding: just a few months earlier, on December 14, 1891, the "German Parliamentary Committee for Arbitration and Peace" had been founded in the German Reichstag, to which about sixty predominantly

---

69   Fried to Suttner, March 26, 1892. Nachlass Bertha von Suttner, Box 19.

liberal-minded parliamentarians belonged, among them Virchow, Dr. Theodor Barth, and Dr. Max Hirsch as the recording secretary.[70] Although Max Hirsch later played an important role in the German Peace Society (DFG), most parliamentarians were and remained in favor of a clear separation of the political arena from the association level.

At the beginning of autumn, while visiting his parents in Vienna,[71] Fried also made a side trip to Harmannsdorf Castle to visit the Suttners. The small castle where Bertha von Suttner lived with her husband, his parents and his siblings was located in the Waldviertel of Eggenburg, about an hour by carriage from the nearest train station and difficult to get to. The stately home with the large study, shared by husband and wife, and the adjoining library, impressed the visitor, even if he already realized that there were problems with the household finances. The main topic of the meeting was the possible formation of a German peace society.[72] Upon his return to Berlin, Fried changed his tactics, and he now increasingly appealed to potential sympathetic members beyond Berlin. Thus he contacted Eugen Schlief[73] in Dresden, who had just published his work *Der Friede in Europa* (Peace in Europe):[74] "Schlief was a lawyer, a member of the National Liberal Party for which he had once been a candidate for the Reichstag. He was a very wealthy man, an impressive character with sophisticated manners [...]"[75]

Schlief's book, which even thirty years later Fried called "the best and most politically mature explication of a League of Nations in the new era," made a strong impression on the young Fried, despite its challenging language: "Schlief's book was for me, particularly in the critical part, a revelation. I thought I could see in this factual account of the topic the basis for the successful creation of a peace society. And although I did not at all approve of the rejection of ethics, I wrote to Schlief, begging him to become a member of a German peace society."

In Schlief's scientific approach Fried intuitively recognized the antithesis to Bertha von Suttner's emotional appeal; he also saw that Schlief could be of great importance to his own work in Berlin. Schlief's rational concept, which excluded all ethical aspects, was appropriate, as Fried emphasized later, to the Zeitgeist, in which "the politicians of the period were stricken by the fear

---

70 Cf. Scheer, *Deutsche Friedensgesellschaft*, 43.
71 Cf. Hamann, *Bertha von Suttner*, 91ff.
72 Cf. Fried, *Jugenderinnerungen*, 30f.
73 In his *Jugenderinnerungen* (31) Fried misnames Schlief as "Emil," but there is no doubt that the person in question in Eugen Schlief.
74 Eugen Schlief, *Der Friede in Europa. Eine völkerrechtlich-politische Studie* (Leipzig, 1892).
75 Fried, *Jugenderinnerungen*, 31f.

that they might be regarded as men of feeling." From the beginning Fried perceived Schlief's position not as an antithesis but as a complement to Bertha von Suttner, to whom he subsequently wrote: "While you, Madame, represent the south with your way of fighting, Dr. Schlief represents the north. Heart and mind, as if one or the other could act alone."[76]

Although Fried's path would later follow the direction of a material pacifist theory, one that put aside all ethical and moral aspects, around 1892 he was still much closer to the Suttner approach, but even at this time, he recognized the need to connect the one approach with the other. What modern research today likes to proclaim an antithesis, between the scientifically oriented approach of Fried's organizational pacifism and the neo-Kantian-ethical approach of, say, Ludwig Quidde, were, at that time, for Fried the cornerstones of a single, multi-faceted movement that ought to be capable, precisely because of their different styles, of joining many people to one another.

Schlief was initially open to participation and came to Berlin for further planning. Together they went to Richard Grelling: "I had already contacted him over the summer about the peace society and had found him to be sympathetic and inclined to cooperate. Schlief and I quickly worked things out with him. The three of us now formed a solid core around which a society could crystallize."[77]

Attempts to find other collaborators encountered various obstacles: in addition to the reluctance of the liberal parliamentarians, another obstacle was the rise of new reform movements (the result of the non-renewal of the Socialist Laws in 1890), since many other peace-loving forces were involved with different groups. Fried mentioned in his memoirs, for example, that the "Ethical Society," founded by Wilhelm Foerster only a few weeks before the German Peace Society (DFG), attracted almost the same people that the peace society needed.[78]

It was the same with Moritz von Egidy's[79] new movement. Von Egidy had moved from Dresden to Berlin in the autumn of 1891. He too was fundamentally

---

76 This was also printed in *Die Waffen nieder!* 3 (1894), 70. Cf. the letter from Fried to Suttner, February 8, 1894.
77 Fried, *Jugenderinnerungen*, 33.
78 Ibid. However, the example of Foerster, who was also a founding member of the German Peace Society, shows that membership in the one association did not preclude working for the other association. Cf. Scheer, *Deutsche Friedensgesellschaft*, 69 for a discussion of the advantages and disadvantages that grew out of the personal connections with other reform movements.
79 On Christoph Moritz von Egidy, see, among others, Josephson, *Biographical Dictionary*, 246ff. and Donat/Hall *Die Friedensbewegung*, 95ff. Both Fried and Bertha von Suttner, who

pacifist, but in contrast to Schlief he placed ethical-moral aspects in the foreground. When Fried personally asked Egidy to collaborate, he refused: "I can still see him standing in front of me in the middle of the room: 'Join us, we have unfurled the banner,' he said in a solemn tone with the vision of a seer. He thought that the doctrine he preached could become the center of all reformist movements."[80] A few years later, however, Egidy did join the Peace Society and, until his death in December 1898, dedicated all his energy to advancement of the Tsarist Manifesto.

In addition to Foerster and Egidy, Fried addressed all those who had in some way written about peace, such as Moritz Brasch in Leipzig, Dr. E. Harmening in Jena, and the emeritus pastor Hetzel in Fürstenwalde, who had recently published a book *Die Humanisierung des Kriegs in ihrer kulturgeschichtlichen Entwicklung* (The Humanization of the War in its Cultural-Historical Development).[81] Fried had success with the old man because he too was interested in founding a peace society, and he too joined the effort.[82] A young student in contact with Bertha von Suttner was also actively involved in the first phase, but he would later withdraw disappointed. Albert Südekum later became a socialist leader and Prussian finance minister.

Even at the first meeting of the committee, which was held at Knoop's wine tavern near Fried's apartment, there were contentious arguments with Schlief. His idea of a purely politically oriented society, possibly even a peace party, was not shared by the others: "First, because we felt too weak to enter the arena armed only with a political program, and second because we feared we could not win over the masses with such a program. Also, the law restricted the freedom of movement of the political associations to a large degree. Women, whose participation was indispensable, for example, were not allowed to join. [...] In short, we felt (and rightfully so) that we would not be able to be effective in Germany at that time with a purely political program, while the establishment of the association as an ethical community would allow the prospect of further activism and, in the long run, political influence."[83] The inaugural meeting of the Peace Society, which met in the more respectable wine bar of the Hotel Kaiserhof on November 9, 1892, finally took place without Schlief. However, that did not detract from the high spirits of those present, as Fried

---

in her memoir called Egidy a "Mensch von Kristall" ("a beautiful person") (Suttner, *Memoiren*, 256), held Egidy in particularly high regard and admiration.

80　Fried, *Jugenderinnerungen*, 34.
81　H. Hetzel, *Die Humanisierung des Krieges in ihrer kulturgeschichtlichen Entwicklung* (Frankfurt an der Oder, Trowitzsch, undated [1891]).
82　From 1893 to 1894, he even served as president of the German Peace Society.
83　Fried, *Jugenderinnerungen*, 36.

later recalled: "After the meeting, Theodor Barth approached me and shook my hand with the words: 'You have done it, Octavio.'"[84]

For Fried, however, this personal triumph was short-lived. The provisional board of directors with its 15 members[85] had at first no chairman; this was due to the lack of appeal of the "largely thankless office, which from the start was certainly exposed to countless hostilities."[86] But it also had to do with the fact that, following the example of the Austrians, Fried only sought out well-known names, for whom membership in the new society was less attractive. Even Bertha von Suttner finally advised against Fried's recruitment plan: "So you democrats need a title, do you? Do not think that that is necessary. The baby born in Bethlehem did not have a title, and his association is flourishing."

However, Fried insisted on his plan and, in the end, managed to find a seemingly suitable person. At the board meeting on December 21, 1892, Josef Kohler, a Berlin law professor, was elected chairman, but he was replaced by Pastor Hetzel just a few months later. Presumably, Deputy Chairman Richard Grelling bore the administrative burden from the beginning.[87] Yet he too could not prevent the mood of the society from quickly turning against its founder.

Fried may have seemed disagreeable to the other members for a variety of reasons: his unrestrained temperament and dominating manner may have had an off-putting effect on the older members, and his lower social status and lower level of education may have had a negative impact on the predominantly university-educated board members. It is also possible that the Austrian, with his close ties to Bertha von Suttner, was a thorn in the side of the deeply nationalistic propensity of the German pacifists from the outset. In any case, it was certainly not just his editions of erotic literature that led to Fried's isolation, because at least some of the members, such as Grelling, must have known about this part of his publishing business beforehand. Nevertheless, the *Sammlung Fried* (Fried Collection) provided them with a convenient excuse to get rid of him for the sake of the good name of the new organization: sometime between December 1892 and January 1893 he was removed from the

---

84 Ibid, 37.
85 The provisional executive board consisted of Count A. von Bothmer, Colonel (retired) (Wiesbaden), Dr. M. Brasch (Leipzig), Privy Councillor Professor Dr. Förster (Berlin), publisher Alfred H. Fried (Berlin), Colonel (retired) von Gizicky (Berlin), Reichstag representative Dr. Harmening (Jena), Dr. Mühling (Berlin), Attorney Nelson (Berlin), Dr. Richter (Pforzheim), Richard Schmidt-Canabis (Berlin), Friedrich Spielhagen (Berlin), Franz Wirth (Frankfurt am Main).
86 This and the following quotation are taken from Fried, *Jugenderinnerungen*, 37.
87 Cf. Scheer, *Deutsche Friedensgesellschaft*, 47f.

board.[88] It was the first of several bitter experiences that he would have with the German Peace Society (DFG).

For the young society itself, his exclusion was a decision that had fatal consequences. Without Fried's driving force, the German Peace Society was not able to publish its first proclamation until October, in which it set out its goals: its theme centered on countering the claim that the German people were less peace-loving than other peoples who had already formed peace societies. Accordingly, the German Peace Society should "be a point of unity for all who consider it desirable that the mutually connected states commit themselves by treaties to submit all disputes arising among them to international arbitration tribunals for resolution."[89]

Despite his feelings of deep disappointment, Fried had no intention of withdrawing from peace work. He was still convinced that the success of the peace movement required that it become a mass movement. But since the German Peace Society did not develop as he had hoped, Fried began to look for new ways to nurture the society. Earlier and more clearly than his fellow travelers, he recognized the necessity of clear and understandable publications and articles that could present the idea of peace to a broader range of the population. In 1893–94, he worked on a question-and-answer booklet intended to "educate the uninitiated about the status, causes, and goals of the peace movement as well as to provide those who already have some basic knowledge a primer to answer questions that may exceed their knowledge. I have quite faithfully sought to collect the clichés of our opponents and to refute them."[90]

Fried subdivided the text into five main chapters and an appendix, in which he reprinted the proclamations of the Austrian Peace Society and the German Peace Society, a list of local groups, and a directory of "outstanding writings and journals of the peace literature," which, besides Bertha von Suttner, Schlief, Grelling, Hetzel, and other pacifists, also listed Kant, Tolstoy, and two works by Wilhelm Liebknecht.[91] The fifth chapter contained various quotations about the peace movement by famous people. In the first four chapters Fried tried to give short and clear answers to 119 questions around such themes

---

88 Cf. Roger Chickering, *Imperial Germany and a World Without War. The Peace Movement and German Society, 1892–1914* (Princeton, 1975), 49. While Chickering dates the forced exit to the beginning of January 1893, Fried cites December 1892 in a letter to Otto Umfrid. Cf. Fried to Otto Umfrid, February 2, 1907. Nachlass Fried, Box 84.

89 Cf. Scheer, *Deutsche Friedensgesellschaft*, 48. The appeal "An das deutsche Volk!" was reprinted in *Die Waffen Nieder!* 1893, 402, and in *Die Waffen Nieder! Hundert Jahre Deutsche Friedensgesellschaft (1892–1992)*, ed. Guido Grünewald (Bremen, 1992), 20ff.

90 Forward to the first edition of *Friedens-Katechismus*, June 3, 1894.

91 Cf. Fried, *Friedens-Katechismus*, 84ff.

as war, armed peace, nation, animosity between nations, and the goals of the peace movement. He calculated the cost of a cannon shot, dealt with the social Darwinist question of whether war was a variation of the struggle for existence, explained the position of the army vis-à-vis the peace movement, and described the existing political situation in Europe as anarchy, a condition that was no longer consistent with the cultural level of modern Europe. Fried probably addressed all of the usual questions surrounding the promotion of peace.

In the summer of 1894, Fried published his *Friedens-Katechismus. Ein Kompendium der Friedenslehre zur Einführung in die Friedensbewegung* (Peace Catechism: A Compendium of the Doctrine of Peace as an Introduction to the Peace Movement).[92] It was dedicated to "the tireless warrior-couple for their work toward the salvation of our time, Baroness Bertha von Suttner and Baron Arthur Gundaccar von Suttner, in sincere admiration." The pamphlet appears to have been so successful that a second edition had to be printed five months later, and in 1896 yet another. Although Fried later referred to this booklet as a youthful folly, probably because of the absence of theory,[93] it was particularly useful to the peace movement, especially since the German Peace Society did not develop its own program until November 1898.[94]

Fried had virtually given up his publishing house at this time, although he did not officially make it public until the beginning of 1895 at the Börsenverein (German Publishers and Booksellers Association). All that remained was a mountain of debt. As early as the beginning of 1896, he had an income of scarcely 250 marks, but he had debts amounting to several thousand, as he reported to a friend.[95] He repeatedly filled out job applications for positions in the publishing field hoping to consolidate his finances by finding permanent employment, to no avail. In the end, he was forced to try his hand at journalism.

There was also bad news from his family in Vienna. Otto, who early on had been in trouble with the law and had been imprisoned for theft and embezzlement, was sentenced in May 1894 to ten months' imprisonment in Munich for counterfeiting. According to a newspaper article located in Fried's papers,[96] Otto, who had worked as a waiter in Munich, justified his deeds in court by claiming that he had wanted to emigrate to America with his friend but that they did not have enough money.

---

92 Fried, *Friedens-Katechismus. Ein Kompendium der Friedenslehre zur Einführung in die Friedensbewegung* (Dresden, Leipzig, Vienna: Pierson Verlag), 1st and 2nd edition, 1894; 3rd edition, 1896.
93 Fried to Wehberg, December 15, 1911. Nachlass Wehberg, vol. 59a, Bundesarchiv Koblenz.
94 The program comprising five points is reprinted in Grünewald, *Nieder die Waffen,* 21f.
95 Fried to Krisch, January 24, 1903. Nachlass Fried, Box 32.
96 A clipping from a newspaper that cannot be identified. Nachlass Fried Box 30.

By 1895, at the latest, Fried's marriage finally failed. Gertrud was no longer able to bear life with her increasingly insufferable husband and became involved with Richard Calwer, a Social Democrat from Berlin. He would become her second husband a few years later. Albert Südekum wrote to Fried in 1898: "In my opinion, the whole catastrophe was only caused by financial circumstances; everything else is secondary. [...] You had become an embittered household tyrant and you were able to control your bad mood with everyone but your wife."[97]

It is hard to imagine the pressure that the young Fried was under at this time. He tried to conceal his precarious economic situation not only from his friends, but probably also from his family in Vienna. The household account books preserved in his estate show that while he was married to Gertrud, he continued to send money to Vienna, amounting to almost one third of his total monthly expenditures.[98]

Despite everything, Fried did not give up. He moved to Hauptstraße 145 in Berlin-Schöneberg and then later to Steinmetzstraße 25 in the western part of the city. By way of artistically designed inserts, he offered newspapers and magazines exclusive reports about important events at home and abroad, such as the Antwerp World's Fair in the summer of 1894 and other social events of interest. In his *Verzeichnis von 1000 Zeitungs-Artikeln Alfred H. Frieds zur Friedensbewegung* (Directory of 1,000 Newspaper Articles by Alfred H. Fried on the Peace Movement), published in 1908, Fried noted that the fall of 1894, more precisely the Antwerp Peace Congress, marked the actual beginning of his journalistic activity on behalf of the idea of peace.[99] It is easy to get the impression that from this point on he devoted himself exclusively as a journalist to the promotion of peace. But the writings of the first few years in fact only comprise a small part of his journalistic work; in addition to those efforts, he wrote feature articles, travelogues, and reports on various exhibitions and congresses. Nevertheless, the deeper Fried immersed himself in the theory and practice of European pacifism, the more his emphasis shifted towards peace journalism, so that one may legitimately call him the first real peace journalist in German-speaking countries at the turn of the century.

As early as the fall of 1894, Fried once again tried to exert his influence on the direction of the German Peace Society (DFG) by calling for the establishment of an independent promotion committee to further spread the idea of

---

97 Dr. Albert Südekum to Fried, April 8, 1898. Nachlass Fried, Box 42.
98 Cf. Nachlass Fried, Box 18, file 287.
99 Cf. *Verzeichnis von 1000 Zeitungs-Artikeln Alfred H. Frieds zur Friedensbewegung* (*Bis März 1908*) (Berlin, 1908), 4.

peace and, in collaboration with Maximilian Stein, he developed concrete plans. The German Peace Society reacted with caution. On October 11, 1894, Richard Grelling replied: "Dear Mr. Fried! In possession of your letter from the 10th of this month. First, I want to thank you for your suggestions, excellent in every respect, I fully endorse them. The execution, however, depends on the more basic notion that we first have to bring together a number of younger people to form a committee to promote the idea of peace, because at the moment our greater need is labor not ideas. [...] In the interest of the unity of our movement, however, this committee can only function as an organ of our society, albeit with complete freedom. The relationship with the board must be maintained; accordingly, it is the board that must appoint members to the committee. With such a composition, I believe our society will experience the greatest benefit, and above all, I ask you to again become a member of our society and devote your valuable talents to the Promotion Committee."[100]

Fried was not willing to agree to that, so in the end the plan went nowhere. Instead, in February 1895, he made a motion to relocate the headquarters of the Peace Society from Berlin to Frankfurt, the center of the peace movement for southern Germany, because of the complete failure of the executive board in Berlin. In order to make this proposal more appealing, he wrote a piece for the Swiss peace journal *Der Friede*, which – as intended – caused a considerable stir. In the article, "Pro domo!",[101] he contrasted the high-flying plans of the founding days with the real impact of the German Peace Society: "It held four meetings, including two general assemblies required by statute, enrolled 3,000 members from a population of 51 million, and has a treasury of 602 marks and 35 pfennig, as per the candid declaration by the last General Assembly of December 1894, this in a country that has a military budget of 650 million per year!"

Fried ruthlessly analyzed the situation, the complete ineffectiveness of Berlin as the headquarters of the local groups, and especially the lack of real individual leadership: "We built the coachman's box in Berlin, and there is no driver sitting on the coachman's seat. The person who should be driving, the most suitable driver, the oldest of the German movement, who was predestined to be the leader, is running behind the wagon and pushing the rusted wheels forward." The only effective thing to do, he claimed, was to take the

---

100 Richard Grelling to Fried, October 11, 1894. Nachlass Fried, Box 35 (German Peace Society).
101 "Pro Domo!" (anonymous) in *Der Friede. Organ des akademischen Friedens-Vereines Zürich sowie des Allgemeinen Schweizerischen Friedens-Vereines. Wochenschrift für Friedensbestrebungen und für einheitliche Jugenderziehung und Volksbildung*, Zurich and St. Gallen 7/8 (February 15, 1895): 2–5.

wagon to its rightful coachman, to where, *pace* Fried, the real center of the peace movement lay and where the man who was the only right choice lived: to Frankfurt am Main, to Franz Wirth. Retired patent attorney Franz Wirth founded the Frankfurt Peace Association in 1886, at the age of 60, and had been its chairman ever since. Later he was not only involved in founding the German Peace Society (DFG), but had also begun to agitate systematically for peace in southern Germany and had founded nearly twenty new peace societies by the end of 1895.[102] The number of members of the peace association in Frankfurt had also risen steadily as a result of his promotional work. At the time of Wirth's death in 1897, it reached 353. Just like Fried, with whom he maintained a lively correspondence, Wirth was "outraged by the tepidity and inactivity of the Berlin Executive Board and often complained bitterly about it." As an effective and necessary recipe for successful promotion, Wirth, using himself as an example, pointed to the necessity of full personal commitment to peace work: "I committed myself totally to the movement and don't do anything else; at my own expense I took on the position of secretary and also stenographer. Last year alone I spent 250 marks on postage! It would also be important for the society to have someone who is exclusively devoted to the cause." Wirth was probably thinking of Fried; contrary to what is sometimes said of their relationship, Wirth was no enemy of Fried.[103] The very extensive and friendly correspondence, which was partly conducted in shorthand, demonstrates the close relationship between the two.

Wirth was the right man for Fried, and Frankfurt was the right place for the headquarters: "A headquarters in Frankfurt can do something powerful, and it will deliver on its promises."[104] Even before the proposal could be discussed in Berlin, the peace society in Frankfurt preemptively refused to accept the official leadership: the executive committee, it claimed, was of the opinion that the head office had to remain in Berlin for the sake of foreign countries. However, if it became necessary, Frankfurt would be prepared to take over the promotion activities for the North.[105] This was a very serious offer, because at about the same time Wirth arranged for the *Monatliche Friedens-Korrespondenz* (Monthly Peace Correspondence), which he and Elie Ducommun had founded two years earlier in Berne, to become the official publication of the German Peace Society, and he would continue to perform the editorial work

---

102 On Wirth's activities, see Dietz, *Franz Wirth*, 33ff. The following quotations are also to be found here.
103 Cf. Hamann, *Bertha von Suttner*, 183.
104 Fried, *Pro Domo*, 5. In the original the letters are spaced out.
105 Franz Wirth to Fried, March 2, 1895. Nachlass Fried, Box 44.

himself. His efforts, however, were not acknowledged by Berlin at all; rather, they led to a serious conflict since Wirth continued to express publicly his criticism of the passivity of the Berlin office. In addition, he was accused in Berlin of having been somehow involved with Fried's articles, so that in the following months both he and Fried were sharply attacked in Berlin. So, in October 1895, Wirth resigned from the editorial staff and shortly thereafter, "deeply disappointed,"[106] he stepped down from the Executive Board of the German Peace Society.

Beginning in March 1895, a roughly two-month dispute arose between Fried and various members of the Berlin Executive Committee. It centered on the issue: whether the article that appeared anonymously in the Swiss peace journal was a mistake by the editors or done so deliberately, and thus "a stab in the back," and how, indeed even whether, the central office should respond to it. Bertha von Suttner also got involved in the controversy from Austria. Finally, on April 26, Richard Grelling suggested to Fried that the matter could be settled through an informal apology; at the same time, he once again invited Fried to return to the German Peace Society, "especially since the reasons that led to your resignation have become irrelevant due to changes that were made on the Executive Board."[107] But Fried was already looking for new arenas in which to become active.

Only a few months later, in November 1895, the party platform of the "Deutscher Verein für internationale Friedenspropaganda von 1874" (German Association for the Promotion of International Peace from 1874) was published in Berlin listing the name of its founder, Eduard Loewenthal, as first chairman and Fried as first secretary. It is a disguised call for the founding of an association, because the date, 1874, was an apparent reference to a long-standing organization. In fact, in 1869 Loewenthal had already founded the "Europäischen Unionsverein" (Association of the European Union) in Dresden and after his move to Berlin in 1874, the "Deutscher Unionsverein für internationale Friedenspropaganda" (German Union for the Promotion of International Peace), but both organizations quickly failed due to a lack of membership.

The new association was entirely focused on international law and hoped to achieve a "legal situation that excluded all war"[108] by means of an "international agreement to be entered into by the various governments and approved by their parliaments." Part and parcel of the agreement was the mandatory

---

106 Dietz, *Franz Wirth*, 35.
107 Richard Grelling to Fried, April 26, 1895. Nachlass Fried, Box 35 (German Peace Society).
108 This and the following quotations are taken from the association's program of November 1895. Nachlass Fried, Box 35 (German Peace Society).

THE BERLIN YEARS 1884–1903

submission to arbitration by an "international peace court that would be established."

Fried thus hoped to have finally found an appropriate platform for his endeavors. In December 1895 he enthusiastically reported on the founding of the new organization to the chairman of the Danish Peace Society, Fredrik Bajer[109] in Copenhagen, with whom both he and Wirth were in close contact. But Bajer showed some hesitation: "I'm sorry that I knew nothing of this new organization to promote peace before it was founded! [...] I am a complete observer."[110]

Even Franz Wirth, informed by Fried of the newly founded organization, had not answered as enthusiastically as Fried had expected. Despite his own quarrels with the German Peace Society, Wirth desperately wanted to keep Fried in the society and warned him that a second association for the promotion of peace could prove harmful. Fried replied that he had agreed to join the board only on the condition "that the new association not publicly oppose the existing peace society and that, in the event of an attack from the other side, he would not take action."[111] Then he explained to Wirth why he was convinced that the new association was useful: "First of all, we have a meeting every week. In the past three weeks we've had three meetings with lectures, which are always well attended and which the newspapers wrote about both before and after the event. Is that not a success? - In two weeks we have our 5th meeting; therefore we will have held more meetings in a month than the great German Peace Society in the four years of their existence. Furthermore, we will have an impact on our members by setting up a library and a reading circle, and we will publish pamphlets. Moreover, in four weeks the first two volumes of our publications on peace will appear: Volume l. Revon, Volume 2. Novicow. Both translated by me. Has a German peace society ever done that? The books are already in print and will be distributed by the book trade, 4,000 copies !!!!!!!"

Fried enthusiastically detailed other plans, which, however, were not very different from those of the other society: they would send out speakers, organize teas and balls for the members, and start a women's group. While there were no famous names to note, there were people who were willing to get involved: "Grelling cannot find a worker among his 900 members, but we already have 90 workers among our 90 members!!!!!" But for all his enthusiasm

---

109   On Fredrik Bajer, see Fried, *Handbuch der Friedensbewegung*, 1913, 322f. See also Peter van den Dungen in Josephson, *Biographical Dictionary*, 49f.
110   Fredrik Bajer to Fried, December 15, 1895. Nachlass Fried, Box 33.
111   Fried to Franz Wirth, November 9, 1895. Nachlass Fried, Box 44. The following quotations are taken from this letter.

there was also a paragraph that probably indicated the reasons for Fried's looming quarrel with the society: "The only concern I have for now is that I am the only practitioner on the board, and that I can therefore easily be outvoted by the other members who have not heard much about the movement itself yet!"

The first activity was the publication of two works that represent Fried's first known translations from the French: *Die Philosophie des Krieges* (The Philosophy of War)[112] by the Swiss Michel Revon, who held the first chair of international law at the University of Tokyo at this time and who was well known within the European peace movement,[113] and *Der Krieg und seine angeblichen Wohltaten* (War and its Alleged Benefits)[114] by the Russian sociologist Jacques Novicow,[115] who was also known in relevant circles. Both works — Revon's focus on international law but especially Novicow's sociological approach, which directly countered the theories of social Darwinism — would later have a decisive effect on Fried's own pacifist theory. However, it quickly turned out that even the new organization did not develop as Fried had hoped. When he told Grelling about his concerns, the latter did not appear surprised: "The development of things in the organization of 1874 does not surprise me, since what Dr. Loewenthal, an engineer, is doing now is what I had expected of him. Obviously, the man is much more concerned with playing the role of president than with the issues of relevance to the organization."[116]

Only a few months after joining, Fried thus returned to the German Peace Society (DFG), which in January 1896, at the urging of retired Franz Wirth, offered him a position as editor-in-chief of the *Monatliche Friedens-Korrespondenz* (Monthly Peace Correspondence). Since this month also marked the end of his short, albeit controversial employment in the publishing house, Verlag der Romanwelt, in Charlottenburg, he accepted the position without hesitation, so that the February issue of the journal was actually published under his leadership.

---

[112] Michel Revon, *Die Philosophie des Krieges. Autorisierte Übersetzung aus dem Französischen von Alfred H. Fried* (Munich, 1896). Original "Philosophie de la guerre," 1896, Paris.
[113] On Revon, see Fried, *Handbuch*, 1913, 396f. and the article by Sandi E. Cooper in Josephson, *Biographical Dictionary*, 801ff.
[114] Jacques Novicow, *Der Krieg und seine angeblichen Wohltaten. Autorisierte deutsche Übersetzung von Alfred Hermann Fried* (Leipzig, 1896). Original "La Guerre et ses prétendus bienfaits," 1894, Paris.
[115] On Novicow, see the article by Sandi E. Cooper in Josephson, *Biographical Dictionary*, 705ff. Cf. also Fried, *Handbuch*, 1905, 409f.
[116] Richard Grelling to Fried, March 18, 1896. Nachlass Fried, Box 35 (German Peace Society).

The assumption of the role of editor and, shortly thereafter, his resignation from the Verein für Internationale Verständigung (Association for International Understanding), as well as Grelling's continued affection now also seemed enough to support Fried's reinstatement to the Executive Committee of the German Peace Society (DFG). Grelling: "In the interest of our collaborative work, I am delighted that you have abandoned the unproductive relationship with Loewenthal's organization, and I now expect you to join us as a member, which is only natural given your position as the editor of our journal. Personally, I can add that for my part I will do everything to ensure that you become a member of the board. In my opinion, your position as editor will bring this about in no time at all, and for us your collaboration on the other tasks facing the Executive Committee is, I believe, as desirable as it is necessary."[117] It was a hope that never materialized. In the years to come, Fried would continue to be an outsider; especially after the election of Max Hirsch, an engineer, to the presidency in 1897, Fried would have no further chance at a leadership position.

Fried's contact with Eduard Loewenthal broke down completely after his subsequent departure from the latter's association. However, in 1912, Loewenthal once again turned to Fried privately, in order to secure Fried's support for his election as a candidate for the Nobel Peace Prize;[118] it was support that Fried vehemently refused. When, after the award ceremony, Loewenthal complained in a flyer about his failure to be nominated, Fried found it necessary to distance himself from Loewenthal in an article that he called "Humoristisches aus der Friedensbewegung" (Something humorous from the peace movement).[119] When Loewenthal died at the beginning of 1917, Fried dedicated a short obituary to him in the *Friedens-Warte*, which ended with the sentence: "He had a highly polemical nature and thus found few friends in the movement, whom he frequently and unfailingly antagonized."[120]

For a short time, it seemed that Fried had finally gained a secure position within the German Peace Society. However, scarcely a year and a half after beginning his employment, on September 30, 1897, the business office surprised him with a letter of termination signed by first chairman Seydel and secretary Georg Haberland: "In view of our unfortunate financial situation [...] and much to our regret we must inform you that the board has decided to cease publication of *Friedenskorrespondenz* (Peace Correspondence) until the local

---

117 Richard Grelling to Fried, March 18, 1896. Nachlass Fried, Box 35 (German Peace Society).
118 Letters by Loewenthal in Nachlass Fried, Box 39.
119 *Friedens-Warte* 3, no. 39/40 (December 23, 1901): 159f.
120 *Friedens-Warte* 19, no. 4 (April 1917): 127.

groups have satisfied their financial obligations to us. For this reason, unfortunately, your services as editor are, for the time being, no longer required, and we must hereby terminate your position as editor in all matters."[121] It is questionable whether the financial situation was the sole reason for Fried's termination or whether, after the death of his supporter Franz Wirth in May 1897, the board in Berlin hoped to get rid of the unbeloved Fried as quietly as possible.

With the discontinuation of the journal, the German Peace Society was without an official publication, and Fried was without employment. So he quickly went about locating a new, more affordable option. This he found in the journal, *Die Waffen nieder!*, which had been published by Pierson since 1893. Fried immediately entered into negotiations with Pierson and was able to come to a reasonable financial agreement between the *Friedens-Korrespondenz* and *Die Waffen nieder!*: "With Pierson, I was able to agree that I would produce a journal that would appear monthly. It will be 12 pages in length and contain content from *Die Waffen nieder!* on nine of those pages. The three remaining pages could be filled with new material. [...] The German Peace Society, which was formerly responsible for 5,000 copies of the *Friedens-Korrespondenz* (Peace Correspondence) at a cost of approximately 4–5,000 marks a year, was now able to obtain a regularly published journal for 2,000 marks."[122] Since Pierson required a guarantee of 5,000 subscribers, Fried tried to compel the local associations to place firm orders. He managed to get 3,000 subscribers, plus a subsidy for 1,000 copies from Heinrich Rössler, an engineer who had assumed the presidency of the Frankfurt Peace Association after the death of Franz Wirth.

Fried hoped to get the final 1,000 subscribers from the local association in Berlin, which had about 1,000 members. But Berlin refused to subscribe to the journal because the members there had already begun preparations for the publication of a journal, *Zwangslose Mitteilungen* that was set to appear at irregular intervals. Although, of all places, southern Germany soon criticized the journal for its unreliability and its inefficacy as a means to promote peace,[123]

---

121   German Peace Society to Fried, September 30, 1897. Nachlass Fried, Box 35.
122   Fried, "Rundbrief," May 1899.
123   Circular of Count Bothmer, April 1898, which urges the necessity of an up-to-date journal that is published punctually every month: "The informal communications are definitely not appropriate for bringing the news of the peace movement to the attention of the world. They merely have the advantage of making it as easy as possible for those who are disseminating the news." Nachlass Fried, Box 20, file 344.

the journal did have one decisive advantage for Berlin: it was cheaper and was published directly by the Berlin board without Fried's involvement.[124]

In order to secure his publication further, Fried forced the convening of a delegate assembly in Frankfurt am Main on March 6, 1898; Frankfurt, where the spirit of Franz Wirth dominated, was the ideal environment for his demands. In any case, the Berliners, whom both Fried and others engaged southern German groups had repeatedly accused of inactivity, were in a difficult position. But Fried was successful, as expected, in achieving his goal and Berlin was forced to relent. Representing his local Berlin association, Georg Haberland ordered the much needed 1,000 copies.[125] However, the victory was not complete. At first, Fried could only count on the assembly's order until January 1, 1899, and he was also subject to the condition that each issue had to be submitted to the chairman of the Berlin Central Committee for approval. Thus the seed of new conflicts was already sown, and the chain of misunderstandings, personal attacks, and intrigues against Fried was not broken. Fried defended himself and acted on his own independent authority as editor of the journal, delayed sending the draft to the new chairman Dr. Max Hirsch,[126] and ignored, where possible, the latter's instructions.

On November 27, 1898, the main office in Berlin convened another delegate assembly, this time in Berlin, without consulting Fried, in order to raise official complaints and criticisms against the editorial office of the *Monatliche Friedens-Korrespondenz* (Monthly Peace Correspondence). But again, the Berliners could not prevail. Fried was allowed to continue as editor for the following year. However, Hirsch now demanded Fried publish the journal in a more timely fashion, and he also took broader editorial control. Of necessity Fried agreed – but the situation still did not improve. Later Fried stated that the board knew from the beginning "how I always resisted any interference

---

124   Dr. Rudolph Penzig, the secretary of the German Peace Society, edited the communications that first appeared in March and were printed by Ernst Boll's print company; Boll was the treasurer of the society.

125   This order was only realized as a result of the extraordinary pressure by other delegates as can be observed from the fact that the pertinent group in Berlin at first refused to accept the 1,000 copies that it received. Since Georg Haberland had gone on vacation from Frankfurt without having informed the executive board in Berlin about the new developments, the members of the board, at the meeting of April 12, 1898, set aside the agreement that had been reached. See "Mitteilungen der Deutschen Friedensgesellschaft," no. 2, April 1898. Nachlass Fried, Box 35.

126   On Hirsch, see Fried, *Handbuch*, 1905, 397f.

in my personal freedom as editor,"[127] thus indirectly acknowledging his own unwillingness to compromise.

In addition to the personal animosities among Penzig, Boll, Hirsch and Fried, there were frequent additional power struggles, large and small, between the editor and main office, especially because Fried undermined Hirsch's desire to document in detail the parliamentary debates relevant to peace (and thus his own work as a member of the Inter-Parliamentary Union). Instead, Fried preferred to publish articles such as a thorough obituary of Moritz von Egidy or an article about general questions of the peace movement.

The conflict came into the open at the end of March 1899, when Fried accepted an article that he himself wrote with the title "1900 nach Paris!" (1900 to Paris!). It reported on an installment payment plan by a Parisian company for travel to the World's Fair;[128] the article was published contrary to Hirsch's express order. At the end of April 1899, Hirsch declared that the *Monatliche Friedens-Korrespondenz* (Monthly Peace Correspondence) was no longer the official publication of the German Peace Society. At the same time, in an official circular letter to all the local groups, the Berlin group canceled its subscription without notice.

The circular was signed by members of executive board, Dr. Hirsch, Dr. Rudolph Penzig, and Ernst Boll.[129] Fried, who was contractually obligated to Pierson until the end of the year and who, in addition to the loss of his earnings, still had to fear the publisher's claims for damages, wrote a counter-circular letter in early May 1899 to the local groups. He described in detail not only the various conflicts surrounding the journal but also explained that they were the result of the board's disdain for his person: "Such a disagreeable colleague who sees shortcomings everywhere and who has the audacity to offer his opinion to a solid majority, one does not like that. I regret this infinitely, but I cannot change my character, I love the straight path, and I put our primary concern

---

127   Fried, "Rundbrief," May 1899.
128   See the exact content of the article in *Monatliche Friedenskorrespondenz* (Monthly Peace Correspondence) 4, no. 4, April 1899.
129   Fried took his revenge on Boll by pointing out in the *Friedens-Warte* how some of Boll's activities were incompatible with the German Peace Society. See "Auch ein Friedensfreund," in *Friedens-Warte* 2, no. 43 (October 1900): 172. "Mr. Ernst Boll … has been publishing a journal with the title "Armee und Marine" that is richly illustrated and thoroughly saturated with a militaristic spirit. Since the Berlin group of the German Peace Society has not called an assembly or a meeting of the executive board since January of this year, it would then seem appropriate if the executive board in Stuttgart would draw Mr. Boll's attention to paragraph #4 of the bylaws and make clear to him that his presence on the board of a peace society could well be a hindrance to business interests."

above the person and have no sympathy for an individual's self-advertising needs."[130] This view was certainly not entirely wrong. Fried's idiosyncratic editorial practice and the close connection of the journal to the revue *Die Waffen nieder!* (Lay down your arms) certainly played a role as did the fundamental differences between Fried and the executive board around Max Hirsch.

In fact, Fried himself had a need for self-advertisement, and many aspects of his often belligerent and stubborn behavior can probably be explained by the fact that he, who was perhaps right to feel that he was the founder and initiator of the German Peace Society, received no recognition during his Berlin years either for his various activities or for his initiative on behalf of the peace movement.

Once again Fried hoped for an intervention by the local groups, but this time most of them were behind Hirsch. The central office's criticism of the article about the World Exhibition seemed justified to them. Even the banker Georg Arnhold in Dresden, a friend of Bertha von Suttner and later patron of Fried, who had just launched his own local chapter, wrote: "In answer to your esteemed question, I write to inform you that I have received 40 copies of the *Monatliche Friedens-Korrespondenz* (Monthly Peace Correspondence) from Pierson. But I cannot distribute them because of the main editorial, which is in extremely poor taste."[131] Responding to Fried's justification that he had been influenced by the negative circular of the Berlin headquarters, Arnhold replies: "You are mistaken if you believe that I have let my decision (...) be guided by the circular letter (...). On the contrary, I have acted on my own initiative and after consultation with the other gentlemen of the local board. If you take into account that this is the first issue that we intend to ship out, then you will surely have to admit to yourself that it would make a very bad impression if it were to be delivered as an advertisement to someone's door."[132]

Although not all of the local groups followed the suggestion of the much disputed leadership of the German Peace Society,[133] they could all see the need for new regulations regarding the association's publication. This time, Fried lost the fight. In an extraordinary general meeting, the German Peace Society decided on July 2, 1899 that it would no longer consider the previous journal to be the official publication of the society, and, instead, it would create the

---

130   Fried, "Rundbrief," May 1899.
131   Georg Arnhold to Fried on May 6, 1899. Nachlass Fried, Box 33.
132   Arnhold to Fried on May 23, 1899. Nachlass Fried, Box 33.
133   Georg Arnhold also continued to order the copies of the *Monatliche Friedenskorrespondenz* for the group in Dresden.

Friedensblätter, which would not be edited by Fried.[134] In September 1899, the last edition of the *Monatliche Friedens-Korrespondenz* was published.

From October to December, the *Friedensblätter* was published in Berlin without Fried's help — but only for a short time. Richard Grelling and Georg Haberland had resigned from the board one year earlier. Since 1898 Max Hirsch had been a representative of the Liberal People's Party (Freisinnige Volkspartei) in the Prussian state parliament and engaged in various activities as secretary of the German IPU group. At the end of 1899 he resigned as chairman. New activists were not easily found.

For a long time, new negotiations, supported by Fried, were underway to move the leadership of the association to southern Germany. On December 3, 1899, the General Assembly of the German Peace Society in Frankfurt am Main decided to relocate the main office to Stuttgart with the consent of the Berlin representatives.[135] Adolf Richter of Pforzheim became the new first chairman.[136] He was a veteran of the movement, whom the international community long considered the leading representative of pacifism in the German Reich. He was also a member of the Berne office and director of the peace congress in Hamburg in 1897. Otto Umfrid,[137] a clergyman in Stuttgart, was to serve as second chairman. He was a highly active and talented organizer and journalist. Fried later referred to him as "the most outstanding theorist of pacifism in Germany."[138]

Although Fried contributed greatly to this vital move to southern Germany, he continued to define his position, even more forcefully, from within the peace movement but from outside of the German Peace Society. One reason for this was undoubtedly that the Berlin local group, which formally continued to exist and which Fried tenaciously observed and criticized, was even less active than before the change of leadership to Stuttgart. In spite of the fact that there were still too few active members in Berlin (as there were in subsequent years), the local chapter never approached Fried. On the contrary, even as a reorganization of the Berlin local group was undertaken in 1902, on his initiative, Fried was quite deliberately kept away. He therefore continued to

---

134 Cf. Scheer, *Deutsche Friedensgesellschaft*, 96f and Reichel, *Pazifistische Presse*, 9f.
135 Cf. the report on the general assembly of December 3, 1899 in the *Friedensblätter*, 12 (1899): 3ff.
136 On Richter, see *Dr. Adolf Richter-Pforzheim*, ed. Georg Grosch (Stuttgart, undated [1920]) and Karl Holl, "Adolf Richter," in Donat/Holl, *Friedensbewegung*, 327.
137 On Umfrid, see Wehberg, *Führer der Friedensbewegung*, 44ff and Chr. Mauch and T. Brenner, *Für eine Welt ohne Krieg. Otto Umfrid und die Anfänge der Friedensbewegung* (Schönaich, 1987).
138 Fried, *Handbuch*, 1913, 208. Cf. also Scheer, *Deutsche Friedensgesellschaft*, 101.

focus on his journalistic activities but also tried his luck in other completely different areas.

4 Experiments

One of these experiments is his marriage to Martha Holländer in 1896. Fried probably first got to know her brother Felix Holländer through the writer Hans Land, who was friends with both of them. Felix Holländer, the son of a physician from Upper Silesia who had been living in Berlin since his youth, had attracted attention with two successful novels.[139] After lengthy study trips away from Berlin, he had returned to the city to create a more secure livelihood in 1894. In 1895 his brother Gustav, a well-known violinist and composer, became director of the Stern Conservatory in Berlin, while his other brother, Victor, a well-known theater bandmaster, still lived in London at the time. A connection with the respected Berlin family must have made a deep impression on Fried.

In March 1896, Fried and Martha, who was then 27 years old and probably already mentally ill, got engaged. The wedding took place in Berlin barely three months later, in June 1896. That this was not a marriage of love can be seen from a retrospective letter that Fried wrote to Therese Frankl, the wife of his friend Siegfried. Therese would later become Fried's third wife. "I took my coffee at the Café Josty yesterday afternoon, where there wasn't a chair to be found. Mutzerl, we too sat there once, and my wife, who was passing by and was only my fiancée at the time, told me that she'd thought for sure that I (Fried) was having a romantic relationship with this lady (you)."[140]

In fact, the secret relationship between Therese and Fried was already two years old[141] in 1896, and it continued during Fried's marriage to Martha. Moreover, it was not until after the breakup of the marriage that Fried first noticed Martha's mental disorders, which had intensified in the course of the marriage. What exactly the young woman was suffering from can no longer be determined. Among the few surviving testimonies, in addition to some letters from 1903[142] when they separated, is a manuscript by Fried of the same year. It deals with "experimental marriages," with the much-lamented habit of many

---

139 On Felix Holländer and his brothers, see: NDB, vol. 9 (Berlin, 1972), 534ff. In 1891, Holländer made his authorial debut with the novel *Jesus und Judas*. It dealt with the miserable conditions of the working class and was followed by the novel *Magdalena Dornis* in 1892.
140 Fried to Therese Frankl, March 28, 1903. Nachlass Fried, Box 92.
141 Cf. Fried to Therese Frankl, March 24, 1903. Nachlass Fried, Box 92.
142 Nachlass Fried, Box 92.

families to "try to heal one of their family members, who is either physically or socially unsound, through marriage."[143] It states: "Imagine what it means when, as in a case I know of myself, a man who had fallen in love with a woman and, after a brief period of marriage, which he had entered into full of hope, and in the steadfast opinion that he had now established his happiness in life, suddenly learns from the maid that his wife had been frequently [...] a resident in mental asylums before she was married, that he had married a mental patient, with whom any intellectual exchange must be forever absent. Imagine such a deception, such a botched life of constant restlessness, constant commotion, constant acrimony, and isolation with a person of impaired mind. Complete economic decline as a result of an inability to work and the world-weariness associated with being the unscrupulously sacrificed object of the experiment were the consequences of the trap that I am speaking of. And the hope of the family performing the experiment, which in cold blood gave their consent to the crime and lent their support to it — even though men respected in public life belonged to this family — was not fulfilled, for the mental illness, which was one of periodic recurrence amid some lucid intervals — and therefore offered no means of saving that marriage — had only worsened in the course of the marriage; the acute seizures became more frequent and the periods of madness lasted longer."[144] Even if some of this may be exaggerated, one can assume that the years after 1896 were not happy years for Fried. His marriage with Martha, as with Gertrud, remained childless and increasingly burdensome. The hoped-for social advancement was not realized, nor was the consolidation of his financial situation.

At first, however, things finally did seem to get better. Thanks to his brother-in-law Felix, who worked as a literary editor for the weekly newspaper *Die Welt am Montag,* Fried got in contact with the owner Dr. Martin Langen and finally received, after some initial exploratory talks in April and May, the much longed for employment contract at the end of June 1896: "I shall hire you from July 1, 1896 for a period of 5 years as a business manager of the newspaper that I publish, *Die Welt am Montag* (The World on Monday), at a monthly salary of 350 (three hundred and fifty marks), and you will receive 25% (twenty-five percent) of my portion of the company's net profit."[145]

This was an apparent stroke of luck, since the contract did not include a probationary period and guaranteed the first year without the possibility of

---

143 Manuscript "Experimentaleben," 1903. Nachlass Fried, Box 8, file 58.
144 Ibid.
145 For this and the following quotation, see Dr. Martin Langen to Fried, June 28, 1896. Nachlass Fried, Box 38.

termination, although it did otherwise restrict literary activity; it still allowed him to write additional paid articles for *Die Welt am Montag* (The World on Monday) and to continue working unconstrained "in the service of the peace movement." But there was a snag; further on, one reads: "If the newspaper, *Die Welt am Montag*, fails, I have the right — even during the first five years of this contract — to cancel this contract within six months of the date of the cancelation notice." In fact, the young weekly, which was printed on Sunday evening and appeared on Monday morning, was losing money by the summer of 1896, and Fried's employment as a "business manager" or "director," as he called himself, did not change that much. Langen presumably hoped that the inclusion of someone with experience in the publishing world would increase the profitability of the advertising section of the newspaper, which Fried would lead. This was likely a last-ditch effort since when no major improvement occurred by the end of the year, he decided to abandon the newspaper. On December 27, 1896, Fried received a tersely worded notice of cancelation, as per the contract, effective July 1, 1897.

Together with Felix Holländer, he began negotiations with Martin Langen to purchase the newspaper. Since Felix Holländer had little money, and Fried none at all, both parties agreed in a preliminary contract in February 1897 to finance the purchase retroactively from the expected profits. But a final contract did not come about, for unexplained reasons, and so Langen sold the newspaper in mid-March to another interested party. Since he did not find Fried in the office that evening, of which he is critical, he informed him of the sale in writing: "I transferred the ownership of the newspaper *Die Welt am Montag* to the publisher Hermann Bousset (publisher of *Zeit*) this afternoon. Since Mr. Bousset will take over the commercial management of the newspaper itself, unfortunately, there is no future use for your services in the company. I would therefore ask you to cease your activities immediately — since Mr. Bousset will take them over tomorrow."[146] In the event that he would renounce his share of the annual profit, which was not expected to amount to anything anyway, Langen continued, he could begin his search for a new position on April 1, but he would draw his salary, as per the contract, until the end of June. This was, however, only ostensibly a good offer for Fried since he was not able to find a permanent job in the succeeding months despite having applied for numerous positions. He did indeed have plenty of work to do, because the editing responsibilities of the *Monatliche Friedens-Korrespondenz* (Monthly Peace Correspondence) and his collaboration on the journal *Die Waffen nieder* left

---

146 Dr. Martin Langen to Fried, March 15, 1897. Nachlass Fried, Box 38.

him little free time. Both, however, brought in virtually no income, so that once again Fried was fighting for his very existence. Just as earlier in Vienna, his life in Berlin was never free of fearing for his existence - even though he worked non-stop, not only as a journalist and writer but also as an inventor.

4.1   Fried's Hygienic Trash Collection and Removal Apparatus

Probably as early as 1893, the *Illustrierte Zeitung* reported in detail on Fried's invention for the improved storage and removal of household waste in the city.[147] It was, accordingly, a construction made of iron sheet metal, about 170 cm high and 70 cm wide, in the lower part of which there was a removable, replaceable garbage box, which was filled from above by means of a folding mechanism. This method of waste collection was said to allow for the waste to be collected dust free, and it was odorless and beyond the reach of vermin and unauthorized persons. Moreover, the removal of the entire lockable garbage container also made it hygienic. Fried even thought about the need for subsequent storage. Instead of throwing the garbage into an open field, one could make use of the "not to be underestimated value of the garbage" and first store the locked crates in barracks, then sort them gradually in large sorting rooms. Whether this system has ever been tried is unknown.

4.2   The Self-Dating Envelope

In the autumn of 1897, Fried filed another application for a patent: the self-dating envelope, an envelope which, by means of an opening in the upper right-hand corner, would allow the stamp to be glued directly onto the document and then canceled; this then ensured the precise monitoring of the timely receipt and posting of official letters. In fact, this invention initially found some interest. Carl Rudolf Bergmann, a prospective customer in Berlin, wrote to his printer: "In the attachment I am bringing to your attention is a new idea, which interested me for my own purposes. I read about it in the newspaper, and the idea seemed in fact quite original and worthy of attention. What is unique about it is that the envelopes, so it seems to me, can be produced in the traditional way and that only a small hole, square or round, needs to be punched out before the adhesive is applied. This hole is said to allow the stamp to be glued directly to the contents of the envelope so that it essentially will have the postmark on it. It is obvious that the courts and many others would very much welcome this."[148]

---

147   Separate publication of the *Illustrierte Zeitung*. Nachlass Fried, Box 8, file 77.
148   Carl Rudolf Bergmann to H. C. Bestehorn, October 21, 1897. Nachlass Fried, Box 33.

Bergmann asked the printer for an estimate and a sample. However, the addressee immediately had serious reservations: buyers would probably not feel like purchasing the much more expensive envelope just for the benefit of the recipient. In addition, the post office might not allow such letters, since other letters could get hung up on the punched out opening. Further, the stamp would have to be set very carefully in the opening, because if it sticks to one part of the envelope, the letter would be damaged when opened. And if you needed several stamps, the whole envelope was useless. Above all, however, the printer saw one serious flaw: "And finally, many senders may find the opening very unnerving, since the privacy of the correspondence and perhaps even the entire contents of the envelope could be compromised."[149] Similar concerns were also raised by the package delivery service, Berliner Paketfahrt-Aktien-Gesellschaft, to whom Fried sent a sample letter in September 1897, a proposal that the company rejected. They even put the sample to a test and returned a torn copy of his unopened letter to Fried.[150]

4.3   *An Election Atlas*

Fried had one more notion that turned out to be a flop: in the fall of 1897 he offered the Cartographic Institute G. Freytag & Berndt in Vienna the idea of an election atlas for the German Reichstag elections as of 1898. It would contain all the information about the last three elections: the electoral district in the colors of the elected parties, the turnout, and the distribution of seats in the German Reichstag. "As you probably know, Germany is to hold an election next year, which, depending on the specific political situation, will be both lively and extended. Seven million voters will go to the polls, showing a keen interest in the political process. The people were politically quite mature as a result of the enormous spread of social democracy and the radical bourgeois parties. Thus, the project that I have suggested would fit within the offerings of your publishing house and have a chance to be a financial success."[151] But the publisher dismissed his idea noting that there have been similar maps since 1893 and it had already decided to publish such diagrams.[152]

4.4   *Supplemental Encyclopedia*

In 1901, Fried registered what was likely his final invention at the Imperial Patent Office in Berlin. It was "an encyclopedia that can be supplemented by the

---

149   H.C. Bestehorn to Carl Rudolf Bergmann, October 22, 1897. Nachlass Fried, Box 33.
150   Berliner Packetfahrt-AG to Fried, September 25, 1897. Nachlass Fried, Box 36.
151   Fried to Freytag & Berndt, November 18, 1897. Nachlass Fried, Box 36.
152   Freytag & Berndt to Fried, November 20, 1897. Nachlass Fried, Box 36.

insertion of a single article into a set of loosely ordered articles."[153] Anticipating later developments, Fried saw the value of his encyclopedia in the fact that it could always be made up-to-date, as obsolete articles could be removed and replaced by new or updated ones. Unfortunately, the existing correspondence does not allow us to see whether the patent was awarded and whether there was any interest in it. However, none of Fried's ideas and inventions contributed to an improvement of his own situation. And even the larger works produced during these years did not lead to a financial breakthrough.

After the great success of his *Friedens-Katechismus* (Peace Catechism), Fried expressed his view on one of the burning questions within the European peace movement in 1895: the legality of the annexation of Alsace-Lorraine by the German Reich. In *Elsass-Lothringen und der Krieg* (Alsace-Lorraine and the War), a bilingual work that appeared simultaneously in Paris and Leipzig in 1895,[154] he tried to offer a way out of the dilemma by means of a "non-solution." The future, he argued, would overtake national thinking one day, and Germany and France, together with the rest of the civilized states of Europe, would then form a community of states in which the question of which country Alsace-Lorraine belonged to would no longer arise. All concrete proposals for the resolution of the Alsace-Lorraine question should therefore be rejected as being harmful to the future development; instead, a cultural bridge was to be built by the best of both countries, "not simply by decorated military leaders, but by the truly human, the princes of intellect." "A German-French League intended to collectively promote the cultural and humanitarian interests of both nations must be founded!"[155] Fried designed a plan of action to accompany the first items of the program of the league: the members of the league should "meet annually at a congress in one of the two countries or on neutral territory for mutual discussion." In addition, there would be special congresses and exhibitions for individual occupations. Congresses for doctors and technicians would be encouraged, as well as school exchanges and agencies to promote the exchange of letters. One of the main issues would be the promotion of contact through literature and the press: "It will endeavor to provide the writings of both peoples in both languages to advance the mutual knowledge of the masses, and thus bring about a most beautiful moment of reconciliation."[156]

---

153   Fried to the Royal Patent Office Berlin, October 22, 1901. Nachlass Fried, Box 38.
154   *Elsass-Lothringen und der Krieg. Ein Friedenswort von A. H. Fried. L'Alsace-Lorraine et la guerre. Une Parole de Paix par A. H. Fried* (Leipzig/Paris, 1895).
155   Ibid, 136.
156   Ibid, 157f.

In fact, at this time Fried was making plans with Albert Südekum for the bilingual revue *Deutsch-Französische Jahrbücher/Annales Franco-Allemandes* (Franco-German Yearbooks / Annales Franco-Allemandes), which was to appear twice a month and, "bypassing the narrow national political points of view, could form a common center for the intellectual life of both peoples and thus impart and expand the mutual understanding."[157] In the summer of 1895, Fried and Südekum solicited financial support for their idea. But since no financier could be found for the bold project, not even a sample issue appeared. The German-Franco League, which was inspired by Fried and for which he predicted a great future, in fact failed due to a lack of interest among their contemporaries, despite the efforts on the German side by Fried and Südekum, and on the French side by Bernard Lazare.[158]

In the end, Fried was left only with a philosophical perspective: "The pursuit of the good, that's what is eternal in us! That is a part of the chain that connects us both to our ancestors and to our descendants. That explains the audacity of those who struggle their whole life for an ideal whose fulfillment is deliberately denied to them, and under whose struggle their ephemeral existence vanishes. [...] whatever we strive to achieve in the service of the good, we are always the pioneers of the future, always the momentary representatives of the Eternal."[159] These and other similar explanations will no longer be found in later works by Fried, but rather they will give way to a sober, more scientific style. Nevertheless, they are fundamental to his self-understanding and, together with his unwavering faith in the inevitable progress of humanity, form the fundamental pillars of his work.

In the same year, *Dschingis-Khan mit Telegraphen* (Genghis Khan with Telegraphs) attracted much wider attention.[160] Following the example of Bertha von Suttner's *Maschinenzeitalter*[161] (Machine Age), Fried published it under a

---

157 Double-sided flyer on the foundation of the *Deutsch-Französische Jahrbücher*. Early July 1895. Nachlass Fried, Box 42. This notion was not developed further until after World War II. Today it is employed, for example, by the television station "Arte."

158 Bernard Lazare (1865–1903) was a writer and literary critic. He was the son of an assimilated Jewish family from Nimes. A resident of Paris from 1886, he was involved in the symbolist movement and in the anarchist movement. He also delved into the roots of antisemitism and became famous for his early position on the Dreyfus Affair. See the correspondence between Lazare and Fried in 1895. Nachlass Fried, Box 38.

159 Fried, "Elsass-Lothringen," 163f.

160 More than twenty years later Fried noted that the Russian writer and publicist Alexander Herzen (1812 - 1879) had come up with this title. Cf. Fried, *Kriegs-Tagebuch*, IV, 439 (June 25, 1919).

161 "Das Maschinenzeitalter. Zukunftsvorlesungen über unsere Zeit," 1889, Zurich. Set in the 21st century, Suttner's text has a professor of history lecture on topics such as "Forms of

pseudonym. The piece is a roughly ordered aphoristic collection[162] of thoughts and minor essays on war and peace, cultural development, emancipation, and progress. The theme of war and peace is clearly the centerpiece; it already shows the seeds of his later theoretical development: the distinction between "struggle" and "war," the analysis of the present situation as a state of war in peace time, the rejection of all efforts to humanize war, and the positive evaluation of universal military conscription as a transitional stage to world peace, "an institution from a time when the necessary level of brutality no longer existed to create voluntary armies." The peace societies, according to Fried, are not there to directly abolish war, but merely to verify an international mass will, "a will that, through its very activation [!], is sufficient to put an end to the activity of armies."

Interesting is Fried's vehement objection to the term "peace association". The peace societies were not social entities, he wrote, and they did not want to be associated with choirs and with bowling clubs. Instead, they were "societies of ideas to which everyone who shares our ideas can belong." The actual (paying) membership is secondary. "We do not want to form an association with long-winded statutes! Our only statute is the watchword "Die Waffen nieder!" (Lay down your arms!). If we follow this maxim, then we will suddenly have more members than Europe has armed men. But those who sign up as members of a peace society should be regarded as soldiers who have responded to the call 'volunteers to the front!' in preparation for an attack." Fried dedicated the work to his parents and noted in the introduction that he was expressing his private thoughts to the public "because I know about ten people who might be interested in my thoughts."

The name of the author did not remain a secret for long. As early as December, 1895, in a review in the journal *Die Waffen nieder!* (*Lay Down Your Arms!*) one reads: "*Dschingis Khan mit Telegraphen* (Genghis Khan with telegraph) by Manfred Herald Frei. A significant enrichment of the literature on peace. Or rather an enrichment of the literature on peace as part of the social sciences. [...] It's a proud, bold book. The language lively and fiery, the thoughts of sometimes surprising depth and novelty. Our friends will welcome the work with

---

Government," "Women," "Sociology and Politics," "Religion," etc. in the present age. The reason that she chose a pseudonym was the legitimate fear that a woman would allegedly not be able to do justice to such topics. In fact, her contemporaries thought that Max Nordau or Karl Vogt authored the work. Cf. Suttner, *Memoiren*, 170ff.

162 This is in fact the lasting impression of the work, even if Fried emphasized in his introduction that he absolutely did not want the work to be seen as "merely a collection of aphorisms," but rather as a book that only sought to do without the "connecting gaps." Cf. Fried, *Dschingis-Khan*, 2. The following quotations are taken from this book.

great satisfaction, and they will draw joy and edification from it. But there is one disappointment that they will not be spared: — At first, one will be pleased that a new, strong fellow-comrade has joined us — but after reading the first hundred pages, there is no doubt that he has been a longtime and trusted companion of ours, who is hiding behind an all too obvious pseudonym."[163] At least in peace circles, the book is a short-term success; a second edition appears in 1896, but then there are no subsequent editions.

As his next book project Fried addressed the death penalty, a hot topic at the time. Since the abolition of the death penalty had been accepted as a fundamental right by the majority of the representatives at the St. Paul's Church in August 1848, the topic was taken up again and again by the liberal side. As the number of executions dramatically increased under the reign of the German Emperor Wilhelm II after a significant decline in the Bismarck era, the opponents of the death penalty became more visible.[164] At the beginning of 1898, Fried planned a compilation of the responses of as many "cultural leaders" as possible to the question: "What do you think about the death penalty?" He wrote an appeal, which he sent out in large numbers; using the *Dogma der Unverletzlichkeit des menschlichen Lebens* (Dogma of the Inviolability of Human Life) as a point of departure, the responses ran the gamut from the hostile and war-ready European armies opposing each other to a belief in the possibility that the courts could administer justice in his own lifetime.

Not all those to whom he appealed responded as Fried had hoped. While the Suttners, Leopold Katscher, Gaston Moch, Moritz Adler and Wilhelm Liebknecht spoke out against the death penalty as expected, Max Nordau, Ernst Haeckel and Alfred Kerr considered it appropriate for the times, and even a die-hard pacifist like the Stuttgart pastor Otto Umfrid spoke in favor of keeping it.[165] So Fried decided to abandon the proposed project and instead wrote a novel. Composed as the diary of an inmate on death row to his beloved, the novel communicated the thoughts, feelings, and mental anguish that the prisoner might experience in the days leading up to his execution.[166] He prefaced the work with the response to the questionnaire given by Ludwig Büchner,

---

163 *Die Waffen nieder*, 4 (December 1895), 451. Column: "On Literature."
164 A comprehensive view of the development of the death penalty can be found in Richard J. Evans, *Rituale der Vergeltung. Die Todesstrafe in der deutschen Geschichte 1532–1987* (Berlin/Hamburg, 2001).
165 All the materials related to this survey can be found in the Nachlass Fried, Box 24, file 351.
166 Either consciously or not, Fried remained close to the content of Victor Hugo's early work *Der letzte Tag eines Verurteilten*. See the commentary on the new edition of this work (1945) by Hans Wehberg in *Friedens-Warte* 46 (1946): 97f, which, surprisingly, does not mention Fried's work.

who considered the death penalty, as Fried himself did, to be a remnant of a medieval worldview, a cold-blooded murder,[167] that is unworthy of a modern state. Fried was aware of the low literary quality of this little book. In a review that he wrote himself, he observed: "When I wrote the book, I made no claim to creating a work of art. I only wanted to underscore the significance of this issue."[168] Although the publisher succeeded, with the help of Victor Holländer, to publish an English edition, a second edition was never published.

5 The Conference at The Hague 1899

The final years of the nineteenth century were a difficult time for Fried, but not only personally. While he was trying to make a living from his journalistic and literary work after his quick and unanticipated termination at the *Welt am Montag*, he was also involved in constant quarrels with the executive board of the German Peace Society in his position as editor of the *Monatliche Friedens-Korrespondenz* (Monthly Peace Correspondence). Moreover, it was not only the German Peace Society that was in crisis, the peace movement as a whole had to fight backslides.

Many were distraught at the disappointing attitude of the USA. Especially the pacifists on the European continent had viewed America as a model for the future; they had placed their hopes on America, especially in the field of arbitration. All the greater then was their disappointment when the US Senate failed to ratify the Anglo-American arbitration treaty in 1896–97. When America declared war on Spain a year later, the situation seemed hopeless. Fried made the following comment on the summer of 1898: "The Spanish-American War was just over. The most democratic state in the world had broken with its fundamental principles and was well on its way to setting a wild policy of conquest. An old cultural state, within whose borders the sun never set, had collapsed within a few weeks and was forced, by the power of its opponent's cannons and rifles, to retreat from its previous political position and abandon its formerly large colonial possessions. Power stood triumphantly over law."[169]

---

167   Fried, *Das Tagebuch eines zum Tode Verurteilten. Mit einer Einleitung über die Todesstrafe von Professor Dr. Ludwig Büchner* (Berlin, 1898). The death penalty, which was restricted to cases of murder in the German Reich, was increasingly employed after 1933 and was expanded to other crimes. It was not abolished until after the war. This occurred in the Federal Republic in 1949 through Article 102 of the Basic Law. It occurred in West Berlin in 1951, in Austria in 1968, and in the German Democratic Republic in 1987.
168   Fried, *Das Tagebuch eines zum Tode Verurteilten*, in *Die Zukunft* 24 (1898): 533. Deutsches Literaturarchiv, Marbach am Neckar.
169   Fried, *Die Haager Konferenz, ihre Bedeutung und ihre Ergebnisse* (Berlin, 1900), 8f.

The thought of a peaceful balance of power seemed farther removed than ever. The arms race was also heating up in Europe. In Berlin, the friends of peace were overcome with deep despondency as they recognized the increasing unpopularity of their ideas and proposals. At the beginning of 1898, Fried's initiative to invite Bertha von Suttner to Berlin to represent the peace society once again was rejected on the grounds that no one would be willing to "bear the financial risk of a major event."[170] And further: "In the present political state of affairs, given the extent of the interest that the public has shown in the forthcoming elections to the Reichstag, the time for the promotion of our ideas is not favorable, and, at least for Berlin, we will be the violet that blossoms in secret." Toward the end of July 1898, Fried wrote to Bertha von Suttner: "Sad, sad, dear Baroness, this momentary backward slide of the peace movement. It is also evident when I realize that the newspapers no longer assign me to report on the two peace congresses. There were only a few assignments, but this year even they are no longer available."[171]

Just at this moment, however, something completely unexpected happened. It came from a source that the pacifists had previously only frowned on: on August 24, 1898, at his weekly reception for the diplomatic corps in St. Petersburg, the Russian Foreign Minister, Murav'ev presented a document to the assembled ministers and ambassadors of the nations that would later go down in history as the Tsar's Peace Manifesto.[172] In the name of the young Nicholas II, who, at the age of twenty-five, succeeded his father Alexander III to the throne in 1894, the manifesto appealed for the "maintenance of general peace and for a possible reduction of excessive armaments"[173] as an ideal "to which the efforts of all governments must be directed." After describing the negative consequences of the European arms race, the tsar invited all the governments represented at the imperial court to a conference in order to put a limit on these "ever increasing armaments and to seek the means to avert the disaster that threatens the whole world."

The Tsar's Manifesto unleashed a new lease on life for the peace movement. The mere possibility that their previous activities, their books and resolutions, could have played a role in this manifesto, wrenched the peace-loving friends out of their crippling sense of powerlessness for a short while. Throughout Europe, the leading pacifists were in the limelight, "commenting on the

---

170 Georg Haberland to Fried, January 10, 1898. Nachlass Fried, Box 35. The following quotation is also from this letter.
171 Fried to Suttner, July 30, 1898. Nachlass Suttner, Box 19.
172 On the following related themes, see Jost Dülffer, *Regeln gegen den Krieg? Die Haager Friedenskonferenzen von 1899 und 1907 in der internationalen Politik* (Berlin/Frankfurt am Main/Vienna, 1981).
173 Quoted from a copy of the manifest in Fried, *Die Haager Konferenz* (Berlin, 1900), 1f.

wonderful event to all who would listen."[174] Congratulatory telegrams were sent back and forth, and they discussed the welcome event with friends and sympathizers. The arguments of the pacifists finally seemed to have been taken seriously in the important centers of power, and finally there was again a clearly defined goal of action: the promotion of the Tsarist Manifesto.

In an editorial in the *Berliner Zeitung* of August 30, 1898,[175] Fried made explicit the connection to the pacifists' work under the headline "Die Waffen nieder!" He describes the ever-widening relevance of the idea of peace among the international intelligentsia, parliaments, newspapers, and peace societies, and he declared—very optimistically—the "pacification of Europe" to be the "ideal of millions," which was resisted only by the rigid attitude of politics, as it continued to move along the "old paths" to the detriment of humanity. Only with the Tsar's Manifesto, he claimed, did this change: "The idea of peace has a victory message to record, a victory message that one had not dared to dream of. The crowned head of the most powerful European state has taken up the banner, which reads "Die Waffen nieder!" (Lay Down your Arms.) Although Fried did not expect quick successes — "the plan is so immense that it could not be put into place with the speed of an ardent wish," he did concede that it would take years to be fully realized; nevertheless, he saw the beginning of an irreversible development: "Its appeal is a kind of progress from which there is no turning back. One can confidently assert that in the last 48 hours the history of the world has taken a detectable step forward, a step that cannot be reversed." He further claimed that now was the time for relentless lobbying in parliaments and in the newspapers, as well as at popular assemblies and congresses. "The call must go out that everyone must be on board, that everyone should take up their intellectual arms: 'Peace has broken out!'"

In their euphoria, those seeking peace did not raise concerns about the person or intentions of the tsar, or, as Sandi Cooper put it, "Pacifists forgot that the tsar was not among their usual gallery of heroes."[176] This was also true of Fried, who because of the decades of pogroms against the Jews was anything but a friend of Russian autocracy, but he did not publicly express any concerns. Conversely, he tried to make light of it: "From the East comes this message of salvation: The absolute ruler of the Russian people seized the initiative and

---

174   Suttner, *Memoiren*, 399.
175   Text in Fried, *Unter der weißen Fahne* (Berlin, 1901), 169ff. The place of publication and the date of publication, however, may be found in the *Verzeichnis von 1000 Zeitungs-Artikeln Alfred H. Frieds zur Friedensbewegung* (Berlin, 1908), 9. All of the subsequent quotes are from this text.
176   Cooper, *Patriotic Pacifism*, 97.

thus put an end to the delusion, which saw in the Russian lack of cultivation the enemy of Europe. Could it be that these savages really are better people?" The answer: "With his manifesto the tsar has exclaimed in a language much more understandable to the peoples of Europe that they should preserve their most holy values, and the peoples of Europe will heed this call and will ensure that the thought is not forgotten. This thought is indeed a child of their spirit, it is an idea of the democratic world, which has asserted its power even upon the mind of a crowned head." For Fried, the real virtue of the western-trained tsar lay solely in the fact that the thoughts, which for some time had been prefigured and worked out in the Western countries, had now become "socially acceptable." To advance the manifesto was thus not to promote the tsarist empire, but rather to advance the ideas that were born long before in the West—ideas that seemed to stem directly from the peace movement.

Most other pacifists also firmly believed that the roots of the Tsarist Manifesto could ultimately be traced back to their own promotion of peace. Connections between Russian diplomats and the peace movement were not something that was known only to today's researchers.[177] Soon rumors were circulating that the tsar had read the novel *Die Waffen nieder!* before issuing the manifesto. However, in her memoirs Bertha von Suttner, who learned of this from Prince Dolgorukov, later decisively disavowed that the novel alone could have prompted the tsar to take his initiative.[178]

However, the influence of Jan Bloch and his work[179] was undisputed among the pacifists. In fact, in May 1898, the tsar seems to have spent some time with the extensive, six-volume work, which described the suffering, and above all, the futility of a modern war, which, according to Bloch, would necessarily lead not to the victory of one state but to the ruin of all states.[180] Not only was the work not banned by the censors, as was customary with books advancing

---

[177] Cf. Dülffer, *Regeln*, 26ff. In September 1896, the Russian Consulate, General Vasily, and his deputy participated as observers in the World Peace Congress and in the subsequent Interparliamentary Conference; they then sent a report to Petersburg. Vasily contributed to the preliminary writing of the Tzar's Manifesto.

[178] "While I was happy to hear that the Tzar had read my book shortly before the publication of the manifesto, I nevertheless was always convinced that numerous influences would have to precede such an action, among which the reading of a novel can only have played a minimal role." Cf. Suttner, *Memoiren*, 402ff.

[179] Jan Bloch, *Der Krieg. Der zukünftige Krieg in seiner technischen, volkswirtschaftlichen und politischen Bedeutung*, 6 vols. (Berlin, 1899). The Russian original was published in Petersburg in 1898.

[180] Cf. Dülffer, *Regeln*, 31f.

pacifist ideas, but it even brought about a meeting between the author and the tsar.

For the pacifists, however, Bloch's influence on the tsar was not as important as the effect of the manifesto on their own standing in society. What they hoped for was a clear gain in the social and political acceptance of their ideas, a "turning point in European history,"[181] or as Henry Dunant, the founder of the Red Cross, put it to Bertha von Suttner: "It is a gigantic step, and whatever happens, the world will not scream 'Utopia!'; our ideas will no longer be so poorly esteemed. And even if their realization does not immediately follow the Congress, which is sure to take place, then it will at least have been set in motion. This initiative will always exist as a precedent."[182]

It was not only Fried who realized early on that as much public support as possible would be needed to overcome the expected resistance within the European governments. Thus, the Russian sociologist Jacques Novicow wrote to Bertha von Suttner that it was now absolutely necessary to support Nicholas II with all our strength, "not only against his opponents but also against his own person."[183] This endeavor, he feared, was so daunting that the tsar could lose heart given these obstacles. "Then it will be necessary for the liberal opinion of Europe, and especially the peace associations, to offer him their tireless, unwavering cooperation."

In fact, the response to the tsar's manifesto outside the pacifist and left-liberal camp was one of caution. Fried later wrote that all the parties in Germany, from the extreme right to the Social Democrats, had viewed the manifesto "with rare unanimity [...] with distrust, even hostility"; the press and scholars were even more opposed to it.[184] Over the next few months, those acting for peace would therefore seek to bring about a change in public opinion, so that states would actually be obliged to meet with each other, but they also wanted to limit too high expectations in the run-up and to develop possibilities for realistic negotiations.

Fried pursued a two-thronged strategy: while repeatedly providing the press with new, enthusiastic articles and campaigning actively for the promotion of the peace movement, he tried to explore the real possibilities of such a state conference, in particular in his *Was kann die Petersburger Konferenz erreichen?*

---

181   Jacques Novicow to Suttner, September 12, 1898, quoted in Suttner, *Memoiren*, 405.
182   Henry Dunant to Suttner, September 21, 1898, *Memoiren*, 405.
183   Jacques Novicow to Suttner, September 12, 1898, quoted in Suttner, *Memoiren*, 405.
184   Cf. Fried, *Die Haager Konferenz*, 13ff. Cf. also Dülffer, *Regeln*, 39ff.

(What can the Petersburg conference achieve?)[185] (At this early date a meeting in Petersburg was still considered probable). "Those who expect nothing from the Petersburg Peace Conference exaggerate as much as those who expect everything and think that they are witnessing the dawning of the Golden Age." The main obstacles to a spectacular outcome were, in Fried's mind, the sovereign states "whose law and morality are the weapons that they are now supposed to weaken," and the diplomats whom they will send to the meeting. "And what kind of people will be sent? [...] Men with antiquated views, old traditions, old things and old customs, who are stuck in the last century (not in the coming century) with respect to their hearts and their spirits, but also with respect to their emotions and understanding." A real disarmament agreement was, in his view, hardly conceivable, at best a reduction in the speed of rearmaments might be achieved. But a decreased rate could possibly increase the threat of war rather than reduce it. Therefore, the elimination of the causes of an armaments build-up was much more important: the construction of a legal system and thus the end of anarchy between the states: "The conference will have to get down to the causes of why states amass armaments and, if it really cares about its work, will finally take the only possible path and the right path, that is, to broaden the legal relationships between states and to expand them to a significant extent."

Fried was not yet speaking of the ultimate goal of those who seek peace, namely a permanent international tribunal, which could be called by any state and whose judgments and resolutions would be binding on all states. However, he did think that a community of common interests of the European states was possible. Turkey and the remaining Balkan states did not count, just as China and Japan did not count, but he did include a "Europeanized America." The community of interests that Fried imagined and that would eventually lead to a codification of international legal principles and the creation of an international court of justice, could be seen in a "European colonization alliance, an alliance that, leaving the current colonial claims to ownership untouched, could work on a joint plan for the areas that were still undeveloped." Since he believed that the states within Europe were saturated and that a major European war would be an economic disaster—"almost an impossibility," he perceived the possibility of real conflict only in the colonies: "The only possibility today of a confrontation between large European states lies in the

---

185 "Was kann die Petersburger Friedenskonferenz erreichen? Ein Vorschlag zur Erreichung der vom Zaren angestrebten Ziele von Alfred H. Fried," (Dresden and Leipzig, 1899), 36 pages. All of the subsequent quotations are taken from this work.

colonial areas." It was precisely there that he sought the key for future peaceful development: "It is sufficient that we have a unification of the states of Europe for a certain purpose, a limited liability company, a society with limited liability to open up China, to open up Africa and goodness knows whatever other undeveloped areas." This step would then provide the seeds for further development. The participating states would approach each other legitimately and at the same time create a unified international law based on common policies and develop common interests in all other fields. Instead of opposing each other, they would get used to interacting with one another: "An international fleet operating with a European mandate will do business much more peacefully, and a congress of European states, the board of this large limited partnership, will direct and regulate its activities." What motivated Fried to propose this adventurous detour via a "colonial union" was a very skeptical assessment of the effectiveness of ethical or moral arguments against economic advantages. Ultimately, he says, "beyond the sensitivity of the moralists" only material interests can lead to cultural advances.

These ideas find broad appeal especially in southern Germany. For example, Otto Umfrid, who at a later date became the second chairman of the German Peace Society, wrote: "Your idea that a colonial alliance among the European nations should be concluded at the conference, analogous to the trusts for which business competitors meet, has something brash about it and something that is not to be underestimated—originality."[186] Count Bothmer, chairman of the Wiesbaden group, also spoke positively, as did Richard Feldhaus, Heinrich Rössler, and the Swiss journal *Der Friede*.[187] However, Fried's suggestions also met with fierce resistance, for example, from the leaders of the Berlin group of the German Peace Society and from Bertha von Suttner, who resolutely rejected a predatory policy in Asia and Africa.[188] However, all pacifists agreed that the tsar's manifesto was an opportunity—for the European states and for the peace movement. It was essential to make the idea of a peace conference so popular that governments would find it difficult to reject. The need for this "pressure from below" soon became apparent when, after the first diplomatic congratulations to the tsar were sent by the governments in question, his manifest received only little enthusiasm and much open criticism. Only by virtue of a second memorandum on January 11, 1899, which, significantly, took into consideration the concerns of the nations, and, as the

---

186 Quoted in *Die Waffen nieder!* 8, no. 4 (April 1899): 159.
187 Ibid.
188 Cf. Hamann, *Bertha von Suttner*, 255f.

pacifists lamented, "represented a strong watering-down of the original points of view,"[189] could the idea be saved at all.[190]

After the publication of the first manifesto on August 28, 1898, the pacifists quickly pushed for an international meeting, since - of all years - this was the year that the World Peace Congress and the Inter-Parliamentary Conference, which had been planned for Lisbon, were canceled due to the Spanish-American War. Instead, the International Peace Bureau now convened an expanded General Assembly in Torino that met from September 26–28.[191] Of course, the manifesto was unanimously welcomed, and a resolution expressed hope that governments would be favorably disposed toward the manifesto and finally that a future conference would be successful.[192] But above all, the national associations were urged to take immediate action. Only the participants in England were able to report that promotional efforts had already begun in their country. Of particular significance was the idea of a peace crusade, initiated by the English journalist William T. Stead, which was supposed to pass through the great cities of Europe on its way to St. Petersburg and which was also supposed to attract leading personalities of all European countries. Although the plan was never realized, Stead's preparations, his conversations, and the broad discussion in the press about the project had the desired promotional effect.[193]

In Germany, too, there were numerous initiatives actions and meetings in support of the Tsarist Manifesto. In Munich, for example, Margarethe Leonore Selenka[194] founded the "Komitee für Kundgebungen zur Friedenskonferenz" (Committee for Demonstrations for the Peace Conference) in the winter of 1898. On January 27, this committee sent out a call to the public supporting the peace conference, and 90 well-known citizens from Munich in the areas of politics, culture, and science signed the document.

Months earlier, Fried had vainly pressed the Berlin group to organize public activities. When the Munich committee began to form in the winter of 1898, without any similar preparations being made in Berlin, his patience was at an end. Over the heads of the board, he invited Bertha von Suttner to come to Berlin. She agreed, leaving him to arrange everything else. Fried managed to get the necessary funds from a friendly Reichstag deputy. In May 1899, he described what happened next: "Well, it would have been easy for me to

---

189 Fried, *Handbuch*, 206.
190 For a more precise description of the way events unfolded, see Dülffer, *Regeln*, 39ff.
191 The IPU met from September 29 to October 1 in Brussels.
192 Cf. Fried, *Handbuch*, 1913, 137f.
193 Cf. Fried, *Handbuch*, 1913, 138f and Suttner, *Memoiren*, 426ff.
194 On Margarethe Selenka, cf. Donat/Hall, *Friedensbewegung*, 352f among others.

arrange an evening with von Suttner in Berlin, completely bypassing the Berlin Peace Society, but I did not. I informed the chairman that I could give him the consent of the baroness and the necessary money to arrange such an evening. A board meeting was convened, attended by six members of the board, who simply out of politeness expressed their gratification for my gift, but nonetheless voiced their petty concerns about bringing a foreigner into the movement!!!!"[195] For Fried, who admired Bertha von Suttner as the founder and the most important personality of the peace movement in the German-speaking world, these were completely absurd objections. Moreover, the misgivings also applied to him, since he too was a foreigner in Berlin.

Fried's initiative came at a rather inopportune time for Max Hirsch, a politician who valued the debates and petitions in the Reichstag more than public gatherings. So he seemed to act consistently when he tried to use the scheduled lecture for his own purposes. Outraged, Fried remarked that the German Peace Society had rented a room that was much too small: "She had to speak in a hall that held only 250 people. Thousands of people had to leave without getting to hear her." In addition, the original initiative to collect signatures for the crusade was replaced by a similar one to support a petition to the Reichstag. Fried's displeasure was intensified when Hirsch tried to torpedo the formation of a honorary committee intended to receive the "crusade" that had prepared for Bertha von Suttner's visit: "A number of notables had been invited to the hotel where Bertha von Suttner was staying. They were all men who were much revered and who were supposed to form the basis of a committee of notables for the reception of the Stead Crusade. Suddenly, Herr Hirsch, who had also been invited, railed against Stead, advocating for a purely national event." In fact, in Germany, Max Hirsch was not alone in his rejection of Stead. "As early as October, 1898, he (Stead) was received by the tsar in St. Petersburg, and since then, at least from the German perspective, he had been considered a hack in the service of Russia."[196] Nevertheless, a committee was formed in Berlin of which Fried was a member; it was dedicated to the promotion of peace until May 1899.

Fried arrived at The Hague on May 14, two days before Bertha von Suttner's arrival and four days before the official beginning of the conference. Unlike the baroness, Fried was there primarily as a journalist, working as a correspondent for the *Berliner Zeitung* and *Pester Lloyd* as well as other newspapers such as the *Hartungsche Zeitung* in Königsberg, the *Berliner Volkszeitung*, and the

---

195   Manuscript of the circular to the local groups of the German Peace Society, May 1899. Nachlass Fried, Box 20, file 343. The following quotations are taken from this document.
196   Dülffer, *Regeln*, 70.

Fränkischen Kurier. For all of these newspapers, he was to provide reports on the conference and on related issues. Bertha von Suttner was able to help him by virtue of her contacts. In addition, Fried was considered the representative of the German Peace Society by the international proponents of peace. On May 18, 1899, as one of only 15 selected individuals, he, along with Bertha von Suttner as the only woman, attended the solemn opening session of the conference. This was not only an honor, but also an adventure, because the journalists were not seated in the hall; they had to stand "on the decrepit parapet under the domed roof of the main hall," to which they first had to climb up a wooden flight of stairs, and then through beams and rafters.[197] Nevertheless, Fried was enthusiastic and believed that he was witnessing a historic turning point, a feeling that he later described with a quote from Goethe: "From here and today a new epoch of world history is beginning and you can say that you were there."[198]

Fried described the atmosphere in the Dutch conference venue as follows: "From all countries, even from across the ocean, came the well-known friends of peace, so that at times it looked as if one were at a recent peace congress. At the Central Hotel in The Hague, the peace-lovers had set up their headquarters, and from the roof of this hotel a white flag was flown, perhaps for the first time in history."[199]

Inside the hotel, the Suttners' salon was a meeting place for the "peace-workers," as Fried called them, numerous members of the diplomatic corps and conference delegates. We cannot examine here the extent to which the pacifists could actually exert influence on the thinking of the conference delegates, but it is interesting that Fried noted in an article for the *Pester Lloyd* that he had to consciously downplay the danger of influencing the course of the conference. Of the Suttner salon he stated: "One has quickly made a great fuss over this group and discredited the intentions of the members saying that they wanted to exert influence on the course of the negotiations in the Haus am Busch, as a kind of 'minority congress' (this phrase was quickly picked up and circulated). This was not the case. The Suttners' salon in The Hague was nothing more than an observation post from which the pioneers of peace looked back on the work that they themselves had begun."[200]

---

[197] See Fried's recollection of the events in his *Kriegs-Tagebuch* IV, 414 (May 18, 1899).
[198] Fried, *Haager Konferenz*, 28. The quote is taken from Goethe's *Kampagne in Frankreich 1792*, written in the years 1820 -1822 (September 19, 1792).
[199] Fried, "Unsere Freunde im Haag," in *Die Waffen nieder!* 8, no. 6 (1899): 228ff.
[200] "Der Salon der Baronin von Suttner im Haag," *Pester Lloyd*, May 27, 1899, reprinted in Fried, *Unter der weißen Fahne*, 193ff.

But the intentions of the friends of peace actually went far beyond the role of mere spectators. Their aim was to provide as much information as possible to the global community, whose continued interest could in fact impact the conference, and to inform the less knowledgeable delegates about the work of the peace movement so far. The Russian Council of State von Bloch,[201] whose monumental work *Der zukünftige Krieg* (The Future War) was said to have contributed to the initiative of the tsar, had expressly come to disseminate his findings among the delegates via brochures and lectures.

For Fried, the personal encounter with Bloch was useful in a completely different way. After the congress, they remained in close contact, and for a short time, until Bloch's death in January 1902, Fried found him to be a generous benefactor who not only supported the newly-published journal, *Die Friedens-Warte*,[202] but also paid Fried for the German translation and the publication of his other shorter works. Fried also handled the distribution of Bloch's brochures. Bloch, who had studied in Göttingen but considered his German writing style inadequate, even went so far as to let Fried revise his articles stylistically for German-language periodicals.[203]

In addition to Bloch, the conference in The Hague also allowed Fried to get reacquainted with the Dutch painter Jan Ten Kate, with whom he had been in contact since the World Peace Congress in Hamburg in 1897 and who, even though he himself had only limited financial resources, supported Fried's trip financially with 300 marks.[204] Ten Kate, who by this time had been producing paintings on peace and anti-war topics for ten years, was a well-known and admired personality among the pacifists, but unlike Vasily Vereshchagin, for example, had had no commercial success with his paintings. Like Fried, he too was always on the verge of ruin.[205] In The Hague, Ten Kate exhibited some pictures of a series designed for the Paris World Fair that Fried enthusiastically reported on.[206] At the center of the exhibition was the allegorical painting "War on War," depicting war, death, and suffering as well as Christ, Bertha von Suttner, Henry Dunant, Tolstoy, and Zola—a gathering that indicated the direction of Ten Kate's Christian-humanitarian pacifism. Fried, who

---

201 On Bloch, cf. the article by Michael Bloch in Josephson, *Biographical Dictionary*, 84f.
202 Cf. Fried's obituary of Bloch in *Friedens-Warte* 4, no. 1 (January 15, 1902): 1. He writes among other things: "It was precisely in these pages, which primarily owe their existence to him, that his efficacy on behalf of peace was reported." Emphasis in original.
203 Cf. the correspondence with Bloch in Nachlass Fried, Box 34.
204 Jan Ten Kate to Fried, May 8, 1899: "In addition, I am sending you 300 marks for the trip." Nachlass Fried, Box 38.
205 On Ten Kate, cf. the article by J. H. Rombach in Josephson, *Biographical Dictionary*, 933f.
206 Fried, "Der Maler der Friedens-Idee," *Die Waffen nieder!* 8 (1899): 234.

was already convinced that a broad-based peace movement could certainly be useful to the cause, had made sure that Jan Bloch was part of the small group of invited guests who were the first to view the paintings: "I found it interesting to observe the man of the real anti-war movement together with the man of the ideal direction of this movement. How far are these two men apart in their view of the same thing, and yet how close they are to each other in their goal [...] One wants to convince, the other inspires. Truly, two opponents of war who would have to join together in order to rein in this century."[207]

Many of the pacifists who were gathered at The Hague already knew Fried from the peace conferences of previous years; Fried met others for the first time, such as the Parisian philologist Charles Richet, "the representative of the philosophical school of the peace movement founded by Michel Revon,"[208] and the French conference delegate Baron d'Estournelles de Constant, who shared an apartment with Revon. To others, like Feliz Moscheles, whom he had previously known only fleetingly, Fried was able to create a closer relationship. On the other hand, Fried's own actions were very important for the promotion of the conference in German-speaking countries. Bertha von Suttner, for example, noted with appreciation: "In this respect, A. H. Fried, who writes extensive reports on the general ambiance of the conference for the *Berliner Zeitung*, the *Pester Lloyd* and for several other newspapers, sent long daily reports from here. There is hardly a more thorough expert and more zealous warrior for peace, a cause for which he has been working for eight years, to be found among the German journalists."[209]

Fried would remain at the conference until June 2. Bertha von Suttner noted: "Dr. Frischauer and A. H. Fried are saying their goodbyes. Both leave today. It is natural, of course, that the papers do not want to leave their journalists in places where negotiations are conducted. And to them, namely the journalists, the role of reporting only what has already been picked up is quite unpleasant."[210]

In fact, after two weeks the public had begun to lose interest in the conference, especially since the information from the individual committees, whose meetings were closed to the public, only trickled out, and the little that was heard did not point to anything sensational. Most of the journalists and many

---

207 Ibid, 235.
208 Fried, "Der Salon der Baronin von Suttner im Haag," in Alfred H. Fried, *Unter der weißen Fahne*, 201. See also the shorter article, which contains some identical passages, in "Unsere Freunde im Haag," in *Die Waffen nieder!* 8 (1899): 228ff.
209 Suttner, *Friedenskonferenz*, 53f.
210 Ibid, 91.

pacifists had long since left when the conference announced its final declaration on July 29. The results were also not very encouraging for the pacifists who were most interested in long-term outcomes. Although the desire for a restriction on future arms production had been expressed and although some bans on certain kinds of weapons had been concluded, only the results of the third commission offered a small spark of hope for the future,[211] namely the establishment of a permanent arbitration court, even if it consisted only of a secretary and a non-binding list of referees and even if an appeal remained merely optional.

For the pacifists, it was a matter of keeping this spark alive. Many of Fried's articles in the following months were aimed at revising the public's perception of the alleged complete failure of the conference or at contesting its vilification by the nationalists. In his article "Das Werk der Haager Konferenz" (The Work of the Hague Conference),[212] he described in feuilleton style the everyday life of a pacifist during these months: "'You were in The Hague?' – 'Yes.' 'That was probably a big flop?' – 'Why?' – 'Well, nothing came of it.' – 'So ...' I had this conversation about 500 times last summer. The first twelve times I tried to convince the questioner that something did indeed come of The Hague Conference; but when I realized that these explanations were not understood, and when these clichéd questions kept coming back, I stopped trying to 'persuade and convert' the questioner. I'm sure that he'd believe his *General-Anzeiger* before he'd believe me."

Nevertheless, Fried did not preach resignation but called on all pacifists to intensify their efforts both in speech and in writing in order to make the actual success of the conference, namely a potential change of values, better known: "It must first of all be made clear that in this first conference, with the cooperation of the highest diplomats of both worlds, war was unanimously condemned in principle, that the principle of arbitration was recognized for the first time by the vast majority of the states of the world, albeit provisionally in a limited way, and that the tremendous burden of arms build-up was officially acknowledged as a social evil such for the first time."

In addition to countless articles, which were published more often in the *Friedens-Warte* and only rarely as editorials in daily newspapers, Fried also

---

211 On the course of the conference and on its outcomes, see Christian Meurer, *Die Haager Friedenskonferenz*, 2 vol. (Munich, 1905). Also see Dülffer, *Regeln*. Another informative source is Arthur Eyffinger, *The 1899 Hague Peace Conference. The Parliament of Man, The Federation of the World* (The Hague, London, Boston, 1899).

212 Fried, "Das Werk der Haager Konferenz," in *Friedens-Warte* 1, no. 13 (September 25, 1889). This piece was also published in Fried, *Unter der weißen Fahne*, 189ff. The following quotations are taken from this source.

wrote an 80-page work on The Hague Conference that appeared almost at the same time as the diary of Bertha von Suttner. It was financed by members of the Berliner Komitee für Kundgebungen zur Friedenskonferenz (Berlin Committee for Peace Conference Rallies) and presumably also by Jan Bloch, the "*Realpolitiker* of peace," to whom Fried dedicated the work.[213] The foreword entailed a letter from Baron d'Estournelles de Constant of March 25, 1900 in which he expressed his delight that Fried wanted to make the results of The Hague Conference as well known in Germany as he did in France. Unlike Bertha von Suttner, whose main aim with the publication of her Hague Diary[214] was to capture an authentic picture of the events there,[215] Fried focused on the pacifist interpretation of the conference and its findings.

Even in the introduction he left no doubt as to the significance that he attached "to this eternally memorable assembly of representatives of almost all civilized states [...] this most significant work of our time."[216] He claimed that the conference was the equivalent of the discovery of America and the French Revolution and that it would inevitably lead to upheavals of far-reaching importance.

To illustrate the immense value of the Russian initiative, he first described the grim situation at the end of the Spanish-American War, the constant increase of militaristic and imperialist tendencies, and the arms race in Europe, which resulted in great national debt and poor living conditions for the population. He juxtaposed this with the needs of the world economy, the international trends in culture and science, and the longing for peace among peoples, which were all expressed in the tsar's manifesto: "Suddenly someone said aloud what millions had long felt, for what the peoples of both hemispheres had so long yearned, namely that the prevailing anarchic conditions were a burden to the national communities, that they needed to be eradicated, that the prevailing peace was neither "true" nor "permanent," and that "there must be a limit to the current ongoing development of armaments" because that "affects peoples' welfare at its core."

---

213   The dedication reads: "Sr. Excellenz Herrn Staatsrat Johann von Bloch dem Realpolitiker des Friedens ehrerbietigst gewidmet vom Verfasser." (To his excellency, the minister Johann von Bloch, a Realpolitiker of peace, dedicated most respectfully by the author.)
214   Bertha von Suttner, *Die Haager Friedenskonferenz. Tagebuchblätter* (Dresden and Leipzig, 1900).
215   In the foreword Suttner writes: "With the following highly accurate notes from those historic days, I hope to have provided those who seek the truth some documentation and points of reference to begin their own study." Ibid, v.
216   For these and the following quotations, see Fried, *Haager Konferenz*.

Fried offered a rather inconsistent explanation as to why the Tsarist Manifesto after some initial astonishment quickly aroused an overwhelmingly skeptical or negative reaction by reference to the "intellectual inertia" of the people; he even spoke of the "great mass of sluggish and thoughtless people" who united to form a strong opposition. The opposition in Germany, he claimed, was quite unanimous; to varying degrees, it included all the parties as well as diplomats and scholars because they had not yet transcended the "outmoded blood-and-iron tradition of the national era of consolidation." However, Fried attributed the responsibility for the lack of popular support among the general public to the press: "The press opposed the Tsarist Manifesto because it believed that the public was not serious, and the public did not take the manifesto seriously because the press opposed it."

This point was especially important to Fried. On the one hand, this had been his experience as a "peace journalist" and, on the other hand, he recognized more clearly than many other pacifists the steadily growing importance of public opinion and the enormous influence of the press. He harshly criticized the press for catering to the expectations of the reading public, and he strongly emphasized their opinion-forming role. Further, he demanded an approach to new ideas that was independent, critical and responsible. "If the press were aware of its great responsibility, if it pursued its craft with more idealism, it would take a new position on every new question, and sometimes dare to step out of the template of party-line thinking and other commonly-held views."

It was obvious to Fried that the press had in no way lived up to this demand. According to Fried, in Germany the press discredited the ideas of the manifesto, declared the conference unfeasible until the very end, and later, when it did come about, ridiculed it as the "Hague Comedy." The press had also deliberately labeled the conference as a disarmament conference in order to be able to clearly demonstrate its subsequent failure. It is interesting that Fried, although he was active for several German papers in The Hague, condemned the German press without exception: "There was no German newspaper that found it newsworthy to explain to the people the importance of this conference and to encourage their active support of the work done there." Of course, this retrospective appraisal also included Fried's recollection of how quickly the newspapers' interest, which had indeed existed, disappeared.

While assigning very poor grades to the press,[217] Fried did see a significant change for the better in the attitudes of the delegates in the course of the

---

217   On the attitude of the German press, see Andreas Gestrich, "Die Haager Friedenskonferenzen und die deutsche Presse," in Christof Dipper, Andreas Gestrich, Lutz Raphael (eds.), *Krieg, Frieden und Demokratie* (Frankfurt am Main, 2001), 231ff.

conference and affirmed "that by far the vast majority of the delegates sought to create something tangible from the negotiations."[218] What's more, he even saw the beginnings of a new school of diplomacy, which would be more internationally attuned and which would deal with "governing and securing the relations between peoples." To this end he drew on personal experiences: "While I was staying at the Dutch residence during the peace conference, I too became convinced that the concept of peace, the idea of a true lasting peace, was opening up new perspectives for the younger diplomats."

Regarding the actual work of the conference, Fried stated: "The proceedings showed that almost all the great political powers complained about the ever increasing financial burden of armaments procurement, that they recognized the dangers of this mounting burden, but that they could not find the means to obviate these dangers." The verdict on the second commission, which had dealt with extending the resolutions of the Geneva Convention and which the pacifists rejected from the outset, was even more striking: "This commission has worked hard, but has produced little." He gave a better grade only to the third commission, which dealt with arbitration and mediation. According to Fried, this is where the emphasis needed to be placed, and the members of the conference recognized this. In order to underline the importance of the decisions made there, he published them in their entirety and then provided a summary.

Fried noted that it was clear to the friends of peace that only the initial steps toward establishing peace could be expected at this conference; truly impressive results were not yet to be anticipated. On the one hand, the negotiations had been made difficult by the untrained diplomats who, with a few exceptions (Descamps, Pauncefote, d'Estournelles, Rahusen and Martens), were not familiar with the new approach to international law; additionally, the number of states attending the conference (some 26 states including some non-European states at various stages of development—"not all states are ready for peace") was too heterogeneous. He called for a much smaller group at the hoped-for subsequent conference.

5.1   *The Founding of the Friedens-Warte in 1899*

The most important event of the Hague Conference for Fried was to be found in a very different area: the founding of his own peace journal, of which he was the publisher and editor. Even before the trip, one could envision a possible end to the *Monatliche Friedens-Korrespondenz* (Monthly Peace Correspondence).

---

218   Fried, *Haager Friedenskonferenz*, 25. The following quotations are taken from this work.

And for some time there had also been problems with the journal *Die Waffen nieder!* The constant struggle to finance the journal had finally exhausted Bertha von Suttner, and so she took the Tsarist Manifesto as a welcome occasion to declare her journal superfluous for the new times ahead.

In early November 1898, she informed Fried that she had announced an end to Pierson's revue. Outraged and horrified, he wrote back to her: "Baroness! [...] you cannot possibly be so rash, so foolish, so impetuous. What are you thinking? How do you view our present situation that you would think we no longer need this journal? How can you believe that the day has come, where we can lay down the arms, where we just observe the events with our hands in our pockets, where we just toss this revue into the fire as something superfluous, after working, worrying, and fighting for seven years? [...] Hasn't this journal held our small but committed group together? Hasn't this revue been a significant part of the greatest and most meaningful progress of the movement? [...] and now, after seven hard years of struggle, after I have secured its existence for another year at great expense, you stand there and say I cannot do it anymore."[219]

For Fried, the continued existence of the journal was not only a theoretical concept, but also a financial necessity, because it gave him at least a small income of 100 marks per month,[220] which he desperately needed. In addition, the end of the revue would also mean the end of the *Monatliche Friedens-Korrespondenz* (Monthly Peace Correspondence), to which Fried had linked it in order to lower the printing costs for both journals. That would then mean the end of his last source of fixed income. When Bertha von Suttner tried to reassure him that he would surely find a job with a newspaper, a resigned Fried replied, "My dear Baroness, stop with the prophecy of a great position in a large daily newspaper! Whether I'll still have my teeth when it really does happen, I doubt very much, because they're already falling out. And at the moment my position as a journalist is very precarious. My predisposition toward peace has cost me any influence with the *Berliner Zeitung*, and my earnings there are almost zero."[221]

Although Fried succeeded in persuading Bertha von Suttner to continue working for the current, financially secured year, he was already able to foresee

---

219   Fried to Suttner, November 2, 1898, in *Collection de 17 lettres de Alfred H. Fried à Berthe de Suttner*, Bibliothéque du Palais de la Paix, Haag, Sig. Y 3462.
220   Fried to Suttner, November 17, 1898, in *Collection de 17 lettres de Alfred H. Fried à Berthe de Suttner*, Bibliothéque du Palais de la Paix, Haag, Sig. Y 3462.
221   Fried to Suttner, November 17, 1898, in *Collection de 17 lettres de Alfred H. Fried à Berthe de Suttner*, Bibliothéque du Palais de la Paix, Haag, Sig. Y 3462.

the end in May 1899. So it was not surprising that his numerous meetings and discussions with other pacifists in The Hague were aimed at seeking financial support for a new journal. And he got lucky. His idea for a *Wochenzeitschrift für internationale Verständigung* (A Weekly Journal for International Understanding), published in the capital city of Berlin, had appeal. The journal was to address any current events relevant to pacifism and at the same time be a forum for domestic and foreign pacifists. A small fund to start the journal was found, so that Fried could begin work.[222]

When he returned from The Hague on June 2, he immediately got to work and, on July 1, while The Hague conference was still in full swing, he was able to present the first issue. The new magazine, with the title *Die Friedens-Warte. Wochenzeitschrift für internationale Verständigung* consisted of eight pages. In his introductory article,[223] Fried claimed that a new phase of the peace movement had begun with the events of the conference in The Hague; the movement was now called upon "to play a major role in the political life of nations." The goals of the movement, as he understood them, were once again explained: the struggle for the expansion and safeguarding of peace through law and reason, which was not directed against the army or against the nation, the renunciation of the dogma "disarmament at any price," and the negation of a quest for "eternal peace." The new journal would stand on these principles; moreover, it would seek to establish relationships among the peoples of the world: "From the perspective of peace, the *Friedens-Warte* will also comment on the events, register the progress of the movement, and, with the help of the most outstanding peace-workers, strive to advance the movement along the path that leads to the well-being of humanity and of the nation."

The big advantage of a weekly publication, according to Fried, was, as stated in an advertisement in the journal *Die Waffen nieder!*, that readers would be able to "keep up with events, take a quick and decisive position, and counter and clarify the distortions and false perspectives of our opponents, and thereby increase understanding."[224] Bertha von Suttner also saw the ability to be current as a great advantage and pointed out to the readers of her own revue as early as October,[225] that *Die Waffen nieder!*, as a monthly journal, "no longer met" the requirements of the age and therefore had to be "temporarily shut down."

---

222 Cf. *Friedens-Warte* 3½ (January 14, 1901): 1.
223 *Friedens-Warte* 1, no. 1 (July 1, 1899): 1f. The following quotes are taken from this article.
224 *Die Waffen nieder!* 8, no. 12 (December 1899): 440. A full-page ad on the last page.
225 Cf. *Die Waffen nieder!* 8, no. 10 (October 1899): 406. Letters to the editor.

In December 1899, the last issue of the journal appeared; it remained in the red until the bitter end. The new journal was also on financially shaky ground. The anticipated collaborators were just as non-existent as the hoped-for subscribers. For the most part, Fried wrote the articles alone, and in the fall, he had to reduce the size of the journal from eight pages to four. Even the end of the journal *Die Waffen nieder!*, which was succeeded by the *Friedens-Warte* as Fried saw it,[226] changed the situation very little. Only in the second half of 1900 can one occasionally find the names of other authors, such as Novicow, Jan Bloch, and Leroy Beaulieu. Frequently, however, the four-page weekly came out as an eight-page double number at two-week intervals.

Although Fried would eventually succeed in preserving the journal (and later turn it into a monthly journal), it would take many years for the *Friedens-Warte* to be on solid financial footing. It would never make a profit. Nevertheless, for Fried, the publication and editing of the journal now became a task that was inextricably linked with his future life. It would remain associated with his name beyond his death.

6 Consolidation Attempts around 1900

Despite his best efforts, Fried's financial situation did not improve at the turn of the century. He continued to live day to day with crushing debt. There is much evidence of this in his estate.[227] There are requests for payment from private money lenders, notices from courts and pawnshops, and tax reminders from the Jewish community and the municipality Schöneberg. It seems that even doctors and lawyers only rarely received their fees after the first notice. All this indicates that Fried had still not been able to achieve a secure existence.

Meanwhile, the Fried family, apart from Pauline and Otto who went their own ways, came to Berlin. After the academic failure of his eldest son, Samuel Fried pressed the younger sons into business apprenticeships, but neither Leopold nor Carl completed them.[228] The youngest daughter Sidonie had begun training in Vienna for a career on the stage, following the example of her aunt Katharina Ganghofer; she also performed under the stage name Sidonie

---

226 Cf. Fried's open letter to the publisher in *Die Waffen nieder!* 8, no. 12 (December 1899): 432.
227 Documents in Nachlass Fried; some are in Box 24, file 349 and 350 and others are in diverse correspondence.
228 Letter to Leopold, February 3, 1904: "I wanted to go to the university at the time and I worked hard to get myself ready. But Papa had this crazy idea that I should become a businessman. With reluctance, I went from one shop to the next until I finally was able to see that I had to earn some money." Cf. Nachlass Fried, Box 31.

Forbeck at the Vienna Raimund Theater.[229] But in Berlin she apparently did not continue her training. When her father, Samuel Fried, died on June 29, 1900,[230] her worried mother urged the 20-year-old to quickly marry. The opportunity to do so came a short time later, when Sidonie met the 22-year-old Alfred Simonsohn, a very successful businessman from Gutstadt in East Prussia who just recently settled in Bernburg on the Saale and was the main shareholder and managing director of two factories there. In January 1902, the two were married and took in Berta Fried.

The prosperity and reputation of his brother-in-law, who was only six years older than Fried himself, stood in stark contrast to Fried's own situation. Even his increasing fame changed nothing. In November 1901, he wrote bitterly to Bertha von Suttner: "I am known in very wide circles, and I know that if I shot myself in the head today, my fate would be regretted, my desires acknowledged, and beautiful, touching phrases would be written about my early death. But to me, still alive, that little bit of fame has become a burden, a barrier. I know that it is my fault; I do not have the robustness I need to stand up and force the world to believe in my work."[231]

In fact, Fried had indeed become so well known in these years that in 1902 he was even included in the planned *Jewish Encyclopedia* by Isidore Singer. In a letter to Fried asking for biographical data, Singer also explained why he wanted the information: "We write not only about the so-called celebrities, but also about all those who have done something really extraordinary in their field, and who deserve mention in a detailed family history."[232] And Fried certainly belonged to this group of accomplished men at this time. However, there was no mention of him in the dictionary. Whether Fried refused to be included in a Jewish encyclopedia or whether he later did not seem significant enough to the editors remains unclear. However, Fried did find a place in another dictionary a few years earlier: in 1897 an account of his life appeared in an encyclopedia by Richard Wrede and Hans von Reinfels; the book was dedicated to the "intellectual life" of Berlin.[233] As stated in the introduction, the authors had set themselves the task "to provide information on all those women and men of Berlin who have been able to rise above the intellectual level of the average

---

229 Newspaper article along with a business card of the budding artist in Nachlass Berthold Simonsohn, privately owned by Trude Simonsohn, now in the BA Bundesarchiv Koblenz.
230 Samuel Fried was interred at the Jewish cemetery at Weißensee.
231 Fried to Suttner, November 1, 1901. Nachlass Suttner, Box 19.
232 Dr. Isidor Singer to Fried, August 8, 1902. Nachlass Fried, Box 38.
233 Richard Wrede, Hans von Reinfels (eds.), *Das geistige Berlin. Eine Enzyklopädie des geistigen Lebens Berlins* (Berlin, 1897), 120.

person by virtue of their gifts, talents, or genius."[234] Since it was always Fried's goal to be counted among these people, he may have been very pleased with his selection. In the short article, which gives a brief summary of his career, previous work experience, and literary works, Fried also named the two pseudonyms that he had sporadically used in those years: Manfred Herald Frei and Leo Karrassowitsch.[235]

Nevertheless, Fried felt rather discriminated against by the Berlin society as a whole and in particular by his employers, the editors of the large Berlin newspapers. In November 1901, in a letter to the *Berliner Zeitung*, he complained that for months he had had to fight for the inclusion of every single article and that on average only one in four was accepted. Fastidiously, he further calculated that his fee in the five-and-a-half years of his collaboration had dropped from a peak of 3,183 marks in 1898 to 360 marks in 1901:[236] "On the other hand, if I consider the extent of growth of your publishing house and how much opportunity for employment was opened up, and also how my contributions decreased from year to year, then I have to think, maybe a little too late, that my collaboration may not even have been wanted. I would be very sad about that, for two reasons. First, I live from the income that my writing generates, and, as you know, the field of journalism is not very large for a man who allows himself the luxury of a mind and a worldview. Secondly, I believe that my selfless activity on behalf of the peace movement is the reason why I have been increasingly pushed aside in my work at the *Berliner Zeitung*."[237]

The editor's answer is not extant. However, things were likely not as bad as Fried feared, because in the years to come, he continued to write articles, feuilletons, and book reviews, as well as pacifist articles, and even when he finally left Berlin, he continued to work as a "Viennese Correspondent." Nevertheless, during these years the position of a pacifist journalist in Wilhelminian Berlin was becoming increasingly difficult. The marginally tangible results of The Hague Conference became even clearer with the outbreak of the Boer War, just three months after the conference ended, and led to an uptick in the

---

234 Ibid, v.
235 To the best of my knowledge, only *Dschingis-Kahn mit Telegraphen* (1895) was published under the name Manfred Herald Frei. For the pseudonym Leo Karrassowitsch [!] only one article in the journal *Die Waffen nieder!* 1, 1892, 17ff, with the title "Phantasien vom Schlachtfelde," could be discovered. It was also published in the anthology *Friedensstimmen* by Leopold Katscher, Esslingen, undated [1894], 334–336.
236 It is quite surprising that Fried only says that he earned 874 marks for 1899, the year of the conference in The Haag at which he was a correspondent for the *Berliner Zeitung*.
237 Fried to the *Berliner Zeitung*, November 18, 1901, in Nachlass Fried, Box 33.

already widespread resentment against England rather than to an interest in pacifist ideas.[238]

Fried's efforts to become a naturalized citizen of Germany, which had begun around 1900, were also not successful, probably due to the fact that he could not show sufficient income. In 1902, his application for naturalization was rejected once and for all.[239] At the end of 1901, ten years after their first contact, Fried drew a devastating conclusion in a letter to Bertha von Suttner: "My innermost core, which was so hopeful at that time, has turned bleak and desolate. A decade, a decade of maximum creative power, has passed me by, unlived, and I have neither internal nor external achievements to show for it. I look with horror towards an uncertain future; a tired man at the age of 37."[240]

But Fried was not a person to give up so quickly, and periods of depression were always followed by periods of increased and heightened activity. He continued to devote a large part of his work to his journal. But since that did not bring him financial gain, he was forced to earn a living by other means. Mostly, he worked as a journalist for newspapers outside of Berlin, for example, for the *Breslauer Zeitung*, the *Hamburger Fremden-Blatt,* the *Königsberger Hartungsche Zeitung*, the *Frankfurter Zeitung*, the *Karlsbader Tageblatt*, the *Kölnische Zeitung* and the *General-Anzeiger für Dortmund und die Provinz Westfalen*. Generally, he wrote feuilletons: short reports and stories, like "Mein bester Freund" (My Best Friend), about the great importance of the letter carrier or the cultural significance of a small invention in "Knöpfe" (Buttons). However, Fried also offered whole series, such as the very successful *Berliner Briefe*, which gave newspapers, particularly those located far away from the metropolis, the opportunity to enhance their publication with a bit of big-city flair. In the letters, he talked in a chatty tone about the social, literary, and artistic events in Berlin, about incidents in parliament or in the courtroom, and about other events in the public life of the capital, but he expressly eschewed political issues, producing pure entertainment. Quite similar was the tone of his travel correspondence, in which he usually reported on his experiences

---

238 On the increasing preparations in Germany for war, see the collection edited by Jost Dülffer and Karl Holl, *Bereit zum Krieg. Kriegsmentalität im wilhelminischen Deutschland 1890–1914* (Göttingen, 1986).

239 The case file could not be located, but there are indications of several attempts to gain citizenship in his correspondence as well as a review report, dated October 9, 1902 by a criminal inspector (Schöne), which was then sent to the Foreign Office: "Alfred Fried, born on November 11, 1864 in Vienna, Jewish, is an Austrian citizen whose recent petition for naturalization was denied." PA/AA, R 8774

240 Fried to Suttner, November 1, 1901, Nachlass Suttner, Box 19.

in ten feuilletons, for example, on his time on the Riviera in April and May 1902: "Feuilletonistic descriptions of the Azur coast (via Nice, Monte Carlo, San Remo, Cannes, Marseille, southern France, etc.), based on my location at the time."[241]

In May of the same year, Fried offered a series called "Wanderungen durch die Düsseldorfer Ausstellung" (Walks through the Dusseldorf Exhibition), an industrial exhibition in western Germany to which he attached great importance for the entire empire. "I will try to create a general picture of the exhibition and its Rhenish milieu in an entertaining, feuilletonistic manner, without going into too much detail."[242] Since the series were inexpensive (ten to thirteen articles for a total of ten marks) and so smaller newspapers could then afford a subscription, he was relatively successful. In 1902, the *Berliner Briefe* were being published in newspapers in 22 German cities—but he still did not get rich on them. Two larger works were also produced at this time: *Kleine Anzeigen* (Small Advertisements), a work on the short classified advertisements in newspapers and magazines, and the polemical *Theaterdusel* (Theater Stupor), which argued against overestimating the value of the theater.

But Fried was still bubbling with ideas, even if only a fraction of them could be realized. He planned a telephone newspaper to be financed through the advertisements of customers and a history of asphalt. He also designed an illustrated streetcar map, which among other things would contain the rules for safe entry and exit. In addition, he worked on plans for a large "library of modern reform movements" that would encompass the progressive currents of the time. First and foremost, of course, was the peace movement followed by: the reform of land ownership, the women's movement, the anti-alcoholism movement, the anti-duel movement, the ethical movement, the Egidy movement, zionism, the free religious movement, the cremation movement, the art education movement, the guest house reform movement, the movement to end the trafficking of young girls, the movement to reform women's clothing, and the movement to combat sexually transmitted diseases, as well as the vegetarian movement.[243] For most of these ideas, however, he was unable to find publishers who were in sufficiently strong financial positions.

Around 1900, Fried's openness toward new developments and his interest in the various reform movements of his time led him to the social-religious "Neue Gemeinschaft" (New Community) around the brothers Heinrich and Julius Hart, who managed a life reform project that emerged in early 1900 from

---

241 Nachlass Fried, Box 25, file 362.
242 Ibid.
243 This and some of Fried's other plans can be found in Nachlass Fried, Box 14, file 270.

a group of Berlin bohemians.[244] The goal of the community, whose innermost circle had established a residential community in the spring of 1900 on the lower floor of a free-standing common building (Gartenhaus), was as follows: "In a profound fusing of religion, art, knowledge and life, the New Community seeks to realize the ideal human being and the ideal humankind, the perfection of the individual and of the community."[245] The members of the community were to be a model of the "right life" for the individual.

Fried probably came into contact with the group through his brother-in-law Felix Holländer, who was close friends with Gustav Landauer and the Hart brothers. Fried's own characteristic enthusiasm quickly opened lots of doors for him, as suggested by Heinrich Hart: "We are pleased to welcome you and thank you very much for your fervent approbation. The enthusiasm that your words breathe also fills us, and together we will ignite the world with the sun in us to create a new spring."[246] By the summer of 1900 Fried had already been invited to the planning sessions of the "inner circle" and, despite his own financial plight, regularly supported the upkeep of the community housing. Nevertheless, the relationship did not last long. Personal differences with Felix Holländer, which had nothing to do with the New Community, prompted Fried to withdraw at the end of the year. "I'll write to the Harts today and announce my resignation from the inner circle. It wouldn't be right of me to inject a lie into this harmonious circle."[247] Heinrich Hart's persistent attempts to change Fried's mind were in vain; there was no further contact with the group after the spring of 1901.

Nevertheless, the encounter left its mark on Fried—the missionary consciousness of the community, which aimed, in word and deed, to help mankind attain higher knowledge and personal development, reflected his own views. In the words of Julius Hart: "But we do not fight an enemy in anyone, but rather someone who has been left behind, who is entrapped, confused and can see things only in one way, someone whom, as far as we are concerned, we also want to encourage in the fight."[248] Fried then used this comment as a motto in a polemical letter to his brother-in-law; the words recall Fried's later remarks that the correct knowledge of the idea of peace is only a problem of intellectual optics. The blind and the reactionary contemporaries need only be taught the correct view.

---

244 Cf. Janos Frescot, "Literatur zwischen Betrieb und Einsamkeit" in *Berlin um 1900. An Exhibition of the Berlin Gallery in Connection with the Akademie der Künste* (Berlin, 1984), 329ff.
245 Excerpt from the flyer "Unsere Feste," quoted as in the above note, 330.
246 Heinrich Hart to Fried, undated [summer 1900], Nachlass Fried, Box 37.
247 Fried to Felix Holländer, undated [end of 1900], Nachlass Fried, Box 37.
248 Placed at the head of an undated letter by Fried to Felix Holländer [early 1900] with the source listed as "Hart v. L.i.L ss 81," Nachlass Fried Box 32.

6.1 *Esperanto*

At roughly the same time as his encounter with the New Community, Fried also came across the constructed auxiliary language Esperanto. Around 1878, the Polish ophthalmologist Dr. Ludwig Zamenhof[249] developed a world language from elements of various European languages; he first introduced it to the public in 1887 under the name "Lingvo lnternacia" in Russian and later presented it in Polish. Its pseudonym "Esperanto," the "hoping one," soon replaced the original name of the language.

It may have been Gaston Moch, the former French officer and well-known pacifist of Alsatian descent, who drew Fried's attention to the importance of this new artificial language. After his first, less encouraging experience with the Volapak language, the articulate Frenchman had learned the new language as early as 1889 and had become its zealous advocate.[250] Surely it was not difficult for Fried, who was always on the look-out for new fields to engage with, to become interested in the promising new "world language." But other pacifists were also involved with Esperanto early on. In England, for example, William T. Stead campaigned for Esperanto especially in his journal "Review of Reviews."

While the new language spread relatively quickly in Russia and France, it was still virtually unknown in Germany around 1900 after some short-lived initial success. In order to explore the possibilities of Esperanto for pacifist purposes and to obtain basic information, Fried turned directly to the inventor, Ludwig Zamenhof in Warsaw, who was overjoyed that Fried had reached out to him: "I am very pleased that you want to work for our cause in Germany. You still have a very wide-open field because, unfortunately, Esperanto is virtually unknown in Germany! [...] L. Einstein was a capable promoter, but he unfortunately died early on. Messrs. Schmidt and Meyer have published grammars, but they dropped out when our cause was in very bad shape, six or seven years ago."[251]

Fried decided to immerse himself in the new language and to explore the possibilities of publishing a German textbook. To this end, he turned to Professor Adolf Schmidt in Gotha, a geomagnetist with whom he had been in correspondence on occasion since 1896 and who had previously created a grammar for Esperanto. In the spring of 1902, both agreed that Schmidt would write a

---

249   Zamenhof himself wrote his name with an 'S', which is why even today the correspondence between Fried and Zamenhof is found in Fried's Nachlass under 'S' and not under 'Z'.
250   Cf. Fried, *Lehrbuch der Internationalen Hilfssprache 'Esperanto'. Mit Wörterbuch in Esperanto-Deutsch und Deutsch-Esperanto* (Berlin, 1903), 14f.
251   Dr. Ludwig Zamenhof to Fried, November 11, 1901, Nachlass Fried, Box 26.

comprehensive German Esperanto textbook by the next summer—followed by a grammar, a dictionary, and exercise and reading books; Fried intended to publish these in his own publishing house.[252]

In order to create a market for the new books, Fried wanted to "quickly set about founding a German Esperanto society, at least a core group,"[253] according to a well-tested formula. Schmidt warned that the work would first have to be published before one could think of founding a society.[254] But Schmidt's work was delayed, and in mid-June it was too much for the impatient Fried. Not only did he begin to work on an Esperanto textbook on his own, but he also started to advertise in the press. At the end of June 1902, an article appeared in *Die Woche* (The Week),[255] in which he outlined the unique advantages of Esperanto: its phonetic spelling, the European linguistic roots, the grammar of only 16 rules, etc.— in short, its ease of learning, which also made it useful for ordinary people who had not learned English or French. At the same time, he argued, Esperanto was also a language that would soon be indispensable to international trade and the academic world.

While Fried was working at full speed on the completion of his manuscript, some legal difficulties with the Hachette publishing house arose, since Hachette had Zamenhof under contract. Zamenhof tried to help as best he could, but after further difficulties Fried decided to publish his textbook without the consent of the Parisian publisher. In his new Esperanto Publishing House, which was to specialize entirely in the publication of Esperanto literature, the textbook went to print in early 1903.

Zamenhof was enthusiastic: "Thank you very much for your textbook; I was very pleased to have received it. I was impressed with the book; I wish you much success with it, and I am confident it will be successful."[256] At the same time, he reminded Fried to be patient. The initial phases would not be easy, but he was convinced that sooner or later Esperanto would shine in Germany.

In the next few months, Fried needed to establish a group or a club for those interested in his new book and other planned Esperanto projects, such as the book of exercises, which he had planned and had already advertised on the cover of the textbook. It was to appear in April. But it was, in fact, never published. In March 1903, he wrote to Therese Frankl in Vienna: "You have now

---

252 Fried to A. Schmidt, May 7, 1902, Nachlass Fried, Box 42.
253 Fried to Adolf Schmidt, May 7, 1902, Nachlass Fried, Box 42.
254 A. Schmidt to Fried, May 8, 1902, Nachlass Fried, Box 42.
255 Fried, "Eine internationale Hilfssprache," in *Die Woche. Moderne illustrierte Zeitschrift* 26, (Berlin 1902): 1197–1199.
256 Ludwig Zamenhof to Fried, March 16, 1903, Nachlass Fried, Box 26.

received the Esperanto book. I have already placed the orders and am beginning with the promotion campaign. I have also begun to work on the exercise book. [...] Tonight there is a meeting of the Esperanto Club in my apartment."[257] However, what Fried called the "Esperanto Club" in this letter was, for the time being, a meeting with two interested 19-year-old boys from Berlin.[258] Even before the small group could establish itself, Fried would leave Berlin in early summer 1903 following his separation from his second wife, Martha, and return to Vienna. The founding of the club took place without him. On November 28, Jean Borel informed Fried of the events: "I am pleased to inform you of the founding of the Berlin Esperanto Group with 20 members. The provisional Board of Directors consists of Prof. Dr. med. Schmidt, M.D. (Potsdam), Jürgenson, Philipp, Seeger and me. We regret that you could not be there, but we hope that you will join our group and that we will soon have the pleasure of seeing you in Berlin."[259]

The offer to become merely a member, however, was not enough for Fried. In December 1903, he wrote with disappointment to Adolf Mehlisch, a friend of the German Peace Society (DFG), whose umbrella group oversaw the Esperanto club: "I take the founding of an Esperanto group in Berlin to be an encouraging sign for the progress of Esperanto in our priggish country, one that is antithetical to new and international things. To put it bluntly, I was troubled by the fact that I, who was among the first in Germany to promote Esperanto and published the first textbook at some financial sacrifice, was not called upon to join the board of this group."[260]

But in the Berlin branch of the German Peace Society, there was no urgent need to firmly integrate Fried in any way. Moreover, given the fact that he was now living in Vienna, the leadership had another good argument against his inclusion. For Fried, these experiences in Berlin became seminal; easily hurt as he was, he would keep his distance from all clubs and associations, as far as possible, in the next few years.

While Fried was primarily living in Vienna from April 1903 on, his brother Leopold looked after the distribution of the textbook and tried to encourage his older brother to complete the exercise book: "If I had the exercise book, I would certainly be able to speak and write Esperanto very well. There is also a great demand for it, i.e., the people who had paid for the exercise book,

---

257 Fried to Therese, March 13, 1903. Nachlass Fried, Box 92.
258 Fried to Therese, March 14, 1903. Nachlass Fried, Box 92. Therese also learns Esperanto, which is why many of his letters of this time include sections in Esperanto.
259 Jean Borel to Fried, November 28, 1903. Nachlass Fried, Box 49. This piece of news was composed in Esperanto in the original. For the translation of the texts I am grateful to Ina Tautorat of the Esperant-Centro Berlin.
260 Fried to Adolf Mehlisch, undated [December 1903]. Nachlass Fried, Box 53.

about 3 or 4 people, right after you left, have repeatedly asked for it. [...] We have returned the money for the exercise book that came in later; we have noted the addresses."[261] In the following year, Leopold again pressed Fried and emphasized his regret that his brother missed out on some great business opportunities.[262]

In fact, under different circumstances, the publishing house could have become quite a promising source of income for Fried. In the summer of 1903, shortly after he left Berlin, the brother of Jean Borel, who worked as a publisher, succeeded in reaching an agreement with Hachette for the German publishing rights of Zamenhof's works, and subsequently the extremely successful Berlin Esperanto publishing house Möller & Borel was founded. Fried had already abandoned his publishing plans. Instead, he tried to secure a larger publisher for his textbook. When the publisher Francke in Stuttgart showed interest in the fledgling world language movement, Fried seized the opportunity. He offered the publisher not only the remainder of his textbooks, including the publishing rights, but also the exercise book and other conversational, reading and correspondence manuals. In 1905, Francke published a second, improved and expanded edition, and in the next three years three more editions followed.[263]

However, the main theme in Fried's writing remained the idea of peace. *Unter der weißen Fahne* (Under the White Flag)[264] was published as early as the spring of 1901; it contained 46 selected articles and essays on topics such as the "Peace Movement," "Peace Politics," "Understanding," "The Hague," and "Cuba - Transvaal - China," all of which were written in the period between 1895 and 1901, the majority in the years 1898 and 1899. The front page was adorned with a quote on the importance of the press for the dissemination of the peace idea by Count Albert Apponyi "the outstanding Hungarian statesman, president of the Hungarian group of the Interparliamentary Union, member of The Hague Court of Arbitration, and the founder of the International Press-Union for Peace and Arbitration."[265] Fried dedicated the whole work "most respectfully" to him.

The Hungarian politician, as chairman of the interparliamentary group of his country, had encouraged the formation of an "International Press

---

261 Leopold Fried to Fried, December 18, 1903. Nachlass Fried, Box 31.
262 See, for example, Leopold Fried to Fried, February 4, 1904. Nachlass Fried, Box 31.
263 In spite of this success Fried did not complete the exercise book and never published any other materials of this nature.
264 *Unter der weißen Fahne. Aus der Mappe eines Friedensjournalisten. Gesammelte Artikel und Aufsätze von Alfred Hermann Fried* (Berlin, 1901).
265 Ibid. Dedication.

Association for Peace and Arbitration" after The Hague Conference and had successfully initiated the formation of a Hungarian branch in March 1900 during a lecture to Budapest journalists.[266] However, Fried's hope that a group could also be formed in Germany was not realized.[267] Only in France, where a similar association had existed since 1895–96,[268] did Apponyi's suggestion fall on fertile ground and breathe new life into the local "Association Internationale des Journalistes Amis de la Paix." Disappointed by the low response in German-speaking countries, Fried joined this organization.

In the introduction entitled "Presse- und Friedensbewegung" (The Press and the Peace Movement), Fried detailed the tremendous importance of the press to the peace movement: "As brilliant as the prospects that are now open to the peace movement are, it must not forget, even for a second, to act in the present; it must go through the press to reach the people. It needs the press and must take hold of it. The professional journals on peace are a stopgap; the idea of peace is not disseminated through them, nor justified; it is only maintained there, where it already exists. New supporters are hardly gained through the professional peace journals. They only appeal to the already converted. The great hunt for supporters must take place in the daily papers, and that's why we must do everything we can to capture the press."[269] Fried saw himself at the forefront of this fight for the "white press." For years, he noted, he had dedicated his journalistic activity exclusively to the propagation of the idea of peace, but he had never found a German colleague at the congresses of the peace societies and the IPU—a claim that may actually be true. However, some parliamentarians and many pacifists did write for the few interested, liberal newspapers, which may then have been less inclined to send their own journalists. So, Fried also saw himself as a journalist, as a member of the peace movement, who was in a special position, not just someone on the margins, but at the forefront of a coming cultural development: "If one wants to put it in a nutshell, one could say that the peace movement is cultural development (Kulturentwicklung). If one wants to be more elaborate, one might say: the peace movement is the sum of all the striving that is carried out in the service of the intellectual development of humanity and the translation of acquired theoretical knowledge into practice. It provides the impetus to the path of modern development, and it denotes the effort from what has already been achieved to what must yet be achieved."

---

266   See also the thorough report in *Friedens-Warte* 2, no. 13/14 (April 2, 1900): 52ff.
267   Cf. *Friedens-Warte* 2, no. 16 (April 16, 1900): 61.
268   Cf. *Die Waffen nieder!* 4: 236.
269   Fried, *Unter der weißen Fahne*, 13. The following quotations are taken from this work.

Fried's equally broad statement, that he dedicated himself exclusively to the advancement of the idea of peace, may also be correct. Between the autumn of 1902 and the spring of 1903, Fried produced, in quick succession, four pamphlets dealing with topics related to the peace movement. The first and probably most interesting, "Die Ausgestaltung der Friedensaktion in Deutschland" (The Formation of Peace Action in Germany), was published at the end of October 1902. Appearing first as the only document of a sixteen-page, double number of the *Friedens-Warte,* which at that time was still published every fourteen days,[270] it was distributed by Fried as a separate publication in November.[271] This little piece was intended to commemorate the 10th anniversary of the German Peace Society; above all, it dealt with the possibility of restructuring the society. He wrote that the time had come to step out of the esoteric circles and into the arena of political life, namely through an effective reorganization of the local groups and a new program that would put the modern scientific-political orientation above the purely ethical-humanitarian. Promotion on a massive scale, he claimed, was the order of the day.

These goals were also to be served by the other three works of the period: "Die Grundlagen der modernen Wirtschaft und der Krieg" (The Foundations of Modern Economy and War), "Die Lasten des bewaffneten Friedens und der Zukunftskrieg," (The Burdens of Armed Peace and the War of the Future), and "Die hauptsächlichsten Missverständnisse über die Friedensbewegung" (The Most Basic Misconceptions of the Peace Movement),[272] the latter of which was supposed to clarify the meaning of the term in their promotional materials. How little, however, the German Peace Society was inclined to acknowledge Fried's unwavering efforts, is best illustrated by the example of the Berlin local group. There was no response in Berlin to the relocation of the headquarters of the German Peace Society to southern Germany, which Fried had long demanded, and to the definitive end of the *Monatliche Friedens-Korrespondenz* (Monthly Peace Correspondence). The small local group finally died out. In the spring of 1902, after his return from the World Peace Congress in Monaco, Fried drew the attention of the headquarters in Stuttgart to the situation in Berlin. In the mailbox of the *Friedens-Blätter,* he received an evasive answer: "A. H. Fr. - B. We energetically regret the unsustainable conditions described

---

270 Cf. *Friedens-Warte* 6, no. 19/20 (October 3, 1902): 145–160.
271 Fried, *Die Ausgestaltung der Friedensaktion in Deutschland. Eine Denkschrift zum zehnjährigen Bestande der Deutschen Friedens-Gesellschaft. November 1892 – November 1902* (Berlin, 1903).
272 Fried,"Die hauptsächlichsten Missverständnisse über die Friedensbewegung," in *Der Türmer* 5, no. 3. As a separate publication, see Verlag der Friedens-Warte (Berlin, 1903).

in your letter about the local group in Berlin and hope that a remedy will be found in the very near future."[273]

Fried himself set out to re-establish the local chapter,[274] not least in the hope that this time he would be able to establish himself in the group and perhaps occupy an important position. Although there was no direct protest from the Stuttgart headquarters, Fried was nevertheless asked to hold off on the re-constitution of the group until headquarters itself could try to reorganize the existing group in the autumn. Until that time, he should draw up a list of possible candidates for the new Berlin board of directors and send it to Quidde in Munich. In fact, in the fall of 1902, Quidde and Richter arranged for personal talks with eight of the people named by Fried, but Fried himself was not interviewed. Fried was not even invited to the General Assembly convened on November 13 by Quidde and Richter in Berlin. Embittered, he wrote to Adolf Mehlisch, one of those whom he suggested: "I also heard this evening how eagerly they sought a person who was living in Berlin and who was central to the peace movement, without any mention of me." And he asked the addressee, to let him know, if in the interview he had heard of any reasons why he (Fried) was not considered. A reply letter has not been preserved. It is quite conceivable, however, that in Berlin, Stuttgart or Munich, there was no great interest in naming to the board a passionate maverick and unconventional activist, who had once again attracted unwelcome attention with his memorandum on the tenth anniversary of the founding of the German Peace Society.

For Fried, however, this rejection was a new and serious setback, because he had long recognized that he also needed a certain reputation for his journalistic work and for his publishing efforts—or, in his own words, "that for the full development of my activities I need an organizational framework that would give my work greater prominence."[275] In Berlin, however, this support was not forthcoming.

7   Flight from Berlin (1903)

1903 was a decisive year for Fried. In January, the situation with his sick wife Martha escalated such that on Thursday, January 15, Fried secretly left his apartment and Berlin, and traveled to Bernburg to visit his mother and sister.

---

273   *Friedensblätter* 5 (May 1902): 64.
274   On this and the following points, see Fried to Adolf Mehlisch, December 5, 1902. Nachlass Fried, Box 39.
275   Ibid.

Upon his return, he vehemently reproached his wife's family: "Dear Gustav! I am moved to express my deep dismay and outrage, not at you personally, but at you as the head of the family, over the fact that Martha, after her mental illness was clearly established, was left alone in the apartment from Sunday night to Monday morning with an inexperienced 20-year-old servant, who did not attend to her until Monday at 11 o'clock. The greatest of misfortunes could have happened. Martha slept in the maid's room; the girl was so fearful that she locked herself in the small front room. Martha was left alone in this situation and endured who knows what torment. I don't believe that something like this, that such recklessness, such selfishness would be possible even among the Botokuden. If the family had at least stated that it did not want to take on the duty of watching over her at night, Frankl would have done so without batting an eyelid. In addition, it would have been appropriate for someone to telephone an attendant. There is no excuse for such behavior, which even the doctors find incomprehensible. In response to the objection that I was not there myself, I have to declare that I had to leave Berlin on Thursday afternoon as a [!] ... after the terrible fight with my wife who had been suffering from the onset of her illness for weeks and who was just no longer able to engage. My cries for help on Wednesday evening, when I urgently requested the presence of a third person, went unheeded. Selfishness may be very useful, but it is not pretty."[276]

The family reacted angrily, and in turn Gustav Holländer accused Fried of irresponsible action himself in a short handwritten letter, because he had left Martha alone and with virtually no money.[277] For his part, Fried defended himself to a more obliging relative in a several-page letter, in which he explained the reasons for his departure in detail: the doctor's recommendation, his nervous breakdown, the need to finish some work in order to maintain some financial viability. "Gustav and probably the other members of the family have never seen Martha in this condition; they certainly have not lived in the same house with her when she was in this state. You cannot imagine what life is like under such circumstances, how it grates on the nerves of a man, especially those of a nervous man."[278] At the end of the letter he explained metaphorically that the tablecloth connecting him and the Holländer family was torn and that any hopes for understanding and accommodation were buried. Fried was at a turning point. He found his marriage to Martha unbearable, and his relationship with Siegfried Frankl's wife Therese, who was similarly unhappy

---

276   Fried to Gustav Holländer, January 20, 1903. Nachlass Fried, Box 32.
277   Gustav Holländer to Fried, January 23, 1903. Nachlass Fried, Box 32.
278   Fried to Krisch, January 24, 1903. Nachlass Fried, Box 32.

in her marriage, was becoming more and more intimate. Only a small push was needed to make an irrevocable change. The dramatic event came two weeks later. While Martha was still in the "asylum for mental patients" in Charlottenburg under the care of Dr. Edel, where she had previously been treated for a few weeks, something happened on February 8, something whose sequence can no longer be precisely determined from the existing documents,[279] but whose result was clear: The long-term relationship between Fried and Therese Frankl became publicly known.

Siegfried was horrified and forbade Therese to see Alfred again, which was not easy since the families had been living side by side in the same house at Grünewaldstraße 40 in Berlin-Schöneberg for a year and shared a telephone line, which could also be used as an intercom. Siegfried therefore decided to send Therese to her sister's family in Vienna for a while, thus hoping to end the affair. Two weeks later, Therese's brother-in-law arrived from Vienna and picked her up. She arrived with him in Vienna on the evening of the 26th.

The plan to separate the two lovers, however, did not succeed. Even before her departure, Fried wrote the first letter to his "Röschen" in "exile in Vienna." He included a poem "An mein Röschen" (To my little rose) in which he expressed his heartfelt grief over their separation but also the certainty that they could no longer really be separated.

From the very beginning Therese was also determined not to deny her feelings, and she too was borne by the same certainty and confidence. In her first letter from Vienna, she wrote: "We complete each other perfectly with our feelings for each other; we will be very happy. We are bound to be happy [...] Come get me soon, and you will lead me to paradise, and it will always be that way—and you will feel forever the love and gratitude of someone rescued."[280]

Ironically, it was at this very time of personal turmoil that Fried had to complete a difficult translation in addition to his normal work: the German translation of the autobiography of the Prince of Monaco, *Carrière d'un navigateur*.[281] When Bertha von Suttner, who was then opening the Peace Institute in Monaco, saw the galley proofs, she was appalled by the many mistakes and began to correct them herself. "There were so many mistakes that the pages

---

279 There are several comments in the letters in Fried's Nachlass that suggest that Josef Wiener, an acquaintance of both families and who was probably in love with Therese himself, informed Siegfried of an intimate meeting of the two and caught them *in flagranti*. In the Nachlass there is a poem written by Wiener to Therese during this time.
280 Therese to Fried, February 27, 1903. Nachlass Fried, Box 92.
281 *Albert I, the Prince of Monaco: Eine Seemannslaufbahn. Aus dem Französischen von Alfred H. Fried* (Berlin, 1903). (New edition 1991, Berlin).

THE BERLIN YEARS 1884–1903   99

that were already printed had to be pulped."[282] For Fried, whose reputation in Monaco, especially with regard to the newly founded Peace Institute, was very important to him, this was a blow, but understandable, considering that even Bertha von Suttner needed six months of intensive and single-minded focus for a good translation,[283] something that Fried even without his personal problems would never have had. Given the tension he felt as a result of Martha's situation and his affection for Therese, it was almost a miracle that Fried had been able to finish the work on time.[284]

Fried to Therese:

No one can force us to love
Where love does not come from itself,
Nor to deny it
When every vein, every fiber loves.
Farewell, my love!

You are mine, my dear, and mine you will stay,
Do not despair in the darkest storm,
What painfully scorches our hearts now,
Is the cement for eternity.[285]

In the first weeks, while Therese was in Vienna and Martha was in the sanatorium, Fried was supported by his mother who, unlike the people around him, showed complete understanding. Almost amused, Fried described to Therese the initial reactions of friends and acquaintances: "Mr. Adolf, whom I see every day, goes out of his way so as not to see me."[286] Many acquaintances responded to the double adultery with disapproval and a lack of understanding, whereby the criticism directed at the unfaithful wife was usually harsher, as Fried reported to Therese: "They disapprove of your actions more than of mine, and they thought that you had gone to Vienna because of me. The moral indignation of the pregnant virgin and her mother as well as of her husband is characteristic of the whole clan."

---

282   Hamann, *Bertha von Suttner*, 316.
283   Ibid.
284   The book first appeared in 1903.
285   Nachlass Fried, Box 92.
286   Fried to Therese, March 1, 1903. Nachlass Fried, Box 92. This is the source of the following quotations.

It was rare that Fried experienced a different reaction in the coming weeks, but he did relate one such encounter to Therese joyfully: "Yesterday, I had a very pleasant experience. I stopped by the Antricks for the first time in months. She was the only one in the shop, and I could not refrain from telling her what was going on. So gradually I came out with it. Well, she nearly fell off the chair. – She always said that we two were a good match, and she also said that she had told you that once before and that you replied quite stoically, 'yes, what's to be done?' She sends you her warm regards and wants you to know that you have her blessing. Well, then."[287]

Reactions like these, however, were the exception. Fried did not find the hoped-for support even from Bertha von Suttner, who had lost her husband in December 1902; he complained to Therese: "[...] when I have hinted to her how I am suffering mentally, she only responds by complaining to me of her own sorrow at the loss of her husband."[288] It is unclear, however, how much Fried had actually told Bertha von Suttner about the events.

In general, the behavior of Fried and Therese was too severe a violation of the morality of times to meet with much understanding. So, quite quickly, they both sought to file for official divorces from their respective spouses.

In order to strengthen Therese in her intention to separate from her husband, Fried had his brothers Leopold and Carl keep tabs on Siegfried Frankl. They were soon able to determine that Siegfried was visiting a prostitute. Fried immediately informed Therese, who was plagued with a guilty conscience vis-à-vis her husband, and he then promptly offered some appropriate language that she could use in a letter to him: "You must be tough. There will be time for leniency later. I would be very short. For example: Dear Siegfried! It has just come to my attention that you have been engaged, for a long time, in an adulterous affair with a prostitute in the Markgrafenstraße, whose name and address are known. Unaware of the importance of this fact, Carl Fried mentioned this to his brother in a conversation. Both he and the prostitute confirmed the affair. [...] Apart from everything else, this incident makes it impossible for me to live with you any longer, and I will now file for a divorce from you."[289] Whether Therese followed Fried's suggestion is unknown, but at least she seems to have successfully confronted her husband with the allegations that she raised, because Siegfried pleaded guilty and did not object to his wife's legal complaint.[290] Nevertheless, the divorce was delayed, as it soon

---

287 Fried to Therese, March 24, 1903. Nachlass Fried, Box 92.
288 Fried to Therese, March 14, 1903. Nachlass Fried, Box 92.
289 Fried to Therese, April 2, 1903. Nachlass Fried, Box 92.
290 See Fried's report to the lawyer Moritz Leitersdorf in Pressburg of December 28, 1904. Nachlass Fried, Box 92.

turned out that Siegfried, as a native Hungarian, also had to be divorced there, something that carried a large and costly administrative burden.

With regard to his own marriage, Fried sought an annulment because of his wife's demonstrated mental illness, but he encountered resistance from all sides. Even an expert that Fried paid, who in mid-March gave an opinion on the prospects of a divorce under these circumstances, offered "a rather unfavorable assessment."[291] Likewise, a court expert was of no help, since Fried, as an Austrian, was subject to the Austrian divorce laws, which did not allow divorce on the grounds of mental illness.

Sometime between the beginning of March and May 1903, Fried and Therese needed to decide how the unacceptable distance between them could be overcome. For Fried, a move to Vienna was initially out of the question. His negative childhood memories of Vienna caused him to feel more angst than hope for the future: "How I pity you, my dear, that you must spend such awful times in this miserable place, when you should really be living in beautiful Berlin. Truly, we who live here in Berlin are gods compared to these wretched inhabitants of Vienna."[292] Fried suggested to Therese that she return to Berlin and live there for a while in a pension, or alone in her old apartment, which he would pay for. But since he once again was lacking all financial resources, this plan was shelved again and again. At the beginning of April, Fried was ready to permanently leave the apartment that he shared with Martha. "On Saturday, the housemaid is leaving; then I'll lock the apartment at Grünewaldstrasse 40 and this era of my life will be over."[293]

He first spent a few days in Bernburg with his mother and sister, and at the end of May he went to Paris. He came to Vienna several times for a quick visit. While Therese lived with her sister's family, Fried had to stay in a hotel, although his sister Pauline lived quite comfortably with her husband, the well-to-do English journalist Reginald Wyon. In a bitter letter in 1908, Fried sought to settle the score with Pauline: "Then there was the time I came to Vienna. You threw out Röschen when she needed help the most. Cold-hearted, you threw her out. You have no idea what you did to me!!!"[294] And the tears that I swallowed when I passed by the palace in which you lived, and I did not know where I would stay. Rose had to live with a crazy woman and five other people

---

291　Fried to Therese, March 16, 1903. Nachlass Fried, Box 92.
292　Fried to Therese, March 10, 1903. Nachlass Fried, Box 92.
293　Fried to Therese, April 8, 1903. Nachlass Fried, Box 92.
294　There are no clear reasons given for Pauline's behavior. Presumably, it had to do with her close friendship with Siegfried Frankl, which she had enjoyed since their childhood, but it may also have involved the many efforts, on the part of her English husband and his mother, to distance themselves from the Fried family. These attempts at distancing can be seen in numerous letters.

in two rooms, and I could not visit her there, while I stayed in a small hotel room and had no choice but to spend the whole day with her out on the street. And all that, while I was going through the hardest time of my life!"[295]

During these months Fried also spent a lot of time in Berlin trying to get the divorce proceedings moved along and also pursue his journalistic work. His troubled life also left its mark on the *Friedens-Warte,* which in these years now appeared every two weeks. At the end of April 1903, he was forced to apologize to his readers for the first time: "Because the publisher has been away from Berlin, the editorial work and production have been a bit delayed. Nos. 7 and 8 will therefore appear together as a single issue. Unanswered correspondence may be attributed to the same cause. We will get to everything."[296] But at the end of May and at the end of June, double issues were once again published; this time Fried declared that there were a number of "grave personal circumstances" that had prevented him from pursuing this work to the fullest extent possible.[297] It would not be until July that the journal returned to its biweekly schedule.

By June at the latest, his decision to move to Vienna had been made. Why exactly Fried finally decided to abandon his plan to live with Therese in Berlin cannot be clearly determined from the available documents. What is certain, however, is that his affair with Therese was widely known in Berlin, and the opposition of the influential Holländer family made his professional life in Berlin difficult. In December 1903,[298] Fried wrote to his friend, the representative Otto Antrick in Berlin, noting that the Holländer family (who maintained in a sworn statement that everything belonged to his wife) had not only had his furniture confiscated, but also made slanderous comments about him in the newspapers and to his publishers, claiming that he had no money to feed his wife. Fried also maintained that the family was forcing him into many costly lawsuits. On the attitude of the rest of society he wrote: "Since the affair with Mrs. Frankl, the philistine society has completely turned away from me." Highly indebted and with little hope, Fried fled to Vienna.

---

295   Fried to Pauline Wyon, November 30, 1908. Nachlass Fried, Box 31.
296   *Friedens-Warte* 5, no 7/8 (April 30, 1903): 60.
297   *Friedens-Warte* 5, no. 9/10 (May 31, 1903): 72.
298   Fried to Otto Antrick, December 17, 1903. IISG Amsterdam.

CHAPTER 3

The Vienna Years, 1903–1915

1 A Reluctant Return Home

In June 1903, after an absence of nearly twenty years, Fried returned to a different Vienna, especially for Jews. In the election for the Imperial Assembly of 1891, the antisemitic parties had achieved an impressive victory. German national groups, militant Catholics, and in particular the Christian social movement increasingly held positions of leadership. In 1895, the Christian Social Party of Dr. Karl Lueger[1] emerged victorious in the election of the city council in Vienna. Besides his emphasis on Vienna as a "German city," Lueger's campaign targeted the Jews as an enemy. While it is true that Emperor Franz Josef had been able to resist Lueger's appointment as Vienna's mayor for two years—he saw in Lueger a danger to the equal treatment of all the city's citizens—he finally yielded to public pressure in 1897. Lueger assumed office and would remain in power until his death in the spring of 1910.[2] This "Lord of Vienna" put his imprint on the city like no other mayor before or since, and even today one often comes across his name in the city's geography.[3] With enormous loans from both domestic and international investors he built Vienna into a modern metropolis, providing gas, electricity, and an up-to-date streetcar system. Between 1880 and 1910 the city's population doubled,[4] and by 1908 it reached the two million mark. Lueger countered the crippling effects of the rivalry between the various competing ethnic groups in Vienna with his claim that Vienna was a German city and would remain so. In so doing, Lueger aimed to take advantage of the locals' xenophobic fears that arose from a scarcity of housing, unemployment, and increasing inflation.

Even if in his collaboration with the Jewish religious community he operated under the dictum "Wer a Jud ist, bestimm i!" ("I determine who is a Jew"), Lueger, a self-avowed antisemite, was a disaster for the Jews in Vienna because

---

[1] For further information on Karl Lueger, see the flattering portrayal by Kurt Skalnik, *Dr. Karl Lueger. Der Mann zwischen den Zeiten* (Munich, 1954). A more critical and precise portrait is offered by Brigitte Hamann in *Hitlers Wien. Lehrjahre eines Diktators* (Munich, Zurich, 1998), 393ff.
[2] My characterization essentially follows that of Hamann, *Hitlers Wien*, 393ff.
[3] Ibid, 398.
[4] This growth came about not only as a result of ever-increasing immigration but also through the incorporation of Vienna's suburbs in 1890.

he was clever enough to reduce all of the city's failings to a simple formula "It's the Jews' fault" and because he could scapegoat the social democrats by labeling them a "stock market Jew," a "newspaper Jew," an Eastern-European "beggar Jew," and the "Jewish protective guard." Again and again, he emphasized that he wanted to reverse the emancipation law of 1867: "In Austria, it is a question of liberating the Christians from Jewish hegemony."[5] Brigitte Hamann summarizes the impact of Lueger, the "people's tribune," as follows: "Politically, it is insignificant whether Lueger privately may have had Jewish friends, and if he did, how many he may have had. On the other hand, the devastating impact of his inflammatory speeches was highly significant. The antisemitism that Lueger conveyed to his adoring masses through his decades-long hypnotic oratory, as well as his refusal to contradict the crude blunders of his fellow party members, poisoned the atmosphere."[6]

Years before Lueger came to power, Bertha von Suttner and her husband had founded a "Verein zur Abwehr des Antisemitismus" (Association for Resistance to Antisemitism)[7] in the summer of 1891. Fried's uncle, Ludwig Ganghofer, is said to have been a member,[8] along with many prominent Viennese, like Eduard Sueß, Wilhelm Exner, Peter Rosegger, and Johann Strauß. Beginning in 1892, the association published a journal, *Das freie Blatt*, which was financed by Baron Friedrich Leitenberger, a textile industrialist. The members offered the defamed Jews free legal assistance, and they publicly opposed the antisemitic slogans. Thus, in response to the call of Prince Liechtenstein, a politician in the Christian Social Party who had exclaimed "Don't buy from Jews," Bertha von Suttner appealed to women: "Don't love antisemites!" Her appeal created a furor.[9] In the final analysis, the association was ineffective. Suttner's engagement resulted in the fusion of the opponents of pacifism and philosemitism, so that now in addition to attacking the "pacifist Bertha" they could also

---

5 Dr. Karl Lueger, "Rede gehalten in Wien am 20.7.1899," quoted in Hamann, *Hitlers Wien*, 418.
6 Hamann, *Hitlers Wien*, 418.
7 In Berlin an association of the same name, "Verein zur Abwehr des Antisemitismus," had been founded in 1890; one can thus see the founding of the association in Vienna as a branch of the Berlin association. But the two associations operated independently. On the German association, see the two-part study by Barbara Suchy, "Der Verein zur Abwehr des Antisemitismus," in *LBI Yearbook* 28 (1983) and 30 (1985). The association was sustained by liberal members of the Reichstag such as Theodor Barth and Georg Gothein, and it remained in existence in Germany until 1933.
8 Cf. Hamann, *Bertha von Suttner*, 203. It is known for certain that Ganghofer was in contact with the Suttners during this period and that his short story "Der Kamerad des Frühlings" was published in the journal *Die Waffen nieder!* See *Die Waffen nieder!* no. 8 (December 1899): 439.
9 "Das freie Blatt," no. 112 (1894): 2f. Hamann, *Bertha von Suttner*, 214.

attack the "Jew Bertha."[10] In 1896, the journal of the association, that is, of the "anti-anti-association," ceased publication, and in 1900 the association was forced to give up its offices.

Under Lueger, antisemitism had become socially acceptable in Vienna. Even the Suttners, who, because of their belief in progress, had been long-time supporters of the assimilation of the Jews, abandoned their hopes for a quick improvement of their circumstances in the Vienna of the late 1890s. When Theodor Herzl founded the Zionist movement with his novel *Der Judenstaat* in 1896 and one year later started the newspaper *Die Welt* to advance his idea, Arthur Gundaccar von Suttner immediately reacted positively. Bertha von Suttner was at first hesitant to support a national movement and wrote to Herzl: "I'm just not sure—assimilation might be better than founding a new state and nation. I wish that all reasonable people could embrace the higher notions of 'European' and of 'humanity' (Kulturmensch), which are only now beginning to take hold and which are concepts that far transcend national, religious and social self-importance and fanaticism."[11] But she too quickly saw that the creation of a safe haven would spare the Jews much misery, so she supported Herzl as best she could. And, indeed, he was always inclined to support the peace movement; in 1899, he sent Bertha von Suttner to the Peace Conference in The Hague to work on behalf of his newspaper, *Die Welt*. In light of the pogroms that were taking place in Russia, Bertha von Suttner requested, to no avail, an audience for him with the Tsar in 1903, one year before Herzl's death.

The pogroms at Kishinew led to another mass exodus across the border and to the worsening of the situation of the Jews in Vienna. With the continuing influx of Jewish refugees from the east, who were very different from the local, assimilated Jews in both appearance and adaptability, the potential for conflict within the Jewish community increased. For the Jewish religious community in Vienna, social interaction with their eastern fellow-believers, who were usually dependent on them for support, proved problematic. On the one hand, one feared the impact of the newcomers whose striking appearance intensified antisemitic propaganda, but on the other hand one could not blame their brothers-in-faith

---

10 Cf. Hamann, *Bertha von Suttner*, 214. The underhanded means that the antisemites employed can be seen in an example that Brigitte Hamann cites. She describes how Schönerer published excerpts from the land register of the Harmannsdorf estate in his journal *Unverfälschte Deutsche Worte* in order to show how indebted the property was, and then hypocritically expressed his regret that the Suttner family had thereby been forced to provide protective services for the Jews.

11 Bertha von Suttner to Theodor Herzl, 1897, reprinted in *Die Welt*, no. 3, 6 (1897), as quoted in Hamann, *Bertha von Suttner*, 219.

for fleeing the horrific pogroms and seeking refuge in the legal protections of the Imperial City, where the police and the state officials were obligated, at least according to the law, to protect them and to treat them equally.

Fried, who returned to Vienna in 1903, was certainly not unaware of these events although he did not have deep roots in the Jewish religious community, but there are no documents suggesting that he concerned himself with the situation of the Jews in any vigorous way. Nevertheless, it does almost seem that the deteriorating situation of the Jews sharpened Fried's consciousness of his Jewish background: perhaps for financial reasons[12] he rejoined the Jewish religious community in 1908, from which he had kept his distance since leaving Berlin.

One indication of his motives may be found in a letter that he wrote to the Stuttgart pastor Otto Umfrid who had suggested that he convert to Christianity to better advance his ideas.[13] After he had pointed out the extent to which his family had accepted Christianity, Fried wrote: "It is not the religious community that binds me to Judaism, for my education taught me very little about the Jewish faith, and my *Weltanschauung* is quite far removed from that of the Jewish faith. What compels me to remain a Jew is the contemporary social circumstances of the Jews. In this time of oppression and persecution, to separate myself from a community to which I am bound by birth and origin, would be, for me, like an act of desertion in wartime. If I were a merchant or a member of some similar profession, that would not be such a weighty decision. But as an intellectual, I believe I have an obligation to stand with an oppressed minority."[14] Even when he married Therese in 1908 he set an example: in contrast to what usually occurs in mixed marriages, Fried did not give up his religious affiliation to marry Therese, a protestant, but rather she did.[15]

For the first few months, Fried found a place in Mödling near Vienna where he and Therese lived. In September 1903 they moved to Müllnergasse 3, and

---

12   When he joined the Viennese Jewish community in 1908, his income was so low that he was permitted to pay only the minimal amount of 20 crowns. Cf. the notices of the Jewish Community to Fried. Nachlass Fried, Box 24, file 350.

13   On May 21, 1909, Umfrid had written: "Might I make a personal suggestion? You should convert to Christianity! Your experiences have surely shown you that Judaism is a hindrance to the promotion of your ideas. From your own standpoint that might seem to be highly unreasonable, but from the point of view of the peace movement it is totally understandable." Nachlass Fried, Box 84.

14   Fried to Umfrid, May 24, 1909. Nachlass Fried, Box 84.

15   Mixed marriages between Christians and Jews were not allowed if one partner did not convert to the other's religion or did not declare himself or herself unaffiliated with any religion. Hamann, *Hitlers Wien*, 471.

one year later they moved again to Währinger Gürtel 118 in Alsergrund, District IX in Vienna, which, like Leopoldstadt, was a part of the city favored by the Jews and, at this time, was especially sought out by Jewish office workers and freelance professionals.[16]

Fried's return home was in no way a happy one. It may be true that Siegfried Frankl emphasized in his recollection of Fried on the tenth anniversary of his death that Fried was very fond of Vienna and that he (Frankl) even believed that Fried dearly loved Vienna,[17] but this view might only be accurate for the period shortly before World War I when Fried had finally established himself in the city. The first years following his return to Vienna are perhaps better described in Fried's own words of 1903: "I would prefer to go back to Berlin, sooner rather than later, but that is, given the animosity of the Holländers, an impossibility. They operate on the principle 'Love me or else I'll knock your block off!' And they've already knocked me around quite a bit."[18] As late as 1905 the address given on the masthead of the *Friedens-Warte* was Berlin-Schöneberg (although no street address was named), and even in 1906 Fried could write "Vienna for the present" as if he were only temporarily visiting Vienna.

Although Fried worked tirelessly, and only rarely gave himself a break, the financial situation of the couple remained rather bleak. When the Holländers released some of his belongings in 1904, including manuscripts, books and family pictures, he wrote to the shipping company responsible for their transportation: "I ask with the utmost urgency that you find the most inexpensive route."[19] And a family argument between his sister Pauline and Fried in 1906 provides evidence of their strained relationship. The virtually destitute Fried had borrowed some furniture from his sister in early 1906, which she then asked him to return in the summer since she was planning to relocate to London. Fried reacted in horror: "Your things are indispensable to me, and I never imagined that you would want them back as long as I still needed them, since you had chosen to lend them to me."[20] Fried consented to buy the pieces of furniture from Pauline, but initially he was not able to, and he wouldn't pay the price that she demanded: "'How very generous of you.' That's how you, by whose side I have stood in difficult times, describe it when I object to your taking away the few objects that make my Spartan rooms a bit more livable, so that I would

---

16 Cf. Rozenblit, *Juden Wiens*, 96.
17 "Vienna, which he loved above all else, where his crib was to be found, and also his grave." Frankl, *Friedens-Fried*, 3.
18 Fried to Otto Antrick, December 17, 1903, International Institute of Social History, Amsterdam.
19 Fried to Starcke & Co, November 11, 1904. Nachlass Fried, Box 31.
20 Fried to Pauline Wyon, July 7, 1906. Nachlass Fried, Box 31.

not have to stack my books on the floor. At least you could ask a price that is in the range of the possible and not one that is four times higher than you might get elsewhere. [...] I have left behind completely furnished apartments worth thousands during my lifetime, but they were not as valuable to me as these four lousy pieces that you are so worried about."[21] Ultimately, Pauline came to an agreement—with Therese, not with her brother. Pauline would give two of the pieces of furniture in question to her—a black bookcase and an American rotating desk—that she could use until May 1907 in exchange for a security deposit of 50 crowns. Fastidiously, Pauline noted that she was forgoing compensation for "damage that might result from the normal use of the objects."[22]

But in spite of his disadvantageous situation, Fried still remained someone with whom his brothers could talk about their difficulties, especially since Pauline did not fare well after the separation from her husband Reginald one year later. That even included Otto, who, after his release from prison, had had little contact with his older brother; he turned to Fried in the summer of 1907 on a visit to Vienna with a desperate request to send some money to his wife, Marie, who was living in London, because she was broke and unable to pay the rent.[23] Since Otto was not able to meet his brother in Vienna because the latter was working as a journalist at the second Peace Conference, he wrote him a nasty telegram. From The Hague, Fried asked Pauline about the actual situation. Her answer was not very encouraging: "It is natural that you would want to know what Otto is doing here – well, he came here with a pretty good idea, one that someone else might follow up on and earn some money – but he is in such a miserable state that he just doesn't have the strength or energy – you can imagine that he is living off of me – to the extent that I can give him something, and yet he grovels from Praterstraße to Döbling by foot just to save a few pennies to get something to eat – [...] send him something – I beg you – so that he won't starve, for I have nothing more to give."[24]

Bad news also came from Berlin where Fried's younger brothers Carl and Leopold had stayed behind in 1903. In the summer of 1904, Carl was taken to the Jewish hospital on Auguststraße. Born with a heart defect, he was never able to establish himself professionally. From Vienna, Fried got in contact with the doctors and learned that Carl was suffering from a weak heart, but that it would surely soon improve.[25] A mistake – Carl's condition never stabilized.

---

21 Fried to Pauline Wyon, October 11, 1906. Nachlass Fried, Box 31.
22 Contract between Therese Frankl and Pauline Wyon on October 14, 1906. Nachlass Fried, Box 31.
23 Otto Fried to Fried, August 24, 1907. Nachlass Fried, Box 31.
24 Pauline Wyon to Fried, undated. Nachlass Fried, Box 31.
25 Hospital of the Jewish community to Fried, June 17, 1904. Nachlass Fried, Box 31.

After his release from the hospital, his mother and sister took him in at Bernburg where he died on September 7, 1904. Leopold, too, had serious health issues. In long letters to his siblings[26] he complained of more and more frequent epileptic fits, which in the end led to his dismissal from his position as a typist and stenographer. Only with difficulty was he able to get back on his feet. His older brother helped where he could, but only rarely did he have the financial means to do so.

Fried found great support and help in Therese whose unlimited devotion to him continued to buoy him up. In spite of all the setbacks and impediments, Therese remained certain that her beloved husband would one day have a great career: "My dear, I am confident in your success, it will certainly come. – I have always had the feeling that you are destined for great things. – It will happen."[27] At the same time, she strove to keep up with him intellectually. Even while she was in Berlin, she began to learn Esperanto; in Vienna she learned French and published short articles in magazines and journals on the theater, fashion, and Viennese cuisine.[28] Fried wrote enthusiastically to Otto Antrick: "I have finally found the woman who suits me in every way and who is a true companion. I have trained her to become a writer. A number of her articles have already been published. With the money she earns, she is able to purchase her own clothes. […] We are living in the holiest harmony, without strife, without conflict, without misunderstandings."[29]

For Fried, his relationship with Therese was the fulfillment of an ideal that he had shared with Bertha von Suttner: the woman's equality and her free, self-assured position next to her husband, and the shared duty to continue their education and to contribute to the ennoblement of humanity. He too strove for a broadly-defined partnership, as described by Bertha von Suttner: "Husband and wife next to each other, well-matched, having equal rights – the woman strengthened, the husband softened, both nobly attuned to an emerging perfected humanity."[30]

Fried was convinced that he had such a relationship with Therese. With complete conviction, he, a married man, characterized his life with a married woman as "a marriage of the purest sanctity."[31] But the Viennese society was

---

26   Cf. Leopold's numerous letters in Nachlass Fried, Box 92.
27   Therese Frankl to Fried, April 9, 1903. Nachlass Fried, Box 92.
28   Evidence of this activity can be found in the Nachlass Fried, Box 25, file 364.
29   Fried to Otto Antrick, December 17, 1903, International Institute of Social History, Amsterdam.
30   *Neue Freie Presse Wien*, August 23, 1909. Bertha von Suttner, open letter to Master Adolph Wilbrandt, in Hamann, *Bertha von Suttner*, 436.
31   Fried to Otto Antrick, December 17, 1903, International Institute of Social History, Amsterdam.

as little convinced of the holiness of this union as was the Berlin society. For example, this was the attitude of Fried's cousin, Tassilo Engel, a Catholic who was ten years younger than Fried; Tassilo was the oldest son of Fried's uncle Moritz Engel and had become the owner and publisher of the *Wiener Salonblatt* upon his father's death in 1897. In February 1906, he wrote to his cousin Alfred: "We can no longer socialize with you directly, on account of your wife, whom you quite reasonably wish to protect from any kind of unpleasant social criticism – she certainly has no need to fear that from me and Katzl, but she likely does from other people with whom we socialize. Therefore no animosity, honesty is always best. See to it that you can somehow tie up your previous bonds, since your wife appears to be a very nice person and deserves to be able to avoid any awkward situation."[32] But that was not as easy as it sounded. Fried's divorce from Martha continued to be delayed since, according to Austrian law, the consent of the wife was required.[33] But Martha refused to give her consent without a sufficient financial agreement.

In February 1907, Fried appealed for assistance to the Imperial Counselor Arnold Goldstein in Berlin and sent him his thoughts on "Experimentalehen" (Experimental Marriages). In the letter he complained about the lawyer for the Holländer family: "He is proceeding against me with a creative cruelty that borders on the perverse."[34] Fried noted that not only did the Holländer family pawn all of his belongings, but they also publicly humiliated him by placing orders of attachment. Fried's lawyer seemed shocked: "I was deeply disturbed to learn from your letter what you have suffered in your second marriage. I am willing to assist you even though I am not quite able to see, according to the statement of facts that has been created, how I can be of help."[35]

Fried then explained to Goldstein that he had agreed with his wife in January 1905 to pay her alimony of 60 marks per month and to cover the costs arising from the divorce, but that he stopped payment toward the end of the year since he had not seen any evidence of his wife's consent to agree to a divorce. He further stated that in the meantime his wife had agreed to the deal but that she now demanded, in addition to the monthly alimony payments of 60 marks, a guarantee from a third party and an automatic increase when Fried's financial situation improved. He wrote that he agreed to the 60 marks but did not want to give a guarantee from a third party nor pay the automatic increase. Goldstein promised to take the case, but then apparently did not receive an

---

32 Tassilo Engel to Fried, December 17, 1906. Nachlass Fried, Box 31.
33 Fried to Otto Antrick, December 17, 1903, International Institute of Social History, Amsterdam.
34 Fried to Dr. Arnold Goldstein, February 21, 1907. Nachlass Fried, Box 60.
35 Dr. A. Goldstein to Fried, February 24, 1907. Nachlass Fried, Box 60.

answer to his letters to Fried, nor did he get a response from his request for his deliberately low fee, which he then cut in half in June. The last warning was dated October 1908. But by this time Fried had already achieved his goal: in May 1907 the district court of Josefstadt declared his marriage to Martha dissolved.[36]

Therese had to wait until July 1908 for the royal court in Pressburg (Bratislava) to rule on her divorce, and she did not receive the documentation until the end of October.[37] The reason for the long delay had nothing to do with Siegfried Frankl, who had already agreed to the divorce in 1903, but with Fried himself. The high cost of divorce in Hungary, for which a Hungarian lawyer was required in addition to the lawyer from Vienna, deterred the impoverished Fried from proceeding too quickly, because he also had his own divorce to pay for. When Siegfried's mother reproached Fried for wanting to delay the divorce, he responded: "You're making a false assumption. The reason we are not expediting the matter is because, at the moment, I don't have the necessary money. The litigation with my wife is taking all of my strength at present. Besides, I don't have any interest in expediting the case now since my own divorce proceeding is more important to me."[38]

But the time between Therese's divorce and her marriage to Fried was much shorter. On December 17, 1908, the forty-four-year-old Alfred Hermann Fried and the thirty-nine-year-old Marie Friederike Therese Frankl, neé Vollandt, were married at the office of the civil registry in Vienna.

2   Fried, von Suttner, and the Austrian Peace Society

When Fried returned to Vienna in 1903, Bertha von Suttner had just recently settled there, reluctantly. Hermannsdorf, the run-down and heavily indebted estate and family castle, had been auctioned off after her husband's death, and Bertha von Suttner had rented a small apartment at Heugasse 20.[39] On the occasion of her sixtieth birthday in June 1903, a large gathering of her friends from around the world raised 20,000 crowns, thereby enabling her to move into an apartment, befitting her social rank, at Zedlitzgasse 7 in the city center; she remained there until her death.[40]

---

36   Cf. Attorney Adolf Altmann to Fried, May 23, 1907. Nachlass Fried, Box 46.
37   Cf. correspondence with the attorney Moritz Leitersdorf in Nachlass Fried, Box 67.
38   Fried to Frau Frankl, October 31, [1904?]. Nachlass Fried, Box 25, file 364.
39   Cf. Hamann, *Berta von Suttner*, 308.
40   Ibid, 320.

Fried lived only two kilometers away on the other side of town. The close proximity and also the fact that Bertha von Suttner had lost her closest confidant in her husband created a tight bond between the two pacifists. Brigitte Hamann's observation about the relationship between Fried and Bertha von Suttner is certainly true: "In her final years Fried was the most important person in Bertha von Suttner's life."[41] In addition to their personal meetings, the two wrote countless letters to each other, and they offer insight into their close collaboration (much to Fried's dismay, Suttner did not have a telephone[42]).

As early as 1903, Suttner began to involve Fried in the activities of the Austrian Peace Society (ÖFG). She organized evening discussion groups, at which they appeared together, and urged him to give his first public lectures.[43] One of the lectures that Fried gave in April 1904 at the Lower Austrian Trade Association on the occasion of the Russo-Japanese War was published by the Austrian Peace Society.[44] According to his own records, Fried had given over 70 lectures by early 1914.[45]

Although he at first remained quite reserved with regard to the Austrian Peace Society, the fact that he had Bertha von Suttner, a leader in the society, as a friend and mentor who could support him, was something that he had lacked in Berlin. Even if he did not himself immediately step into a position of leadership in the Austrian Peace Society (and in October 1906 actually turned down an appointment that had already been announced),[46] Bertha von Suttner saw to it that the Austrian Peace Society supported Fried's projects as well as it could; she also took up many of his ideas in her own work for the society. In addition, she took pains to make Fried, whom she saw as her protégé and potential successor, suitable both for the international stage and for his dealings with the upper circles of society.

---

41 Hamann, *Berta von Suttner*, 328.
42 In Fried's Nachlass there are approximately 5,000 letters from Bertha von Suttner to Fried. Of Fried's letters to Suttner, only about a dozen are extant. They are located today in Bertha von Suttner's Nachlass, Box 19. There are an additional 17 letters by Fried to Suttner, written between 1892 and 1908, in the Bibliothek des Haager Friedenpalastes (Collection de 17 lettres de Alfred H. Fried à Berthe de Suttner - call number Y3462).
43 Cf. *Friedens-Warte* 5, no. 16 (August 31, 1903): 170, and no. 23/24 (December 15, 1903): 191.
44 *Der gegenwärtige Krieg und die Friedensbewegung* (Vienna, 1904).
45 Cf. Fried to Wehberg, February 25, 1914 in Nachlass Wehberg, vol. 59b, BA Koblenz.
46 The protocol of the meeting of the executive board of October 18, 1906, in *Friedens-Warte* 8, no. 11 (November 1906): 219. Notice: "Mr. A. H. Fried and Mr. Johannes C. Barolin were chosen;" the footnote: "Since then Mr. A. H. Fried has explained that he was unable to accept his selection onto the board because of the vast array of pacifist activities that he has undertaken."

Even while he was in Berlin, she had tried, from Vienna, to educate her charge according to her own criteria[47]—but she was not always successful. An aristocrat, she believed that among the skills that an international peace advocate must have was the ability to write and speak multiple languages. So as early as 1900 she advised Fried to learn English, and she critiqued his translations from the French. Given his many activities, Fried found it difficult to meet her expectations, especially since his abbreviated schooling included only a rudimentary knowledge of French. Nevertheless, he made an effort: he took English lessons and in 1902 began to learn Esperanto. He also tried to improve his French, but it would never be good enough for Bertha von Suttner. In 1905, she wrote: "I have to teach you some French. It is part and parcel of the career of a pacifist. I mean correct and elegant French."[48]

It was Fried's translations that were particularly subject to Bertha von Suttner's constant critique, and Fried could only defend himself with meticulous effort. For example, in 1901, he defended himself against her harsh criticism of his translation of the compendious work by Jacques Novicow *La fédération de l'Europe*[49] arguing that he had dictated the text to a stenographer who had had difficulty transcribing her own shorthand: "That's why, and since I am a poor editor in any case, some nonsense, which I did not write, appears in the text."[50] At the same time he highlighted his own financial situation: "In general, you are right that one can notice that I'm under a lot of pressure in my work. Give me a lousy 6,000 marks—a steady stream of income, and I will work like a precise mechanic; I will even read like a conscientious editor. [...] But if you don't give me this annuity, well, then I will continue to work, but it will be like the mason in a sandstone quarry, with the sweat of my brow and imprecisely."[51] In spite of this and probably other attempts by Fried to make clear his situation in Berlin to Bertha von Suttner, it is debatable whether she adequately understood his circumstances. The same can be said for her critique of Fried's flawed manners and his many quarrels.

Although Bertha von Suttner did not stop offering Fried guidance when he came to Vienna (she explained the table manners of finer society to him

---

[47] In this matter and that on the following passages, see Hamann, *Bertha von Suttner*, 324ff.
[48] Suttner to Fried, June 13, 1905, in Hamann, *Bertha von Suttner*, 326. In the same year she expects Fried to learn Italian because, she claims, all three languages are necessary to be a pacifist. Ibid, 326.
[49] Jacques Novicow, *Die Föderation Europas. Autorisierte Übersetzung von Alfred H. Fried* (Berlin/Berne, 1901), 738 pages.
[50] Fried to Suttner, May 22, 1901. Collection de 17 lettres de Alfred H. Fried à Berthe de Suttner. Bibliotheque du Palais de la Paix, Haag (call number Y 3462).
[51] Ibid.

before he traveled to England in 1906), the more personal contact she had with him, the more she grew to appreciate him. In spite of the difference in family background and social standing these two pacifists were indeed similar in their overall viewpoint: both were free thinkers rooted in the tradition of Humanism and the Enlightenment; they both strove toward "noble-mindedness;" neither had children; each declared pacifism to be their spiritual child; and both of them employed their enormous capacity for work and the richness of their ideas to the rearing of their child. Like Fried, Bertha von Suttner would also suffer in her later years from depression and exhaustion after periods of heightened activity, and at these times she would need the encouragement and support of her friend all the more. Fried was also the only one who could remove her fear of "publicly getting old" by urging her to ever greater and more pressing projects that "only she" could complete.[52]

She also acknowledged the impact of his pacifist theory even as it differed from her own to some extent. Having read his *Die Grundlagen des revolutionären Pacifismus* (The Foundation of Revolutionary Pacifism) in 1908, she wrote: "I am pleased that you have been able to remove the emotional appeal in your book"[53] because, she maintained, this gave his book greater impact. She clearly recognized that Fried was able to appeal with his "scientific pacifism" to different groups than she could and that this was good for the movement. Indeed, she was convinced, as she wrote in her diary, that in the final analysis his approach would better advance the peace movement than her own: "Fried will be much more useful than I have been."[54] In 1912, she went so far as to acknowledge: "You are de facto the only one that we have in Central Europe who represents pacifism and can publicly invigorate it."[55]

In the same year Fried wrote a twenty-eight page portrait of his friend for the series "Persönlichkeiten" (Distinguished Individuals):[56] "Aristocracy, as I understand it in this entry, is the self-discipline of the individual in the service of a higher, artistic way of life, which, when it is raised to the level of a categorical imperative, would impart to our collective coexistence a measure of creative harmony. And if we add to this way of living a higher raison d'être, if the individual who is living aristocratically is also moved by an aristocratic spirit, and further if this person is able to own for himself what he has inherited from

---

52 Cf. Hamann, *Bertha von Suttner*, 328f.
53 Suttner to Fried, September 9, 1908. Nachlass Fried, Box 27.
54 Suttner, *Tagebuch*, January 19, 1908. Nachlass Bertha von Suttner, Box 2.
55 Suttner to Fried, September 10, 1908, in Hamann, *Bertha von Suttner*, 485.
56 Alfred H. Fried, *Bertha von Suttner*, Berlin undated [1908?]. The following quotations are taken from this work.

his ancestors through his attained *Weltanschauung*, then a kind of person will develop that we can refer to as a "noble-minded human being," a species that today is largely still being pursued and cultivated, but one that is all too rare today. Bertha von Suttner is such a noble-minded human being."

By virtue of her noble-mindedness, Bertha von Suttner was and remained a model for Fried. But he was also aware that there were advantages associated with her birth that were not available to him: an aristocratic education and the possibility to move in influential circles that were important for the dissemination of one's worldview. In his portrait of her, he suggested that her novel *Die Waffen nieder!* would never have had the broad and lasting effect that it did if it had been written by "Frau Schulze or even by a von der Schulze." "Doors were open to her that are otherwise closed to the average man. [...] She was born to become the representative of an idea at the highest levels of society. In her personal dealings with heads of state, with ministers, and in the halls of diplomacy and higher bureaucracy, she closed the gap and made conservatives receptive to new ideas." Fried's admiration for her was further deepened by the fact that the revered baroness was forever in financial straits and that she had had anything but an easy, carefree life. He saw in her the key to present his pacifist ideas not only to the higher social circles but also to the press. He praised her journalistic work in his portrait, her "particular gift to verbally capture events and characterize them in quick strokes," her rich use of metaphor, and her ability to create incisive neologisms. He called her "a journalist of higher style." Through her unique mixture of talent and social standing, she was able to gain access to skeptical and even adversarial segments of the press.

His deep and lifelong admiration both for the baroness and for her work did not exclude differences of opinion with her on some issues. Ultimately, each of them wanted to spread pacifism to as many groups as possible, and the press would accordingly take on particular significance. In addition to their appeal to those in power, they also repeatedly sought rapprochement with the Social Democrats. Their respective paths to that end differed in part, but basically Bertha von Suttner was not merely an "enthusiast for the good"[57] any more than Fried was merely a sober, scientifically oriented pacifist. Brigitte Hamann's contrastive thesis that Bertha von Suttner believed "more in the significance of personal achievement for pacifism" while Fried, on the other hand, "had counted on a materialistic, inevitable victory of the movement"[58] is not tenable. Fried's assessment of Suttner clearly shows how much he valued her personal efforts and her significance for the movement, and when Bertha

---

57 Cf. Leopold Katscher, *Bertha von Suttner, die "Schwärmerin" für Güte* (Dresden, 1903).
58 Cf. Hamann, *Bertha von Suttner*, 328f.

von Suttner wrote to Fried in 1907 – "Our cause is pursuing its great, certain, and historical course toward its goal"[59] – one can also see her own confident belief in the positive future outcome. In addition, many other attitudes were also in flux. In Vienna, Fried polemicized against the inefficacy of the peace organizations and advised the baroness, after she had returned from America in 1904, to quit the organization she founded because the effect of her personality was being hindered by the small-mindedness of the members of the executive board.[60] When Bertha von Suttner died in 1914, however, Fried took over the leadership and the official presidency of the Austrian Peace Society.

Since both pacifists were often in contact with each another, discussed important events and topics, recommended books to each other, and talked about their thoughts and new ideas together – even if, at least in their writing to each other, they never used the informal form of address ("du") – it might be difficult to determine their respective contributions to each other's works, views, and ideas, but one should not therefore minimize the influence they had on each other.

Bertha von Suttner's influence on Fried's social standing was, nevertheless, quite unmistakable. Not only did she introduce him to important Viennese citizens, like Arthur Schnitzler, Balduin Groller, and Heinrich Lammasch, but she also intervened on his behalf with patrons such as Carnegie and Prince Albert of Monaco, with the result that Fried's financial situation in Vienna stabilized. Moreover, she may have had a hand in his being named the Austrian member of the Council of the International Peace Bureau in Berne in 1907.

As closely as Fried and Suttner worked together in Vienna, and as indisputable as their mutual influence was, they nevertheless differed in one matter, that is, in their opinion of Emperor Wilhelm II. Although from the very beginning the double strategy of the peace movement was to convince not only the common people but also the rulers of the value of its ideas, Bertha von Suttner placed little hope in the German emperor.[61] In 1890, she protested strongly against the suggestion of a friend that she send the emperor a copy of her book *Die Waffen nieder!*, exclaiming "my words are not able to banish the mystical-megalomania and the militaristic-adventurousness that animates this restless Hohenzollern."[62]

Ten years later Fried and Suttner actually had a significant argument about the format of her "review of the times" in the *Friedens-Warte*. The flagrant

---

59   Suttner to Fried, August 29, 1907, in Hamann, *Bertha von Suttner*, 328f.
60   Notes by Fried on his conversations with Suttner, December 11, 1904, Nachlass Fried, Box 20, file 342.
61   Cf. Hamann, *Bertha von Suttner*, 369ff on this and on the following topics.
62   Suttner to Bartolomäus Carneri, September 25, 1890, in Hamann, *Bertha von Suttner*, 396.

criticism of the German emperor that she repeatedly expressed there made Fried feel rather uncomfortable since he was in the process of applying for citizenship. While it was true that the law of 1874 meant that the German press was no longer under direct censorship, there were numerous instances of *lèse-majesté* at the time: "Even at the end of the century it was almost considered a badge of honor for journalists to have spent a few weeks in jail."[63] So in August, Fried asked Bertha von Suttner to refrain from criticizing Wilhelm II. She reacted with indignation: "It is totally impossible to chronicle peace and war without mentioning the person, indeed without criticizing the person who directs the war puppets. Under such circumstances, I can no longer write the column "Zeitschau," and you yourself should give up the *Friedens-Warte*. For to be thrown out 'in so unwelcome a manner' is truly no pleasant sword of Damocles."[64]

Indeed Bertha von Suttner stopped writing the "Zeitschau" that very month. More than four years would pass before she would again contribute her *Randglossen zur Zeitgeschichte* (Commentaries on Contemporary History) in January 1905. The timing of the new beginning is telling: It was only when Fried no longer saw a chance to return to Berlin and got used to the idea of spending substantial time in Vienna that he dared to publish the critical political commentary of his friend. But Bertha von Suttner had also changed her view to the extent that she now saw it as worthwhile, in light of the emperor's substantial powers, to try to exert some pacifist influence on him. Her path went through the Prince of Monaco, Albert I, a friend of hers, who often met with the emperor and whom she encouraged to inform Wilhelm II about pacifist activities and even to get him to meet with some pacifists.[65] Fried, on the other hand, did not have such paths open to him; he tried to reach the emperor through his writings. He started in 1905 with "Kaiser, werde modern!" (Emperor, become modern!), in which he asked Wilhelm II, as "the most popular personality on the planet,"[66] to spearhead the pacifist movement. Fried had convinced himself that the will of the emperor for peace in Europe "was beyond any doubt," as evidenced by the fact that he sought a rapprochement with France at every opportunity. The German army, which the emperor had declared to be the single most important institution of the German empire, was for Fried, therefore, quite clearly only a means to the maintenance of a European peace. This peace, however, could not be guaranteed through national armies but rather

---

63 Andreas Gestrich, "Die Haager Friedenskonferenzen und die deutsche Presse," in Christof Dipper, Andreas Gestrich, Lutz Raphael (eds.), *Krieg, Frieden und Demokratie*.
64 Suttner to Fried, August 21, 1900, in Hamann, *Bertha von Suttner*, 275.
65 Cf. Hamann, *Bertha von Suttner*, 378f.
66 Fried, *Kaiser werde modern!*, 5 and for subsequent references, 9.

only through international agreements, whose realization required a strong leader. Cleverly, Fried thereby used the apparent claim to leadership that Wilhelm II made in Europe in 1905 to suggest to him a totally different and new perspective.

Five years later Fried would once again take up the theme of the special mission of the emperor in his more comprehensive and detailed book *Der Kaiser und der Weltfrieden* (The Emperor and World Peace). This time, however, he sought not only to illustrate the evolution of Wilhelm II toward greater prudence and peacefulness, from "War Lord to Peacemaker,"[67] by citing dozens of quotations from speeches and published conversations of the emperor, but also by noting the significance that other countries ascribed to him in this regard. As the principal witness he quoted from Andrew Carnegie's speech to the New York Peace Conference of 1907 in which he claimed that the emperor was the only person on earth who had the power to abolish war.

In these years, Fried undoubtedly placed great hope in Wilhelm II. Misplaced, as we know today. However, we must consider that Fried did not personally know the emperor or his inner circle; he drew his conclusions solely from the published speeches and the reports of conversations, which could not easily communicate the highly volatile statements of the emperor that circulated in the newspapers at the time. The very fact that during his regency peace still reigned in Europe in 1910 – despite all the fears and warnings – formed the most important argument for Fried's hopes for a peace-loving Wilhelm II. And Fried was not alone in this regard; even the highly critical English writer (and future Nobel Peace Prize recipient) Norman Angell[68] could write in the foreword to the English translation of Fried's book on the emperor in 1912: "Is it not time, therefore, that the English-speaking world tried to judge this ruler in light of facts instead of prejudice and prepossession?"[69]

One should also not overlook yet another, more fundamental reason for the targeted optimism of the pacifists, namely, that the movement "from below," that is, the participation of the masses, was hardly to be counted on in the near future.[70] Even if there had been sufficient financial resources to conduct a massive campaign, it nevertheless seems doubtful that the overall orientation

---

67 Fried, *Der Kaiser und der Weltfrieden* (Berlin, 1910), v.
68 On Norman Angell, that is, Ralph Norman Land (1872–1967), see the short biography by Louis Bisceglia in Josephson, *Biographical Dictionary*, 27ff.
69 Fried, *The German Emperor and the Peace of the World. With a Preface by Norman Angell* (London, New York, Toronto, 1912).
70 In 1896, Suttner wrote to Henry Dunant: "You too have had success with your work because you have appealed to those who are deemed great. That is of course quite natural: the great ones are the powerful ones. In order to have success when starting from

of the pacifists, which was directed mainly toward foreign affairs and ignored burning social issues, would have been able to move the people as a whole to work with them. Since the behavior of the majority of the Social Democrats suggested an aversion to the aims of the pacifists, the matter seemed doubly pointless. The hope for a change in international politics was thus necessarily directed toward those in power: first toward the Russian Tsar Nicholas II, then toward Emperor Wilhelm II, and later toward President Wilson.[71]

3 Work as a Journalist to 1907

Besides his books about the emperor, which were written during the first years of his stay in Vienna and published with the support of Bertha von Suttner and the Austrian Peace Society, there also appeared a number of books and brochures solidifying Fried's significance in the German-speaking peace movement. Offering a clear position, he commented on the themes central to the peace movement, e.g., "Deutschland und Frankreich. Ein Wort über die Notwendigkeit und Möglichkeit einer Deutsch-Französischen Verständigung" (Germany and France. A Brief Comment on the Necessity and Possibility of a Franco-Germanic Rapprochement), "Die moderne Schiedsgerichtsbewegung"[72] (The Modern Arbitration Movement), "Das Abrüstungs-Problem"[73] (The Disarmament Problem), and "Die Nobelstiftung. Ihre Einrichtungen und ihre Bestimmungen"[74] (The Nobel Foundation. Its Institutions and Purpose). However, none of these publications exceeded 2,000 copies since they only reached the small circle of those who were already interested in peace.

But three other works did find greater resonance during this time: *Weder Sedan noch Jena*[75] (Neither Sedan nor Jena) sold 10,000 copies; *Die Friedensbewegung, was sie will und was sie erreicht hat*[76] (The Peace Movement: What it wants and what it has achieved) sold 8,000 copies by 1907 (and even had a second edition); and his most well-known work today, *Handbuch der*

---

below, one has to involve the masses, which can be rather difficult." Hamann, *Bertha von Suttner*, 399.

71 Emperor Franz Josef played no role in this matter since it was believed that he had neither the will nor the international influence to act in the interest of pacifism.
72 Fried, *Die moderne Schiedsgerichtsbewegung*, Berlin undated [1904].
73 Fried, *Das Abrüstungs-Problem*, Berlin undated [1905].
74 Fried, *Die Nobelstiftung. Ihre Einrichtungen und ihre Bestimmungen* (Leipzig 1906).
75 Fried, *Weder Sedan noch Jena*, Berlin undated [1904], 2nd edition, 1905.
76 Fried, *Die Friedensbewegung, was sie will und was sie erreicht hat*, Leipzig 1905, 2nd edition, 1907.

Friedensbewegung (Handbook of the Peace Movement), was published in 1905. In *Weder Sedan noch Jena*, Fried drew on one of the most intensely discussed novels of the day, Franz Adam Beyerlein's[77] *Jena oder Sedan? (Sedan nor Jena?)*, which stirred up a great deal of excitement in Berlin in the spring of 1903 and became a bestseller that year in Germany, with 280,000 copies having been published.

The novel, dedicated to "the German army," offered a thoroughly critical portrayal of the terrible condition of the Prussian-German military; it centered on the son of a peasant, Vogt, who was serving his two-year military service obligation. The portrayal was considered by many contemporaries to be thoroughly realistic, and consequently elicited opposing perspectives by those in military circles as well as others. Beyerlein's criticism of the soulless drilling of the soldiers and of the arrogance of the officer corps was met with full agreement by the pacifists. Even if Beyerlein intended to point out the danger of a future defeat of the German army (as earlier at Jena) and even if his criticism aimed to make the German army more able to defend the homeland, the pacifists were nevertheless able to use the novel for their own propagandistic purposes.

But, to Fried, the formulation of the question itself was wrong. The answer must be: neither Sedan nor Jena. For him, the disintegration of the army, which Beyerlein had rightfully recognized, was actually a symptom of a great change that had taken place in the relationship among the states, which subsequently had an impact on the army. Through the creation of national states of equal strength, which were constantly caught up in an arms race, war in Europe had become an incalculable risk and therefore not feasible. The recognition of the changing international situation, which was already taking place, had to lead, according to Fried, to obvious changes: first the army had to be reorganized along the lines of the Swiss army, that is, it needed to become a militia that all citizens participate in for defensive purposes only. Professional soldiery had to be abolished, and officers were to be selected according to intelligence and their capabilities, not according to social standing. Anticipating the objection that such an army was not appropriate for a major power, Fried pointed explicitly to a work by the French artillery captain, Gaston Moch,[78] which he had translated four years earlier. Moch had published a concrete proposal for

---

[77] Franz Adam Beyerlein (1871–1949) founded the *Literarische Gesellschaft* in Leipzig and made a name for himself as an author of realistic novels with an anti-militaristic tendency.

[78] Only three years earlier Fried had translated *Die Armee der Demokratie* by the French pacifist Gaston Moch (Stuttgart, 1900), which had unleashed a discussion of the role of the military within the peace movement.

just such a reorganization in France. This restructuring of the armies would expedite the transformation of the developing international reorganization of states into an internationally recognized legal framework. The states would work increasingly closer together, and the existing differences, which at the time could only be detected below the surface, would be settled peacefully by means of a court of arbitration. In the long run, this would produce a change in the function of the armies: "The defensively-oriented armies of the individual states would become the defensively-oriented armies of the common international order and by virtue of their superb organization would be the force responsible for protecting international order. They would become armies that no longer fought against each other but alongside each other with a common task and a common purpose."[79]

Fried's proposal must have sounded bold to his contemporaries in 1904, but it sounds quite familiar nowadays. It shows that belief in progress, which had always been directed toward some unspecified long-term goal and which Fried believed was easily adaptable to different conditions, can still be of interest today – especially today – in some areas.

During his first two years in Vienna, Fried directed his energies toward writing his *Handbuch der Friedensbewegung* (Handbook of the Peace Movement), in which he summarized all of his beliefs and findings. The idea arose from a six-part lecture cycle that he held in early 1904 in the Wiener Akademischen Friedensverein (Vienna Academic Peace Union) and whose publication Bertha von Suttner had encouraged.[80] The significance of the handbook for Fried can be seen in the fact that he dated the foreword November 11, 1904, his 40th birthday.

Like his "Friedens-Katechismus" (Peace Catechism) ten years earlier, this more comprehensive book was directed toward those "who are working for the advancement of peace." It was supposed to serve as a useful reference book in their recruitment efforts and in their discussions. In the first chapter Fried explained the differences between a pacifist notion of peace and a military notion of peace, between conflict and war, and between cosmopolitanism and internationalism. He further explained the fundamental importance of an international system of law, which made use of force not "instead of" but "in the service of" the law, and he differentiated the ideas of the peace movement from such concepts as "eternal peace" and other conventional notions of peace. It was important to him to emphasize that the internationalism of the peace

---

79 Fried, *Weder Sedan noch Jena*, 47f. In the original, this was printed, in part, as extended text.
80 Fried, *Handbuch* (1905), v. The following quotations are also taken from this book.

movement signified "a patriotism of the highest order" and that the peace movement was therefore "the most patriotic movement of the present age."

In the second chapter, which bears the title "Die realen Grundlagen der Friedensbewegung" (The real foundations of the peace movement), Fried briefly examined the situation and trends of the time, the international linkage between economics and technology, the developments in arms technology, and the relations of states to each another. In the end he concluded: "The armed peace, which we have borne for three decades, is a hindrance to cultural development and thwarts the natural tendency toward a higher organization of humanity. The costs of a future war demonstrate convincingly that such a war would bring about the total collapse of the European economy and of European cultural life. The threat that emerges from the excessive build-up of armaments is death and destruction. Armaments intended to prevent war are unproductive and hinder real progress." As the only way out of this dilemma, Fried proposed an international organization of states and an international system of law, whereby the peace movement, as the most consistent representative of these ideas, could become the "savior of Europe." At the same time, he also showed that "this movement is not built on some speculative idea but is itself a necessity, born of objective reality, 'a release valve' that will preserve Europe from its annihilation." Or more accurately, we would say today that it could have preserved Europe. But Fried saw the movement as having already progressed quite far, and so his third chapter focused on the gradual emergence of the "organization of world peace" as a contrast to the current dominant model of international anarchy.

Fried next considered the history of the peace movement, proceeding from the ancients to the period just after the Congress of Vienna, to the founding of the first peace societies and world peace congresses, and finally to the conference in The Hague and the present situation: "This review is necessary in order to show that the peace movement is not, as its detractors have incorrectly assumed, a purely fashionable whim that will disappear just as quickly as it is said to have arrived; the movement has rather been in existence for a long time and it is still developing, albeit gradually, on a clearly recognizable, ascendant path in conjunction with the general development of the human race and the expansion of civilized behavior. The logical conclusion of the continual, unstoppable development and the ultimate victory of the movement will become obvious." Ultimately, it is a matter of noting Fried's belief in progressive evolution, which he shared with most of his contemporaries, and of seeing it as a source of motivation and strength for him to carry on despite all the hostility and negative tendencies of the present.

The final section was concerned with basic information about the institutes, the groups, the political entities, and the leading personalities of the international peace movement: here Fried noted 1) the descriptions, addresses, and the lists of members of the Inter-Parliamentary Council of the IPU, of the International Peace Bureau, of the *Institut du droit international*, of the International Peace Institute in Monaco, of the Nobel Foundation, among others; and 2) the addresses, boards of directors, the local chapters of the peace societies, and a biographical section that introduced some 85 leading pacifists of various nations. Fried emphasized that in spite of all his efforts this list should not "be seen in any way as complete." Although Fried expressly referenced people of all nations in the introduction to this chapter, he recorded only Europeans and individuals in North America, as indicated by his own statistics. Accordingly, the French have nineteen representatives, followed by the English with 15, the Germans have nine, and the U.S. Americans have eight. With Novicow as its only representative, Russia is last. It is also striking that Fried recorded a lot fewer women than men (13 to 72) although women made up a significant percentage of the members of the societies. This was probably not the result of an arbitrary decision but rather may be attributable to the fact that women constituted only a small portion of the members of the boards and governing bodies.

The extent to which Fried tried to remain objective in his selection can be seen in the fact that besides Otto Umfrid, M. L. Selenka, Eugen Schlief, Adolf Richter, Richard Reuter, Ludwig Quidde, and Richard Feldhaus, he also included Max Hirsch whom he disliked. However, he emphasized the latter's role as parliamentarian and founder of the German Group of the Inter-Parliamentary Union, and he established Hirsch's connection to the German Peace Society only in the final sentence, where he noted that Hirsch was its president from 1897 to 1900. The final section of the chapter provides a survey of the existing literature on pacifism in which Fried recorded the current pacifist newspapers with their addresses, the frequency with which they were published, and their subscription rates.

The exceptional significance of the *Handbook* lies in its uniqueness; there was no other book of its kind in German, and so Fried essentially was the "first peace researcher in the German-speaking countries."[81] Usually, the leading pacifists only expressed their views in articles and brochures on specific issues, or they wrote replies to the defamatory brochures of the nationalists and militarists. But the *Handbook* was too voluminous and expensive to be used in

---

81 Scheer, *Deutsche Friedensgesellschaft*, 133.

large numbers as a means of publicity for peace. Flyers and brochures were used for that, e.g., "Die Friedensbewegung, was sie will und was sie erreicht hat" (The Peace Movement, its Goals and Accomplishments), which was published shortly after the *Handbuch*. What is especially striking in this publication is the absoluteness of Fried's claim to speak for "the peace movement," which he does not limit to particular nations of different groups or organizations. Presumably, he felt justified in this approach by virtue of his position as an outsider in both the German and Austrian peace movement. As an attempt to legitimize his work, the title page notes "Alfred H. Fried, Member of the International Peace Institute."

The *Institut international de la Paix*, which was founded in February 1903 at the recommendation of Gaston Moch under the patronage of Prince Albert I of Monaco and which was housed in a small former chapel, took as its task the collection and documentation of scholarly research on the various branches of pacifist activity and the expansion of internationalism.[82] The number of members had been limited from the very beginning to 60, of which at least ten had to reside in Monaco.

When the names of those selected were announced in March 1903, Fried along with Carl Ludwig von Bar, a professor in Göttingen and member of the court of arbitration in The Hague, were the only Germans chosen (Fried was still considered a resident of Berlin until 1905).[83] His presence in this notable group, which included members of the court of arbitration in The Hague, members of the Inter-Parliamentary Union, professors of international law, and long-time pacifists, was his first sign of success. He wrote to Therese with pride: "This appointment as a member of the academy [...] is a big deal for me. Very important men have been selected, and it is a title that one can make use of: 'Member of the International Peace Institute.' I will include this in my books and other publications."[84]

Even during the celebration of the founding of the institute in Monaco on February 25, 1903, which Fried could not attend, the designated president, Gaston Moch, encouraged the publication of a *Jahrbuch des internationalen Lebens* (Yearbook of International Life), which Fried had originally proposed. It was to list all the international conferences and associations in the fields of science, art, commerce, and transportation.[85] In March, at the time of his nomination,

---

82 Cf. on this topic *Friedens-Warte* 5: 23, 32, 34, and 60.
83 The list of members can be found in *Friedens-Warte* 5, no. 5 (March 15, 1903): 37. Bertha von Suttner represented Austria there.
84 Fried to Therese Frankl, fragment of a letter [March 1903]. Nachlass Fried, Box 92.
85 Cf., *Friedens-Warte* 5, no. 5 (March 15, 1903): 34.

Fried was officially named the general editor of the journal. However, he was at first unable to convert his idea into reality. "The cost for the yearbook is calculated to be about 52,000 francs. But this amount exceeds the funds of the institute, and we have to find a publisher who would be willing to accept such a risk in the hope he would secure a future return."[86] But since no such publisher could be found in 1904, the first volume, as a product of the institute itself, did not appear until early 1905.[87] The small volume, which Fried presumably put together himself, was, in spite of its slight size, a diligently researched but nondescript piece of work, for "the editor was only able to gather his information through the newspapers and through the willingness of a few individuals who were kind enough to answer his questions."[88] In the forward to the 1905 volume, Fried defined the goal he set (but had not yet attained in this year): "To illustrate the totality of contemporary international life, to identify the essence of the current state of internationalization, and to show that the internationalization of civilization is already further advanced than one generally thinks."[89]

The next two issues, for which Fried had sole editorial responsibility, were noticeably longer; they also strengthened his belief in the steady and organic growth of the integration of individual nations. The compensation for his labors, however, did not increase, for it soon became clear that Albert I devoted much less time to the Peace Institute than to the two other institutes that he had founded, i.e., the Institute for Oceanography and the Institute for Paleontology.[90] In fact, so little funding was available that the project was moved to Brussels in 1908, to the International Institute for Bibliography, which was founded by Henri La Fontaine, the president of the International Peace Bureau. Fried remained a part of the editorial board along with Henri La Fontaine and Paul Otlet, but the real work was now done in Belgium.

An important reason for the move had to do with the fact that the institute in Brussels provided greater access to data; this can be seen in the edition of 1908–1909 and particularly in the edition of 1910–1911, both of which contained a massive amount of data. Fried seemed to be less involved in the publications produced in Brussels, for at this time he was already working on a more modest chronicle and, since 1909, had been publishing an annual report on

---

86 *Friedens-Warte* 5, no. 7/8 (April 30, 1903): 60.
87 Alfred H. Fried, ed., *Annuaire de la vie internationale* (Monaco: Institut internationale de la paix, 1905).
88 Cf. the manuscript containing the preface to the first volume of 1905. Nachlass Fried, Box 7, file 35.
89 Ibid.
90 In 1906, due to a financial shortfall, the institute reduced Fried's honorarium for the translation by half. Cf. Hamann, *Bertha von Suttner*, 384.

the development of pacifism, which he called "Der Weg zum Weltfrieden"[91] (The Path to World Peace). The little brochure, which Fried and other pacifists had continued to send out as a New Year's greeting until 1914, was much more suitable for promotional purposes than the compendious *Annuaire de la Vie Internationale*, because it was concise, handy, and inexpensive, but hardly less effective since it could be produced and distributed in greater quantity.[92]

4 Impulses from The Hague

From the end of the first conference in The Hague the pacifists had constantly urged the continuation of the work that had begun there. But the unfavorable international climate caused a new meeting to be delayed. An initiative by President Roosevelt in 1904 failed because of the smoldering Russo-Japanese War. In 1905, the Russian government continued the initiative but was impeded by the domestic unrest that had broken out. The result was that a date for the conference could not be determined until March 1906. But the proposed date for the summer of 1906 had to be postponed once again since it conflicted with the date of the third, planned pan-American conference in August 1906 in Rio. Finally, the date was set for July 1907.

Fried had carefully followed and commented on the developments in the *Friedens-Warte*. When the plans were finalized, the conference became the main theme of the *Friedens-Warte* from January 1907 on. In April, Fried held a lecture cycle of three talks on the themes of the conference at the Viennese Technical College, which, as he proudly noted, "was attended by a thoroughly distinguished audience."[93] It was, as he wrote, also thoroughly covered by the Viennese press. In addition, with an eye toward the upcoming conference, Bertha von Suttner and Fried founded PoPaKo, the "Politisch-Pazifistische Korrespondenz" (Political-pacifist Correspondence) in the spring of 1907. This one-page information sheet was sent to some 300 newspapers in the German-speaking countries with an offer to reprint the articles at no cost; it was an offer that did not find great resonance.

Fried, Bertha von Suttner, and many other pacifists were present at the second conference in The Hague, which began on June 15, 1907 and which attracted participants from 44 nations. But Fried did not live with the baroness, who as president of the Austrian Peace Society had appropriate living quarters

---

91 Cf. Fried, ed., *Der Weg zum Weltfrieden im Jahr...* (Berlin, 1909–1913).
92 Cf. Nachlass Fried, Box 4, file 17.
93 *Friedens-Warte* 5, no. 5 (May 1907): 98.

with Eduard de Neufville, the official representative of the German Peace Society. Fried lived with Leopold Katscher and Fritz Decker, two committed pacifist writers, who contributed to Stead's *Courrier de la Conférence*.

As at the first conference, many pacifists attempted to influence the delegates and the course of the negotiations through their conversations, presentations, and media work: "sometimes it appeared as if a small conference of pacifists were taking place."[94] Fried himself represented twelve German and two Austro-Hungarian newspapers in The Hague.[95] Presumably this number grew in the course of the conference because the unexpected length and the meager results led many pacifists and journalists to leave The Hague early. At the end of August, Fried reported that beside himself only Stead, Barclay, Davis, and de Neufville were still present.[96] Bertha von Suttner herself had already left on August 25. Fried stayed until the beginning of the World Peace Conference, which took place in Munich from September 9–14, that is, he was away for thirteen weeks as he meticulously noted in his account book.[97] During this time he also participated with his wife Therese in the 8th Zionist conference, which was likewise taking place in The Hague.[98]

Fried was not present for the last five weeks of negotiations, that is, until October 18. After the conference, he tried to develop a pacifist assessment of the results.[99] Among the most notable outcomes for him was the creation of the International Prize Court: "this prize court [is] the first transnational court whose judges will rule in the name of the international community and whose rulings will override national law. The Prize Court is the first true court of law of the international community."[100] For Fried, it represented the beginning of the reversal of the judiciary system. According to Fried, whereas up until then national law had always superseded international law, there was now hope that one day international law would become the basic law and thus outweigh national law.

But juxtaposed with this positive evaluation is his harsh criticism of the actions taken by Germany. For Fried, Germany alone bore responsibility for the failure of the negotiations since it had influenced its allies and many smaller states in a negative way. In so doing, it harmed its political position

---

94   *Friedens-Warte* 9, no. 7 (July 1907): 133.
95   Ibid, 134.
96   *Friedens-Warte* 9, no. 9 (September 1907): 171.
97   Cf. Nachlass Fried, Box 20.
98   Cf. Printed invitation, Nachlass Fried, Box 74.
99   Cf. *Friedens-Warte*, 9, no. 10 (October 1907): 181ff. No. 11 (November 1907): 204ff; No. 12 (December 1907): 226ff.
100 Fried, *Zweite Haager Konferenz*, 185; the following quotation, 195.

and "isolated itself from other countries before the whole world." Compared with his comments after the first conference in The Hague, Fried's tone was clearly sharper after the second conference, and he was not willing to excuse Germany's behavior because of any particular considerations or other circumstances.

Although Fried had spoken out against increasing the number of participating states before the conference, these additions did indeed prove productive in retrospect. He now believed Europe might actually be able to organize itself along the lines of the American continent; he subsequently saw it as his task to make the pan-American movement better known. Immediately following the conference he began preliminary work for a comprehensive study of the pan-American movement; it would be completed in March 1910. The difficulties that he had to overcome were enormous: "I have had to draw my material from the most diverse sources, and I must note that there is only one review article on the topic in German at this time, and it comes from an American."[101]

Nevertheless, he succeeded in putting together an impressive volume. The three-hundred-page book covers the history of the pan-American movement from its inception in 1810, to the three pan-American conferences, and finally to the participation of the Latin American countries in the second conference at The Hague and in the formation of the States of Central America. Fried devoted the final chapter to the significance of the pan-American movement for Europe. He observed that while America was growing ever more integrated, Europe was splitting further apart and was thereby causing a divide between itself and America, one that threatened to grow even larger: "I don't think that I am exaggerating when I claim that Europe will no longer be more important than an organized America, much like the Balkan countries are with respect to the British empire." Europe, he claimed, must finally become Europe, not in the way that the cosmopolitans of the nineteenth century dreamed, that is, as a "United States of Europe," but through a modernized organization: "Instead of wasting the vitality of their people on armaments, without ever achieving the desired security, something which also cripples the possibilities for development, the states of Europe must get to work bringing their institutions into harmony with one another, facilitating transportation, internationalizing their administrations, and creating security through mutually beneficial treaties of protection." That is the only way that a modern Europe can arise, not against America, but by its side. As a first step Fried proposed the creation of a pan-European bureau. When his book appeared in 1910, he had already taken the first steps toward initiating such a bureau. In October 1909 Fried suggested to

---

101   Fried, *Pan-Amerika* (Berlin, 1910), iv.

the International Peace Bureau that it champion the creation of a Pan-European Bureau.[102]

Fried saw areas of common interest in commerce, transportation, agriculture, social policy, hygiene, law, and international politics. If a consolidation of the already existing international consortia in these fields could be organized in one place, the other areas could also be drawn into a similar collaboration.

Fried's proposal was received with great applause at the General Assembly,[103] but there were objections from his own ranks, which contended that a European Bureau might possibly lead to serious economic tension with America, and that would mean a step backward rather than a step forward with respect to a world organization. But Fried's aim was to pursue this policy in small steps: "In my view, first the will to organize must be awakened in those governments in Europe that are involved in the most intense conflicts. This desire is currently lacking in Europe. The first order of business is to overcome this psychological barrier. This can best happen if we start with what has already been achieved and shown to be advantageous to Europe."[104] This would not impact the ultimate goal of a world organization, Fried argued, just as the already existing institutions would remain untouched. In addition, he pointed out that there were certainly some matters that were exclusively European, and that the example of a pan-American organization showed the extent to which even a very limited union could become an ever more powerful promoter of the world organization.

The disunity in the movement, however, finally caused the project to fizzle out. The expanded General Assembly of the Berne Bureau toward the end of September 1911, which replaced the World Peace Conference in Rome (which was itself canceled because of the outbreak of a cholera epidemic), had to address other, more acute worries. The eleven resolutions passed by the General Assembly were concerned with the conflict in Morocco and the question of Tripoli,[105] i.e., contemporary political events that caused the prospect of a pan-European Bureau to be put on the back burner. It was only after the First World War, in 1923, that the idea for a pan-European Bureau was taken up by Count Coudenhove-Kalergi in Vienna. The first account of his ideas can be found in the *Friedens-Warte*.[106]

---

102 Cf. *Friedens-Warte* 11, no. 11 (November 1909): 203ff.
103 Cf. Report "Die Brüsseler Generalversammlung," in *Friedens-Warte*, 11, no. 10 (October 1909): 186.
104 *Friedens-Warte* 11, no. 11 (November 1909): 203ff.
105 Cf. *Friedens-Warte* 13, no. 9 (October 1911): 292f.
106 Cf. Dr. Richard Nikolaus Coudenhove-Kaergi, "Die Europäische Frage," in *Friedens-Warte*, 23, no. ½: 9ff.

In 1909, Fried attempted another project that grew out of his experiences at the Second Hague Conference: the creation of an international association of publishers dedicated to peace. Even while he was in Berlin, Fried had sought, albeit in vain, to link together all the presses in the German-speaking countries that were friendly to the peace movement. In May 1904, while he was living in Vienna, he made a similar appeal through a circular, "An die Führer der deutschen Presse der Linken" (To the Leaders of the German Presses on the Left).[107] Writing to 150 German newspapers, he called upon them to collaborate in founding a "union of publishers sympathetic to the idea of a court of arbitration ... in order to prove to the people of Europe and America that the people of Germany intend to fulfill the obligations of a modern civilized society."[108] But this excessively long, awkward, and in part clumsily worded appeal found little resonance and did not lead to any further action.

Nevertheless, in April 1909, Fried again tried to establish such an association under the name "International Association of Peace Presses" (I.U.F.P). From Vienna he sent out a circular written in German and French to "several hundred potentially interested people in Europe and America." In particular, it was sent to writers and journalists affiliated with pacifism but also to other significant pacifists or "extraordinary members," i.e., sponsors of the association, whom he wanted to invite. In his appeal[109] he explained that the peace movement should no longer attempt to recruit journalists for whom the idea of pacifism was a foreign concept; rather it should seek to enlist those many, yet diffused journalists who were already working for pacifism and to bring them under one roof. Through its very existence, he claimed, such an international organization would carry more weight than a single journalist, and it could also become "a crystallization point to which the other, better elements of the publishing world would gradually want to connect."

The appeal ended with an urgent invitation to all like-minded colleagues to offer vigorous support for the founding of the International Association of Peace Presses and to suggest the names of anyone else who might be interested. At the same time, he called upon all those whom he was addressing to immediately join the association: "I therefore expect that all the recipients of this circular* [*including the readers of *Die Friedens-Warte*] will register to

---

107 Several copies of the appeal can be found in Nachlass Fried, Box 3. The text is in *Friedens-Warte*, 6, no. 5 (mid-May 1904): 90ff.
108 Ibid. In the original it is printed in bold in extended spacing.
109 *Friedens-Warte* 11, no. 5 (May 1909): 88f. All the quotations of this section are taken from this source unless otherwise indicated.

become ordinary or extraordinary members of the core group, and I ask that they do so as soon as possible."[110]

The assertive tone apparently was successful: "The International Association of Peace Presses is taking shape. We have received over two hundred requests for membership, from all over Europe. And colleagues in South America and the United States have also taken steps to recruit members in their respective countries.[111] The association was, in fact, founded in the same year, albeit not in Stockholm, since the planned world peace conference had to be cancelled due to a general strike in Sweden, but rather in Brussels at the expanded general assembly of the International Peace Bureau at the beginning of October, at which the Pan-European Project was also considered.[112]

On October 9, Fried presented the plan for the foundation of the press association along with his report on the creation of a pan-European bureau. On October 11, the constitutive meeting of the "Union internationale de la Presse pour la Paix" was held. Agreement was reached to set up the office of the association in Vienna and to appoint Fried as its director. He was to work up a proposal for the statutes in such a way that "it meets the requirements of Austrian law with respect to the rights granted to the union as a legal entity."

After the assembly had elected an eight-member working committee (which included Fried, La Fontaine, G. H. Perris, Prudhommeaux, and others) and an international committee, composed of the working committee and six other people, it was then "decided in principle, that in May of the following year a first assembly or a conference of the Peace Press would be called in Brussels." By then, the bureau was to have created a network of representatives "in all major locations"[113] and to have worked on a catalogue that would record the political leanings, the significance, and the circulation of all the known newspapers.

There was no required membership fee for active members, and for sponsors the minimal dues were 5 francs per year—a ridiculously small sum, especially at the beginning of a campaign, since no large sponsor was even in sight. No wonder that the grand plan quickly ran into trouble. At the next meeting in Berne toward the end of April 1910, Fried had to tell the members "that due

---

110   Emphasis in the original.
111   *Friedens-Warte* 11, no. 7 (July 1909): 137.
112   *Friedens-Warte* 11, no. 10 (October 1909): 187. The following quote is also taken from here.
113   The organizational structure is very similar to the one that Fried suggested for the restructuring of the German Peace Society in 1902.

to funding issues he has not yet been able to set up the bureau that was voted on in Brussels."[114] The planned conference was then put on hold indefinitely.

In the end, the international association of peace presses remained merely a statement of intent despite the fact that Fried was repeatedly concerned with the importance of the press and with the possibilities of influencing it in the next few years and despite the fact that he still referred to himself as the general secretary of the association[115] in the second edition (1913) of his *Handbuch der Friedensbewegung* (Handbook of the Peace Movement).

5 *The Foundations of Revolutionary Pacifism*, 1908

Far more important to Fried than the above-mentioned projects during this time, however, was the formulation of a theory of pacifism. In 1908, he summarized his ideas in *Die Grundlagen des revolutionären Pazifismus* (*The Foundations of Revolutionary Pacifism*),[116] which would soon become one of his most well-known books. But this slight volume really only presented a summary of his views that had already long been in print; only in the final chapter did he offer a newly developed program of action that was intended to realize his views.

In point of fact, many of the basic ideas of "revolutionary pacifism" can be found in the writings of Jacques Novicow and especially in Eugen Schlief's *Der Friede in Europa*, albeit in an unpopular and not easily readable style, a fact that Fried had actually criticized in 1904. Noting that Schlief's writings could hardly win over the masses, he wrote: "Your writings are Gothic masterpieces and every sentence can be dissected into a chapter."[117] Since Schlief was happy to see the significance of his theory for the peace movement compared to that of Marx for the social democrats, Fried added: "The three million voters of that party were not won over by Marx but by the wordsmiths that grew up around the party." Popular propaganda with catchy slogans, according to Fried, was indispensable in speaking to the masses, and it was only when the masses got behind the peace movement that it would be able to have an impact on government. Fried was convinced of that and tried—albeit in vain—to convince Schlief of it as well. He himself pursued this writing strategy consistently, and in the future he always tried to formulate his own theory in the simplest of terms and to illustrate it with succinct catchwords.

---

114   *Friedens-Warte* 12, no. 5 (May 1910): 88.
115   Cf. Fried, *Handbuch* (1913), 351.
116   Fried, *Die Grundlagen des revolutionären Pazifismus* (Tübingen, 1908).
117   Fried to Schlief, May 3, 1904. Nachlass Fried, Box 81.

Practically out of necessity, Fried took another step in shaping his theory when the Russo-Japanese War broke out. In the opening pages of his *Der gegenwärtige Krieg und die Friedensbewegung* (The Present War and the Peace Movement), he observed: "The outbreak of the Russo-Japanese War has once again given the opponents of the peace movement an opportunity to announce to the world, with an enviable feeling of superiority and an undisguised *Schadenfreude,* the bankruptcy of this theory and the unattainability of the goals it pursues."[118]

The powerlessness of the peace movement in acute, dangerous situations was the point of departure for its opponents from the very beginning. In spite of all their resolutions and calls for action, the small group of pacifists was neither in a position to prevent war nor to curtail it, and so when war broke out, they were forced to come face to face with the futility of their efforts. The necessity of finding a new starting point was obvious. For Fried, this concern comprised the final step toward the initial formulation of his theory.

As early as August 1905, he presented his "system of revolutionary pacifism"[119] in *Die Friedens-Warte*. In his article he distinguished "revolutionary pacifism," which was directed against the causes of war, from the prevailing "reform pacifism," which only sought to counter the phenomenon of war. Reform pacifism, accordingly, wanted to prevent or to curtail long wars, and it ascribed too great a role to the arbitration process. Revolutionary pacifism, on the other hand, aimed to attack the evil at its core; it sought to replace the anarchy of the states with a system of international cooperation. With this approach Fried thought he could take the wind out of the sails of his opponents: "One will no longer be able to reproach the pacifists when war breaks out that their work is pointless; pacifists can quite calmly reply that their actions cannot prevent war as long as the causes are not removed."

Similarly, the opponents' reference to the half-measures of arbitration agreements and to the ineffectiveness of the courts of arbitration in essential questions was no longer an argument against the pacifists, for they, the pacifists, viewed the development of the formal arbitration process as a "barometer that only shows us the current state of international law." Only after the creation of a stable international order, Fried argued, could a court of arbitration display its real function, so that, given the existing state of anarchy, it necessarily remained imperfect. Nevertheless, Fried maintained, the peace movement could quite easily applaud the conclusion of an arbitration agreement as an indication of the continued development toward an international

---

118   *Der gegenwärtige Krieg und die Friedensbewegung* (Vienna, 1904), 3.
119   Fried, "System des revolutionären Pazifismus," in *Friedens-Warte* 7, no. 8: 145–148. The following quotations are also taken from this source.

order. For Fried, this perspective was "logical, natural, and thus singularly purposeful in itself," for it not only pointed out the right path for the promotion of pacifist ideas, but "with one stroke it also [threw] into disarray the whole arsenal of our opponents."

Although Fried promised further formulations, it was not until January 1906 that he once again took up the topic, this time using the slogan "organize the world!"[120] From January 1906 to 1915, this slogan, in combination with a series of interlocking cogs, formed the emblem of the *Friedens-Warte*. Quite consciously, he broke with the traditional symbols of peace, i.e., the peace angel, doves, olive branches, and broken swords. Seeking to provide his new form of pacifism with a new image, he rejected these former emblems as too sentimental. That this image found favor with many pacifists can be seen in the fact that the logo soon appeared on the stationary of southern German pacifists,[121] and in 1908 the peace society in Hamburg produced and distributed it as its identifying symbol.[122]

At the same time, Fried replaced the prevailing Christian metaphors of the pacifist "doctrine of salvation" and the "peace apostle" with more everyday designations such as the "peace technician"; he also tried to offer more precise definitions of war and peace. In 1905, he had already concerned himself in his *Handbuch* with the distinction between "struggle" and "war"; he defined the former as the broader concept that comprised both physical violence (such as war) and psychological forms (such as competition). Then he examined the various meanings of "peace," which, he wrote, could signify calm, quiet, and death, but could also designate longer or shorter ceasefire in a military sense. In the pacifist sense, however, peace was to be understood as something much more comprehensive than the harmonious coexistence of civilized peoples governed by hard and fast legal norms, according to which conflicts would be resolved by the particular "ruling of an international court."

Based on this definition, the slogans of the opponents of the peace movement could more easily be countered: one could accuse them of confusing their ideas, specifically their claim that war is the "father of all things," which

---

[120] "According to the feature article of the first issue of this volume, this catch phrase was first used in America. We can update this knowledge today: a Dr. Edwin D. Mead made use of the title 'Organize the World' in a brochure published the previous year." *Friedens-Warte* 8, no. 3 (March 1906): 56.

[121] Around 1908–09 in Nachlass Fried: Letters of southern German pacifists that were written on stationary paper, the head of which contained cogs and the motto "Organisiert die Welt!" Cf. Nachlass Fried, Box 53.

[122] Cf. Nachlass Fried, Box 53. The circular stamp showed several cogs printed in white and centered on a blue background. The cogs were bordered by the motto "Organize the world," radially ordered in several languages.

now, through the substitution of "struggle" for "war," could be refuted as an argument against the idea of peace. Similarly, the reproach that the peace movement was opposed to natural law could also be negated, for the struggle, namely the competitive struggle, would not be called into question as an indispensable means of development; in contrast, war could be questioned, which is to say that physical struggle is no longer an acceptable means to resolve conflict for advanced cultures. In a similar way, Fried opposed the military notion of peace—"si vis pacem para bellum"—as well as the often quoted remark by Moltke that peace is a dream and not even a beautiful one: "Moltke was thinking in terms of a biological notion of peace, but he applied this thinking to a militaristic notion of peace."[123]

But more important was the fact that the new kind of pacifism that Fried advocated could only be realized if the concepts were more clearly differentiated. For without greater differentiation, Fried's assertion that "we are not only fighting the war of our opponents but also their peace"[124] would hardly be intelligible. And so he was able to work out the "essential equivalence" between hot wars and the periods of cold war that lie between them, namely, the limited ceasefire that is characterized by permanent preparation for war and attention to developing the most effective weapons possible. He concluded: "Under the hegemony of a system of international anarchy, war and peace yield the same results: they both impede human development as well diminish the value of humanity. With respect to their harmful effects, there is no real distinction between a war that is raging at the moment or what passes for peace. Pacifism thus had to do battle with two opponents: war and peace. Its task is to fight the whole system."[125]

The new system that Fried wanted to advance was more or less a comprehensive organization of states within an international legal system, acknowledged by and binding on all of the member states. If one nation were to act contrary to the law, the community would make use of the international legal system, even if that required force. But what was important about the new orientation, which was based on *Realpolitik*, was also the sense of the progressive character of the desired peaceful order and its dynamic components, which anticipated the ideas entailed in some of today's definitions of peace.[126] This was why Fried avoided prescribing a definite framework of the desired

---

123 Fried, *Handbuch* II, 16. Gross has established that this thesis is not supported by the facts. See Gross, 84.
124 Fried, *Die Grundlagen des revolutionären Pazifismus*, 33.
125 Ibid, 33f.
126 In his discussion of Fried, Dieter Senghaas emphasizes that peace has to be understood as "a political process that is free of violence and directed toward the prevention of the use of violence." Senghaas, *Dimensionen*, 156.

organization: "Our aim is solely and exclusively to proclaim the world organization; it is our task to show that for the most part it already exists, that it is expanding daily, that it is growing and becoming more powerful whether those who are blind unleash war or fear war, and that a thoughtful humanity need only to put on the final touches, need only to refine it, to give a uniform façade to the whole structure. One can call this façade whatever one wants: united states, federation, world empire. Its essence must be organization [...]."[127] Although the goals of revolutionary pacifism had thereby already been defined, Fried nevertheless could not give a precise answer to the question about how to best promote pacifism at that time.

The two-part article "Neue Bahnen des Pazifismus" (New Directions of Pacifism) first appeared[128] in 1908. In the first part Fried once again referenced the notion of arbitration. In pacifist circles he felt this notion was overvalued, something that he attributed to the fact that most wars were not fought as a result of a dispute, but rather "to gain additional room in the skies above one's country or on the ground in order to secure a country's continued existence in a stifling atmosphere of disorder." They were not preventable by a legal institution. "We are just as unlikely to get to peace through arbitration as we are through disarmament. Both are consequences that will simply fall into our laps once we have altered the causes." Thus, he reasoned, the task of the pacifist was to make observable progress in that direction, to support it, and when possible to accelerate it.

In the second, more theoretical part, Fried further examined the difference between a military and a pacifist peace. He explained: "Given the predominance of international anarchy, war and peace are essentially the same. It is only really a matter of two examples of one and the same thing." Even in times of peace, the costly military expenditures, which could clearly be better spent elsewhere, resulted in countless victims through avoidable diseases, workplace accidents, undernourishment, and premature death. Accordingly, to the pacifist it did not really matter whether war or peace predominated within the old anarchical system. If that were not the case – and here Fried made clear concessions to those representing the opposite view, then it was only because a hot war had impeded the progress toward an international organization. "From the standpoint of the pacifist it is therefore of great importance to

---

127 Fried, "Organisiert die Welt!" in *Friedens-Warte* 8, no. 1 (January 1906): 1–3.
128 Fried, "Neue Bahnen des Pazifismus," Part One, in *Friedens-Warte* 10, no. 1 (January 1908): 2–4. Part Two, *Friedens-Warte* 10, no. 3 (March 1908): 41–46. Subsequent quotations are taken from these articles.

prevent war as much as possible in spite of the essential equivalence between war and peace in the present anarchical system."

Fried then depicted the development of the international order as an irreversible, quasi-evolutionary process that arose from a natural tendency toward a higher form of organization and the accompanying decrease in an individual's expenditure of energy. "Our task thus consists in the first place of sharpening the eyesight of our contemporaries. They should learn to recognize the trajectory of the development, so that they can adapt their actions accordingly." Fried further claimed that the second task included the need to weaken the factors that have had a debilitating effect on the process and conversely to strengthen those factors that were beneficial to the developmental process.

But aside from these general guidelines Fried did not offer any concrete recommendations for action at this time; that did not occur until the summer of 1908 when his *Grundlagen des revolutionären Pazifismus* was published. The 68-page work, which sold for one mark, consisted of the articles noted above in a slightly edited form,[129] supplemented with a chapter entitled "Abrüstung" (Disarmament), and sections of the comprehensive chapter "Die Aktion" (The Plan for Action).[130] This booklet contained Fried's first attempt to develop a detailed plan of action that would show revolutionary pacifism to be "a pacifism of deed."[131] He saw two areas where engagement was needed: on the one hand, it was necessary to shield the natural developmental process from retarding influences and, on the other hand, to actively promote the process. Acknowledging that war was always caused only by a small group of people within the state, he argued that one first had to take steps to prevent the desire for war from being spread to the masses who were actually needed to conduct the war. It was therefore necessary to raise the level of education and to dismantle national prejudices through the rigorous promotion of personal and intellectual exchanges among the peoples of various nations. Besides trips abroad and international correspondence, Fried contemplated exchange programs for students, teachers, officials, merchants, and workers, and he even suggested the possibility that young men be required to spend six months in a foreign country. Since Fried was aware that this "immunization of the masses" was a tedious process and that in times of great urgency it might not succeed, he demanded at the same time the establishment of mobile, permanent, and above all binding investigative commissions whose task would be to "neutralize the passions of the people once they are unleashed." They were

---

129   Cf. the data provided by Fried in *Friedens-Warte* 10, no. 8 (August 1908): 158f.
130   The chapter is new from page 42.
131   Fried, *Revolutionärer Pazifismus*, 42. The following quotations are taken from this work.

to contribute to a quieting of the passions and to a greater sense of objectivity through a deliberate, impartial investigation of the conditions at hand. In addition, Fried favored the adoption of binding mediation. But since neither was possible without the participation of the rulers and the diplomatic corps, he insisted that "international politics be placed more and more under the control of parliaments and that diplomats stop operating in secret and align themselves with the modern spirit."

Fried saw the principal task of revolutionary pacifism to be the advancement of an international organization. Above all, he had in mind the improvement of transportation, the development of international law, and the consequent alignment of policies in support of these new institutions, in particular, the mutual representation of interests and administrative units, as well as the above-mentioned modernization of diplomacy.

Taken as a whole, Fried's plan resembled more an agenda for internationalism than for pacifism. His program demonstrated his intention to align his theory with the current ways of thinking and thereby lead pacifism out of isolation. But there were obvious weaknesses. Many of the premises of Fried's argument were debatable: the gradual decline of the use of physical force in disagreements, the efficient and effective progression from chaos to order as well as from the individual into the larger totality, and the steady development of the individual to a noble-minded human being. Moreover, the belief in an inevitable, linear development to a higher organization, which could only be accelerated by human engagement, could be seen as a great temptation to passivity. This point was particularly emphasized by the German pacifists around Ludwig Quidde, who, grounded in Kantian ethics, were absolutely convinced that war would only disappear from the world if humanity would act decisively for its abolition, and so they supported human free will over any form of determinism.

Nevertheless, in this work Fried was able to formulate an independent ideology with a philosophical basis, a scientific character, and a political program, as well as create a closed system.[132] Of course, one must not underestimate the mistakes and limitations of his effort, in particular its renunciation of all ethical and human motivation, the exclusion of inner-political approaches, and the dangerous exaggeration of economic cooperation as a driving force to the formation of an international organization. Nevertheless, this is the first time that the attempt was made to "to consider systematically the presuppositions and conditions that make peace possible and that might allow it to come into

---

132   Cf. Scheer, *Deutsche Friedensgesellschaft*, 134ff.

being."[133] So Fried's theory, as the peace researcher Dieter Senghaas emphasizes, is "comparable to today's attempts to bring about a contemporary theory of peace." Fried thus became the leading pacifist of the Imperial Age, and his approach, taken together with the democratic pacifism of Ludwig Quidde, substantially influenced the development of pacifism up to World War One.

The designation "revolutionary" pacifism was to remain controversial for a long time. In 1905, at its first mention, Fried saw himself compelled to define the concept "revolution" as "the transformation of a principle" in contrast to reform, which he viewed as a "transformation of a phenomenon," because for the bourgeoisie the concept revolution was negatively charged. "Do not fear! – The word 'revolutionary' is not to be equated with pitchfork violence. Revolution is not identical with the building of barricades, assassination, mutiny, incendiary acts, and street fighting."[134] Six months later Fried introduced the new cogwheel emblem for the *Friedens-Warte* to his critics and emphasized that this should provide reassurance to anyone who was anxious about his use of the concept "revolution."[135] But even as late as 1908 Fried had to defend his concept and to clarify that it was in no way meant politically. He even admitted "that this was not a very fortunate choice of word since, if considered only superficially, it might lead to incorrect assumptions."[136] But, he maintained, it would not be difficult to find a more suitable expression at some future point.

And indeed in due course there were other suggestions. Fried noted that Professor Schücking had suggested the adjective "organizational," and others proposed "scientific." He himself thought that the word "causative" ("ursächlich") was the most analogous term.[137] In 1916, a new edition of his book appeared with the title *Grundlagen des ursächlichen Pazifismus*. After Fried's death, owing to the influence of Hans Wehberg and Walter Schücking, an expert in international law, the designation "organizational pacifism" became the common phrase to describe Fried's pacifism.

This reveals indirectly that Fried's theories found resonance in some parts of the field of modern international law, and they were indeed further developed there to some extent. Fried thereby helped to advance a kind of law that was later to develop in a different mode from the general trend in law, namely,

---

133 This and the following quotation are taken from Dieter Senghaas, *Zum irdischen Frieden. Erkenntnisse und Vermutungen* (Frankfurt a. M., 2004), 26f.
134 Fried, "System des revolutionären Pazifismus," *Friedens-Warte* 7, no. 7 (mid-August 1905): 145.
135 Cf. Fried, "Organisiert die Welt!" *Friedens-Warte* 8, no. 1 (January 1906): 1.
136 Fried, *Die Grundlagen des revolutionären Pazifismus*, 2.
137 Fried, *Die Grundlagen des revolutionären Pazifismus*. Second revised and expanded edition, 1916, 5, note 1.

one that viewed the sovereignty of a national state as inviolable.[138] Around 1905, while Fried was still forming his theory, some experts in international law began to consider the advantages of an international organization through their engagement with the work of The Hague and its possible expansion; this led some to question the necessity of unfettered sovereignty. For this group, which in fact gained influence only after the war, Fried's theory was of decisive importance for the shaping of a pacifist-oriented system of international law, one that no longer wanted to simply regulate war, but also sought to dispute its legitimacy. Schücking wrote on this development: "The whole direction of my thinking on international law was determined to a large extent by Fried's writing."[139] Wehberg and Lammasch also often emphasized their intellectual indebtedness to Fried's influence.

In 1908, however, Fried was most interested to bringing his "theoretical system" to the attention of those who were not already supporters of pacifism and to have it acknowledged in scholarly circles. "I had the pleasure of seeing my system acknowledged by scholars and its influence on the development of international law recognized."[140] The first step to the long-desired goal for recognition as a scholar and scientist was thus accomplished.

6   Integration and Recognition

The year 1908 represented a step forward for Fried in several respects. His private life also underwent some changes. Fried and Therese Frankl were finally able to marry after they had divorced their respective partners. The new union was doubtless a marriage of love, even if they were only able to live in relative peace for a few years and were forced to endure numerous strains on their relationship. In 1918, Fried wrote Therese in a personal note: "You have made me completely happy. I am grateful to the fates that allowed me to find you. I cannot say how much I love you, and I will love you until my last dying breath."[141] His marriage seemed to bring a consolidation phase to a close. Fried found his new/old home in Vienna; in the coming years, he would find friends and other like-minded colleagues in Vienna who existed on the margins of and fully

---

138   Cf. on the following, among others, Peter K. Keiner, "Bürgerlicher Pazifismus und 'neues' Völkerrecht" (Diss. Freiburg, 1976), 145ff. Detlev Acker, *Walter Schücking 1875–1935*, Münster, 1970, 34ff.
139   Quoted in Acker, 44, note 44.
140   Fried, *Grundlagen des ursächlichen Pazifismus*, Foreword, 3.
141   The document was drafted on July 5, 1918 in Berne and since then has been in the personal possession of Trude Simonsohn. It was placed in Fried's papers (Nachlass Fried) in Geneva in 2003.

outside of the peace movement. His reputation would grow and he would gain access to circles that were previously closed to him despite the efforts of Bertha von Suttner to promote him. In 1910, Fried reported how proud he was to have participated in the banquet honoring Heinrich Lammasch, the Viennese privy councilor and member of the House of Lords (*Herrenhaus*): "It was an illustrious gathering of people who accepted the invitation to honor the great jurist of international law. The heads of the government were in attendance; also present were the diplomatic corps, the members of the House of Lords and of Parliament, and, in great numbers, the luminaries of the university."[142] And among them was Alfred H. Fried, as yet without his Nobel Prize and doctor title, and who, as a member of the non-parliamentary peace movement and of the peace bureau in Berne, was nevertheless allowed to give a speech. It is not hard to imagine the feelings of this poor Jewish boy from Vienna, whose education had been cut short.

Even the Frieds' financial situation improved during these years although it would not become stable until he received the Nobel Prize. Until that time, Fried remained dependent on the donations of friends and benefactors to continue his work. But the fact that he was becoming more famous opened doors to many newspapers and awakened the interest of some publishers, even those who did not publish on pacifism. In 1908 alone, Fried authored seven works, among them the slim booklet "Die moderne Friedensbewegung in Deutschland und Frankreich" (The Modern Peace Movement in Germany and France), "Internationalismus und Patriotismus" (Internationalism and Patriotism), a portrait of Bertha von Suttner, a detailed account "Das internationale Leben der Gegenwart" (Today's Internationalism), and "Die zweite Haager Konferenz" (The Second Conference at The Hague).

1908 also saw the publication of *Ein Verzeichnis von 1000 Zeitungs-Artikeln Alfred H. Frieds zur Friedensbewegung* (A Catalogue of 1,000 Newspaper Articles by Alfred H. Fried on the Peace Movement), which was intended to demonstrate his unparalleled activity as a journalist for peace. This catalogue, organized around specific themes, listed Fried's articles in 95 domestic and foreign newspapers from 1892 to 1908. Among them, 350 were about the work in The Hague – in all, an impressive collection.

Fried's only non-pacifist work of this period, a comparison of Vienna and Berlin, was published in 1908;[143] it provided evidence of how much Fried's view of Vienna as a "city of squalor" had changed. Now the "city of idiots" of 1903

---

142   The Lammasch celebration in Vienna, *Friedens-Warte* 12, no. 12 (December 1910): 223–227, here 223.
143   Fried, *Wien-Berlin. Ein Vergleich*, Vienna/Leipzig, undated, 1908. The following quotations are taken from this work.

came off better than Berlin—in spite of all his efforts to present a balanced picture. In particular, he now saw in Vienna the impact of the older and more highly developed culture, which, to be sure, was less innovative and flexible than that of the young, modern Berlin and offered fewer chances for upward mobility, but it did provide a slower-paced life, one worth living—a life that the 44-year old Fried had since learned to value.

What was especially positive about Berlin were the modern institutions, in particular the efficient transportation network. On the other hand, Fried viewed the Berliners themselves rather negatively: he conceded that the Berliners were industrious and had a sense of duty and of order, but the "hard struggle with nature had overdeveloped their intellectual abilities to the detriment of their emotional well-being." These essential traits were also mirrored in the attitudes of the social classes, the political parties, and the interest groups. He noted a prevailing "spitefulness, resentment, and envy even within closed groups that appeared to be directed outward." Closer relations, according to Fried, between the Berliners and the Viennese were hardly possible: "The contrast between the Berliners and the Viennese in their personal characters was too great to allow them to find favor with one another. And the many Viennese living in Berlin could accept the great institutions there, but not the people themselves, and least of all their customs and habits." According to Fried, the differences in Vienna were less harsh. Even the greatest political opponents were able to collaborate on certain topics, and one could clearly differentiate between the group and the individual, between the person and the opinion. In contrast to life in Berlin, one knew nonpolitical moments in Vienna, "where one finally could stop being a fighter, and just be a human being." As an example, Fried pointed to, of all people, Dr. Karl Lueger, the mayor of Vienna: "Here civil servants collaborate on the newspapers of the social democrats, here a social democrat can speak his piece even in a bourgeois newspaper, and even the famous antisemitic Dr. Lueger is said to have courteous relations with Jews; he is said to be responsive to poor Jews who turn to him for help."

These are astounding sentences from a Viennese Jew even if one assumes that at this point Fried might only rarely have been exposed to antisemitic attacks in Vienna. Contrary to the masses of Eastern European Jews who were flooding Vienna at the time, Fried was not identifiable as a Jew from his outward appearance. In addition, in the Austrian Peace Society, the general lack of public scrutiny directed toward him did not render him a preferred target. Nevertheless, the reference to Lueger can only be explained by the fact that Fried, as he had indicated in this work, was not intending to offer an in-depth analysis. One finds no critical comments that would give some indication that there was social tension in Vienna as well, that ethnic groups were fighting against each another, and that antisemitism was growing. Fried was only critical of a few institutions in Vienna, such as the inadequate transportation system, the expensive carriages, the evening curfew at ten o'clock, and the lack of openness to innovation. And thus he came to the conclusion that the Viennese could benefit from the Berliners if they would imitate some of the institutions found in Berlin. However, "only the institutions are to be imitated, not the people."

Clear signs of Fried's ongoing integration into Vienna's social life and of an improvement of his own personal circumstances from 1908 onwards can be seen in his participation in the clubs and associations to which he belonged, most notably the Freemasons. Although the cosmopolitan Freemasons were not themselves explicitly pacifists, their ideals of individual perfection, commitment to a humanitarian ethic and to a peaceful, socially just communal life, as well as their opposition to any form of fanaticism, chauvinism, and class-thinking, including the categorical rejection of any form of antisemitism,[144] were not too far removed from the goals of the peace movement. Many well-known pacifists[145] were members of the various Freemason lodges, among them Elie Ducommun, the director of the International Peace Bureau in Berne, who was much admired by Fried. In February 1908, Fried was accepted as an "apprentice" in the "border lodge" in Pressburg (now Bratislava, Slovakia).

The so-called "border lodges" came into being as early as 1869 because the Austrian law governing the associations (Vereinsgesetz) permitted governmental commissioners to participate in all meetings of the association, something which the Freemasons strictly opposed. The "border lodges" carried out the humanitarian work of the association under the control of the local officials in the city where they were founded, but they then met in the Hungarian border towns of Ödenburg, Neudörfl, and Pressburg, where the establishment of the Freemasons had been allowed since 1867, to carry out the actual work of the lodge. The border lodges were then officially subject to the Great Lodge of Hungary, but they carried out their missions in Austria.[146] On February 9, 1908,

---

144   *Internationales Freimaurer-Lexikon*, keyword antisemitism: "In the view of the association, antisemitism and free masonry are irreconcilable concepts." Lennhoff, Posner, Binder: *Internationales Freimaurer-Lexikon*. Quoted from a new edition, revised and expanded and based on the edition of 1932. Munich, 2000, 82.

145   Members of the Free Mason lodges included: Elie Ducommun (Nobel Peace Prize 1902), Leon Bourgeois (Nobel Peace Prize 1920), Charles Richet (Nobel Prize for Medicine 1913), Michael Georg Conrad, Franz Bucher-Heller, Friedrich Hertz, Henri Marie La Fontaine (Nobel Peace Prize 1913), Edouard Quartier-la Tente, Elihu Root (Nobel Peace Prize 1912), Carl von Ossietzky (Nobel Peace Prize 1935).

146   The official return of the lodges to their native cities in Austria was only made possible by the founding of the Republic of Austria in 1918.

Fried was admitted to the border lodge "Socrates" in Pressburg, having been assigned the registration number 228.[147]

Simultaneously, he also thereby joined the "non-political association 'Humanitas,'" which was part of lodge and published its own newspaper, *Der Zirkel* (The Circle), under the direction of the Viennese writer and dramaturg Heinrich Glücksmann.[148] Glücksmann, who also had contact with Bertha von Suttner and who acquired her *Randglossen zur Zeitgeschichte* (Commentaries on Contemporary History) from the "fine journal *Friedens-Warte*,"[149] asked Fried to work with him on the journal. And, in point of fact, Fried published several articles there in the course of the next few years: some were reports about the particular events and meetings of the lodge "Sokrates," and some were lead articles from *Die Friedens-Warte*, which were published as advance copies or as reprints.

The lodges in Vienna at this time were closely aligned with the current thinking about peace, as can be seen in a reprinted article that Fried published in *Die Friedens-Warte*[150] under the rubric "Aus der Bewegung" (From the Movement). There he reported on a Peace Festival in Vienna sponsored by the united Austrian border lodges, at which Bertha von Suttner and Heinrich Glücksmann gave invited speeches, the former about the significance of the conference in The Hague and the latter about the relationship of the Freemasons to the idea of peace. Beginning in 1908, *Der Zirkel* (The Circle) included more and more reports about the activities of the Austrian Peace Society, reprinted an essay by Andrew Carnegie entitled "Die Rüstungen und ihre Ergebnisse" (Armaments and their Results), and advertised both for Fried's publications and for the *Friedens-Warte* itself.[151] Up until 1914 one can observe a growing convergence between the Austrian Peace Society and Vienna's border lodge, which no doubt can be attributed in part to Fried.

Fried did not underestimate the significance of his acceptance into the Freemasons. Else Frankl, the wife of Fried's friend and attorney Emil Frankl, both of whom likewise belonged to the Freemasons, wrote a commemorative article[152]

---

147   He attained the second degree on July 7, 1909 and the third on January 22, 1910. The lodge identification cards can be viewed in Nachlass Fried.
148   The newspaper was published from 1871 to 1917 (the volumes were numbered from September/October until August of the following year, e.g. no. 1, vol. 36, October 15, 1905) After the border lodges were dissolved, the newspaper continued as the *Wiener Freimaurer-Zeitung* with Glücksmann as editor, beginning in 1919.
149   Cf. Heinrich Glücksmann, ed., *Der Zirkel* 36, no. 17 (February 4, 1906): 257.
150   *Friedens-Warte* 10, no. 6 (June 6, 1908): 118.
151   Cf. *Der Zirkel* 41, no. 17 (1910): 247ff.
152   Else Frankl, "In memoriam Br. Alfred Hermann Fried," *Wiener Freimaurer-Zeitung* 3, no. 1/2 (June 1921): 9–13. The following quote, 13.

for the Viennese Freemason newspaper in 1921. She is certainly correct when she observes: "In the circle of the Freemason brothers, who all served unappreciated ideals, Fried was able to count on some sympathy for his own misinterpreted and often ridiculed struggle for world peace. Here he found a home for his spirit as well as companions who willingly and without prejudice acknowledged the ideal that he strove for and the work that it entailed." In April 1909, Fried rose to the second degree, and on January 22, 1910, he became a Master Mason in the lodge "Socrates."

The increasing fame of their brother filled the Viennese border lodge with great pride. Commenting on the peace conference in Stockholm in 1910, *Der Zirkel* noted: "Among the most prominent members of the peace movement participating in the conference was our brother Alfred H. Fried, who attended with his wife."[153] When it was announced in early 1911 that many of his colleagues had nominated Fried for the Nobel Peace Prize, *Der Zirkel* wrote: "Brother Fried, who has been a frequent and enthusiastic champion of world peace both in our lodge and in *Der Zirkel*, is to be counted among the most zealous and resolute leaders of the pacifist movement and is fully deserving of this award. [...] This honor pleases us in particular because it is to be awarded to one of our own, and so some of the luster is also shone on our group and our ethical goals. We act in support of nothing less than the establishment of a brotherhood of humanity through a just settlement of conflicts, not through the use of brutal force or sanctioned mass murder."[154]

When the award became a reality, the lodges were among the first to congratulate him. From Budapest, the Grand Master of the Symbolic Grand Lodge in Hungary wrote to Fried that the brothers had read the happy news: "We have been witness to your continual and indefatigable work for peace, which has been ongoing for over two decades. You have carried out your outstanding Freemasonic work, both past and present, with true zeal, especially in the service of the royal art of peace. We had to tell ourselves and have to tell you, beloved Brother, that you have fulfilled your Freemasonic obligation to the fullest measure. We are very pleased that the recipient of the Peace Award this year has been one of the brothers of the Symbolic Grand Lodge of Hungary [...]"[155] The brothers' pride in Fried will accompany him in the coming years and will provide him with encouragement. Even after the war broke out in 1914, the brothers remained faithful to him.

One year before Fried joined the Freemasons, he became a member of the newly founded "Soziologische Gesellschaft" (Sociological Society) at the

---

153 *Der Zirkel* 41, no. 1/2 (1910): 10.
154 *Der Zirkel* 41, no. 18 (February 1911): 266f.
155 Nachlass Fried, Box 17.

University of Vienna. From the very beginning, he was involved in the planning and preliminary discussions of the society: "[...] and so we ask you not only to contribute your valuable experience to the planned endeavor but also to vigorously make known your interest in the project through your kind participation."[156] This request did not fall on deaf ears, for Fried was currently working on the translation of *Gerechtigkeit und Lebensexpansion* (Justice and Life Expansion) by the Russian sociologist Jacques Novicow, a work that he considered "one of the most genial sociological tracts ever written."[157] When the society was founded in 1907, he was one of its first full members.

The purpose of the new association, which "all educated people, without regard to gender" were invited to join, was to gain an understanding of the essence and significance of sociology and "to nurture and disseminate the acquisition and awareness of sociological facts in a strictly scientific manner."[158]

Leading the association was Rudolf Goldscheid, who hailed from a rich Jewish family in Vienna. He had spent several years in Berlin and had become a convinced socialist through his acquaintance with August Bebel. Having broken off his studies, Goldscheid returned to Vienna and became well known through his writings on ethics; he now turned his attention to economics and sociology.[159] Goldscheid, who only gradually warmed up to pacifism, developed a theory of "Menschenökonomie" (Human Economy), which pacifists would later come to esteem. The theory highlighted the progressively ascending economic value of human life, of human labor, and of public health in a culturally advanced society.[160] His views developed at the same time as Fried was working on his "revolutionary pacifism," but Goldscheid, a convinced socialist who saw social problems as consequences of domestic not foreign matters, kept his distance from the Austrian Peace Society at first.

Although Fried and Goldscheid got to know each other only gradually, their mutual influence is unmistakable. While Fried participated in the activities of the Sociological Society through his lectures and discussions (and in so doing involved Goldscheid more and more in peace movement), it is quite clear that the *Friedens-Warte* from 1908 on deals increasingly with the perspectives of the Social Democrats. That Fried himself at this time had no direct contact with

---

156 Invitation to Fried, Nachlass Fried, Box 80.
157 Cf. the advance notice of this work in *Friedens-Warte* 9, no. 5 (May 1907): 98.
158 Statutes of the "Soziologische Gesellschaft," §2, Nachlass Fried, Box 80.
159 On Rudolf Goldscheid and his activities, see Donat/Holl, *Handbuch*, 160f. and *Friedens-Warte* 30 (July/August 1930): 193–202. See also Josephson, *Biographical Dictionary*, 342f. The Nachlass of Rudolf Goldscheid is thought to have been lost.
160 Cf. Rudolf Goldscheid, *Entwicklungstheorie, Entwicklungsökonomie, Menschenökonomie* (Leipzig, 1908).

the Austrian Social Democrats (but was aware of Goldscheid's contacts) can be seen in a letter that Fried wrote to him toward the end of 1912 or early in 1913. Fried asked him for his assistance in securing the support of the leading members of the Viennese Social Democratic Party since Fried planned to nominate the socialist bureau in Brussels as a candidate for the Nobel Peace Prize in 1913. Fried wrote: "Since I have no connection with these men, would you please speak with your colleagues in the party so that I may have an opportunity to meet with them."[161]

In 1912, Fried published Goldscheid's short text "Friedensbewegung und Menschenökonomie" (Peace Movement and Economy of Human Beings), which was based on his lecture to the Austrian Peace Society, in his series "Internationale Verständigung"[162] (International Understanding). In the lecture Goldscheid described the special relationship between his theory and the peace movement. Starting from the socialist view that work is "the mother of all things,"[163] Goldscheid emphasized the "modified role that war plays in the current system of production," which he labeled "an anachronism" because of the obvious negative balance sheet. Equally disastrous, in his opinion, was the economic balance sheet of armed peace, for it was the cause of much poverty, exploitation, and widespread disease. The only solution to this condition, in Goldscheid's view, was to be found in international rapprochement and organized internationalism, whereby a more just international economic system and a balance of the mutual economic interests of the various countries were accorded greater weight than international law. In so doing, Goldscheid was actually describing the dependency of domestic exploitation on international exploitation. Thus he claimed, it was not right—and here he sees a gap in the Marxist system—to expect the solution to come from the increasing the power of the working class: "It is a fact that at some particular point the relationships between nations prevent any socialist movement from achieving its desired progress." Accordingly, both had to grow together simultaneously and to support one another. That was why, in Goldscheid's view, the peace movement, if it really wanted to accomplish something, needed socialism as a substratum just as socialism needed the organized internationalism of the peace movement.

For Goldscheid himself these thoughts led directly to his work with the pacifists. In December 1912, he wrote the lead article in the *Friedens-Warte*

---

161 Fried to Goldscheid, undated [end of the year 1912/1913], Nachlass Fried, Box 60.
162 The series is later renamed "Internationale Organisation."
163 Goldscheid, *Entwicklungstheorie, Entwicklungsökonomie, Menschenökonomie*, 6. Subsequent quotations are from this work.

for the first time,[164] and one year later the Austrian Peace Society announced his (and Fried's) appointment to the executive board.[165] In the coming years Goldscheid would play an important role in the peace movement: during the war, he was especially involved with the "Bund Neues Vaterland" (Federation of the New Fatherland); later, from 1923 until his death in 1931, he would become the president of the Austrian Peace Society as Fried's successor; and finally he would serve on the council of the International Peace Bureau.

7 The Association of International Understanding

Encouraged by the early reactions of several scholars of international law, sociologists, and economists, Fried began, around 1909, to work on expanding the pacifist base in Germany to include the academic class, a group that until then had been generally dismissive of the peace movement. "The time is now ripe to win more people for the idea of peace. But even riper, it seems to me, is the academic world. The way has been paved, and I can now tell you, that in the very near future an organization will be created that will have as its primary task the inclusion of German academics to our cause."[166]

What Fried is suggesting to Hans Wehberg here toward the end of 1910 is the founding of a new society that he would initiate himself. The original idea likely came from Eugen Schlief, who believed that there was a need for a coalition of pacifist academics in addition to the peace societies, which he saw as less than effective. He subsequently turned to Fried, who took to the idea right away: "Regarding your suggestion that we form a committee of the peace movement, I am certainly willing to help, but aside from Nippold in Germany I don't know of any others who might be won over. Quidde is too much aligned with the 'association', and it seems to me that given his candidacy for parliament he would not want to alienate the 'association'."[167]

While Fried was passing along Schlief's suggestion to Otfried Nippold, a lawyer specializing in international law and a university professor (Privatdozent) in Berne with whom he had been in frequent contact since 1905, it quickly became apparent that Schlief was more interested in founding a party than a committee. Schlief suggested that the party be called "Partei der

---

164 "Krieg und Kultur. Die Lehren aus der Krise," *Friedens-Warte* 14, no. 12 (December 1912): 441–446.
165 *Friedens-Warte* 15, no. 7 (July 1913): 279.
166 Fried to Wehberg, April 27, 1910, Nachlass Wehberg, vol. 59a, BA Koblenz.
167 Fried to Schlief, February 27, 1907, Nachlass Fried, Box 81.

Internationalen Ordnung" (Party of International Order) and that a committee of thirty to forty people be formed to establish the party. Fried replied that a dozen would likely suffice for the initial phase and suggested that the core consist of himself, Schlief, Nippold and Schücking.[168]

But these colleagues did not respond particularly well to his proposal, for Fried's own euphoria for the project had cooled, and his communications with Schlief became less frequent. Nevertheless, Fried did publish Schlief's article "Die Partei der internationalen Ordnung," in which Schlief called for the creation of a party "to which people from the most diverse states can be recruited."[169] This was, however, not really a specific call to establish such a party, but rather a document for discussion, rooted in Schlief's thinking. In a "note by the editor," Fried himself spoke only vaguely "of the project that had been discussed for some time both in conversation and in writing among several German pacifists," namely, the project to create a party, and he found it necessary to distance himself both from Schlief's rather polemical remarks about the peace movement in its current form and from the related activities.

At the same time, however, Fried pursued a somewhat different course in his correspondence with Nippold: "I hope to start a large academic-political society to stand beside the peace societies, one that is quite distinct from the previous tea parties and the tables reserved for pub regulars in its composition and its effectiveness. Such a society is sorely needed. This will quickly win over public opinion and will enable the associations to focus on their real values."[170] Once again, the criticism of the shortcomings of the existing peace societies formed the core of the initiative, and Fried found himself in agreement with both Schlief and Nippold: "There are some garrulous blockheads who have chosen the peace movement as a platform to satisfy their own ambitions—people with the intelligence of their cooks, who have received honorary positions and are placed in the front ranks because they create a 'good impression'—who are able to purchase positions of honor [...]. Of course, this whole mess must remain concealed from the outside world, because, even if the peace societies are in a terrible way, they do have some advantages. They do effect some changes, so one just has to accept them."

Fried wrote that he had been working for a number of years as a "guerilla" and that he was the most hated man among the leaders of the German Peace Society. However, he also believed that it was advisable to stay connected with

---

168   Fried to Schlief, January 8, 1908, Nachlass Fried, Box 81.
169   *Friedens-Warte* 11, no. 2 (February 1909): 25ff., 27; the following quote is on 25.
170   This and the following quotation are from: Fried to Nippold, September 29, 1907. Nachlass Fried, Box 72.

the associations in the interest of peace, even if from a distance, and also to try to exert some influence at the conferences. Nippold answered him in January, writing that he would be happy to meet with him if he came to Switzerland in the next few months to talk about his proposal further.[171] It is, however, not clear if such a meeting took place or whether, as Fried would later maintain, the two were frequently in touch about founding a group.[172]

It is certain that from 1908 on Nippold was involved in an international collaboration of like-minded experts in international law. In his *Meine Erlebnisse in Deutschland vor dem Weltkriege*[173] (My Experiences in Germany before the World War), he described how, as a student of international law, he wondered about the possibility of taking the notion of international understanding to the masses, and that he therefore took a trip to Germany in February 1909 in order to confer with experts in international law, statesmen, parliamentarians, and others about founding such an organization.[174] He made no mention of Fried in this context, and Fried is not mentioned elsewhere in his *oeuvres*.

After his move from Berne to Frankfurt in October 1909, Nippold began to work on concrete plans to form a larger organization with Walter Schücking, a professor of international law in Marburg. Fried seems to have distanced himself from this effort. Later he wrote: "Although it was my idea to found an academic-pacifist organization in order to better represent pacifist thinking—and the two of us discussed it quite thoroughly—when I noticed that you wanted to work on the idea with Schücking but without me, I discreetly stepped back from the project. First, I knew that you were in good hands, and second I absolutely did not want to push you aside."[175]

It may indeed be true that Fried withdrew because he had little contact to those university and political circles in Germany that Nippold wanted to interest in the project and that he was already overburdened with his own work. Nevertheless, he followed the development closely and did not shy away from chiming in on occasion. When Schücking sent him the draft version of the call for the establishment of the party, Fried expressed his disapproval, in rather strong terms, of the sentence "All German men and women, no matter what party, are welcome." To Nippold he justified his opposition on the grounds that

---

171   Nippold to Fried, January 2, 1908, Nachlass Fried, Box 72.
172   In Nachlass Fried, there is little correspondence about this period so that this claim cannot be made with certainty.
173   Prof. Dr. Otfried Nippold, *Meine Erlebnisse in Deutschland vor dem ersten Weltkriege, 1909–1914* (Berne, 1918).
174   Ibid, 9. Nippold names specifically: Jellinek, Zorn, Schücking, von Bar, von Liszt, Kohler, Piloty, and von Ullmann.
175   Fried to Nippold, April 5, 1910. Nachlass Fried, Box 72.

it was now a question of attracting the intellectual elite but that this sentence would address the same people who were already working with the peace societies, a group from whom they wanted to distinguish themselves. Nippold appeared to be hurt by this response and reproached Fried for wanting to trip him up and hamper the creation of the organization. When the call was published in May, the sentence that Fried had objected to had not been altered.[176]

In October 1910, Fried mentioned "some differences of opinion" that might possibly prevent him from participating in the founding meeting in Frankfurt.[177] In May 1911, he gave notice that he would not be attending the meeting. As his rationale he explained that Nippold had "preferred to drop me and carry on the work alone,"[178] once the work itself began to take concrete form. But above all he accused Nippold of having rejected him as a candidate for the executive committee for "tactical reasons," despite Schücking's suggestion to nominate him during a preliminary meeting of the organizing committee back on March 13, 1911.

To Nippold himself, he wrote: "With the creation of the new organization, I had thought that I would have a political home for myself. Since I always stood apart from the Peace Society and always worked on my own, I longed for a community of like-minded people that I could join, and now, as this community is being formed, the door is closed to me and I am once again homeless. That is a great disappointment to me, and I don't yet know how I will respond to it."[179]

In fact, the decision not to elect the well-known Fried to the executive board arose from the ongoing fear that many of the founding members had had about being identified with the socially ostracized pacifist. Schücking had proposed Fried "because of his accomplishments in the area of international law" and also in order to signal at least an indirect connection to the pacifist circles.[180] It was not a question of separating the new organization from the peace societies but rather of not giving in to all their fundamental pacifist demands. The clear hesitancy of those whom they sought to attract caused the founders to further weaken the original program and finally to put the whole idea of an

---

176 Cf. *Friedens-Warte* 12, no. 5 (April 1910): 84f.
177 Fried to Wehberg, October 11, 1910. Nachlass Wehberg, vol. 59a, BA Koblenz.
178 This and the following quotation are taken from Fried to Wehberg, May 31, 1911. Nachlass Wehberg, vol. 59a, BA Koblenz.
179 Fried to Nippold, May 29, 1911. Nachlass Fried, Box 72. Fried's disappointment was all the greater as he emphasized to Nippold in September 1910 that he would be willing to work directly with the association. He asked about the position that Nippold had in mind for him he was the person who came up with the idea. See Fried to Nippold, November 6, 1911, Nachlass Fried, Box 72.
180 Cf. Scheer, *Deutsche Friedensgesellschaft*, 148.

international organization that Schücking had emphasized—as had Fried—on the backburner. Despite Fried's support, an international organization was not pursued, and a commitment to mutual understanding was put in its place.[181]

Fried was not quite correct in his belief that Nippold had rejected his leadership simply because he believed that Fried was too closely allied with the peace societies from which the new organization wanted to distance itself: "You are mistaken if you try to see me as a representative of the pacifism that the new organization wants to overcome. On the contrary. I was the first to have overcome that pacifism."[182] It was rather a question of Fried's name recognition as a pacifist and of his (radical) theories that might frighten off potential members. Moderate pacifists, especially if they were academics, were precisely the people that were needed. Apart from that, it was, for Nippold, also a question of his own leadership in the organization, whose founding he wanted to represent as his work, and which he did not want to establish as a branch of the peace movement; rather, he wanted an organization that positioned itself "in the broad stream of the movement for greater mutual understanding."[183]

In spite of his personal disappointment Fried continued to place his hopes on the organization and asked Hans Wehberg to report on it for the *Friedens-Warte*. In a preface to the article, Fried wrote a few lines in which he emphasized that he was the initiator, although this was not necessary because Wehberg did that anyway. Fried wrote: "The editor of these pages is proud of the fact that he gave the first impulse to establish such an organization, whose necessity he had long advocated and promoted in these pages. Not for personal fame do I mention this but rather in an effort to point out the umbilical cord that ties the new organization to pacifism."[184]

In his article Wehberg, too, did not forget to emphasize Fried's authorship, which was "warmly emphasized" by several speakers at the conference, especially by Schücking and Nippold. In doing so, he cited the world peace congress in Lucerne in 1905 as the origin of the first conversations on the topic, according to Nippold.[185]

Among the 41 participants at the gathering there were also members of the German Peace Society and the Interparliamentary Union, some of whom, like Ludwig Quidde and Richard Eickhoff, had also been elected to the twenty

---

181 Cf. Detlev Acker, *Walter Schücking, 1875–1935* (Münster, 1970), 52.
182 Fried to Nippold, May 29, 1911. Nachlass Fried, Box 72.
183 Scheer, *Deutsche Friedensgesellschaft*, 149.
184 *Friedens-Warte* 13, no. 6 (June 1911): 171.
185 The correspondence between Fried and Nippold (in Nachlass Fried) indicates that the topic was not taken up until 1907.

-member executive committee of the society. By and large, there was indeed an effort to recruit men who up to that point had not been pacifists but who were active in the fields of economy, science, and politics. Fried was pleased by the words that were spoken in his honor at the gathering, and for the next few months the conflicts abated. Without making further demands, Fried became a member of the organization and frequently reported on it in the *Friedens-Warte*. But then, unexpectedly, a new conflict quickly arose.

In April 1912, there was a new and serious dispute, which, for Fried, came totally out of the blue. On April 17, Fried asked Wehberg to inquire of Prof. Robert Piloty in Würzburg whether he (Fried) might publish a lecture, given by Piloty, in his series "Internationale Verständigung," in which he had already published a speech by the British Lord Chancellor Haldane on German-English relations.[186] At the same time, he mentioned that in the near future he wanted to publish several additional works in this series.[187] This inquiry caused quite a stir because the "Verband für internationale Verständigung" (Association for International Understanding) feared that there could be some confusion between Fried's series "Internationale Verständigung" (International Understanding) and a series that it was itself planning. It also wanted to prevent a direct connection between itself and the *Friedens-Warte*, i.e., its editor. So Piloty refused to allow Fried to publish his lecture and immediately informed Nippold, who, speaking on behalf of the association, demanded that Fried immediately change the title of his series. Fried at first refused to do so: "There is no way that I can change the name of my series since it is the German equivalent of 'International Conciliation,' and there is no other translation. Moreover, the gentlemen should not behave as if 'international understanding' characterizes their endeavor because I coined this term for my own efforts. You know that the *Friedens-Warte* used to be called 'Organ für Internationale Verständigung'." (Journal for International Understanding).[188] Since Fried was also the General Secretary of "Conciliation Internationale" for Central Europe, he felt doubly justified in continuing to publish his series under this title. In the first half of 1912, he published four small volumes in the series, all with the

---

186 The Right Honourable Viscount Haldane, J. B. M., State Secretary of War, "Deutschland und Großbritanien. Eine Studie über nationale Eigentümlichkeiten," authorized trans. by Dr. Rudolf Eisler (Berlin/Leipzig, 1911), published in *Internationale Verständigung*, no. 1. The Carnegie Endowment paid $4,000 for the distribution of the 250,000 copies of the brochure. Cf. Carnegie Endowment for International Peace. *Year Book for 1911*, 60f.
187 The letter is dated April 27, 1912, but from the correspondence it is clear that this must be a typo. In fact, the letter was written on April 17, 1912. Fried to Wehberg. Nachlass Wehberg, vol. 59a, BA Koblenz.
188 Fried to Wehberg, April 29, 1912. Nachlass Wehberg, vol. 59a, BA Koblenz.

motto "Conciliation Internationale" ("pro patria per orbis concordiam") on the title page.[189] To avert possible objections, he printed an explanation on the back of the front cover page, in which he officially distanced himself from the Frankfurt association.

What Fried did not know at this point is that in the meantime Nippold, through conversations with the European President of the "Conciliation internationale," Baron Paul Henri d'Estournelles de Constant, was able to arrange an affiliation between his association and the international organization, thus acquiring for the entire general association the exclusive rights for the German publications. In spite of Fried's explanation on the cover page, Nippold, representing the association, felt provoked to act. In July 1912, he wrote to Fried: "In so doing, you are guilty of violating our intellectual property, and certainly there is no doubt that, after we had warned you last year, you are doing so with malicious intent. You are therefore hereby summoned to immediately suspend the distribution of the books you intend to publish. We reserve the right to make known to the public your illegal activities and to argue for the confiscation of these books via a judicial decision."[190]

Fried was devastated at the tone of the letter. On the very same day, he composed a four-page letter defending himself; he sent it to Schücking and Wehberg along with a copy of the letter he had received from Nippold.[191] In his letter he not only emphasized that he was the General Secretary of the "Conciliation internationale" for Central Europe,[192] that he had been publishing books under the rubric "Conciliation internationale" since 1907, and that the American branch had been helping to finance the book series, but he also underscored once again his own authorship: "I was the first to have used these words as the hallmark of the peace movement. From 1899–1908 they served as the subtitle of the *Friedens-Warte*."

In the conclusion of his letter he asked both men to intercede on his behalf: "I ask you to judge, what right Mr. Nippold has to write me the kind of letter

---

189   No. 2/3: Goldscheid, "Friedensbewegung und Menschenökonomie." No. 4: Alfred H. Fried, "Kurzgefasste Darstellung der pan-amerikanischen Bewegung." No. 5: David Starr Jordan, "Krieg und Mannheit." No. 6: Bertha von Suttner, "Die Barbarisierung der Luft."
190   Nippold to Fried, July 1, 1912, according to a copy of the letter in Nachlass Wehberg, vol. 59a, BA Koblenz.
191   Fried to Wehberg (and Schücking), July 3, 1912. Nachlass Wehberg, vol. 59a, BA Koblenz.
192   "I am the general secretary of 'Conciliation Internationale' for Central Europe. That can be seen on the inside of the envelope on all the brochures of the French group. In the most recent report about the general assembly of the French Conciliation, page 11, one can also read a report about my activity as general secretary for Central Europe." Nachlass Wehberg, vol. 59a, BA Koblenz.

that I am forwarding to you, and I ask that you do everything in your power to prevent Professor Nippold from making the matter a public scandal. It will harm the cause of "International Understanding" more he or I have been of service to it."[193] In a handwritten note that he included with the letter to Wehberg, he noted that Nippold's letter had upset him to such a degree that he could no longer work.

Wehberg did in fact write to Nippold[194] on Fried's behalf four days later, and he was critical of the fact that the negotiations with the foreign associations were carried out behind Fried's back. He also criticized the "unjust stridency of the letter of July 1." He advocated that the association apologize and seek a reconciliation with Fried. "The thought that the Association for International Understanding would take the most accomplished pacifist in Germany to court is absolutely outrageous. In any case, the matter would involve additional groups of people and many of Fried's friends would perhaps feel compelled in the course of the matter to take an unequivocal position against 'International Understanding'." But it was already too late. By July 4, the association had already made its accusation of Fried public, and for his part Fried now considered taking legal action and threatened to involve the Americans in the dispute.

But even there Nippold beat him to the punch. At a meeting in Paris, Butler and d'Estournelles agreed, influenced by Nippold, to ask Fried to change the title of his series. They also made very clear that the fault for the dispute lay solely with them.[195] Fried gave in and not only agreed to rename the series in the future but also to provide the existing stock in the warehouse with new covers. From this point on, the series was called "Internationale Organisation" (International Organization) and the published books no longer included the motto. But in so doing, the money from America, which now went to the new book series of the Association for International Understanding, dried up for him, and the next volumes did not appear until 1914.

The reason for Fried's unusual compliance is certainly to be found in the fact that Butler, as president of the American Association for International Conciliation and also director of the department of development and education at the Carnegie Foundation, had provided the funding for Fried and the

---

193 Fried to Wehberg (and Schücking), July 3, 1912. Nachlass Wehberg, vol. 59a, BA Koblenz. Fried also sends copies of this letter to Professor Ullmann and to Nippold himself.
194 Wehberg to Nippold, July 7, 1912. Nachlass Wehberg, vol. 59a, BA Koblenz. The following quotations are from this letter.
195 Fried quotes Butler: "From no fault of your own but rather from oversight on the part of Baron d'Estournelles and myself." Fried to Wehberg, July 29, 1912. Nachlass Wehberg, vol. 59a, BA Koblenz.

Friedens-Warte. Since the founding of the Carnegie Foundation in 1910, Fried was employed as a special correspondent for Austria in the department "Intercourse and Education," and beginning in 1912 he received an annual subsidy of $6,000.00 for the journal.[196] So under no circumstances could Fried afford to be in conflict with Butler, and even less so with D'Estournelles de Constant, who had installed Fried as the secretary for Central Europe of the French "Conciliation internationale."

But Fried remained cold toward Nippold and continued to threaten him with a lawsuit. What was more difficult for Fried was the fact that he believed that Nippold had discredited him among his foreign friends. Having just been awarded the Nobel Peace Prize only six months earlier, Fried felt that he had been cast aside through no fault of his own. Frustrated, he wrote to Wehberg: "My dear Herr Doktor: the disgust I felt during the last few weeks was so strong that I wondered whether it might not be best for me to stop my work altogether. Given these circumstances, it is becoming very unpleasant."[197]

Fried nevertheless attended the first meeting of the association in Heidelberg in October 1912 and reported on it with enthusiasm in the *Friedens-Warte*: "I must publicly admit that a shiver ran down my back when I saw those important figures of society in the auditorium in Heidelberg, the representatives of science and the academic world who had been missing from the work for international understanding in Germany, who were now willing and able to work with obvious seriousness. I had the same feeling that I had on that beautiful May morning in 1899 when I attended the first peace conference, sitting in the gallery of the Buschhaus at The Hague."[198]

One reason for this euphoria can certainly be found in Fried's personal experiences in Heidelberg. He proudly reported that d'Estournelles had described him at the banquet as his "collaborator and a man of the first hour" and referred to him as an old friend, "and in so doing he cleared my name before the whole gathering of the advocates for peace."[199] He further reported that Nippold, too,

---

196 Cf. Carnegie Endowment for International Peace. *Year Book for 1912* (Washington 1913), 66ff.
197 Fried to Wehberg, July 29, 1912. Nachlass Wehberg, vol. 59a, BA Koblenz.
198 *Friedens-Warte* 14, 380.
199 This statement by d'Estournelles was important to Fried in light of his position both nationally and internationally, since the conference of the association was attended not only by German pacifists such as his sponsor Georg Arnhold, Alexander Dietz, Wilhelm Foerster, Adolf Heilberg, Adolf Richter and Magarethe Senka, but also by several, well-known foreign pacifists such as Theodor Ruyssen, Henri La Fontaine and Franz Bucher-Heller, the president of the Swiss peace association. Cf. the participant list in Nachlass Wehberg, vol. 67.1 (Nippold), BA Koblenz.

toasted with him, and, with a handshake, he took back the content of his letter. But Fried remained doubtful that the peace would be permanent.[200]

He tried to counter the increasing efforts, which he attributed to Nippold, to separate the new association from the peace societies, i.e., the "old pacifism." In an article, Fried sought to emphasize that the two groups were essentially going in the same direction and that it was just a normal condition of survival for the new association to distinguish itself from the old society: "But it was not necessary to do so in such a drastic manner."[201] And once again he pointed out that pacifism consisted of many different strands: "One need only point to the science of internationalism, which the pacifists created, and to the fact that the leaders of pacifism are quite close to the association in their views." It might not have been too hard for the readers of *Die Friedens-Warte* to guess to whom Fried was particularly referring.

He reported positively and optimistically on the events of the second day of the association's meeting, in which he, the recently named holder of an honorary doctorate, also participated.[202] It was once again only Nippold's policy of differentiation via a polemical degradation of the existing peace societies to which Fried objected, claiming that the association "has no need to put down all other peace activists and pioneers in order to demonstrate their own savvy. Its task is only to present the old and salutary ideas with new means in new forms. It should replace the petty bourgeois character of the present peace societies with the broad-mindedness of an association of scholars and politicians. Its raison d'être, as well as its strength and significance, lies in the altered form, not in its essence."

With the outbreak of World War I, it became evident that it was not only Nippold but also most of the members of the association who viewed the matter differently and sought to distinguish, not just superficially, their less than genuine pacifist convictions from those of the members of the peace societies. While Nippold himself left the association at the outset of the war (but immediately got in touch with Fried from Switzerland in order to found a new association there), many prominent members of the association publicly dissociated themselves from the organization, and several of these former members were among those who signed the famous "Aufruf an die Kulturwelt" (Manifesto of the Ninety-Three) of October 1914.[203]

---

200   Fried to Wehberg, October 7, 1912. Nachlass Wehberg, vol. 59a, BA Koblenz.
201   *Friedens-Warte* 14, no. 10 (October 1912): 381. This is also the source of the following quotation.
202   *Friedens-Warte* 15, no. 10 (October 1913): 363–368. This is also the source of the following quotations.
203   Among those who signed were: Lujo Brentano, Wilhelm Foerster, Ludwig Fulda, Ernst Haeckel, Gerhart and Carl Hauptmann, Karl Lamprecht, Friedrich Naumann, Wilhelm Ostwald, Max Planck, Wilhelm Röntgen und Max Reinhardt.

By this point, at the latest, Fried's hope for the association as a "House of Lords of the peace movement"[204] was permanently shattered: "It is truly regrettable that the association is failing, but that is the result of having too many 'half-hearted' members in it. That is now taking its toll."[205]

Fried had a little more success with the Austrian branch of the movement for international understanding, called "para pacem," which was founded in 1914. This branch acknowledged Fried's "revolutionary pacifism" as its theoretical basis and made an effort, from the very beginning, to work together with the Austrian Peace Society. Among the leaders of the Austrian association, who, like those of the International Understanding in Germany, sought to interest groups in its work from outside of the peace society, were: Heinrich Lammasch, an international lawyer, Konstantin Dumba, who later became president of the Austrian League of Nations, the theologian Johannes Ude, and the feminist Rosa Mayreder. They all remained true to their convictions during the war and sought a quick negotiated peace. An attempt to form a peace cabinet after the death of Emperor Franz Josef I under his successor Emperor Karl in the summer of 1917 and then to negotiate a separate peace was begun under the leadership of Lammasch and the businessman Julius Meinl,[206] who, in 1915, had founded the Österreichische Politische Gesellschaft (Austrian Political Society) consisting of members of this group.[207]

8   Nobel Peace Prize in 1911 and Honorary Doctorate in 1913

Around Easter 1911, Fried wrote the foreword to the second, fully revised and expanded edition of his *Handbuch*, in which he explained why it was not merely a slightly improved edition but was factually a completely new book.[208] He argued that the enriching impact of the second conference at The Hague had provided an impulse for the development of an organization of states, had enlivened the science of international law, and had further developed the

---

204   Fried makes use of the concept in the preface of an article by Hans Wehberg about the association. See *Friedens-Warte* 13, no. 6 (June 1911): 171.
205   Fried to Wehberg, March 20, 1915. Nachlass Wehberg, vol. 59a, BA Koblenz.
206   On Julius Meinl, see also Donat/Holl, *Friedensbewegung*, 267f.
207   Cf. *Die Friedensaktion der Meinlgruppe 1917–1918. Die Bemühungen um einen Verständigungsfrieden nach Dokumenten, Aktenstücken und Briefen,* ed. Heinrich Benedikt (Graz/Cologne, 1962).
208   Fried, *Handbuch der Friedensbewegung.* Part One: *Grundlagen, Inhalt und Ziele der Friedensbewegung.* 2nd ed. revised and expanded (Berlin and Leipzig, 1911), vff.

notion of peace in Germany. In addition, as a result, the peace movement had created a firm, scientifically developed theoretical base.

Because of the considerable size of the *Handbuch* Fried decided to publish the work in two volumes. Only the first volume appeared in 1911; the second was not published until the spring of 1913.[209] Taken as a whole, the *Handbuch* was a thoroughly useful tool especially for the peace activists of his time, but it is also useful for peace historians today because of its meticulous collection of data, its well-researched overview of the history of the peace movement, and its analysis of the movement's subsequent development. As such, it remains a singular accomplishment. Moreover, it enabled Fried to further expand his standing in academic circles, which then led to the much longed-for recognition by the public.

In December 1911, he shared the Nobel Peace Prize with Tobias Asser; this was the first official acknowledgement of his work for peace. Fried had been recommended for the award once before, in 1909; at that time, however, Fredrik Bajer, the Nobel Prize recipient of the preceding year and a long-time friend of Fried, was the only one to nominate him.[210]

In 1910, he was nominated by eight people: Jacques Novicow, Walter Schücking, Theodor Niemeyer, H. Rehm, Ernesto T. Moneta, L. Oppenheim, Eduard Wavrinsky, and once again Fredrik Bajer. Oppenheim emphasized that Fried, who was living only from the income generated by his writings, had particularly influenced the experts in international law, most especially through the publication of *Die Friedens-Warte*. Oppenheim wrote: "Mr Fried seems to be the most worthy" of all those who had come from these ranks and were awarded the Nobel Peace Prize. And he continued: "But I must emphasise this – that he has put the movement of Pacificism on a Scientific basis, that he has founded the science of the so-called "Internationalism," and that he has by his arguments compelled most representatives of the science of International law to become his followers in the pursuit of the Ideal of Permanent Peace."[211]

---

209 Fried, *Handbuch der Friedensbewegung*. Part Two: *Geschichte, Umfang und Organisation der Friedensbewegung*, 2nd ed. revised and expanded (Berlin and Leipzig, 1913). The deadline, however, fell in the fall of 1912.

210 Bajer suggests that Fried be considered for the position of editor of the *Friedens-Warte* since he had been working tirelessly and exclusively to publicize the idea of peace since 1891. Together with Fried, Bajer also recommends the International Peace Bureau in Berne. Cf. Bajer to Notske Storting Nobel Committee, January 12, 1909. Library of the Nobel Institute in Oslo, Pfl 7/09.

211 L. Oppenheim to the president of the Nobel Institute, January 27, 1910, Library of the Nobel Institute, Pfl 32/1910. The underlined sections are also in the original.

Schücking, too, emphasized in his four-page nominating letter that "the reactionary spirit of the age that we in Germany have experienced during the last thirty years"[212] has also dominated the fields of international law and constitutional law, and through the professors at the universities it has impacted the parliamentary system inasmuch as many statesmen are also jurists. "It was therefore extremely important for the peace movement to establish contact with the official experts in international law. No one other than A. H. Fried brought this about. His brilliant writings, in particular the superbly managed *Friedens-Warte*, were, more or less, able to attract the majority of German experts in international law to the cause of pacifism."[213]

After the deadline had passed and nominations could no longer be considered, an additional vote arrived in Kristiana. It came from Dr. Ferdinand Lentner, a professor of constitutional and international law at the University in Innsbruck: "Given the fact that the notice from the Ministry of Education in regards to the awarding of the Nobel Foundation for 1910 reached me on the second of this month, and that I valued the input of my professional colleagues before giving my vote, I would like to request that my vote be considered, even though the deadline has passed. I am honored … to support the nomination of Mr. Alfred Fried."[214] The unanimous decision by a group of Austrian faculty to nominate Fried for the Nobel Prize is curious especially given the fact that one year later Hans Wehberg tried in vain to find a university that would be willing to award Fried an honorary doctorate.

In January 1911, the list of those nominating Fried grew once again, to fourteen. In addition to Ferdinand Lentner, whose recommendation arrived punctually this time, and others such as Moneta, Novicow, Schücking, and Bajer who renewed their recommendations of the previous year—Bajer now for the second time—the list also included Gaston Moch, Leon de Montluc, Karl Lamprecht, Ludwig von Bar, and Baron Ernst von Plener, as well as Anna Zipernowsky, the best-known woman of the Hungarian peace movement,[215] and Bertha von Suttner. Not only did Bertha von Suttner point to Fried's extraordinary publishing activity, through which he had enriched the literature on

---

212   Dr. W. Schücking to the Nobel Institute, January 7, 1910. Library of the Nobel Institute in Oslo, Pfl 2/1910.
213   Ibid.
214   Dr. F. Lentner to the Nobel Prize Committee, February 5, 1910. Library of the Nobel Institute in Oslo, Pfl 47/1910.
215   Anna Zipernowsky was a member of the International Peace Bureau in Berne, a member of the executive committee of the Hungarian peace association, and president of the peace division of the federation of Hungarian women's associations. Cf. Fried, *Handbuch* (1913), 422.

peace "like no other," she also emphasized his total, pacifist character: "What I can say personally by way of justification of my recommendation, has to do not only with the well-known journalistic work of Mr. Fried, but also with his life, his character, and his overall outlook, which—no less than his work in publishing and in promoting peace—render him an appropriate candidate to receive the award initiated by Alfred Nobel and thus be encouraged to continue such work."[216]

Of significance for the positive decision of the committee this time might well have been the fact that Eduard Wavrinsky, a member of the Swedish Parliament who had previously spoken individually on behalf of Fried, was now able to get the whole Swedish interparliamentary group behind him. So, in 1911, the Nobel committee decided against a number of other proposed candidates, such as Wilhelm Foerster, Henri La Fontaine, Gaston Moch, Felix Moscheles, and Adolf Richter, who had been Ludwig Quidde's candidate, and for Fried. The committee made the award to him and Tobias M. C. Asser, a Dutch legal scholar and a member of the Court of Arbitration in The Hague.

The first to learn of Fried's good news was Berta Fried-Engel. On December 5, Fried sent his mother, who was living in Bernburg, a telegram, which she immediately answered, "shaking for joy."[217] She quickly began to prepare to travel to Vienna and in fact arrived a few days later. On December 8, Fried sent Wehberg a postcard informing him of the award that he was soon to receive.

Then he visited Bertha von Suttner. In her diary entry of December 9, she described how this visit unfolded: "Fried comes – weeping, he throws himself at me – I'm thinking that his wife must have died. No, he speaks of the misfortune like this: 'I have won the Nobel Prize.' Now, that is good news. Long conversations. Unfortunately, the prize is to be shared with Asser. But he is content anyway. It will grow by investing it. And Fried and his wife are now over the worst."[218]

When the news of Fried's selection became known officially, congratulations came in from all parts of the world. By December 11, the telegrams had added up: from Walter Schücking, who "rarely has been so happy,"[219] from Adolf Heilberg in Breslau, who extended his congratulations not only on behalf of his

---

216 Suttner to the Nobel Committee, January 21, 1911. Library of the Nobel Institute in Oslo, Pfl 30/1911.
217 See Berta Fried's telegram of December 5, 1911 from Bernburg. Nachlass Fried, Box 17.
218 Suttner, diary entry, December 9, 1911. Nachlass Bertha von Suttner, Box 3. Cf. Hamann, *Bertha von Suttner*, 485. However, Hamann cites the date as December 6.
219 Congratulatory telegrams, cards and letters along with many other items in Nachlass Fried, Box 17.

local chapter but also "especially from the whole family," and from Georg Arnhold, who not only underscored the "young age" at which Fried was awarded the prize but also emphasized his conviction that "[...] there was no one else who was more deserving of the award."

Likewise on December 11, the imperial German legation in Kristiana sent a report to Berlin that offered a thorough explanation behind the rationale for the selection of Fried: "He is to be thanked not least for his having influenced the general mood in Germany in favor of a peaceful conclusion of the German-French Morocco crisis."[220] When Emperor Wilhelm II read the report a week later, he wrote angrily in the margin: "What an outrageous decision. I have never even heard of this idiot."[221] In Kristiana one may indeed have exaggerated Fried's influence and his celebrity. As well-known as Fried was outside of Germany, most Germans would have agreed with the emperor's assessment.

Since the news of the award reached England through the "Daily News" and other newspapers that same day, congratulations also arrived from there, e.g., from William T. Stead and Leopold Katscher, who was living in Letchworth at the time. While Katscher wrote that Fried would have certainly been the sole recipient of the award if he had been able to bring about the planned union of the peace publications, Stead emphasized: "But, anyhow, it enables you to rank as one of the Peace worthies of the world, and we have at least the consolation of knowing that you will not follow the example of Moneta, and betray the cause to which you are pledged."[222] Even Otfried Nippold, who was always at odds with Fried, acknowledged Fried's accomplishments unconditionally: "In my eyes you have performed the greatest, most valuable deeds for peace, and therefore you are most deserving of the Nobel Prize."

Of course, serious criticism was not to be expected in a congratulatory telegram, and so among those offering congratulations there was hardly a note of skepticism. All the more striking then is the ironic tone of Ludwig Quidde when he wrote from his hotel in Ansbach on December 19 "half-dead from the campaign:" "So snowed under with work for the last few weeks that I rarely

---

[220] Report of the imperial embassy in Kristiana (Oslo) of December 11, 1911, Götz, PA/AA, R 8360 (1A, Norway no. 1).

[221] On the previous page, however, the emperor had written the comment that future generations will praise the achievements of the recipients of the award, but he followed that up with: "No one has ever heard anything about them."

[222] The shock that pacifists felt in 1911 when the Italian Nobel Peace Prize recipient of 1907, Ernesto Teodoro Moneta, became a staunch proponent of the conflict between Turkey and Italy was still fresh at this time. On Moneta, see, among others, Verdiana Grossi, "Ernesto Teodoro Moneta – Gebrochene Stimme des Friedens," in *Der Friedensnobelpreis von 1901 bis heute*, ed. Michael Neumann, vol. 2 (Zug, 1988), 106ff.

have had time to read a newspaper, and so I have only just learned that you have been awarded the Nobel Prize, admittedly it is to be shared. That is actually bad luck because a few years later you would have certainly been the single recipient of the prize. You probably viewed the news yourself with one dry eye and one teary eye. Right?" And he did not even hide the fact that Fried was not his ideal candidate. His support went to the first president of the German Peace Society: "You probably know that last year I put in a good word for Dr. Richter for his invisible but truly inestimable efforts on behalf of the German branch of the peace movement."

Quidde was presumably not alone within the German Peace Movement in this opinion since a rather clear distinction between the German and the Austrian pacifists had been established so that one could not feel joy at the other's success. Richter himself, on the other hand, had written a very warm letter to Fried on December 12 expressing his joy "that your accomplishments on behalf of the peace movement have found their appropriate recognition."

The great resonance about the award among the pacifists was equaled by the lack of its acknowledgment in the Austrian press, for at the time it was preoccupied with the Hötzendorf affair[223] and a possible preventative war against Italy, which made an interest in pacifist news even less desirable than it normally was.[224] On December 15, Fried complained to Wehberg: "Let me express my most heartfelt thanks for your congratulations and especially for the excellent article in the *Kölnische Zeitung* [...] The newspapers here, on the other hand, had no idea what to do with me. They knew about Asser, since they got their information about him from me, but the *Neue Freie Presse* mentions as my main work my *Friedens-Katechismus*, a booklet that was my first pacifist work and which today I am ashamed of and which is fortunately out of print today."[225] So he asked Wehberg to write an article for the *Neue Freie Presse* and added that he was not asking this out of vanity but rather so that he might be able use the award, granted to someone from Vienna, to capitalize on it in Austria for the idea of peace. Wehberg complied with his request. The article was accepted, but for some unknown reason it never appeared in print.

---

223   Conrad von Hötzendorf, chief of staff of the Austrian-Hungarian army since 1906, was removed from his position for his public advocacy of a preventative war against Serbia and Italy in 1911. One year later he was reinstalled.

224   Cf. Brigitte Hamann, "Bertha von Suttner und Alfred Hermann Fried," in *The Nobel Peace Prize and Laureates. The Meaning and Acceptance of the Nobel Peace Prize in the Prize Winners' Countries*, eds. Karl Holl, Anne C. Kjelling (Frankfurt a. M., 1994), 83ff.

225   Fried to Wehberg, December 15, 1911. Nachlass Wehberg, vol. 59a, BA Koblenz.

In fact, there was neither in Austria nor in Germany much interest in the news or the person[226] either by the state, the government, or the press and consequently by the public; most newspapers were content to write a few lines about the award on page three, if at all. Only a few of the papers on the opposing side, like the *Danzer Armee-Zeitung* or the antisemitic *Kikeriki*, took a polemical interest in the award. Both focused on the amount of money awarded, and they disparagingly claimed that Fried's engagement for peace was a pure business deal that had finally paid off. This reproach was fed by the news from Holland that Asser had earmarked his share of the award to begin a foundation. Besides this "poor press" it was only the newspapers for which Fried himself wrote, i.e., the *Neues Wiener Tagblatt* and the *Pester Lloyd*, that reported on the award in positive terms. The article in the *Pester Lloyd*, a liberal German-language newspaper, totaled 36 lines, the most of any publication.

As important as the public awareness of the award was to him, Fried nevertheless remained disinterested in a longer acknowledgment in his own newspaper. He returned such an article to Wehberg on January 8, 1912 with the comment: "You will no doubt understand that I don't want to publish this."[227] In the December issue Fried mentioned the award rather laconically in his *Pazifistische Chronik*: "10 December: the Nobel Peace Prize is awarded to the minister of state Asser and Alfred H. Fried."[228] Under the rubric "Aus der Bewegung" (From the Movement), he wrote somewhat more expansively. Following a substantial appreciation of Asser, one reads: "In light of this broad array of deeds, the other laureate is quite aware of his own modest accomplishments. He views the high honor that was bestowed on him firstly as an honor of the social class to which he belongs and then as encouragement for the journalists and writers who are working for peace." But Fried was not quite as modest as he seemed, for he continued: "He feels deeply touched by the fact that he is the youngest recipient of the Nobel Prize and understands the great obligation that it places on him: to work for the sacred goal with redoubled energy and to serve the cause until his final breath, without compromise and without hesitation."

Fried was indeed the youngest of the 13 awardees up to that point—and likely the one with the lowest social status using the standards of the time. Perhaps only Henry Dunant in Heiden, the impoverished and ostracized founder of the Red Cross, was in a financially worse position at the time of his award. But he was already 79 years old when he was awarded the prize. On the other hand, Theodore Roosevelt was only one year older than Fried when he won the

---

226 Cf. Hamann, "Bertha von Suttner und Alfred Hermann Fried," 83ff.
227 Fried to Wehberg, January 8, 1912. Nachlass Wehberg, vol. 59a, BA Koblenz.
228 *Friedens-Warte* 13, no. 12 (December 1911): 365. Subsequent quotations, 374.

award in 1906. Most of the fighters for peace were over 60 years old when they were selected; some were in their 70s, such as Frederic Passy, Ernesto Moneta, and Fredrik Bajer.[229] Almost all of them had studied at the university and lived comfortably as lawyers, professors, or politicians. Fried was quite right to be proud even if the award did not noticeably enhance his reputation with the German and Austrian public.

More important to Fried was the fact that the prize money provided him with some financial security. On December 13, the Nobel Foundation informed him that his share of the award, 70,347 Swedish crowns, had been transferred to the Wiener Bank-Verein. This meant that Fried was now not only able to look forward to a future without debt and with financial security, but that he could also afford some luxury, such as hiring a secretary and looking for a new, larger and quieter apartment.

When an individual has officially accepted the prize, he or she is obliged, by statute, to hold a speech within six months, but for Fried that was not to be the case.[230] In March 1912, Fried established contact with the secretary of the Nobel Prize Committee of the Norwegian Storting, Ragnvald Moe, in Kristiana in order to settle on a date for his speech. His idea to give a speech in August while he was attending a conference of the Institut de Droit International in Kristiana was not acceptable. They did, however, agree on a date at the beginning of June 1912. But in early May 1912 Fried canceled the trip for health reasons and requested an extension since the original deadline would have passed on June 10. Moe agreed. In January 1914 a new date is set. Moe asked Fried to come to Kristiana at the end of June or the beginning of July: "This is usually the most beautiful time of year in the city, and the vacation period has not yet begun."[231] Fried notified him that he was planning to come to Kristiana between June 20 and June 27. But, once again, the trip had to be cancelled. The increasing work for the World Peace Congress in Vienna and the severe illness of Bertha von Suttner, who had been bedridden since the beginning of June with no hope of recovery (she died on June 21), did not allow Fried time for a longer trip. Once again, he canceled the trip, now for the final time because World War I would not give him a chance to choose another date.

---

229 Among the relatively younger recipients, who were still 10 years older than Fried, were Albert Gobat (59), Paul d'Estournelles de Constant (57), and also Henri La Fontaine (59), who received the award two years after Fried.

230 On the following, see the correspondence with the Norsk Storting Nobel Committee in Nachlass Fried, Box 72.

231 Ragnvald Moe, Nobel Committee of the Norwegian Storting to Fried, March 11, 1912. Nachlass Fried, Box 82.

But in any case, Fried could now finally afford to hire a real secretary. In early January 1912, he placed an ad in the *Neue Freie Presse*. Among the applicants was one that he found particularly interesting. Written by Leonore Mundy, who gave her address as Mondscheingasse, she had obviously given a false name, which could be explained by the fact that, as she noted in her application, she had not yet given notice concerning her current position with a well-to-do family in Vienna. The applicant claimed that she had sufficient experience in accounting and correspondence to meet all the requirements of the job. Fried selected her in particular because she was multilingual: "I was born and raised in Romania, but I speak and write French, German, Romanian, English, and a little Italian. I can also type and take shorthand."[232]

Over the course of the next few days Fried invited the young woman, whose real name was Rosamunde Schwalb (but she called herself Mundy) to several interviews. On March 18, he finalized a contract with her; she was to be his secretary at a salary of 150 crowns per month.[233] She was a good choice and quickly became indispensable. Both as secretary and friend, she would be at his side until his death. She even immigrated with him to Switzerland in 1915. Even well after his death she remained linked to his family and especially to Therese; from England, she wrote affectionate letters to "Aunt Rose" as late as 1946.[234]

In the first few years, Mundy Schwalb had to prove her talents, especially during Fried's frequent absences from Vienna; it was her job to keep him abreast of all that was happening, to send him important mail, and at the same time to order his affairs or at least prepare them to the extent possible. Fried was usually out of town for days at a time, sometimes weeks. In May he was in Paris, in September in Geneva, in October in Bernburg. In 1913, he was on the road even more often: in the spring he was away for two months and in the summer from the middle of July to September. On July 14, he was supposed to begin a course of treatment in Dr. Lahmann's sanatorium "Weißer Hirsch." It was primarily intended to relieve stress and to make him fit for the following two events—the World Peace Congress and the ceremony at which he was to receive an honorary doctorate. But Fried had overtaxed his energies in the spring and summer of 1913, as he had so often before. "At the moment my

---

232   Letter of application by Leonore Mundy [Rosamunde/Mundy Schwalb] to Fried, March 11, 1912. Nachlass Fried, Box 82.
233   See the contract written by Fried for Mundy Schwalb, March 18, 1912, privately held by Trude Simonsohn.
234   Mundy Schwalb to Therese Fried, Pentecost 1946, privately held by Trude Simonsohn.

nerves are once again a bit frayed and I have to take a break,"[235] he wrote to Wehberg on July 3. Bertha von Suttner noted at the same time: "Fried's nerves are shot. Nicotine poisoning. Agoraphobia."[236] The doctor at the sanatorium prescribed walks, sour milk, gymnastic exercises, and massages. Underlined twice is the entry: "Less smoking."[237]

Accompanied by Therese, Fried traveled from Dresden to The Hague to attend the twentieth World Peace Congress, which took place from August 18 to August 23 and at which Fried was to be one of the speakers. Only five days later he was invited to the official dedication of the Peace Palace there, which was funded by the Carnegie Foundation. But the most important event for Fried—perhaps the most important event in his life—occurred between these two dates: the conferral of an honorary doctorate by the University in Leiden.

Ever since he received the Nobel Peace Prize, Fried had allowed himself to hope that he might attain the academic recognition that he so desired. The first steps in this direction emanated, without his knowledge, from Wehberg, who had made inquiries of the President of Columbia University, Nicholas Murray Butler, in New York in January 1912. Fried was not unknown to Butler. In 1909, Fried had translated an important speech by Butler for inclusion in Fried's *Amerika gegen die Rüstungen* (America against Armaments). Later he worked with Butler as a special correspondent for the Carnegie Foundation (first division), of which Butler was president. Butler responded positively to Wehberg, but he explained that the conferral of an honorary doctorate presupposed that the honoree be present.[238]

The hope for a doctorate in America was thus for the time being impossible, since Fried was not planning such a trip in the near future—and, in fact, never made such a trip. When Wehberg told Fried of his efforts, Fried was touched: "Your kind endeavors with Butler on my behalf have surprised and pleased me enormously. That is truly very kind of you. I admit that an honor of this kind would indeed fulfill a longstanding wish of mine. It won't be possible in Germany, unfortunately; it would sooner happen in Switzerland or in England. In any case, please accept my most heartfelt thanks for your efforts."[239] But Wehberg also received a negative response from Switzerland. From Zurich, Professor Sieveking wrote that he had once before proposed to the faculty of

---

235 Fried to Wehberg, July 3, 1913. Nachlass Wehberg, vol. 59a, BA Koblenz.
236 Diary entry, July 4, 1913, quoted in Hamann, *Bertha von Suttner*, 505.
237 Course of treatment from Dr. Lahmann's sanitorium at "Weißer Hirsch" near Dresden, July 14, 1913 to September 3, 1913. Nachlass Fried, Box 20, file 324.
238 Cf. Butler to Wehberg, January 23, 1912. Nachlass Wehberg, vol. 59a, BA Koblenz.
239 Fried to Wehberg, February 15, 1912. Nachlass Wehberg, vol. 59a, BA Koblenz.

constitutional law that Fried receive an honorary doctorate, but the request had found no resonance, and that at the moment he was not in a position to propose it again.[240] But, he added, it might be possible in two years when the new university was to be dedicated. When a negative response came from England, Wehberg made a request of Athens, but this too was in vain. Then Fried received a surprise telegram on June 18, 1913, which he copied and sent to Wehberg the next day: "In the year of the inauguration of the Peace Palace, the senate of the University in Leiden has awarded you, Asser, Renault, and Root a doctorate *honoris causa* in political science – Rector magnificus Eerdmans"[241]

The unsuccessful schoolboy and apprentice book seller, who was brought up in poverty and who—surrounded by doctors and professors in the leadership of the international peace movement—had struggled for recognition his whole life, finally stood on equal footing with them as a Nobel Prize recipient and as the holder of an honorary doctorate. He was thus officially recognized as an intellectual and scholar, something that he had always considered himself to be.

Of course, Fried suspected that Wehberg was behind the honor: "I don't think I am mistaken in my assumption that you have had a hand in this, admit it. That I am very happy about it, you can be sure."[242] Wehberg answered the next day in an effusive congratulatory letter and admitted to having played an indirect role; among his many efforts in the summer of 1911, he had contacted Professor van Vollenhoven in Leiden, who then presented Wehberg's suggestion to the senate. But, Wehberg added, it was highly unlikely that the current honor had anything to do with that: "They arrived at your name all on their own because you simply were someone to consider in the first place."[243] Moreover, Wehberg predicted an illustrious future for Fried: "It is a great victory that not only you but also our cause has achieved. I predict today that many other greater honors will follow. You will be appointed to the House of Lords. The recognition of your work will have a powerful effect on our opponents. Won't a German university now want to follow this lead?" Fried was skeptical: "Your predictions amuse me. Be assured that I have no further ambitions. I openly admit that I did indeed desire an academic title, but I need nothing more. That this all came so suddenly and unexpectedly was a great surprise. The congratulations are piling up, just like in December 1911. The newspapers in Vienna, as

---

240 Sieveking to Wehberg. Nachlass Wehberg, vol. 59a, BA Koblenz.
241 See the copy of the telegram in Nachlass Wehberg, vol. 59a, BA Koblenz.
242 Fried to Wehberg, June 19, 1913. Nachlass Wehberg, vol. 59a, BA Koblenz.
243 This and the following quote are taken from Wehberg to Fried, June 20, 1913. Nachlass Fried, Box 85

well as the *Berliner Tageblatt*, the *Frankfurter* and the *Vossische* all reported on the award."[244] He observed that he would make use of the academic title since it was important to him, and he wouldn't act as if that were not the case. At the end of the letter, he asked: "Apropos: May I use the title before the meeting in Leiden?"[245]

Wehberg's answer was likely affirmative because the *Friedens-Warte* of July 1913 included, besides the mention of the honorary doctorate, an important note from the Austrian Peace Society that Dr. Alfred Fried had been named to the executive board of the society,[246] which this time he accepted.

The official, written communication of the senate of the university reached Fried in the middle of July 1913: "It is our great honor to inform you, honorable sir, that the senate of the University of Leiden, in its meeting of June 18 of this year, has awarded you the title Doctor of Philosophy, *honoris causa*, in Political Science and thereby extends to you the highest academic honor that it has at its disposal."[247] At the same time, the senate asked Fried whether he would like to personally accept the award at a celebratory senate meeting on August 27. The appointed date was favorable since it would fall between the 20th World Peace Congress, at which Fried's presence was required since he would give a talk entitled "Presse und Friedensbewegung" (The Press and the Peace Movement), and the long-anticipated dedication of the Peace Palace in The Hague on August 28. Fried agreed to go in person to Leiden.

Through his nominator, the *jonkheer*, Professor Willem Jan Marie von Eysinga, Fried learned of the details of the award ceremony: the meeting was set for 4 PM, a toast in the senate chamber was to follow as well as an evening dinner, to which the law faculty invited the newly awarded doctors. Eysinga himself took care of the travel plans from The Hague to Leiden, the welcome at the train station, and the seat reservations for Therese and several other pacifist friends who wanted to accompany Fried. He also provided suggestions about what to wear: "When degrees are conferred, the members of the Senate dress formally with a white tie and medals of distinction; I would recommend that you do the same so that you do not have to change before dinner and you will be able to spend a half-hour at leisure with one of the professors after the celebrations."[248] Eysinga also sent along the speech that he, Eysinga, was to give

---

244   Fried to Wehberg, June 25, 1913. Nachlass Wehberg, vol. 59a, BA Koblenz.
245   Ibid. Underlined, by hand, in the original.
246   *Friedens-Warte* 15, no. 7 (July 1913): 279.
247   Senaat der Rijks-Universiteit Leiden to Prof.[!] A. H. Fried, July 10, 1913. Nachlass Fried, Box 57.
248   Eysinga to Fried, August 20, 1913. Nachlass Fried, Box 57.

at the award ceremony. It was exactly the kind of academic recognition that Fried had long hoped to receive: "In full acknowledgement of your vast and inspirational work as a journalist, the senate of the University of Leiden has bestowed upon you the title 'doctor honoris causa,' that is to say, it would like to express its full recognition of the inherent and essentially academic value of your work. Free of any exclusively sentimental pacifism, your numerous writings stand on the positive foundation of international law, a law that can no longer be denied. In contrast to others who depict pacifism in a fragmentary manner—without an understanding of the whole—you offer a full picture that every educated person can understand but also one that can provide even legal specialists with new avenues of exploration. Please accept, most esteemed Mr. Fried, this honorary doctorate with the assurance that the academic importance of your work has found its due appreciation at this institution, which is dedicated to the pursuit of pure knowledge."[249]

For Fried, this honor and his recognition as a serious researcher was much more important than his acceptance of the Nobel Peace Prize. Unfortunately, the speech he gave is no longer extant. But the tone of the speech can clearly be seen in a description by Elsbeth Friedrichs: "In his short but characteristic speech on the significance of his honorary doctorate h. c., Dr. Alfred H. Fried, now the academically acknowledged exponent of scientific pacifism, emphasized in a modest and personal way that he was pleased to accept the honor on behalf of the peace movement, and in so doing he has in fact done nothing less than pave the way for the entry of a new science into the history of humankind."[250]

The German press took even less notice of this award than it had of his Nobel Prize. In an article of nineteen lines entitled "Zur Einweihung des Haager Friedenspalastes" (On the Dedication of the Peace Palace in The Hague) only the *Kölnische Zeitung* reported on the awarding of the doctorate to Renault, Root, and Fried. It noted: "Fried explained that the honor is not his alone but that it also belongs to the great idea of the peace movement."[251]

To Fried, however, the clearly increasing social prestige that accompanied the title was important. Combined with the fact that by virtue of the Nobel Prize he was no longer impoverished, the official ascent into the ranks of the educated finally garnered him a position among the middle-class intellectuals (*Bildungsbürgertum*), one that he had always aspired to. As an external sign of

---

249 Manuscript of a speech by Prof. von Eysinga at the degree award ceremony in Leiden. Nachlass Fried, Box 5
250 *Friedens-Warte* 15, no. 9 (September 1913): 335.
251 *Stadtanzeiger der Kölnischen Zeitung*, August 30, 1913.

the change, Fried moved into a newly built apartment in 1913 in the "Dürwaringer Hof" at Bastiengasse 54, on the outer limits of Währing. It was a large garden apartment on the third floor with a balcony. In addition to the four rooms, it also contained another small room, a kitchen, a bath, and a vestibule, as well as a room for servants, and, as stated explicitly in the description, a toilet.[252] Given the size of the apartment and the steep yearly rent of 3,000 crowns, it was a luxury apartment for the childless couple, and it certainly marked Fried's social ascent. At 49 years of age, he seemed to have reached the goal of his youthful dreams and to have finally left the "morass" of his youth behind him.

9 Before the Great War

But his happiness was short-lived. In spite of his personal triumphs, Fried followed the conflicts in the Balkans very closely and commented on them in the *Friedens-Warte* with a mixture of helplessness, rage, and hope.[253] When the first Balkan War broke out in October 1912, he wrote cynically under the headline "Die Propaganda der Tat" (The Propaganda of the Deed): "In the Balkans, 'active' politics is being created. That is to say, one attempts to gain an advantage through means that appear antediluvian to us today, namely the crushing of human bone and the shredding of human tissue as well as the incineration and destruction of property."[254]

The pacifists could do nothing but use the written and spoken word to confront these medieval ideas. Fried could then hope that the experiences and predictable misery of this war, which he thought the great powers of Europe could have and should have prevented, would contribute to the "propaganda of the deed" for pacifism. It was clear to him that the spark could quickly leap onto all of Europe, and he asked, what the scope of the "propaganda of the deed" in the end might look like: "Must we experience a general European debacle before Europe can be organized in the way that it needs to be organized? On the day when the civilized people of Europe, thanks to the narrow-mindedness

---

252 Cf. the correspondence with Josef Bauer, who rented the rooms to Fried, in Nachlass Fried, Box 48 and the floor plan in Box 7, file 25.

253 Cf. Fried's article "Der Krieg am Balkan," *Friedens-Warte* 14, no. 11 (November, 1912): 401–403; "Krise," *Friedens-Warte* 15, no. 1 (January 1913): 1–2; "Die Überwindung des Balkankonflikts," *Friedens-Warte* 15, no. 5 (May, 1913): 161–63; "Der dritte Balkankrieg," *Friedens-Warte* 15, no. 7 (July, 1913): 241–42; "Der Balkankrieg als pazifistisches Dokument," *Friedens-Warte* 15, no. 12 (December, 1912): 441–443.

254 *Friedens-Warte* 14, no. 10 (October 1912): 363. The following quotation is from the same volume, page 364.

of their diplomats and the weakness of their governments, go about slitting each other's throats, we will wash our hands in innocence. We have expended the whole of our life's energy to warn them [...] Pacifism can emerge victorious from this broad European war, but this is not the only way to prevail."

In the early weeks and months of the war, Fried considered it important that precise and critical coverage of the war from the pacifist perspective be maintained, and, in November, he criticized the treatment of reporters and the budding censorship of the press: "The war is being prosecuted without the public's awareness. It is not as if the reporters had been excluded [...] no, they have been incarcerated in concentration camps [...]. Full of trust, the gentlemen were allowed to enter headquarters; respect of all kinds was shown to them, they had access to all kinds of comforts—it was just that they could not carry out their duty as reporters. They were not allowed to report on anything that had not been submitted beforehand to a censor."[255] According to Fried, there was a concerted effort not to give the "parties opposed to the war any effective ammunition." This was also the reason why the cinema was censored in Europe. It was to prevent normal citizens from seeing any films that may have been made at the front: "One does not want to prevent war, but, for reasons of morality, one does aim to prevent reflection on the war by non-participants."

Fried, nevertheless, was able to detect some positive signs in the course of the conflict. He had some confidence that the turmoil in the Balkans would temporarily lead to a coalition of the European Great Powers.[256] In May 1913, he saw in the temporary abatement of the conflict a precedent for Europe: "The dissolution of the Balkans has passed without a European war. Can one imagine a crisis on this earth that can only be solved by bloodshed? The influence and effective powers of the pacifists, which have prevented a European clash in this crisis [...] have created values of the highest order for the future. The war of 1913, which was in fact prevented, has put an end to the use of war as a means to resolve all future European disputes."[257]

While he still believed, even as late as December 1913, that peace would come to the Balkans,[258] the much-feared greater war seemed to him to have been prevented at least for the short term. In his "Pazifistische Chronik 1913" (Pacifist Chronicle 1913), which he would send out "as the author's New Year's greeting" to his friends and acquaintances for the last time, he wrote: "One

---

255 "Der Krieg am Balkan," *Friedens-Warte* 14, no. 11 (November 1912): 401. This is also the source of the following quotation.
256 Cf. Fried, "Im Namen Europas," *Friedens-Warte* 15, no. 4 (April 1913): 121ff.
257 "Die Überwindung des Balkankonflikts," *Friedens-Warte* 15, no. 5 (May 1913): 161.
258 Cf. Fried, "Der Balkankrieg als pazifistisches Dokument," *Friedens-Warte* 15, no. 12 (December 1912): 441ff.

can note that the greatest event of this year is that the fire that burned in the Balkans did not leap over to Europe."[259] He believed that the reason for this could be found in the fact that alongside the excessive arms build-up of the European states one could also recognize a "partially developed organization of states," which would then have "a preventative impact."

As early as 1912 Fried had expressed his views on the Triple Alliance[260] and concluded that it was simply outdated for the times. However, he did believe that it could promote peace indirectly and unintentionally since it could help prevent the outbreak of a hot war and grant more time for the further development of an international organization of states, which he considered necessary to transform the current state of non-war into one of true peace and to convert the existing alliance systems into a "union of European states."[261]

Fried hoped that the European powers that could prevent a war would maintain the upper hand, and he tried to support these forces from Vienna, because here, not far from the flash point, was where the great World Peace Congress was set to gain the public's attention.

The Austrian pacifists wanted to catch up to their neighbors since up to that point Austria had not served as a host for the congress while Germany had already held two such conferences (1897 in Hamburg, 1907 in Munich). At the same time, the members of the Austrian Peace Society hoped for a positive impact on their own society, which to that point had shown only rather weak growth. They also hoped for a role as an intermediary between the West and the Balkan states, whose participation in the World Peace congresses had been somewhat limited. Precisely the events of 1912–1913 had shown how important a strengthening of the Slavic pacifists could be for Europe. In addition, there was hope that Italy would become more engaged so that the Austro-Italian Friendship Committee, which was evolving only rather slowly, could also be given new life. The one-hundredth anniversary of the Congress of Vienna 1814–1815, "which formed the foundation of today's Europe,"[262] therefore offered the Austrian pacifists a welcome opportunity to host the congress. The driving

---

259 Fried, *Der Weg zum Weltfrieden im Jahre 1913. Pazifistische Chronik* (Berlin, Vienna, Leipzig, undated [1913]), 4. The following quote is also taken from this source.

260 Fried, "Der Dreibund und die Friedensfrage," in *Der Dreibund*, ed. Siegfried Flesch (Leipzig, 1912), 7–15. With contributions from A. H. Fried, G. Hildebrand, Timon, Prof. A. Ghisleri, and Bernhard Stern.

261 Fried introduced the concept "Zweckverband Europa" (Common Purpose Europe) in March 1912 in an editorial whose title was also "Zweckverband Europa." See *Friedens-Warte* 14, no. 3 (March 1912): 81–84. Later, he incorporated it into his program (page 62, point B3) in the second edition of *Grundlagen des revolutionären (ursächlichen) Pazifismus*. It does not yet appear in the *Handbuch* (1911/1913).

262 *Friedens-Warte* 15, no. 7 (July 1913): 269.

force behind this idea was Fried himself. At the first meeting of the executive committee of the Austrian Peace Society in mid-October 1913, he was not only officially chosen to be on the board—together with Rudolf Goldscheid—but he was also elected to the three-member executive committee that was charged with planning the congress. Bertha von Suttner and Alexander von Dorn, a member of the Viennese city council, worked with him on this committee.[263]

The tasks were enormous.[264] In the heated atmosphere of the capital, the result of the numerous espionage affairs, neither the sought-after fellow campaigners from the upper classes nor the anticipated subventions were forthcoming. In addition, during the winter of 1913–1914 Emperor Franz Josef once again took seriously ill, which raised doubts about whether the congress would actually take place.[265]

But it was not only the difficulties within the empire that needed to be overcome. At The Hague, a resolution of the general assembly of the Berne Peace Bureau was passed in August 1913; it mandated completely new rules for the organization of the events of the congress. This led to some early delays since the new rules were not passed in Berne until the middle of March 1914, and the committee in Vienna had thus no sound basis for planning.[266] In addition, in March, the dates of the congress (September 7–17) had to be shifted by a week since it was learned that the twenty-ninth conference of the International Law Association and an international conference on education, sponsored by the Dutch government, were to be held in the same week.[267] Nevertheless, the small planning committee, spurred forward by Fried, was able to overcome these hurdles. In May, Fried proudly reported that the Austrian foreign minister, Count Berchtold, had agreed to become the president of the honorary committee.[268]

By early June, the various committees had been formed and the program was finalized despite Bertha von Suttner's serious illness.[269] While Fried served as the chairman of the executive committee, Fried's wife Therese and Marie Goldscheid, Rudolf Goldscheid's spouse, were members of the Women's Committee, and Mundy Schwalb worked in the secretary's office. The program that had been prepared was ready for the public to view: in addition to a gala

---

263   Cf. "Protokoll der Vorstandssitzung vom 14 October 1913," in Nachlass Fried, Box 12a, file 237.
264   How extensive the preparatory work must have been can be seen in the working documents in Nachlass Fried, Box 12a and 12b.
265   Cf. *Friedens-Warte* 16, no. 8 (August/September 1914): 318.
266   Cf. *Friedens-Warte* 16, no. 2 (February 1914).
267   Cf. *Friedens-Warte* 16, no. 3 (March 1914): 120.
268   *Friedens-Warte* 16, no. 5 (May 1914): 199.
269   On the following, see *Friedens-Warte* 16, no. 6 (June 1914): 235–240.

performance by the Court Opera, an excursion to the Kahlenberg, and a closing banquet sponsored by the city of Vienna, there was to be the premiere of the just completed film, "Die Waffen nieder!" by Nordisk Films Co. from Copenhagen, a film based on the eponymous book by Bertha von Suttner. At the end of April 1914, a camera team had filmed the author at her desk for the opening credits.[270]

Unexpectedly, the film took on a whole new significance. While the work for the conference was underway, the seventy-nine-year-old Bertha von Suttner grew increasingly weaker and tired.[271] In April, she began to suffer from nausea and indigestion, harbingers of the later diagnosis of stomach cancer. Since she rejected any nourishment besides milk, she grew still weaker. On June 13, before departing for Paris, Fried spoke with Bertha von Suttner for the last time. When he returned home on the morning of June 21, he was alarmed at the news of her condition, and he rushed to her apartment with Therese, but the baroness was already unconscious. Ten minutes later she was dead. At her bedside were the Frieds, her niece Luise, her servant, and the attending physician. For Fried, the death of his long-time friend was a harsh blow: "Suttner's death has hit me hard, because now there is one less person in Vienna who understands our work."[272]

Presumably it was the animated intellectual exchange that Fried missed most, but he no doubt also missed his friend's abiding support and encouragement. As an expression of sympathy, the July edition of *Die Friedens-Warte* was dedicated to the memory of Bertha von Suttner. The title page featured a poem by Herbert Eulenberg commemorating her death. In the introduction Fried likely described his own feelings when he wrote: "She did not take her own death too seriously, and so it will be all the more difficult for us to come to terms with it. It is as if a new chapter in our lives, in our work, is about to begin. [...] A later generation will come to view her legacy as a palladium. For us, who have lived with her and campaigned with her, the bitter sorrow that this great individual, to whom we had grown so accustomed, will never disappear as long as we shall live. Our own lives have suffered a great loss with her death. The burden of ennui that has come over us will weigh on us as long as

---

270 On the history of the film, see Andrew Kelly, "Film as Antiwar Propaganda. Lay Down your Arms, 1914" in *Peace and Change* 16, no. 1 (January 1991): 97–112. Since the war prevented the premiere of the film, Fried himself was only able to see the film in December 1916 while he was in exile in Switzerland.
271 Cf. Hamann, *Bertha von Suttner*, 512ff. and the article by Fried, "Die letzte Lebenszeit," *Friedens-Warte* 16, no. 7 (July 1914): 248ff.
272 Fried an Wehberg, July 9, 1914, in Nachlass Wehberg, vol. 59a, BA Koblenz.

we continue to work."[273] But he also quickly saw the new task before him: "Our life's mission now, which has been bestowed on us like a sacred duty, is to preserve her memory, to maintain the weapons that she has given us." Fried would in fact cherish the memory of Bertha von Suttner in the roughly seven years that he had to live, and he would commemorate the anniversary of her death. He would forever endeavor to prevent her writings from falling into obscurity.

Bertha von Suttner left Fried a sizeable inheritance upon her death. A year earlier she had made him the sole heir of her entire literary estate; besides the royalties of the already published works, this included the possibility of future publications. In August 1914, Fried was able to begin compiling and editing *Randglossen zur Zeitgeschichte* (Commentaries on Contemporary History), which had appeared in the journals *Die Waffen nieder* and in the *Friedens-Warte*. It was published in 1916, midway through the war. Later he would make an effort—albeit unsuccessful—to obtain permission to publish her diaries.

In addition, Fried now had to worry about the absence of a leader of the Austrian Peace Society. Three days after Bertha von Suttner's death, he was elected in absentia executive vice-president in a meeting of the executive board. It was not considered appropriate to elect a new president at the time, but arrangements had been made for Fried to take over. According to a motion by Balduin Groller,[274] a member of the executive board, "[...] the man who appears most competent by virtue of his writings, his great passion for our cause, and finally by the international reputation that he has acquired over course of his life is our Nobel Prize recipient Dr. Alfred H. Fried, who will take over the position of executive vice-president. [...] We will postpone the selection of a president until after the holidays when we will be able to do justice to the urgent demands of the day. I believe that everyone will be of the opinion that this qualified pacifist should take the place of our deceased baroness."[275]

Fried thus also became the heir to Bertha von Suttner in the peace society. However, he would have little more to do with the society, since the board officially held its final meeting on July 20, 1914. While there were some meetings afterward, two of which were directed personally by Fried (on August 7 and on September 11), the Austrian Peace Society was officially prohibited from conferring about anything but humanitarian relief at this time.

---

273 *Friedens-Warte* 16, no. 7 (July 1914): 242f.
274 Balduin Groller, actually Adalbert Goldscheider (1848–1916), was a famous popular writer in Vienna and confidant of Berta von Suttner.
275 "Protokoll der Vorstandssitzung der Österreichischen Friedensgesellschaft vom 24. Juni 1914," in *Friedens-Warte* 16, no. 7 (July 1914): 275f.

In the July-August issue of the *Friedens-Warte,* Fried announced the changes in the program for the upcoming congress: on the evening of September 17 there was to be a memorial service instead of the planned festive gathering: "On the same day the screening of the film *Die Waffen nieder!* will serve as a commemoration of the deceased. [...] And so, we will be able to see Bertha von Suttner one more time alive and at work."[276]

Although the death of Bertha von Suttner was indeed a hard blow for Fried and the Austrian Peace Society, the preliminary work for the congress continued. Even the assassination in Sarajevo only slightly interfered with the work. Fried evidently did not believe that the murder of the heir to the Austro-Hungarian throne was of any greater significance than similar events in years before. In the *Friedens-Warte,* he published an article[277] on this topic, having changed only the names in a similar article by Bertha von Suttner, which she had written on the occasion of assassinations of King Karl I of Portugal and the crown prince. In her article, she mainly criticized the difference between the way society views the killing of individuals and that of mass killings on the battlefield. Fried emphasized his certainty that Bertha von Suttner would have written a comparable article on the "catastrophe of Sarajevo."

In an attached commentary, he saw the cause of the assassination above all in the militaristic *Zeitgeist* and the "nationalistic demagoguery," "which is artificially cultivated in many parts of Europe in order to demonstrate the necessity of an arms buildup." So he objected vehemently to the agitation directed against Serbia. It is also clear that Fried quite obviously underestimated the danger: "The assassin at Sarajevo and his co-conspirators are Serbians. This is enough to cause some blinded patriots and their newspapers to intensify their agitation against Serbia and to demand war. The assassin was a schoolboy. By the same logic one could demand that all schools be closed."[278]

But by this point, it was clear that the matter did not involve only a few blinded patriots, as Fried seemed to believe. The extent to which Fried followed and analyzed the developments of the next couple of days and weeks cannot be fully determined (if he did so at all) since his work on the congress left him little time for his usual correspondence. Even Wehberg only occasionally heard from him. The last pre-war letter, dated July 9, 1914,[279] contains no indication of his fear that war may be on the horizon; on the contrary, Fried wrote, "I'm in a

---

276   Ibid, 277.
277   Ibid, 269.
278   Ibid.
279   Fried to Wehberg, July 9, 1914, in Nachlass Wehberg, vol. 59b, BA Koblenz.

hurry because I have a great deal of work to do," but he also noted that he was pleased that Wehberg was bringing his wife to the congress in Vienna.

Even at the end of July, the planning committee still thought that the congress would take place since it had just learned that the Austrian ministries agreed to make a financial contribution to the congress. Later on, Fried wrote: "One day before the memorandum to Serbia the Finance Ministry approved a considerable amount of money so that the congress could be held [...] The Ministry of the Interior requested materials on July 21 to prepare for the opening of the congress and even the War Ministry informed the committee on July 27 that it would send delegates to the congress."[280]

Reassured by the intentions of these offices, the action committee did not decide to cancel the congress until July 30, two days after Austria-Hungary declared war on Serbia. Months of intensive, exhausting work had been in vain. What remained was a shortfall of some 4,000 crowns and the feeling of gratification that the congress in Vienna would have been one of the largest world peace conferences ever.[281] On the same day, Fried called a special meeting of the board. The main agenda item was to pass a resolution, presumably written by Fried himself, that would be published in the August-September edition of the *Friedens-Warte* along with the second flyer of the German Peace Society of August 15, 1914 and other documents illuminating the activities of pacifists.

The resolution stated that the executive board of the Austria Peace Society recognized the "severity of the complaints that the government of the monarchy has raised against its southern neighbor," but it regretted that no peaceful means in accordance with The Hague Convention had been attempted to resolve the matter. In addition, the resolution stated that the war had disproved the principle "si vis pacem, para bellum" and had actually demonstrated the necessity of a modern approach to peace. Finally, the board expressed the hope "that a quick return to normal social conditions would make it possible for the society to work for the welfare of our fatherland along those lines." With this resolution, the society essentially stopped its political activity.[282]

---

280   *Friedens-Warte* 16, no. 8 (August/September 1914): 319. Emphasized in part in the original. The attitude of the Minister of War seems to demonstrate that the Austrians were initially not so eager to wage war against Serbia, but ultimately did so because of German pressure. (Cf. *Die europäische Krise und der Ausbruch des Ersten Weltkriegs*, ed. Imanuel Geiss (Munich, 2nd 1980), 21f.) It is possible that on July 27 parts of the ministry had not yet been informed about Austro-Hungary's intention to declare war on Serbia the next day. But it is also possible that the pacifists, because of their international connections, were consciously left out of the loop regarding the plans for war.
281   Ibid, 319. The following notes are based on the same text, 309.
282   Since there have been no new studies of the history of the Austrian Peace Society or its activities during the World War, apart from Josef Bauer's dissertation *Die Österreichische*

On July 31, the council of the International Peace Bureau in Brussels, of which Fried was a member, convened a special meeting to consider their future activities. All the nations were represented at the meeting, with the exception of Austria, which, according to its own records, received notice too late.[283] Since all the participants were invited by telegraph and delays in the communication system had already begun, it is quite possible that the invitation did arrive late. On the other hand, it cannot to be ruled out that at this point in time Fried shied away from discussing Austrian politics with the representatives of the other nations. At any rate, the resolution of the Austrian Peace Society did recognize the gravity of the accusations against Serbia and so placed itself, more or less, on the side of the government. By contrast, even the German Peace Society had judged the situation more critically in its first flyer of July 29: "The Austro-Hungarian government has made demands intended to guarantee not only the satisfaction of its well-justified claims, which have been patiently put on hold for quite some time, but also to deeply humiliate the Serbian state in both form and content, as the whole world can see. In so doing, it has taken on a profound responsibility."[284]

Fried spent the first week of August waiting and hoping that "something must yet happen that can put an end to this madness."[285] He felt helpless and overwhelmed by the speed of the events: "That is what is frightening, the suddenness, the surprise,"[286] he noted. In the general euphoria of the first days of the war he felt alone, misunderstood, and isolated, which was further intensified by the fact that letters from friends and fellow pacifists were delayed by days and weeks.[287]

Friedensbewegung (Vienna, 1949), the question about what possible political activities or meetings the members may have undertaken during the war must remain unanswered. It seems, however, that only within the association "Para Pacem" might activities other than those of a humanitarian nature been undertaken.

283   Cf. Helmut Mauermann, *Das Internationale Friedensbüro 1892 bis 1950* (Stuttgart, 1990), 148. Cf. also the report "Die außerordentliche Sitzung des Berner Büros," in *Friedens-Warte* 16, no. 8 (August/September 1914): 310.

284   First flyer of the war by the German Peace Society, Munich and Stuttgart, July 20, 1914. Kriegsflugblätter ZSp. 1–29/13, BA Koblenz.

285   Fried, *Kriegs-Tagebuch I*, foreword, viif.

286   *Friedens-Warte* 16, no. 8 (August/September 1914): 282. The text can also be found in Fried, *Kriegs-Tagebuch I*, 2.

287   Cf. Fried, *Kriegs-Tagebuch I*, 19. Other pacifists also suffered from isolation. In a telegram that Quidde wrote to Fried on August 13, which was to inform Fried of the death of Adolf Richter, he mentioned that he too had received "no news from Vienna, Berne, and Brussels." Nachlass Fried, Box 77.

It is unclear whether the Fried family was seized by the war euphoria. Photos of Fried's brother Otto in uniform, striking a proud pose,[288] possibly suggest that he joined the military as a volunteer, something that his sick brother Leopold in Berlin would not have been able to do even if he had wanted to. Dr. Bernhard von Jacobi,[289] a resident of Munich and the husband of Therese's niece Lucy, with whom Fried and his wife enjoyed an especially close relationship, was ordered to report to the western front as a staff sergeant during the first few days of the war, but not as a volunteer; a few months later he was killed. Of the rest of the family there is evidence that only Fried's uncle, Ludwig Ganghofer, was enthusiastic about the war. Toward the end of 1914 he published a book of war songs with the title *Eiserne Zither*[290] that glorified the war. A reviewer of the book for the Freemasons' newspaper observed: "But the intense experience, which this tremendous war represents for him, gives the book tones of particular allure and unique power. It is a war in which he would have gladly participated as a soldier, but, rejected as a volunteer, he can only watch with envy as his son and son-in-law go off to war."[291]

In early January 1915, Ganghofer traveled to the "Supreme Headquarters" as a war correspondent on behalf of the German government and then to the front. Just as an advertisement says,[292] not only did he give the people an understanding of Germany's leading military figures, for example, the "highly regarded and profound pronouncements" of the emperor, but he also depicted "the horror and the grandeur of the new war" and the young soldiers "who in steadfast heroism emulate the glory that their fathers had earned."

In contrast to the enthusiasm of his uncle, with whom Fried admittedly had only slight contact for a number of years (as opposed to his sister Sidonie who had a better relationship with him), Fried was essentially paralyzed by the impact of the events. While he did not have to fear being drafted since he had already received his discharge papers[293] in 1906 from the Viennese imperi-

---

288 Privately held by Trude Simonsohn.
289 Bernhard von Jacobi (1880–1949) was an actor who, in 1907, married Lucy Goldberg from Vienna, a daughter of Therese's sister. Cf. also NDB, vol. 10, 221. Vgl. Fried, *Kriegs-Tagebuch* I, 142f. (October 27, 1914).
290 Ludwig Ganghofer, *Eiserne Zither. Kriegslieder* (Stuttgart, 1914).
291 *Der Zirkel* 45, no. 5/6 (November 1914): 64.
292 Advertisement in the *Börsenblatt für den deutschen Handel* 82, no. 96 (April 26, 1915) in *Aus alten Bösenblättern*, ed. Klaus Gerhard Saur (Munich, 1964), 164.
293 Document of the royal-imperial home guard command (k.k. Landsturmbezirkskommando) No. 1 in Vienna, dated December 31, 1906: "Alfred Hermann Fried, born in Vienna in 1864, registered in the federal state of Lower Austria, served in the army with the infantry regiment no. 44 and no. 4 for 10 years and 3 months as an infantry soldier, and then further with the militia no. 1 (Landwehr-Infanterieregiment) for two years as an infantry

al-royal local militia (*Landsturmbezirkskommando Nr. 1*), his outlook remained unchanged. In the first entry in his diary (August 7, 1914), he described his mood: "A horrific pain troubles me. The war weighs on me like hundred-kilo weights. As if every one of life's values were suffocated. [...] Since July 25, the day when relations between Austria and Serbia were broken off, I have not been able to work or to read a book. Restless, I just hang out. I read the newspaper and wait for the next editions. I am unable to work or think."[294] Nevertheless, on this evening he led a meeting of the executive board of the Austrian Peace Society, which did little more than confer about the distribution of the donations to the public, the Red Cross, and the families of reservists.[295]

Only gradually did Fried find his way back to his work. His main concern was the continuation of the *Friedens-Warte* and the layout of its contents. The outbreak of the war complicated his communication with his printer in Berlin and with his authors. He was unable to publish the August edition, which had been completed before the war, since the proofs were not sent from Berlin until August 1 and they took several weeks to get to Fried. In any case, the content of the journal of August 1 was already obsolete. But in September Fried succeeded in publishing a double-edition, which he filled primarily with his own articles. His *Kriegs-Tagebuch* (War Diary), which he began on August 7, provided the bulk (16 pages) of the main section of the journal: "I wanted to express my feelings, my insights, my fears and my hopes. I wanted to capture the events and discuss them from a pacifist perspective, to make clear the mistakes of the past in the course of this disease in feverish Europe and to point the way to recovery."[296] However, the concept of "diary" is misleading in as much as it implies intimate, uncensored entries, since: "From the very beginning it was my intention to publish my entries at least in fragmentary form. They were supposed to appear monthly in my *Friedens-Warte*, which was published in Berlin. But I wrote them down in Vienna, where I was living. This set of circumstances can explain the detectable reserve and the euphemisms that I chose in the first months of the war."

The diary also formed the bulk of the next issue of the journal (October 1914), which appeared for the final time as a full forty-page issue in Berlin. The views that Fried expressed became a bone of contention for the national

---

soldier. He is entitled to wear the Jubilee-Memorial-Medal (Jubiläums-Erinnerungs-Medaille). After he completed his service with the home guard, he received this official certificate." Privately held by Trude Simonsohn, not in Nachlass Fried.

294   Fried, *Kriegs-Tagebuch*, I, 1 (August 7, 1914).
295   Cf. *Friedens-Warte* 16, no. 8 (August/September 1914): 320 and 319.
296   For this and the subsequent note, see *Kriegs-Tagebuch* I, viii.

press in Germany and Austria, and they then also involved the board of censors. Beginning in November, the censors closely monitored the *Friedens-Warte* and, ultimately, were the reason why its operations were moved to Switzerland. In the end, Fried tried to keep a moderate tone because he did not want to lose sympathy for his cause in Germany or in Austria—but he only partially succeeded. "The *Kriegstagebuch* (War Diary) gives me a great deal of encouragement, but it is also the cause of many odious attacks in the German press. I can indeed only publish "fragments" since today one cannot say everything that one would like to say. I have to sound creditable for the coming battle in Germany and Austria."[297]

Indeed, the first issue of September triggered responses in various German newspapers that were filled with biting polemic. The first to make his voice heard was Professor Benno Imendörffer from Vienna in an article in the *Süddeutsche Zeitung* in October 1914. The inflammatory article, entitled "Aus dem Tagebuch eines 'Pazifisten'" (From the Diary of a 'Pacifist'), was framed by a quote from Treitschke and a heroic poem.[298] Imendörffer called Fried "the most famous champion of the butter-soft idea of peace" and defamed him, in spite of his Austrian citizenship, as a "perfect representative, by disposition and career, of an international kind of literature that does not bear any trace of nationalism." Imendörffer was most concerned with Fried's *Tagebuch,* which, he observed, "takes up two-thirds of this annoying journal." The professor was especially agitated at the "emasculated nationalism of the peace sentimentalists," who denied first that the German Empire was fighting for its existence and then also that only a complete defeat of the Western powers could guarantee a longer European peace. In addition, Imendörffer discovered "veiled attacks on the German Empire," which could be found both in the insinuation that the Germans were fighting a preventative war and also in the effort to protect England. He wrote: "The passages in which the author's veiled animosity toward everything German and his preference for the allegedly 'cultured nations of the west' are clearly in evidence and are too numerous to be fully addressed here." Imendörffer then rigorously opposed the implied goals of the pacifists, namely, to mediate for a quick and honorable peace agreement that did not harm either side, since he was certain that this would inevitably harm the German empire given the pro-western attitude of the pacifists. He concluded his article with this sentence: "From the German perspective, the

---

297 Fried to Dr. John Mez, December 1, 1914. Wiener Stadt- und Landesbibliothek, collection of handwritten documents, LN 225.950.
298 Prof. Dr. Benno Imendörffer, "Aus dem Tagebuch eines 'Pazifisten," *Süddeutsche Zeitung* 46 (28 October 1914), supplement "Aus großer Zeit." The following quotes are taken from this source.

activity of the 'friends of peace' seems to be, simply put, dangerous to the public not only for as long as the war lasts but also for as long as negotiation for the subsequent peace takes place."

This is only one example of a series of similar attacks in the German-speaking press. More factual but at the same time no less aggressive is the article, for example, by the university professor (Privatdozent) in Heidelberg W. Schoenborn; it appeared in the *Kölnische Zeitung* and was likely the cause of the censor's intervention regarding *Die Friedens-Warte* in mid-November. Quite similar tones were heard at the same time in the Austrian journal *Roseggers Heimgarten*, which, under the direction of the writer Peter Rosegger, had previously quite clearly taken the pacifists' side,[299] but now under his son Hans Ludwig had noticeably sailed into the nationalistic straits. In the column "Postkarten des 'Heimgartens'" (Postcards of the "Home Garden") of December 1914, Hans Ludwig Rosegger addressed someone from Bosnia who had written a letter to the editor: "I share your dismay at the publication of the *Kriegstagebuch* of Alfred H. Fried in the *Friedens-Warte*. The 'pacifist' shows sympathy for the barbarism of the French and the Belgians and excuses it [...] and then incriminates Germany and Austria! We are all friends of peace—but not of emasculation, infamy, and even treason—and precisely for that reason we condemn the whining of Mr. Fried, who from enemy territory belittles our strength and our power, and in doing so he reduces the imminent, favorable prospects for peace."[300]

At first view it may surprise us that the diary, published in a relatively "small trade journal," caused such a stir. But the real reason for the uproar can be found in a paragraph by Imendörffer where he wrote that the diary "makes quite clear, indeed frighteningly clear, what we, especially we Germans, can expect from the other side if the 'pacifists' are able to participate in the final peace talks. From this perspective, the diary writer's emotional outpourings, in themselves trivial and insignificant, are dangerous; incredibly, this man is in close contact with many influential men who have been infected with the plague of peace."

In fact, by virtue of their international connections, the pacifists were held to be much more influential than they actually were. Additionally, since the *Friedens-Warte* was read abroad, in particular in Holland and in the United States, it was feared that Fried's comments about a preventative war and his other critical remarks could influence the neutral states to take the side of the Western powers and provide propaganda for the oppositional press.

---

299   Cf. Hamann, *Bertha von Suttner*, 156.
300   *Roseggers Heimgarten* (Graz) 39, no. 3 (December 1914): 240.

After the death of Bertha von Suttner, the attacks on Fried by the nationalistic press had nearly seamlessly found a new target among the pacifists. But he was not particularly suitable for mockery and ridicule; both Fried's character and the times themselves challenged most of the journalists to a more serious examination. Precisely his denunciation as a "dangerous person," however, made living in Vienna more and more precarious.

Fried felt this right away, and, by August, he was likely toying with the idea of leaving Vienna; at any rate, he granted power of attorney to his lawyer, Dr. Emil Frankl, which permitted Frankl "to have the same power as he does over his existing bank account at the Wiener Bank, and in particular to withdraw money and receive money in his name, to give orders to purchase or sell securities, to invest securities, to take receipt of all of the correspondence that was sent to him, to take care of his account with the Wiener Bank-Verein, and to disencumber the same."[301]

On September 11, Fried presided over a meeting of the executive board of the Austrian Peace Society for the final time, at least for the time being. At the meeting, he reported to those present that one could not rule out the notion that the board of directors of the Berne Bureau would soon come together in a more permanent manner and that he intended "to participate in this meeting as a member of the board."[302]

But it was not until October that Fried was prepared to realize this plan and—temporarily, as he believed—move to Switzerland. There was nothing more to do in Vienna for this pacifist, and as a journalist he also saw little possibility for actually doing something. Even within the groups of journalists that were friendly to him he felt marginalized, especially when the Austro-Hungarian army was forced to make a large-scale retreat in September 1914: "Among my journalist friends it was asserted yesterday that now is the time to consciously lie, i.e., to portray the mood as confident and strong. I claimed that that would be Jesuit morality. But – that's just part of war. Instilling hatred and demonstrating confidence are essential weapons."

But Fried was not willing to become a part of that weapon. Instead, he wanted to find out and depict what was really going on and to continue his work for peace—now for a true peace in the future. Berne, the capital of neutral Switzerland, seat of the embassies and of the International Peace Bureau and located in the German-speaking part of the country, seemed to be the most suitable place.[303]

---

301 Dr. Emil Frankl received Fried's power of attorney in August 1914. Nachlass Fried, Box 91a.
302 *Friedens-Warte* 16, no. 8 (August/September 1914): 320.
303 Fried, *Kriegs-Tagebuch*, I, 111 (September 9, 1914).

CHAPTER 4

In Swiss Exile 1914/15–1919

1   The Move to Berne

On October 18, 1914, in the evening, Fried traveled with his wife Therese from Vienna to Zurich; from there, the couple moved on to Berne where they were welcomed on October 20 by Otfried Nippold and Walther Schücking. The reunion was the result of a desire to form a new committee headed by the former director of the *Frankfurter Zeitung*, Dr. Curti; the committee was to study the basic principles of a durable peace treaty.[1] For Fried, this now became the main task of pacifism.

As a neutral state, Switzerland was an appropriate place for this task. In a letter to the American John Mez, Fried noted: "Since mid-October, I have been in Switzerland with my wife to breathe in the freer air, to gain a better overview of the events of the world, and also to participate in various planning meetings concerning the future."[2] To Wehberg, he wrote: "I have been here for a month; I intend to stay here a long time. It is very healthy to live outside the belligerent atmosphere. One sees and hears a lot."[3] Fried had not yet given up his apartment in Vienna, and his "office" as well as Mundy Schwalb remained there. He was still reluctant to burn bridges, because for someone like him life was also not easy in Switzerland.

In their constant shifting between pensions, hotels, and other kinds of guest accommodations, which occurred under the surveillance of the authorities of the host country as well as of their own country, the emigrants were outsiders. The general attitude toward the German pacifist émigrés was by no means friendly, especially during the first few months of the war: "In fact, it is indisputable that German-speaking Switzerland admired the organizational and political power of the German Reich, took only little offense at the undemocratic-feudal character of Germany, and was rather reluctant to condemn the violation of Belgian neutrality."[4] Critics of the conduct of the Central Powers

---

1   See Fried, *Kriegs-Tagebuch*, I, 137f. (October 25, 1914).
2   Fried to Dr. John Mez, December 1, 1914. Wiener Stadt- und Landesbibliothek, collection of handwritten documents, LN 225.950.
3   Fried to Wehberg, November 18, 1914. Nachlass Wehberg, vol. 59b, BA Koblenz.
4   Dieter Riesenberger, "Deutsche Emigration und Schweizer Neutralität im Ersten Weltkrieg," *Schweizerische Zeitschrift für Geschichte* 38 (Basel, 1988): 133.

were not all that welcome. Despite his high profile, Fried could therefore not be certain whether he would be able to find a source of income by writing for the Swiss newspapers and magazines.

But there was no going back. When Fried once again returned to Vienna for two weeks at the beginning of February 1915, one experience in the city center made his situation clear: "Last night on the busy Kärntnerstrasse, someone shouted to me 'high treason'. I knew him to be an unbalanced, military writer who has often been the subject of public scandals. Obviously, not someone normal. I had to pretend that I did not hear him. But the incident concerns me a great deal. Unrestraint on the Kärntnerstraße would have been dangerous in the current atmosphere. The fate of Schuhmeier[5] and Jaures[6] flashed through my head."[7] In the heated atmosphere of the warring countries, there was increasingly little room for dissenters.

Fried returned to Switzerland at the end of February intending to spend the "months" until the end of the war there. He did not yet suspect that it would be four whole years before he would see Vienna again, in January 1919. Accompanied by his wife and Mundy Schwalb, and later by Mundy's sister Irene, whom Fried hired as a second secretary, he first went to Zurich[8] to contact publishers and newspapers. The situation weighed heavily on him: "March 3 (Zurich): The days of emotional depression are adding up. The repercussions of the war are becoming increasingly unbearable. Above all, it's the impossibility to speak out that most depresses me. Having to be silent when you have so much to say is torture. There isn't one newspaper in which I could speak halfway openly. [...] The consciousness of being 'without a homeland' likewise torments me. Countless plans run through my head, but I don't have the necessary peace of mind under these circumstances, not to mention the technical wherewithal to carry them out."[9]

But he did have some luck. After intensive talks with the *Neue Zürcher Zeitung*, the newspaper hired him as a staff writer in March. At the same time, Fried found a partner in the Orell Füssli publishing house. Starting in June, it would take over the *Friedens-Warte* and would also publish any new works that Fried produced.

---

5 The Social Democrat Franz Schuhmeier (1864–1913) was murdered in Vienna on February 11, 1913.
6 The French Socialist and pacifist Jean Jaurès, who had keenly sought to promote better understanding between the French and the Germans, was murdered in Paris on July 31, 1914.
7 Fried, *Kriegs-Tagebuch*, I, 297 (February 13, 1915).
8 Presumably Pauline Wyon-Fried and her sons, Lionel and Gordon, were with them; in contrast to Fried, they permanently settled in Zurich.
9 Fried, *Kriegs-Tagebuch*, I, 307 (March 3, 1915).

But Fried himself did not stay in Zurich. In March, he traveled first to Lugano, still unsure where he was going to settle in Switzerland, and then to Thun, where Otfried Nippold and Romain Rolland lived. He then met Rolland in early September. Of this first encounter, Rolland wrote: "Visit by Dr. Alfred H. Fried (Nobel Peace Prize). In appearance he is still youthful and agreeable, more French than German, with fine fingers and gentle eyes. But confident. Speaks bad French; almost always ends his sentence in German. He now lives in Thun [...] he feels very lonely and bored there. Otherwise, he lives in Vienna because he likes the city. But he says he feels German, not Austrian."[10]

After their rather long conversation, Rolland visited Fried the very next day. Fried painted a rather negative view of Viennese society for Rolland: on the one hand, he accused Vienna of thinking only via the *Neue Freie Presse*, and on the other hand, he accused it of placing the theater at the center of its life. But Rolland, who was in a similar situation as Fried and, as an emigrant, was often subject to attack by writers from his own country, was nevertheless struck by Fried's moderate statements about Germany and Austria, but he ascribed these sentiments to a rather different trait: "He speaks generously of Germany and Austria. (Under the appearance of gentleness, however, he must be choleric and furious, and it is strange to hear the passion with which he assures me that he is immune to passion. He reminds me—though he is much more gracious—of the militant pacifist Frida Perlen.)"[11] Just a few days after this meeting, Fried returned to Berne with Therese and Mundy Schwalb and decided to live there, taking a few rooms in an inn.

Berne was the location of the International Peace Bureau, several other international organizations, and the European embassies. To Fried, it seemed a most suitable place to prepare for a future peace. At this time, he still expected a peace agreement within a few months: "It is often said that Berne could be the city of the peace agreement."[12]

Although he gave up his rented apartment in Vienna in February 1915, most of his possessions remained in storage and did not follow him to Switzerland. Even his assets (the Nobel Prize) remained in the care of his friend and lawyer, Emil Frankl, in Vienna. Fried did not regard himself as a "deserter" or a traitor to his country; on the contrary, he saw himself as a patriot who wanted to help his country, as best he could, to get back on the right path. He also resolutely defended himself against the apprehensions of his friend, Georg Gothein, a member of the Reichstag, who thought that he could be drawn to

---

10   Romain Rolland, *Das Gewissen Europas*, vol. 1 (Berlin, 1963), 684 (September 1, 1915).
11   Ibid, 686 (September 2, 1915).
12   Fried, *Kriegs-Tagebuch*, II, 54 (September 17, 1915).

the side of the Entente in Switzerland. "My stay in Switzerland need not exert the influence on me that you fear. Having originally planned to stay for only a few weeks, I extended it for the entire duration of the war because I recognized that I would have no longer a complete overview of the events if I were to permanently remain in Vienna. I know that many of our fellow pacifists will only be able to form an opinion after the war, something which I am already able to do here."[13] These words clearly reveal Fried's further motive for living in exile: his claim to be the leader and intellectual pioneer of pacifism. It was more important to him to be able to establish, even during the war, a community of pacifist intellectuals in Europe and to gather together as many of them as possible for joint discussions and deliberations in Switzerland. Most important of all, he placed his hopes on the International Peace Bureau in Berne, that is to say, on the "Berne Bureau," as most pacifists called it.[14]

However, the situation within the bureau during these months was extremely tense. Just as the Austrian Peace Society (ÖFG) had been shaken by the death of Bertha von Suttner in June 1914, so too had the International Peace Office lost its leader on March 16, 1914 with the death of its longtime director Albert Gobat (Nobel Peace Prize 1902).[15] Many pacifists feared that the paralysis of the national societies might also affect the Peace Office in Berne.[16]

For the Germans and Austrians there was a further problem: the Standing Committee of the International Peace Bureau consisted of three people from French-speaking Switzerland who in two telegrams to Germany and Austria[17] had already taken a clear position on behalf of France and against the Central Powers. Further statements of a similar tone were to be feared and would have placed the German and Austrian members in a very difficult situation. Their presence in Berne therefore seemed very important.

Still, together with Otfried Nippold,[18] Fried managed to assemble some of the members of the council for a first meeting in Berne on October 31, but no representatives from France and England attended. Even when, after much

---

13 Fried to Georg Gotheim, July 1, 1915. Nachlass Gothein, Nr. 20, BA Koblenz.
14 Cf. Fried, *Kriegs-Tagebuch*, I, 139 (October 25, 1914).
15 On Gobat, see, among others, Karl Holl, "Albert Gobat," in *Friedensbewegung*, ed. Donat/Holl, 159f, and also Hermann Böschenstein, "Albert Gobat – der unfriedliche Friedensförderer," in *Der Friedens-Nobelpreis von 1901 bis heute*, vol. 1: *1901–1904*, ed. Michael Neumann (Zug, 1987), 148ff.
16 Mauermann, *Internationales Friedensbüro*, 149.
17 Ibid, 150.
18 That this initiative was put forth by Fried and Nippold is made clear in Ludwig Quidde, *Der deutsche Pazifismus während des Weltkrieges 1914–1918*, eds. Karl Holl and Helmut Donat (Boppard, 1979), 51. Published from the Nachlass.

hesitation, an official council meeting finally was convened on January 6 and 7, 1915, most of the members of the Entente states categorically opposed it; they demanded a clear condemnation of German-Austrian politics and the violations of international law, and they did not believe that this could be achieved in a body that included representatives of both warring parties. The drafting of guidelines for an early negotiated peace, which was especially sought by the German and Austrian representatives, was also rejected by many representatives of the Entente, as they believed that the victory of the pacifist ideas could only be achieved by a complete victory of the Allies over Prussian militarism.[19] In addition to the representatives of the Central Powers, there were delegates from the neutral countries at the council meeting; the only representative of the Entente was the Englishman Alexander. However, some of the delegates had transferred their votes to representatives of the neutral countries in order to exclude theoretically a majority vote by the Central Powers. Surprisingly, the vote ended in a tie, as the representatives from the Netherlands and the Swiss German Franz Bucher-Heller voted with the German and Austrian-Hungarian representatives. Just as Fried, Quidde, and the other representatives of the Central Powers had desired, only carefully worded statements on the political events were circulated.

In the end, the council only issued three previously agreed upon appeals, proposed by Fried, to the "intellectual leaders of all nations," to the "International Organizations," and to the "peace societies of all countries."[20] The intellectual leaders of all nations were reminded of their duty to reestablish international relations immediately after the war: "Be the bridgeheads that must remain intact so that the bridges that are being blown up everywhere today can be reconstructed."[21] Similarly, the international organizations were called upon to "maintain their efforts and pursue them with all their energy."[22] But the appeal to the peace societies included much more than that: in addition to a brief exposition of the discussions and decisions of the council meeting, it contained an appeal, to the extent that the situation in the individual countries allowed, to both maintain and to expand their own organizations, to establish contact with possible allies, or even to form new organizations, following the model of the Dutch Anti-Oorlog-Raad. Thereafter, the nine-point demands of the International Peace Bureau for future peace negotiations were put forward for discussion: among these were, first and foremost, the participation of the

---

19   See Mauermann, 152 and 157ff on this matter.
20   *Friedens-Warte* 17, no. 1 (January/February 1915): 3–9.
21   "An die geistigen Führer aller Nationen!" *Friedens-Warte* 17, no. 1 (January/February 1915): 3.
22   "An die internationalen Organisationen!" *Friedens-Warte* 17, no. 1 (January/February 1915): 4.

neutral countries in the peace negotiations and the rejection of all annexations that did not receive the consent of the population involved.[23]

While Fried attempted to portray the meeting in the "peace room" as a success, emphasizing that it was indeed an achievement in the midst of war to "see pacifists of all countries united in common work,"[24] he nevertheless wrote in his diary: "Woe to us if the people themselves continue to hate in this manner, if it cannot be overcome even by those who are likeminded and who have worked together for a long time!"[25] In addition, the group was unable to create a plan of action for the International Peace Bureau, which, paralyzed by inner division, then sank deeper and deeper into passivity. In the subsequent war years, the office confined itself predominantly to humanitarian tasks, such as the search for prisoners of war, in which Fried too participated.[26] In a reply to an article by Hermann Hesse in November 1915,[27] who accused the pacifists of merely talking and writing instead of actively providing assistance, Fried wrote: "In Berne, for example, the International Peace Gazette, which ceased its pacifist activities during the war (unfortunately!), has employed its working committees and its worldwide international connections to serve as a means of communication for prisoners and civil internees and as a conduit in the search for missing persons and evacuees. According to one report, published in November of this year, it has thus far processed over 15,000 individual cases and over 100,000 items of correspondence."[28] The inclusion of "unfortunately" is indicative of Fried's attitude. As much as he is shaken by the boundless suffering of war, he still does not believe that it is the task of pacifism to simply alleviate the consequences of the war, but rather the pacifist must seek to render harmless the evil that is war.[29] In mid-January 1915, Fried met an old

---

23 "An die Friedensgesellschaften aller Länder," *Friedens-Warte* 17, no. 1 (January/February 1915): 5–9. The additional demands pertained to (3) the creation of an international organization of states with common, permanent bodies of representation and executive powers, including a permanent international court; (4) arms control and arms reduction; (5) control of diplomacy by the parliaments and the prohibition of privately negotiated agreements; (6) the prohibition of all offensive and defensive alliances; (7) the opening of trade to all the colonies and the introduction of a development toward free trade; (8) international agreements for the protection of indigenous peoples in the colonies; and (9) criminal and secured protection of every person from defamation while they are abroad. *Friedens-Warte* 17, no. 1 (January/February 1915): 7.

24 Ibid, 17. Fried knowingly does not mention that not all the countries were represented.

25 Fried, *Kriegs-Tagebuch*, I, 261f (January 11, 1915).

26 Cf. Fried, *Kriegs-Tagebuch*, I, 417 (June 2, 1915).

27 Hermann Hesse, "Die Pazifisten," *Die Zeit* (Vienna), November 7, 1915.

28 *Friedens-Warte* 18, no. 1 (January 1916): 21.

29 After listing the humanitarian activities actions of the pacifists in all the countries, Fried emphasizes in his reply to Hesse: "All these actions, carried out by pacifists in order to be

acquaintance in Berne, Richard Grelling, who had retired to an estate near Florence shortly after the turn of the century. The visit did not come unexpectedly: "In December 1914, in Berne, I was informed by a well-known German Reichstag delegate that Grelling, who was then living in Florence, would visit me with his 'daughter.' I was to be asked if I would like to take care of the 'girl.'"[30]

The "girl" was a manuscript that Grelling produced in December 1914 after having studied the colored-coded official documents of the governments[31] of Germany, England, and France; in his manuscript he asserted that the German government bore the lion's share of the guilt for the war. Grelling hoped to find a publisher for his work in German-speaking Switzerland. When he read it aloud to Fried, the latter was shocked: "I cannot describe the mood that prevailed in that small Bernese pension room back then, when Grelling showed me, for hours on end, the evidence of the criminal culpability of Germany for the World War."[32]

However, Fried, unlike Grelling, did not support the immediate publication of the book: "I wanted to delay the publication of the book, until the post-war hour of reckoning." Fried still assumed that the war would be over in a matter of months, and that's when he wanted to begin a discussion of the guilt for the war. Despite his skepticism, he helped Grelling find a publisher: "For days on end we crawled from publisher to publisher, from printer to printer, and Grelling offered to pay out of his own pocket to cover a portion of the printing costs of *J'accuse*. He tried to make the content clear. The publishers were very decisive, assuring us they would give the work due consideration, and then, just one day later, they claimed that there was no real appetite for this kind of publication during the war."

Fried attributed the rejection to the lack of interest by the "public at large" and to the massive (and free) German propaganda material. But, in fact, the very pro-German attitude in Switzerland at the time might also have been the reason for the rejection. Only when Grelling accepted Fried's advice to turn to publishers in the French-speaking part of Switzerland did he find success.[33] The book appeared on April 4, 1915, anonymously, under the title *J'accuse! Von einem Deutschen* (I accuse! By a German) in Lausanne and immediately found

---

helpful during war, have nothing to do with pacifism. They are private activities actions that do not reflect the movement in the least."

30 A manuscript of an article "Die Angelegenheit Grelling," from 1920. Nachlass Fried, Box 9, file 124.

31 Official administrative dossiers were in specific colors of the country. The official publications on foreign policy and on diplomacy were always white in color in the German Foreign Office.

32 Fried, MS "Grelling." Nachlass Fried, Box 9, file 124.

33 Cf. Richard Grelling in Goldscheid, *Gedenkblätter*, 33.

great resonance in all the disparate camps.[34] Grelling would later say that Fried was the book's "midwife" because of his intercession and described Fried as the one "who stood faithfully as a godfather at its cradle."[35] Fried kept his own view of the matter to himself at the time. Only when his *Kriegs-Tagebücher* (*War Diaries*) appeared in book form in 1918, did he comment on Grelling's work: "The book *J'accuse! Von einem Deutschen* has appeared. I finished it yesterday and am deeply moved by it. The German and Austro-Hungarian guilt for the war is convincingly demonstrated through the published documents such that one cannot simply gloss over the claim."[36]

In fact, in the summer of 1915, Fried was not yet ready to publicize this opinion and thus take the side of the Entente against the German Reich, even as the Entente soon broadly disseminated Grelling's book dropping thousands of copies on the German soldiers at the front.[37] Although he himself was convinced that Germany and Austria bore the main responsibility for the outbreak of the war, Fried was also aware that an unambiguous statement in support of this position would not only lead to a break with most of his pacifist friends in Germany, but it would also create further fragmentation among the pacifist forces. In addition, there was the danger that the fronts would harden, which would have obviated the negotiated peace that he had been working for. The preparation of an early, lasting, and sustainable peace was the most important thing for Fried at this time.

At the beginning of January 1915, when the council meeting of the Berne Bureau displayed a hopeless fragmentation and inability to act, representatives of the Swiss committee and of the Dutch Anti-Orlog-Raad decided to organize an international congress in 1915. In his diary, Fried attributed the initiative to himself: "At my suggestion the Dutch agreed with Nippold and me to convene an extraordinary peace conference in Berne or The Hague at Easter."[38] When the first meeting took place in April 1915 with 30 delegates from

---

34   On the impact of this work, see Hans Thimme, *Weltkrieg ohne Waffen. Die Propaganda der Westmächte gegen Deutschland, ihre Wirkung und ihre Abwehr* (Stuttgart/Berlin, 1932). Thimme even assumes that it was precisely the enormous success of Grelling's book that moved the Entente to make the question of culpability for starting the war the basis of their own propaganda.
35   Richard Grelling in Goldscheid, *Gedenkblätter*, 33.
36   Fried, *Kriegs-Tagebuch*, I, 381 (May 7, 1915).
37   Thimme relates that French bombers dropped more than 20,000 copies of the work across the German front. They were in miniature form like the pocketbook edition of the bible, had black-white-red covers, and bore the title "Die Wahrheit" (the truth). Cf. Thimme, *Weltkrieg ohne Waffen*, 70.
38   Fried, *Kriegs-Tagebuch*, I, 262 (January 11, 1915).

ten nations, Fried was not present. He had been in Lugano for several weeks working on the conclusion of his first book to be written in exile; he explained to Wehberg that the distance and his work prevented him from attending.[39] Perhaps Fried underestimated the importance of this meeting especially since it was only supposed to be a preparatory meeting for the congress and was not intended, as the discussion on the ground actually showed, to create a central coordinating group of all the national efforts towards a lasting peace. The group, named "Zentralorganisation für einen dauernden Frieden" (Central organization for a durable peace), was founded in The Hague and had its permanent seat there under the leadership of the Anti-Oorlog Raad. Nippold was personally offended by this decision because he had wanted the central office to be in Berne under his direction, and so he withdrew from further work with the group.[40]

Nevertheless, a major international convention, organized jointly by both The Hague and Berne, was planned for the near future. Cooperating with the Swiss committee, Fried helped plan this meeting and also participated in one of the nine international commissions, whose reports were to be discussed at the congress.[41] The final date was set for mid-December, but war-related problems, in particular the refusal to grant entry or exit permits, complicated the arrangements, so that it was not until November 1917 that a subset of the committees was able to gather in Berne. In the meantime, Fried had only his writing as consolation.

Fried's very first project of the exile period, completed in April 1915, focused on the conditions and prerequisites for a future durable peace; the title *Europäische Wiederherstellung* (European Restoration) was a little misleading because Fried did not want to restore the old order in Europe, but rather wanted to see "a real peace that governs the relations between the members of the community of nations as they move along their necessary developmental paths and create a whole kind of interaction."[42] Based on Bloch's assumption that there would be "no victors in the old sense" in this war and thus no imposed

---

39 See the letter from Fried to Wehberg, April 6, 1915. Nachlass Wehberg, vol. 59b, BA Koblenz.
40 Cf. Wehberg, "Die Zentralorganisation für einen dauernden Frieden," *Friedens-Warte* 44, (1944): 319.
41 Cf. Christian L. Lange, *Organisation Centrale Pour Une Paix Durable*. "Développement de l'Oeuvre de la Haye. Organisation de la Conférence de la Paix," (La Haye, Mars, 1917). Rapport présenté par une Commission. Composée de M. M. Fried (Autriche), La Fontaine (Belgique), Hull (Etats-Unis), De Louter (Pays-Bas), Schücking (Allemagne) et Lange (Norvège).
42 Dr. h.c. Alfred Fried, *Europäische Wiederherstellung* (Zurich, 1915), 76. The following quotation is also from this source.

peace, Fried dealt above all with the possible course of the peace negotiations and proposed a step-by-step approach. It was essential, he maintained, "to anticipate the way out of the present war from two separate actions, one of which will be primarily the conclusion of hostilities in a so-called 'peace agreement', while the other will serve to establish a real future peace through the formation of a new European Union." Only when the belligerent states would have abolished war, could the real, more time-consuming work of peace be tackled. But even during the first stage, certain guidelines had to be adhered to in order to pave the way for the second: "The agreement to abolish war, taken by those who conduct the war, will have to avoid any humiliation of a particular people, any economic paralysis or exploitation, and will have to acknowledge the fundamentals of the subsequent European Congress! In addition, the second assembly, in which both the warring nations and the neutral nations will take part, must be given the right to abrogate or supplement provisions of the agreement."

Fried left unstated how he envisioned the Peace Congress exactly, but he stressed that he did not mean a third Hague Conference, which would follow (and make sense in his view) only after the conclusion of the "Peace Agreement." His own proposals for a new order in Europe touched on earlier prerequisites: the abolition of the diplomatic class, the participation of representatives of the people in all negotiations with foreign governments, the abolition of the old system of alliances, and the creation of a Pan-European Bureau, modelled on the Pan-American Union, which would have a wide range of powers, have its headquarters in a large city of a neutral country, and organize conferences at least every three years. In addition, there would be a reduction in the armaments under the auspices of an international armaments control court, the nationalization of the armaments industry or at least strict state controls, and a decisive course of action against the nationalist and hateful yellow journalism, also with the help of legislation. In the end, it was clear to him that the war confirmed the teachings of pacifism and that after the war they must reach out to other pacifists and their supporters. The great hour of pacifism was fast approaching, for the "age that is now beginning is a pacifist one."

All of Fried's publications during the initial war years were imbued with the belief that the war did not disprove pacifism, but rather confirmed and justified it, that a general rethinking after the war would rehabilitate the pacifists who to date had been maligned and despised, and that it would catapult them into the leadership of society. This belief was quite likely the engine of his unbroken zeal in Swiss exile.

2 1916: In the Crossfire of the Critics

Throughout this whole period, the *Friedens-Warte* remained Fried's primary concern and the main focus of his work. As was the case before the war, Fried was keen to include in the journal the voices of those who represented different pacifist orientations. At the same time, he did not shy away from the possibility of clarifying his own divergent position or giving other authors an opportunity to speak out on the same topic, so that often there were sequences of related articles. However, the limited space and the monthly publication of the journal were not suitable for such extended controversies.

The *Neue Zürcher Zeitung* (NZZ) offered a better forum.[43] On August 16, 1914, the newspaper had committed itself to absolute neutrality. From early April 1915, when Albert Meyer[44] took over the role of chief editor, the newspaper saw its task, increasingly, as a place for a mutual discussion of differing views and opinions. This tact approximated Fried's personal views. From the end of March 1915 and continuing even into the postwar period, Fried was one of the paper's most diligent contributors and soon significantly influenced the perspective of the newspaper.[45]

With his very first article, "Die tieferen Ursachen des Weltkrieges" (The Deeper Causes of the World War),[46] Fried launched a lengthy discussion of both the causes and possible outcomes of the war as well as of the possibility of a lasting peace in Europe.[47] While he left to the post-war period the question of who was to blame for the war that had begun in July 1914, the most profound cause was already established for him: the anarchy between the nations, which had led to mutual distrust and competition, to a state of "non-war," to the "latent war," which was wrongly labeled peace: "Only the abolition of this anarchy can help us. The only goal of this war should be the recognition that the old peace must not return after the war, that is, the peace that produced the war. We must recognize that the states are not the enemies of each other,

---

43 On the history of the newspaper in the First World War, see the exhaustive description in Gustav A. Lang, *Kampfplatz der Meinungen. Die Kontroverse um Kriegsursachen und Friedensmöglichkeiten 1914–1919 im Rahmen der "NZZ"* (Zurich, 1968).
44 Cf. Lang, *Kampfplatz der Meinungen*, 20.
45 Ibid, 43.
46 NZZ, no. 349 and 352 (March 25, 1915). The article can also be found in the "Blätter der zwischenstaatlichen Organisaton" (April 1915): 41–46, from which the following quotations are taken.
47 See the chapter "Die Auseinandersetzung um die pazifistischen Theorien," in *Kampfplatz der Meinungen*, ed. Gustav Lang, 105ff.

but rather that it is the manner of their previous coexistence that crushed them. This anarchy is the only enemy of us all."

It was precisely this conclusion that met with opposition, and not only from the nationalist circles. The majority of French pacifists, for example, believed that the establishment of an effective peace had to include a clear victory over the German Reich, which they equated with Prussian militarism, while on the other hand German nationalists dreamed of a European peace under German hegemony. In addition, the discussion of whether only democratic forms of government were suitable vehicles for the creation of a durable peace had already begun. Questions about whether an international order, in Fried's interpretation, could bring about a lasting, "eternal" peace in Europe and whether this kind of durable peace was even desirable remained a matter of controversy.

In addition to his numerous articles in the NZZ and the *Friedens-Warte*, Fried also wrote shorter books and brochures this year. Just as important, perhaps even more important, was the publication of Bertha von Suttner's articles in *Randglossen zur Zeitgeschichte* (Commentaries on Contemporary History). Barely two months after her death in August 1914, he had begun work "to numb me and to focus my energies on a good project for the future."[48] – "The normal state will indeed come back. And then Bertha von Suttner's time will come. One will remember her, one will begin to understand her work, to understand her writings." Two years later, in the fall of 1916, he completed this extensive project. It probably appeared as early as the end of 1916, but is dated 1917, under the title *Der Kampf um die Vermeidung des Weltkrieges* (The Battle for the Prevention of the World War).[49] Fried thus fulfilled the deceased's wish and also provided a new expression of his veneration, by not showing her as the novelist or the "enthusiast for goodness," as the Austrian pacifist Leopold Katscher called her,[50] but as a fighter, a most intelligent social critic, "a journalist in the best sense,"[51] as a figure the way he wanted posterity to see her.

But such a time was still far away.[52] Like the *Friedens-Warte,* most of Fried's writings in Germany and Austria were banned in 1916. A reversal of opinion

---

48 Fried, *Kriegs-Tagebuch*, 1, 28 (August 21, 1914). The following quotation is also taken from this entry.
49 Bertha von Suttner, *Der Kampf um die Vermeidung des Weltkriegs. Randglossen aus zwei Jahrzehnten zu den Ereignissen vor der Katastrophe (1892–1900 und 1907–1914)*, ed. Dr. Alfred H. Fried, Vol. 1: *Von der Caprivischen Heeresvermehrung bis zum Transvaalkrieg* (Zurich, 1917), Vol. 2: *Von der zweiten Haager Konferenz bis zum Ausbruch des Weltkriegs* (Zurich, 1918).
50 Leopold Katscher, *Bertha von Suttner, die "Schwärmerin,"* (Dresden, 1903).
51 Fried/Suttner, *Randglossen* 1, iv.
52 This characterization did not change until the pioneering biography by Beatrix Kempf titled *Bertha von Suttner: Das Lebensbild einer großen Frau* (Vienna, 1964) (a new edition:

had not yet come about, and the press had something to do with that. In the first months of the war, the national and nationalistic press had harshly attacked Fried and his diary, but then the number of attacks dropped significantly, only to rise again in 1916 as the situation on the battlefield changed. As the most important German-speaking pacifist, Fried became the preferred target of the right-wing press, although it should be mentioned that he, unlike, for example, Hermann Fernau[53] and others, was usually attacked only as a leader of pacifism, and not as a Jew. In fact, the first article attacking Fried, which appeared anonymously on February 17 in the *Rheinisch-Westfälische Zeitung* under the title "pacifist shenanigans," demonstrates the tenor of the accusations: "The *Friedens-Warte*, now published in Berne, contains the most provocative reading material. Its publisher, Dr. Alfred H. Fried, is writing a 'war diary,' as if to prove that he and his 'pacifists' are the biggest troublemakers and agitators. Not a single word can be found in these pamphlets that betrays a trace of patriotism, but this 'German' and his allies constantly stab Germany in the back. After his world peace had collapsed like a house of cards, our country was attacked from all sides, and now has to fight for its very existence; someone who had true feelings for Germany should really be saying that any criticism directed against Germany only strengthens her enemies. But this sad fellow, blinded by disgusting vanity, usurps the role of judge and fuels the Entente's belligerence through his pronouncements."[54] Germany, which was fighting for its survival, was always portrayed as the victim of a smear campaign by unpatriotic fellows, who by their exaggerated, one-sided criticism were said to play into the hands of the enemy—the first steps leading to the subsequent stab in the back legend. The accusation that Fried was vain and arrogant is even further from the truth than the criticism that he lacked patriotism or that he was cooperating with the Entente.

At the end of March, the *Kreuz-Zeitung* launched a campaign against Fried and the *Friedens-Warte* with the goal of having it banned in Germany. It began on March 26 with the article "Schleichendes Gift" (Creeping Poison),[55] in which the author demanded that the import of the journal be prohibited. Although the anonymous author wrote that there really was no need to fear that the

---

Freiburg im Breisgau, 1980), the subsequent work by Gisela Brinker-Gabler, among others), and then Brigitte Hamann, *Bertha von Suttner: Ein Leben für den Frieden* (Munich, 1986)

53   See the hostile article "Gerade weil ich ein Deutscher bin" in the evening edition of the *Norddeutsche Allgemeine Zeitung*, reprinted in *Neue Preußische (Kreuz-)Zeitung*, no. 89 (February 28, 1916). The article takes pains to emphasize that Fernau was a "Polish Jew."

54   *Rheinisch-Westfälische Zeitung* (February 17, 1916), reprinted in *Friedens-Warte* 18, no. 3 (March 3, 1916): 93f.

55   "Schleichendes Gift," *Neue Preußische (Kreuz-)Zeitung*, no. 157 (March 26, 1916), the Sunday supplement. The following quotations are taken from this article.

population in Germany would be influenced by the "vague action of unpatriotic pacifists," it was nevertheless important to draw attention to the "creeping poison" "that the former socialist journalist Alfred H. Fried is importing with his *Friedens-Warte* to Germany" and to "keep such weeds out of our gardens." And following a few brief excerpts from the *Friedens-Warte*, he emphasized at the end of the article: "In the interest of the fatherland one must demand that such journals be prohibited from entering the Reich!"

Ten days later there was another attack: "Herr Fried bei der Verleumdungsarbeit" (Mr. Fried and his slanderous work),[56] which on this occasion was picked up by numerous newspapers.[57] Fried tried to defend himself this time and wrote a correction to the editor-in-chief of the *Kreuz-Zeitung*, "assuming that I might be dealing with men who also respect the humanity of their opponents."[58] In fact, the newspaper published most of his letter, but the editorial staff succeeded through commentary and layout in ensuring that the article had its desired effect.[59] The *Deutsche Tageszeitung* completely rejected Fried's differing position. Fried noted bitterly: "One then becomes fair game in this 'great' time. If I reflect on the fact that the *Deutsche Tageszeitung* or that the *Hamburger Nachrichten* (!) may write with impunity, that it was 'my old tradition before the war' to 'supply our adversaries with material for their smear campaigns,' I who for 25 years have only acted to promote understanding and communication, while the news outlets of foreign countries, such as *Matin* and *Daily Mail*, agitated against Germany and spread hatred just by quoting from the *Deutsche Tageszeitung* and *Hamburger Nachrichten*, then one cannot help but feel anger at such baseness as well as a sense of disgust that arises from deep within one's being."[60] The campaign of the *Kreuz-Zeitung* was successful: in the beginning of April, the Army Corps Command (stellvertretendes Generalkommando) in Leipzig forbade the publication of the 1916 edition of the *Friedens-Warte*.[61]

The "Foerster Case,"[62] a smear campaign against the ethicist and pacifist, Friedrich Wilhelm Foerster who had been a member of the philosophy faculty

---

56 "Herr Fried bei der Verleumdungsarbeit," *Neue Preußische (Kreuz-)Zeitung*, no. 177 (April 6, 1916), morning edition.
57 Cf. *Friedens-Warte* 18, no. 5 (May 1916): 159.
58 Ibid, 158.
59 "Herr Fried will kein Verleumder sein," *Neue Preußische (Kreuz-)Zeitung*, no. 196 (April 16, 1916), Sunday supplement.
60 *Friedens-Warte* 18, no. 5 (May 1916): 161.
61 Fried, *Kriegs-Tagebuch*, 11, 253 (April 7, 1916). The paragraph about the prohibition of the *Friedens-Warte* is missing under the corresponding date in Fried's diary. Cf. *Friedens-Warte* 18, no. 5 (May 1916): 154.
62 Cf. the characterization in *Friedens-Warte* 18, no. 7 (July 1916): 203–208.

in Munich since 1914,[63] also contributed to the ban against the *Friedens-Warte*. Foerster had written an article for the *Friedens-Warte* on "Bismarck's oeuvre in light of the critique of Greater Germany,"[64] an article that Hans Wehberg later described as one of the "most valuable essays ever published in this leading German pacifist journal."[65] Attacks against Foerster and the *Friedens-Warte* proceeded quickly and simultaneously,[66] especially because part of the argument against Foerster concerned the fact that he had published his article in an anti-German, foreign journal.[67]

The ban on the *Friedens-Warte* in Germany did not put an end to the attacks on Fried. While in early June the *Kreuz-Zeitung* included him among "those literary figures who were guilty of high treason" and the *Friedens-Warte* was placed at the top of the list of "nurseries of unpatriotic sentiment and lack of character" in Switzerland, which itself was suspected of working for the Entente,[68] there now came sharp criticism from the other side. An editorial published on June 12 in the *Gazette de Lausanne*, one of the leading newspapers in French-speaking Switzerland and one that was also widely read in France, raised the suspicion that the *Friedens-Warte* and its publishers actually worked for the German government. But the most vehement attacks came from Fried's homeland Austria. There, under the national conservative hegemony of Prime Minister von Stürgkh, the government launched an investigation into Fried for acts of high treason, which only ended with the change of government after the death of the aged Emperor Franz Joseph and the assassination of von Stürgkh in early 1917.

The criticism from Fried's own quarters was also painful. In hindsight, he would write: "What I wrote (...) did not please the perpetrators, those addicted to conquering others, those certain of the victory, and those who alleged an attack from abroad; they condemned me, insulted me, slandered me; but the

---

63   On F. W. Foerster, see *Friedensbewegung*, ed. Donat/Holl, 118ff, and the short biography by Hans Kühner-Wolfskehl in *Biographical Dictionary*, ed. Josephson, 284ff.
64   *Friedens-Warte* 18, no. 1 (January 1916): 1–9.
65   Wehberg, *Führer der Friedensbewegung*, 57.
66   Fried connects the general prohibition against the *Friedens-Warte* to the case of Foerster in his article "Die *Friedens-Warte* und die Militärzensur," in *Friedens-Warte* 20, no. 11 (November/December 1918): 291f.
67   See *Friedens-Warte* 18, no. 7 (July 1916): 204f. Fried repeatedly emphasizes that the *Friedens-Warte* is a German journal with predominantly German and Austrian readers. The temporary, forced move to Zurich, he claims, has not changed anything in that regard. "It is therefore an egregious distortion and a fabrication to claim that Prof. Foerster had his essay on Bismarck published in a 'foreign' journal." (205)
68   Vgl. Fried, *Kriegs-Tagebuch*, II, 282 (June 14, 1916).

arrows did not only come from the front, sometimes they came from the rear, from my own ranks, and those were more painful."[69]

Although most pacifists merely stopped working or did not speak publicly, let alone attack the leaders of the movement, there were some who did not exercise this restraint. One of them was Oskar Schwonder,[70] a pseudonym for Carl Ludwig Siemering, a journalist from Königsberg who had been active in the peace movement since 1897. He had helped to draft the first edition of the *Handbuch* (Handbook)[71] and for years was among Fried's personal friends. By 1914, he had published numerous articles in the *Friedens-Warte*.[72] At the beginning of the war, however, this editor of the *Konigsberger Hartungsche Zeitung* completely turned his back on Fried and his kind of pacifism.[73]

When in early 1917, another former contributor to the *Friedens-Warte*, Dr. Max Seber, authored a pamphlet with the title "Die Schicksalsstunde des Pazifismus" (The Fate of Pacifism),[74] which offered a devastating critique of international pacifism and especially of its director, Fried, Schwonder wrote an enthusiastic foreword. In it he vehemently complained of the "notorious excesses of Dr. A. H. Fried's war diary," and he boasted that he was the only one within the German Peace Society who, despite his previous friendship with Fried, had early on openly turned against him: "As it was one of my greatest joys in life, when my best friend and highly respected teacher Fried received a half of the peace prize of the Nobel Foundation in December 1911 (this halving seemed to me a grave injustice to the pioneer of the modern peace movement), so it was also perhaps the deepest, almost overwhelming pain of my life, that shortly after the outbreak of the European war I had to recognize more clearly with each passing month how Fried spoke of the question of guilt and the events of the war in such an unmeasured, superficial, prejudiced and rigidly doctrinaire manner, and they were, for the most part, harmful to his own fatherland." For Schwonder, it was beyond question that the time for a

---

69   Fried, *Kriegs-Tagebuch*, IV, 446 (June 30, 1919).
70   On Oskar Schwonder, see Fried, *Handbuch* (1913), 405f.
71   See Fried, "Vorwort," in *Handbuch* (1905), x. Here Fried thanks "Herrn Karl Ludwig Siemering in Königsberg, Prussia, who helped him read the author's corrections and who put together the index. In addition, he thanks Elie Ducommun and the office of the Austrian Peace Society."
72   His final article "Fichte und Wir. Zum 100. Todestag am 27. Januar" appeared in 1914 in the February issue of the *Friedens-Warte*. See *Friedens-Warte* 16, no. 2 (February 1914): 57ff.
73   This characterization follows the information provided by Schwonder in Seber's book (see note 74). Comments by Fried in the *Friedens-Warte* or relevant references in Fried's Nachlass could not be found.
74   Dr. Max Seber, *Die Schicksalsstunde des Pazifismus, Eine Neu-Orientierung* (Basel, 1917). The following quotations are taken from this work.

new form of pacifism had come, one that was German-national and aligned with the hegemonic pacifism of the Central Powers. This was the pacifism that Seber had described, and he ended with the words: "But you, dear Doctor Seber, deserve the warmest thanks for your fundamentally damning critique of Fried's inept conduct from all those in the German-speaking countries who have the best of intentions for the future of a progressive pacifism."

In spite of all this hostility Fried continued to strive to disseminate his ideas, and in particular he tried to influence the powerful people that he came into contact with. Although many initiatives ultimately failed, it should be noted that Fried, who usually remained in the background, was in close contact with all the pacifist groups in Switzerland and saw it as his task to make connections between the various individuals and to forward them pertinent information. Even if he himself had no direct political influence, he was undoubtedly one of the important personalities of the Swiss exile movement.

As early as November 1915, Fried had, for the first time, arranged a remote yet hopeful mediation session: he brought about a conversation between the Russian envoy in Berne, State Councilor von Bacheracht, and Carl René, a consul in Stettin, who officially was acting as a private person but was in fact, as the files of the Foreign Office indicate, acting in the service of von Bülow. René was to meet with contacts of the Russian government in Zurich, but he was also in Berne to meet with "the author Dr. Alfred H. Fried, a friend of many years and the well-known Nobel laureate,"[75] but without informing him of his real intentions. Nevertheless, Fried had picked up on René's vague hint and facilitated contact via the Russian ambassador's private secretary, whom he knew. The extent to which absolute secrecy was attempted can be seen in René's description of the meeting: "On November 17 of this year, Dr. Fried showed up at ten-thirty in the morning, at the Hotel Bellevue in Berne, to meet me for a walk. – Then, later, Mr. Frankenthal appeared. To remain inconspicuous, Fried, Frankenthal and I first rode a trolley for a few streets and got off near Ensingerstraße. – Nobody had followed us. – Frankenthal then accompanied me to the building in which the Russian ambassador has his private apartment, and I appeared before him at precisely 11 o'clock."

Not only did the one-hour conversation fail to produce significant results, but in retrospect it was a trap, since René had acted without any consultation with Berlin. When a Geneva newspaper declared the meeting a "peace offer from a representative of Prince Bülow," the Foreign Office (Auswärtiges Amt)

---

75   Report of the Consul of Stettin, Carl René, to the Foreign Office on November 21, 1915. R 20459, IA, Weltkrieg. WK No. 2 bound. Vol. 13, PA/AA Berlin. The following quotations are also taken from this source.

demanded that René justify his behavior,[76] while at the same time the imperial German embassy in Berne recommended to Chancellor Bethmann-Hollweg that René be withdrawn from of all exploratory meetings: "At any rate, it seems doubtful to me whether Mr. René would be a suitable person to arrange a meeting with a Russian after this experience."[77]

Fried tried a completely different kind of mediation on behalf of the Freemasons in June 1917, when he sought, unsuccessfully, to mediate at a festive event held at the Swiss Grand Lodge in Basel between the lodges of the Central Powers and those of Switzerland, which had been estranged since the beginning of the war. Even in exile, Fried never completely lost contact with his brothers in Vienna, who in turn were loyal to him during the war. In November 1914, the *Zirkel* extended cordial words to the "world-renowned champion of the brotherhood of mankind" on the occasion of his fiftieth birthday: "This day has offered the numerous friends and devotees of the jubilarian, who has spent it in neutral Switzerland, a pleasant opportunity to say to Brother Fried how dear and valued he is to them, how much they cherish his exemplary cultural work, and how cordially they wish to be able to see him enjoy the fruits of his labor and its long-term success."[78]

As the war continued, Heinrich Glücksmann kept his lodge brothers as well-informed as possible about the activities of the pacifists and especially about Fried. However, the censors would soon restrict him. In February 1915, Fried's pamphlet "Ein Dutzend Wahrheiten"[79] (A Dozen Truths) was printed in its entirety. But at the end of March, the appeal to the International Peace Bureau in Berne "An die Friedensgesellschaften aller Länder" (To the Peace Societies of All Countries) was completely axed, whereas the simultaneous appeals "An die Intellektuellen" (To the Intellectuals) and "An die Internationalen Organisationen" (To the International Organizations) were permitted to be published. In April, an article by Fried "Die Zukunft des Internationalismus"

---

76 See the correspondence between Carl René and Director Sobernheim in Berlin on December 6, 1915 and on December 10, 1915 in R 20460, IA, WK Nr. 2, bound volume 14, PA/AA Berlin.

77 See the report by Dernburg, the imperial German ambassador in Berne, to Reichskanzler Bethmann-Hollweg of December 24, 1915. Marked top secret. R 20460, IA, WK Nr. 2, bound volume 14, PA/AA Berlin.

78 *Der Zirkel* 14, no. 5/6 (November 1914): 57. But it should be noted that the same issue also contains an advertisement for the "Eiserne Zither," the war poems of Fried's uncle, Ludwig Ganghofer, that can hardly be labeled pacifist.

79 The flyer can also be seen on the cover of the December edition of the *Friedens-Warte*. See *Friedens-Warte* 16, no. 12 (1914): 370.

(The Future of Internationalism) was allowed to appear unabridged,[80] and in the same issue an appeal by the Austrian Peace Society to all the members of the border lodges to join the Peace Society met with no objection.[81] As late as September 1915, the short article "Ein Jahrhundert Friedensbewegung" (A Century of the Peace Movement) was published, but then the censorship seems to have grown harsher since there were hardly any expressions of pacifism in the newspaper until the summer of 1917.

3   Swiss Exile from 1917 to the End of the War

America's entry into the war on April 16, 1917 marked a turning point for Fried and for the whole of warring Europe. For Fried personally, it meant first of all the end of the Carnegie subsidies; he was then forced to pay for the ongoing deficits of his journal out of his own pocket. At the same time, there was now also someone on the Entente's side in Woodrow Wilson, on whom Fried set his hopes, cautiously in 1916,[82] but then ever more clearly. The American president's appeal to the world for a negotiated peace treaty on January 22, 1917, one without victors and vanquished, and for the establishment of a League of Nations was "the greatest historical act of this war" for Fried. And even more: "Wilson's message is, alongside the tsar's manifesto of August 24, 1898, the most important document of the onset of the pacifist doctrine. [...] He is proclaiming the pacifist doctrine, which we have been expressing and disseminating in all our writings for a generation [...] This message is our victory, our justification, the crowning of our work."[83]

As in 1898, Fried once again hoped that a change of heart in a head of state would give pacifism some authority. While he did not fully abandon hope that this turnaround would occur immediately, Fried did expect scorn rather than agreement in the poisoned political atmosphere of the World War, but still he believed that Wilson's words would fall on fertile ground after the war had ended. He also hoped for new talks aimed at a peace of understanding.

For Fried, as for many pacifists and leftists, Wilson was the focal point of their hopes. And, appropriately, he was soon recognized in other camps as the primary opponent: "The more the ideas of a negotiated peace and democracy on the one hand and the idea of a peace secured by victory and the

---

80   *Der Zirkel* 45, no. 15/16 (April 1915): 162ff.
81   Ibid, 171.
82   Fried, *Kriegs-Tagebuch*, II, 145, 272, 301, and 310f.
83   Fried, *Kriegs-Tagebuch*, III, 143f.

authoritarian state on the other were perceived as two sides of the same coin, the more prominent the position of the American president appeared in the political consciousness of the Germans, the president who was both the most outstanding promoter of the idea of international understanding and the most impressive representative of a powerful, democratic state."[84]

This was not the only reason that the German government had vigorously rejected Wilson's mediation attempts in the summer of 1916.[85] The government was neither willing to give up the monarchy nor to part with the hope of securing a peace through victory. In contrast, clearly speaking in favor of Wilson's goals was the revisionist wing of the SPD, the "ethical socialists" around Eduard Bernstein, Hugo Haase, Karl Kautsky and Kurt Eisner; so too were several liberal politicians and, above all, the various pacifist groups under the leadership of the "Bund Neues Vaterland" (Federation for a New Fatherland). Fried met many of these politicians personally when the conference on the foundation of a durable peace, planned since 1915, took place in Berne from November 19 to 22. However, once again it was not a full congress, as the representatives of the Entente were denied passports by their governments.[86] Only 48 representatives of the Central Powers and of the neutral states attended the conference. Nevertheless, Fried was delighted with the congress, and he emphasized the "splendid pacifist and democratic spirit"[87] that invigorated the gathering. Indeed, many of Fried's friends and acquaintances were among the participants. Of particular importance, however, was the fact that the meeting in Berne had attracted not only pacifists and experts in international law but also some deputies of the German Reichstag,[88] whose parties had voted in favor of the peace resolution in the Reichstag in July 1917.[89] These included: Bernstein for the Independent Social Democratic Party of Germany (USPD), Gothein for the Progressive People's Party (FVP), Blunck for the National Liberals, Heine for the SPD, and Erzberger for the Center Party. However, the efforts to reach an understanding failed, but not only because the Entente stayed away from the

---

84 Ernst Fraenkel, "Das deutsche Wilsonbild," in *Jahrbuch für Amerikastudien*, vol. 5 (Heidelberg, 1960), 73f.
85 Cf. Fraenkel, *Wilsonbild*, 69ff.
86 On this matter, see *Friedens-Warte* 20, no. 1 (January 1918): 19 and 26.
87 Ibid, 19.
88 See Zechlin, 171ff for a discussion of the positions taken by the governments and the Foreign Offices in Germany and Austria and of the effort by the Foreign Office to influence the German participants. Cf. Zechlin, 471ff.
89 At the instigation of Matthias Erzberger, a representative of the Center Party, the majority of the members of the Reichstag, consisting of the Center Party, the SPD, and the Liberals, demanded a negotiated peace in a peace resolution on July 19, 1917.

conference. Fried had already been critical of the Reichstag resolution noting "two serious mistakes" that might hinder possible negotiations: the imprecise language of the announcement that Germany wanted to participate in international rights organizations and especially the introductory statement that Germany had only taken up arms to defend its freedom and independence.[90] Nevertheless, it was clear to Fried: "This pre-convention has proved that the world is ripe for sane negotiation, a powerful final act against insanity."[91] But the much desired joint conference with the states of the Entente would not be realized before the end of the war; the obstacles were just too great.

By the end of 1917, Fried had long ceased to be among like-minded people in the emigrant community in Berne. Beginning toward the end of 1916, the number of exiles in Switzerland had been skyrocketing, and some of these more radical forces saw only the overthrow of the monarchy in Germany and the establishment of a federal republic through a victory by the Entente powers as the basis for a peace agreement and an anti-militarist German Reich. This group, which included Richard Grelling, Ernst Bloch, Hugo Ball, and Hermann Rösemeier, among others, was essentially centered around the twice-weekly *Freie Zeitung*, which, founded in 1917, was openly pro-Entente and understood the war as a fight between the governments.[92] In contrast to Fried, who endeavored to guide the *Friedens-Warte* cautiously and objectively, the *Freie Zeitung* and its contributors "probably consciously violated the Swiss neutrality regulations and also carried out highly targeted propaganda."[93]

Although there were individual contributors who worked for shorter or longer periods for both papers, there was no real opportunity for a close working relationship or even a private relationship; the positions, at least until shortly before the end of the war,[94] were too different for such relationships. For a longer period of time, however, it was thought that the *Freie Zeitung* "punished Fried by ignoring him."[95]

---

90 Fried, *Kriegs-Tagebuch*, III, 293ff. (July 17, 1917).
91 *Friedens-Warte* 20, no. 1 (January 1918): 19.
92 See Dieter Riesenberger, "Deutsche Emigration und Schweizer Neutralität im Ersten Weltkrieg," *Schweizer Zeitschrift für Geschichte* 38 (Basel, 1988): 127ff., 136f.
93 Ibid, 143.
94 But it is also true that the *Freie Zeitung* had contacts to the left wing of the German Peace Society and to the pacifist wing of the USPD through its publisher Hans Schlieben, who was a member of the Bund Neues Deutschland. See L. Wieland, "Die *Freie Zeitung*," in *Handbuch der Friedensbewegung*, ed. Donat/Hall, 133f.
95 Martin Korol, "Deutsches Präexil in der Schweiz 1916–1918" (Diss. Bremen, Tartu, 1999), 133f.

Fried's endeavor, however, was to unite as many currents of the peace movement as possible, be they in the movement or only on the fringe. In the summer of 1918, he adopted Otto Flake's idea to constitute in Switzerland a "League of Intellectuals;"[96] it would consist of German and Austrian intellectuals who wanted to commemorate the fifth year of the war in a special edition of the *Friedens-Warte* by publishing contributions by exiles holding most diverse views, including Hermann Hesse, Stefan Zweig, Romain Rolland, Alexander von Hohenlohe-Schillingsfürst, and Wilhelm Mühlon, as well as Andreas Latzko, Richard Grelling, Leonhard Frank and Ernst Bloch.[97] Even if not all of the addressed emigrants were willing to contribute to the special issue and, subsequently, actually very few were interested in joining the group, it is remarkable how many of them Fried was able to unite in this edition.[98]

The trench warfare among the emigres made life, already difficult in exile, even more problematic. Stefan Zweig also felt this and wrote to Romain Rolland: "Incidentally, Berne is hell. Everything is one gigantic chaotic mess; the revolutionaries are simultaneously agents of their own governments, the journalists are spies, and most people have been living this double life for so long that they no longer know what idea their lives really serve."[99] In this poisoned atmosphere of mutual distrust it was hard to find fellow colleagues or even friends. But it was not impossible. Fried found such a friend in René Schickele, the editor of the *Weiße Blätter* (White Pages), which had been published in Zurich since 1915 (from 1918 in Berne).[100] Especially the expressionists such as Gottfried Benn, Johannes R. Becher, and Walter Hasenclever gathered around the publication, but so too did other anti-war literati like Leonhard Frank, Andreas Latzko, Henri Barbusse, and radical pacifists like Kurt Hiller.[101]

There was far more overlap between the *Weiße Blätter* and the *Friedens-Warte* than there was between the *Freie Zeitung* and the *Friedens-Warte*, and Fried clearly nurtured these more intensive contacts, especially with regard to the editor himself, René Schickele. Born in Alsace, Schickele[102] was 19 years younger

---

96   See the article by Otto Flake, "Die Aufgaben der deutschen Intellektuellen," in *Friedens-Warte* 20, no. 6 (June 1918): 153–156.
97   In total, 34 authors wrote the article with Fried. See the list of authors at the beginning of the issue. *Friedens-Warte* 20, no. 7/8 (July 1918): 176.
98   For a good overview of the mutual attacks and accusations, see Korol, "Präexil," 476ff.
99   Stefan Zweig to Romain Rolland, April 20 1918. Quoted in Korol, "Präexil," 297.
100 On the *Weiße Blätter*, see the article by M. Rooney in *Friedensbewegung*, ed. Donat/Holl, 416f.
101 Cf. also Korol, "Deutsches Präexil," 213.
102 On Schickele, see the short biography by A. v. Borries in *Friedensbewegung*, ed. Donat/Holl, 333f; Dr. Friedrich Bentmann, ed. *René Schickele. Leben und Werk in Dokumenten* (Nuremberg, 1974); and Holger Seubert, *Deutsch-französische Verständigung: René Schickele* (Munich, 1993).

than Fried and thus could have been drafted into the war, but because of his extreme short-sightedness he was deemed unfit for military service. Schickele was an early supporter of a negotiated peace between the Germans and the French, and in early 1915 he took over the editorship of *Die Weißen Blätter* in Berlin. Like Fried, he too reacted to the pressure of German censorship by relocating to Zurich in the autumn of 1915. Although toward the end of 1914 Schickele had temporarily embraced the general enthusiasm for war,[103] he was nevertheless one of the staunchest pacifists both before and after the war, and he therefore rejected in principle the orientation of the *Freie Zeitung*. Fried and Schickele had been in contact since 1912, as the evidence in Fried's *Nachlass* in Geneva demonstrates.[104] Over time, they drew closer together, especially since they had a common friend: the French-German writer Annette Kolb.[105]

Annette Kolb, a pacifist from Munich, had had contact with René Schickele since 1915 and worked with him on the *Weiße Blätter*, which Fried closely followed. On February 8, 1916, Fried expressed his admiration for her *Briefe an einen Toten* (Letters to the Dead) and counted her among the few "steadfast individuals who were immune to the war."[106] At the beginning of September, he had a chance to meet her in person. Having been persecuted in Munich for her pacifist speeches and publications and forbidden from any pacifist activity or even correspondence, Annette Kolb was then spending two months in Switzerland where she not only visited Fried but also Rene Schickele and Romain Rolland. Rolland had been living in Switzerland since 1915, and he was also in close contact with her. On February 1, 1917, she finally moved to Berne, where she would remain until the end of the war. In 1921, Kolb published a literary diary (a kind of *roman à clef*) about her time in Switzerland under the title *Zarastro – westliche Tage* (Zarastro – Western Days),[107] in which she also mentioned Fried (as A. H. Pax) in several places. At the end of February 1917, she wrote in her diary: "Spent the evening with A. H. Pax. With him, one can say whatever one wants without running the risk that it will be distorted as it swirls into the wind. This early champion of the idea of peace, who knows how to speak with such solemn earnestness, is, objectively speaking, the most easy-going man in the world, someone in whose presence one can recover one's humor and one's lost laugh for a moment."[108]

---

103 Cf. the critical characterization by Seubert, *Schickele*, 94ff.
104 Cf. Nachlass Fried, Box 81.
105 On Annette Kolb, see Richard Lemp, *Annette Kolb. Leben und Werk einer Europäerin* (Mainz, 1970).
106 Fried, *Kriegs-Tagebuch*, II, 202 (February 8, 1916).
107 Annette Kolb, *ZARASTRO – Westliche Tage* (Berlin, 1921).
108 Ibid, 41.

At the end of April, she accepted an invitation from the Frieds to visit them in Lugano; she spent several weeks with Fried and his wife there. The three met with one of Fried's old acquaintances. Annette Kolb recounted this encounter anecdotally: "A war profiteer living in Berlin, whom the Paxens knew from Vienna, came to visit them. He was the first such person I ever recall having met. We got to hear that one had never eaten so well as with the Hillers and had never drunk so much champagne as with the Borchards. Further, the world now would have to get to know German military might. What Ludendorff commanded was absolutely the right thing, and no criticism was permitted (that was meant for me!); God, how comfortable was this setting here while nations slaughtered one another. (He said this as one speaks of a snowstorm raging outside by the warm chimney.) Not everyone could have it so well, he observed. 'Enough!' cried Mrs. A. H. Pax. He looked a bit puzzled. 'It's terrible what's happening with our currency,' he said. 'And especially with our intellectual currency!' A. H. Pax interjected."[109]

To the end of the war, Annette Kolb maintained close contact with the warring parties as she tried to help war victims, for which she was attacked more often than were others. She was even accused of committing espionage for both opposing sides. In Switzerland she felt constantly under surveillance. She viewed her visits with the Frieds as a respite, as she later remembered: "He was the cornerstone of peace around which we, who were uprooted and cast into the wind, sought to collect ourselves. He was the one without whom we were never complete, whom we missed when he wasn't there, whom we will always miss. [...] During the war years they met in the ever-decreasing smaller parlor of the Fried family in Berne, as the family's resources were slowly being depleted. This was where they managed to shelter themselves from the atmosphere created by the agents, the eavesdroppers, the top news service, its headquarters and branches. Fried's presence seemed like a vaporizer in this atmosphere. He cast out the poisoned microbes."[110] Fried was likewise very fond of the "dear soul" and wrote to her in the summer of 1919 from his summer home in Interlaken, telling her how much he missed her and Schickele, and that now, finally, they should extend the informal you ("du") to one another: "As you know, my dear, I am very fond of you. And when you come to Interlaken, we have to toast our new relationship. Right?"[111]

---

109   Ibid, 81f.
110   Goldscheid, *Gedenkblätter*, 45.
111   Fried to Annette Kolb, June 14 1919, in Nachlass Annette Kolb, 455/68, Münchener Stadtbibliothek.

Shortly before the end of the war, Fried was unexpectedly delivered a hard, personal blow when, quite suddenly, his nephew Lionel Wyon, the oldest son of his sister Pauline, passed away. The belated October edition of the *Friedens-Warte* reported: "Lionel Wyon, who sought out the good and strove for great things, has unexpectedly died in the radiance of his youth. He silently passed away on the morning of the first of October, a month before his twenty-second birthday. In the middle of work, in the midst of an abundance of hopes, plans, and worries. Lionel Wyon was precocious, which made him a searcher. He had always expected an early end; he even spoke of it. But he did not suspect that it would come so soon. So even at a young age, he was engaged with the world. In the 1911 edition of the *Friedens-Warte*, he—then a fourteen-year-old—published his first emotional outpourings against the war. 'Woe to those who sought war. May the blood of so many be on their hands.' That concluded the great work in 1911! – In Zurich, in 1915, at the age of 18, he began to work for the peace movement. He gave lectures and even edited a journal, *Das Wort*, which did not last very long. But it contained forceful examples of the now-lost talent. In his youthful idealism, he wanted to establish a 'European Society,' and he was able to recruit people of reputation to his project. He was restless and eager to engage with the world, unwilling to take the gradual approach. With his sudden death, a thousand plans and projects also perished. I lost not only a hope for the future but also a nephew. A.H.F."[112]

From around 1908, Fried had begun to intensify his efforts to help his nephews Lionel and Gordon, whose parents, Fried's sister and her husband, had "withdrawn" them from him, as a previous letter made clear.[113] After Reginald Wyon left his wife in 1906 and returned home (to London), the two children lived in a boarding school in Baden near Vienna. Their stay was financed by their London grandmother, while Pauline tried to slog her way through without any financial support. At times, she even had to fight for visitation rights at the boarding school.[114] During this difficult time, she had rejoined her brother and probably went to Switzerland with him. There is no evidence that Pauline herself was a pacifist. Of Fried's siblings still alive at the time, only Leopold, who lived in Berlin and followed his older brother in his commitment to Esperanto, seems to have been interested in pacifism and Fried's ideas—this is reflected not only in the letters in Fried's *Nachlass* labelled "Poldis" but also

---

112   *Friedens-Warte* 20, no. 10 (October 1918): 263.
113   Cf. Fried to Pauline Wyon, November 30, 1908. Nachlass Fried, Box 31.
114   The above-mentioned details are taken from a letter by Fried to the director of the boarding school on March 31, 1908, in which he advocates for the right of his sister to have access to her children. Nachlass Fried, Box 31.

in the fact that he attended the eighth German pacifist congress in Berlin on behalf of his brother in 1919.[115]

Not surprisingly, Fried was pleased with his nephew Lionel's development, and in April 1911 he published the fourteen-year-old's long epic poem titled "Was ist Mord?" (What is murder?) in the *Friedens-Warte*,[116] which as a general rule eschewed lyric poetry of any kind.[117] The poem, which is made up of six stanzas, describes the course of a battle from "the morning before the battle" to the death of those who are wounded and must remain on the battlefield the next day.

Lionel matriculated at the University of Zurich to study in the Faculty of Philosophy for the winter semester of 1915, but after only four semesters, presumably because he had other plans, he broke off his studies without a degree. Although Lionel Wyon was not employed by the *Friedens-Warte*, but rather sought his own way within the broad pacifist movement, his view was likely not too different from that of his uncle, and Fried may well have hoped to see in his nephew a successor who would continue his work.

4   After the War – the Final Months in Switzerland

When Wilson announced his fourteen-point program to end the war in January 1918, Fried once again believed that there was a chance for a negotiated peace agreement. On January 10, he wrote: "The hope for peace is brightening. There could now be peace, if the conflict in Germany between the leadership of the military and that of the state, understood in the Bismarkian sense, were to be decided in favor of the latter. Supported by the desperate Pan-Germans who are fighting for their very existence, Ludendorff is in a struggle with Kühlmann, who has the support of all sane people." It was, however, not Kühlmann, but Ludendorff who was to arrange for the German truce based on Wilson's Fourteen Points nine months later, much to the great disappointment of all Wilson supporters.

---

115   Cf. *Achter deutscher Pazifistenkongress. Verhandlungsbericht.* Account of the proceedings, (Charlottenburg, 1919), 174. The name of Leopold Fried is to be found on the list of participants in this account.

116   Cf. *Friedens-Warte* 13, no. 4 (April 1911): 122ff. Under the column "miscellaneous."

117   According to the editor's note: "In principle, the *Friedens-Warte* does not publish poems. But this is the work of a fourteen-year-old pupil at an Austrian *Gymnasium* (college preparatory school). As such it is a document that shows that the anti-war spirit cannot be fully suppressed by our patriotic schools and their war-worshipping curriculum." Ibid, 122. The fact that the author is his nephew goes unmentioned.

The hopes that moved Fried in these months were no long-term match for the reality of the situation. On December 11, 1918, he wrote: "In the midst of the jubilation over their victory, the statesmen of the Entente are forging the conditions for peace. A strange peace agreement, which is more likely to resemble a court session, where the verdict is conveyed to the defendant as a *fait accompli*."[118]

Although the pacifists continued to place their hopes on Wilson, who was to arrive in Europe on December 13, "people are apprehensive that he will have the power to influence those intoxicated with victory."[119] The "central organization for a durable peace" ceased its activity and completely embraced the promotion of Wilson's idea for a League of Nations in order to salvage at least a small part of their own vision of the future. To Fried, the prospects seemed bleaker than ever. At the end of 1918 Fried wrote in a dejected tone: "As the year ends, we are more hopeless and more dejected than we ever were in these unfortunate four-and-a-half years of the World War. In the past, a conclusion to the severe crisis that seemed favorable to humanity seemed possible; today, this slight possibility is barely perceptible. The war is over only in theory; it still rages on, more terribly than before. We are not fooling ourselves; it can still get worse."[120]

In January 1919, Fried unexpectedly had the opportunity to travel to Vienna for two weeks as the guide for a study commission of American officers. For him, it was a brief moment of triumph: "So I return home, I who was persecuted as 'someone guilty of high treason,' in the lounge car of the government. In addition to this being a personal highlight, it is also one for pacifism."[121] The joy was only short-lived. Shaken, Fried registered the devastation of the war, which had affected all areas of life in Vienna. He described the dirty, neglected houses and streets, the failing public transportation system and communication system, the absence of businesses, the lack of public safety, which was particularly noticeable in the sudden increase in crimes against property. Above all, however, he sees how the misery of the disabled war veterans and that of the starving population was further aggravated by the coal shortage: "In the flats, the lighting is restricted to a minimum by legal statute, as is the heating. The desolation wrought by darkness and coldness joins the starvation."[122]

---

118   Fried, *Kriegs-Tagebuch*, IV, 362 (December 11, 1918).
119   Fried, *Kriegs-Tagebuch*, IV, 363f (December 14. 1918).
120   Fried, *Kriegs-Tagebuch*, IV, 367–68 (December 31, 1918).
121   The entry of January 11, 1919 did not appear in the book edition, but can be found in *Friedens-Warte* 21, no. 1 (January 1919): 23.
122   Ibid, entry of January 28, 1919. This entry also does not appear in the book edition.

He clearly recognized that the 'republican spirit' in this situation had little chance and that the great mass of people were "too lethargic," too concerned with fundamental existential worries to deal with their new rights and possibilities. Fried was left with little hope as a result of the anticipated victory in the upcoming elections by a majority of the reactionary Christian Social Party, whom he saw as a warmongering party and to whom he ascribed unmistakable complicity for the outbreak of war, and even "the main responsibility for all the misery."

In the course of these weeks the news of the Spartakus uprising in Berlin and in other German cities reached him in Vienna; he immediately denounced them as the "foul product of militarism," vehemently rejecting the violence as equivalent to that of the militarism. But he did fully acknowledge the idealism of its leaders: "These theoretical idealists, when they get down to practical action, commit crimes against humanity. The Crown Prince, Tirpitz, Ludendorff are not at all different from Liebknecht, Radek, and Luxemburg. They are all the result of the same cause. Within the human family, the militaristic spirit is not limited to the old order."[123] The triumphant return of pacifism and its teachings to Austria, which Fried saw embodied for a moment in his own journey, was no more to be found here than in Germany or in Paris, where at the same time, on January 18, 1919, the "Peace Conference" had begun.

Fried returned to Berne in early February to attend the International Socialist Congress as an observer.[124] For him, this post-war international conference offered more than a glimmer of hope for the renewal of international cooperation; he saw it as an "historic event" of far-reaching significance, especially in light of the negotiations in Paris: "It has become increasingly clear in the negotiations that this congress in Berne is the antithesis of the Peace Conference in Paris, that the concentrated will of the people who desire peace here in Berne stands in contrast to those diplomats and militants in Paris who want to preserve the old divisive and blood-stained ideas in a new guise for the post-war world to come. [...] Therefore, the congress dedicated the beginning and the main part of its work to the idea of a league of nations, and so it was primarily pacifist before it even dealt with social issues."[125] Above all, Fried emphasized those aspects of their work that were relevant to pacifism, such as a call for the abolition of armaments and military service and for the establishment of a

---

123 Fried, *Kriegs-Tagebuch*, IV, 368 (January 11, 1919).
124 Annette Kolb: "Immovable, as if he were a palm tree, A. H. Pax kept to himself in the background..." Annette Kolb, *ZARASTRO – Westliche Tage* (Berlin, 1921), 196.
125 *Friedens-Warte* 21, no. 1 (January [?], 1919): 26. Entry of February 8, 1919. This article was not included in the book edition of the diary.

democratic international league that could lay the foundation for a true peace agreement. Although he also addressed some sensitive issues, such as the often hotly debated questions surrounding nationality, he nevertheless sensed the initial efforts at a reconciliation between the nations as well as the "possibility of a better time to come!" – "Journalists and interested listeners gathered around the delegates, and one detects what Berne, what Switzerland has to offer by way of its internationally minded intellectuals; this is a different kind of international congress, which completely captivates its attendees."[126] For Fried, who is part of this "different" congress, Berne offered the opportunity to finally exchange views with like-minded colleagues. "After a few days, we knew almost everyone," wrote Annette Kolb, who was also present at the congress.[127] Fried also met Kurt Eisner,[128] whom he later described as "surely the most interesting figure [...]."[129] Unlike Karl Liebknecht, whose idealism Fried acknowledged, but whose willingness to use violence he sharply condemned,[130] the undogmatic Eisner rejected all violence, sought to mediate between the various currents in his own camp, and personally advocated for peace and reconciliation.[131] He struck Fried as an admirable politician with a "warm heart" and "great intellectual gifts;" his assassination only a few days later affected Fried profoundly. Deeply pessimistic again, Fried wrote: "The murder of Kurt Eisner is an act that lets us see where we are, where we are heading."[132]

As Fried received only discouraging news from Germany and saw the rapidly progressing "social disintegration,"[133] he learned of the first peace terms

---

[126] Ibid, 25. Entry of February 8, 1919.
[127] Annette Kolb, *ZARASTRO – Westliche Tage* (Berlin, 1921), 197.
[128] On Eisner, see the article by L. Wieland in *Friedensbewegung*, ed. Donat/Hall, 100f. Eisner, who as early as November 1914 had been among the first members to join the Bund Neues Deutschland, assumed the presidency of the USPD after the split in the SPD and, on November 7, 1918, overthrew the existing government. Like Fried, he too saw the blunt admission of German guilt for the war as a precondition for a democratic government and also for more generous peace conditions offered by the allies. On February 21, 1919, on the way to the Bavarian parliament, Eisner was shot dead.
[129] Fried, *Kriegs-Tagebuch*, IV, 380 (February 23, 1919).
[130] Cf. the entries of January 11 and 16, 1919 in Fried, *Kriegs-Tagebuch*, IV, 368. On the occasion of Liebknecht's death, Fried wrote: "He was a sympathetic figure to the extent that he, who despised war, remained patient and suffered, but he was a terrifying figure when he used the confusion of the situation to bring civil war to the capital and the country." (369)
[131] Like other pacifists, Eisner too placed all his hopes on Wilson for a quick and permanent peace. On November 11, 1918, he tried to negotiate a unilateral peace for Bavaria. It was sent to Wilson through Switzerland and named Friedrich Wilhelm Foerster as the Bavarian Ambassador to Berne. See Andreas Kraus, *Geschichte Bayerns* (1983), 634ff.
[132] Fried, *Kriegs-Tagebuch*, IV, 378ff. (February 23, 1919).
[133] Ibid, 383. Entry of March 2, 1919.

emerging from the peace conference in Paris. These included the desire of the Entente to reduce the German army to 100,000 men. This was a demand that ran counter to Fried's view; he had advocated that disarmament occur simultaneously on all sides once an intergovernmental order was established. Resigned, he noted: "That would be disarmament, just not the one we pacifists aspire to. Mandatory disarmament of a single state while the others remain armed is an absurdity."[134] And, he cautioned, "This kind of peace will reinvigorate the militarist circles, which the revolution had defeated, and it will prevent their complete demise. It is blindness that is operating in Paris, that is preparing the next bloodbath with unavoidable certainty [...]"[135]

Like the German government, the pacifists had also assumed that Wilson's fourteen points would be the basis of the Treaty of Versailles.[136] Anticipating future developments, Fried had placed all his hopes in Wilson, as early as December of the previous year: "It is my hope that Wilson, who is seemingly the only one capable of sober and clear thinking, might exert a powerful influence such that this peace will become what it indeed must become to a deeply troubled humanity, namely, the first true peace that condemns war for all time."[137] And a few days later, when the American president arrived in Europe, he noted that for all those who might see clearly, "all hope rests on the arrival of this man."[138] Even worse for Fried were the rumors and the preliminary announcements about the intended content of the treaty: "Will this peace become what it seems now? I still want to bet on Wilson, but he must not let himself be pushed around. He embodies the good principle; his defeat would be the defeat of the better part of humanity [...]."[139]

By now at least, Fried realized that his own position and that of all the other pacifists and Wilson supporters depended on the outcome of the negotiations. In fact, the consequences would be even more serious, because large parts of the German population would soon believe in a double stab-in-the-back legend—domestic and foreign—with Wilson and his supporters becoming the mastermind of the latter and the pacifists playing the role of mastermind in both scenarios.[140] The roots of the "tragic fate of progressive-democratic politics of the Weimar Republic"[141] can be found here.

---

134   Fried, *Kriegs-Tagebuch*, IV, 385 (March 19, 1919).
135   Ibid, 386. Entry of (March 19, 1919).
136   Cf. Fraenkel, *Wilsonbild*, 81ff.
137   Fried, *Kriegs-Tagebuch*, IV, 362 (December 11, 1918).
138   Ibid, 362 (December 14, 1918).
139   Ibid, 397 (April 18, 1919).
140   Cf. Fraenkel, *Wilsonbild*, 89.
141   Ibid, 85.

As the details of the treaty became known, Fried wrote in shock: "And how are we pacifists supposed to tolerate Wilson's bankruptcy? Let's face it, we wagered everything on him. It was right for us to do so since Wilson was proclaiming our doctrine, our ideals, the content of our decades-long struggle, the content of our lives, we who made the creation of a new world order our life's task. It is not merely the peace that is at stake, it is the honor of an idea that, if realized, could save humanity."[142] If the head of the most powerful country in the world could not succeed in establishing a true peace after such a war, then "all action to this end is futile," and only socialism might be able to help.[143] Fried now appeared completely fatalistic, but then, as always in crisis situations, his fighting spirit and the "The Principle of Hope" returned.

The pacifists seemed to move closer to the demands expressed by their conservative opponents for a revision of the Treaty of Versailles. Fried did not even want to use the term "treaty" since it was not based on a negotiation but on a conviction.[144] His objection was also raised by the *Bund Neues Vaterland* (Federation for a New Fatherland) and other democratic-pacifist organizations. Later historians have also seen that the critical weakness in the pacifists' struggle against Versailles lay in the fact that the pacifists insufficiently distanced themselves from the propaganda of the chauvinistic anti-Versailles forces.[145] On the other hand, however, it has also been argued that the pacifists never missed an opportunity to distinguish their own position from that of the conservatives.[146]

Fried emphasized again and again that the mission of the pacifists lay, above all, in confronting the calls for revenge and in making it clear to the people that the essential revision of the Treaty of Versailles could only occur within the framework of the League of Nations and its resources. "Any effort to encourage the different groups of the German people to engage in a war of revenge is an attempt to murder them,"[147] he cautioned, and "Resorgimento ["rising again"] comes through the gates of pacifism. There is no other path." Yet, like many others, Fried was always aware of the immense danger of another war: "We can never consider this war to have ended. The curtain falls even on a prelude. If, in

---

142 Fried, *Kriegs-Tagebuch*, IV, 409f. (May 10, 1919).
143 Ibid, 413 (May 17, 1919). However, by "socialism" Fried means the direction espoused by the USPD; he categorically rejects the positions of the radical leftists as well as the theories of Lenin. (397)
144 Ibid, 421.
145 Cf. Günther Höhne, "Zur Stellung führender Pazifisten zum Versailler Vertrag," in *Jenaer Beiträge zur Parteiengeschichte* 26/27 (Erfurt, 1970): 124–136.
146 Cf. Scheer, *Friedensgesellschaft*, 361f.
147 This and the following quotation are taken from Fried, *Kriegs-Tagebuch*, IV, 433.

the intermission, we are able to thoroughly overcome the misery, then the possibility of peace is given; if not, after a short pause, the violent madness of the war will erupt anew. More terrible, more bloody, more devastating than were the last four years of bloodshed."[148] The warning against a new war and the search for the means to prevent it now became his main focus. His next work *Der Weltprotest gegen den Versailler Frieden* (The World Protest against the Versailles Peace)[149] was ultimately written to advance this mission. Immediately after the announcement of the peace terms of the Treaty of Versailles, Fried began to collect letters, newspaper articles, and speeches by former opponents of the war or by those who remained neutral but objected to this kind of peace agreement. In the summer of 1919, he compiled a 78-page booklet intended to show the German people what a sensible protest might look like.

As clear as it was to Fried that the "old men in Versailles" had squandered the chances for a real peace, "had swept away the ideas of both Wilson and pacifism," and had created only "this blind work of revenge and punishment," he was just as certain that only a Germany that renounced any thought of revenge and revanchism and turned to democracy and pacifism had a chance to revise the treaty and become a member of the international community. This was the only way to disempower the militarism that had created the war as well as the military victory by the Entente and to strengthen the progressive forces in all nations so that they could take power: "If the German people would make the ideas of democracy and pacifism their own, then their isolation would end; they could then enter into a covenant with the people of the victorious nations who want freedom for a pacifist and democratic Germany and who want to be in a community with such a Germany." To achieve this goal, however, far more than lip service to peace was required: "Only when the desire for democracy and for a peace that is guaranteed by law is honest, can we create the key that will unlock the dungeon! – But to achieve this, it is necessary to break with the past, with the old idols and the old ideas, to break as well with the old people who have fallen into disrepute through the former German policy and are still

---

148   Fried, *Kriegs-Tagebuch*, IV, 432f. Fried's views here show clear parallels to the perspective of historians today who characterize the close interconnection of the two wars and speak of "the second Thirty-Years War." See the series in *Der Spiegel* of February and March 2004 with essays by various historians on the topic, especially the essay by Hans-Ulrich Wehler, "Der Erste Weltkrieg als Auftakt und Vorbild für den Zweiten Weltkrieg," *Der Spiegel*, 8 (2004): 82ff.

149   Dr. Alfred H. Fried, *The World Protest against the Versailler Frieden*. Collected, edited, and introduced by Dr. Alfred H. Fried (Leipzig, 1920). The following quotations are also taken from this work.

infected with this mentality. New leaders of a new nation are needed; only a new nation can join a community of other nations."

The break with the past that Fried demanded could only be achieved through an engagement with the past. For Fried, the German admission of culpability for the war became one of the most important demands of the hour. With unmistakable sharpness he criticized any effort to deflect this guilt: "Instead of frankly admitting one's guilt for the world war now and drawing a clear and redemptive line between the present and the old regime, the white-washing continues and quite clearly leads to confusion.[150] However, even within his own camp, Fried's argument that the German government bore the main responsibility for the war, which had already linked him during the war with Richard Grelling but also with other pacifists like Hermann Fernau and Friedrich Wilhelm Foerster, was not completely acceptable. In particular, the moderate wing of pacifism under Ludwig Quidde, supported by internationalists like Walther Schücking, opposed what they considered a premature admission of German guilt; this wing demanded that all the archives must first be opened to an independent commission of inquiry.[151] Fear may well have played a major role here in that such an unconditional acknowledgement of guilt could prevent a possible revision of the Treaty of Versailles, something that some foreign pacifists also feared at that time.

For Fried, however, it was clear that the Austro-Hungarian ultimatum sent to Serbia in the volatile pre-war atmosphere touched off the explosion. "The German government approved of the ultimatum and supported the actions of the Austro-Hungarian government. Without this support, the responsible leaders of the Habsburg Monarchy would never have been able to carry out this act of arson."[152] With a swipe at the position taken by the moderate pacifists, Fried wrote: "Whoever is willing to look, can indeed recognize the blame in its full clarity just from what is already known. Some timid souls, who want to wait until all the archives of the world are opened before forming an opinion, are like lawyers who want to obscure a trial by requesting a continuance, a trial that has already been deemed hopeless [...]." The claim "my country right or wrong" should be of no significance. On the other hand, it was important to emphasize "that the clarification of the war guilt does not imply the guilt of the German people, but rather the guilt of the system of government that dominated the German people." Through the revolution, Fried claimed, the

---

150 Fried, *Kriegs-Tagebuch*, IV, 417. (May 27, 1919).
151 Cf. Scheer, *Deutsche Friedensgesellschaft*, 367f.
152 Dr. Alfred H. Fried, *Auf hartem Grund* (Hamburg, 1919), 13. The following quotation is also taken from this work.

people have separated themselves from that government, and now, through a clear admission of guilt, they could show how they were different from the old system.

As early as July or August of 1918, Fried had called for "the minds to be disinfected,"[153] which he considered the most important task of the post-war period. He warned against the deep-seated traces left behind by "four years of intellectual morass," in which "ineffectual people, uninspired bunglers, subservient creatures" busily sought to "twist opinions and facts, cover up the grinning truths, enshrine laziness, ban truth and its heralds, torture, and annihilate." The end of the war demanded a radical, far-reaching change: "But one must not restrict oneself to simply eliminating the contamination of the mind. It is rather a question of prevention, the assurance that something like this could never happen again, that the lackeys never be allowed to take control of the intellectual life of a people in the Temple of Ideas."

One way to achieve this, according to Fried, was to confront publicly the main players of July 1914. And nearby in Berne, not far from him, lived one of the most guilty, the former Austro-Hungarian Foreign Minister Count Leopold Berchtold, who had formulated the ultimatum to Serbia after the assassination in Sarajevo and who was now enjoying asylum in Switzerland. In his very emotional article "Schweizer Gesichte" (Swiss Visions),[154] Fried described the terrible conditions of the Viennese children who were sent to recuperate in Switzerland and the distress, hopelessness, and despair they left behind. He then contrasted them with the count's appearance: "Those who live in Berne can see him often, this Count Berchtold. From the green hat, balanced on the long, narrow crétin head, down to his well-polished boots bedecked with spats, in impeccable elegance. His hands always covered with white gloves, playing carefree with his little walking stick, his face always cheerful, he strolls through the arbors."

One can clearly sense the author's anger when he reported how the count traveled by car through the region from his newly acquired properties directly on Lake Thun, "an Adam in reverse, who came to paradise only after the Fall of Man." And he fervently appealed to his compatriots, that, in spite of their worries about their own personal existence, they should not forget to settle the score with the man who cold-heartedly paved the way for the attack on Serbia, who first assured himself of the help of Wilhelm II, and then in the

---

153 Fried, "Die Desinfizierung der Gehirne," in *Friedens-Warte* 20, no. 7/8 (July/August 1918): 188f. The following quotation is also taken from this work.
154 Fried, "Schweizer Geschichte," in *Arbeiter-Zeitung. Zentralorgan der Sozialdemokratie Deutschösterreichs* 32, no. 11 (January 11, 1920). The manuscript is located in Nachlass Fried, Box 9, file 123. The following quotation is also taken from this work.

Council of Ministers, on July 7 and on July 19, ushered in the war against Serbia knowing full well that this would necessarily lead to war with Russia and thereby set Europe ablaze." According to Fried, it was the duty of the people of German-Austria to put the criminal on trial, "in our court, not that of the foreign victors," and to pass judgment on him, notwithstanding the fact that neither the victorious powers nor Austria could compel Switzerland to hand over the native Czech Berchtold. Fried was not concerned with the execution of a sentence, but only with a public demonstration of guilt: "The people who ruthlessly brought about this war should be ostracized, first and foremost the chief offender, the smiling lord of the castle of Lake Thun."

But even if Fried cursed all those who started this war "in the summer of 1914, frivolously and recklessly, as well as incomprehensibly and unscrupulously,"[155] it remained the case that neither in Germany nor in Austria had efforts toward a serious discussion about the question of guilt and the guilty parties found broad appeal. On the contrary, prompted by the Germans' anger and disappointment about the Treaty of Versailles, the political right managed only too quickly to shift the blame for the misery and the defeat onto the "defeatists" and "traitors" already disdained in the war, and above all onto pacifists like Fried who had emigrated.[156] It soon became clear to them that they would not return as revered representatives of reason ready to take power, but, as before, only to continue to belong to a fringe group that had been ostracized more than ever. Nevertheless, Fried made plans to return to Germany in 1919—he had felt compelled to make such plans because his personal situation at the time offered little reason for optimism. The moderate wealth that he had accumulated (from the Nobel Prize) became almost worthless due to the collapse of the Austrian currency. His meager income, earned through his journalistic work in Switzerland, was scarcely enough to live on, especially because the *Friedens-Warte*, after the Carnegie subsidies were ended, had again become dependent on other sources of income. In June 1919, Fried wrote to Wehberg, who had suggested an expansion of the *Friedens-Warte*, that he did not even know whether the next issue could be published. The end of the letter includes a handwritten sentence: "I'm done, also privately. The economic collapse of German-Austria has made me a beggar."[157]

In desperation, he wrote to Annette Kolb: "Isn't living 'in peace' terrible? Now we have it. Don't we look grand."[158] She had earlier asked him about

---

155 Fried, *Kriegs-Tagebuch*, IV, 447. (last entry of June 30, 1919).
156 Cf. Scheer, *Deutsche Friedensgesellschaft*, 354f.
157 Fried to Wehberg, June 2, 1919, in Nachlass Wehberg, vol. 59b, BA Koblenz.
158 Fried to Annette Kolb, June 14, 1919, in Nachlass Annette Kolb, Stadtbibliothek München.

the possibility of nominating the musician Busoni, who was also in difficult straits, for the Nobel Prize for Literature. He asked half-jokingly, half-seriously, whether she might know of someone who would want to buy his own Nobel Prize: "I would be happy to give my own away, if someone would make me a good offer. It is in Austrian bills. Perhaps you know a rich man who would like to receive the Nobel Prize (second-hand, antique, no longer needed). He would just have to pay me the equivalent in crowns at face value. Then he could print on the business card "Recipient of a Nobel Prize."

Fried first returned to Germany at the end of October 1919. Four months earlier he had canceled his participation in the pacifist congress in Berlin, since he could not "risk the excitement and danger[159] of a trip to Germany,"[160] and merely set out his positions in a long letter to the assembly. But now the trip to Germany became very important to him because his situation in Switzerland had become increasingly critical. The relocation of the journal and its editor to Germany or Austria seemed urgent not only for tactical but also for financial reasons. Although there is no documentation, it can be assumed that Fried used the congress in Kassel to seek support for his relocation plans and to explore his personal standing within the German Peace Society. Evidence that he was still one of the leaders can be seen in the fact that Fried, along with Quidde and Nicolai, personally addressed the assembly.

By the middle of November, the decision to move the *Friedens-Warte* to Germany seems to have already been made. Peter Reinhold in Leipzig agreed to become the publisher, but he demanded some financial assurances. Fried looked for a new home in Germany, although his friends strongly advised against it. Among them was his longtime friend Elsbeth Friedrichs, who had settled in Locarno with her husband. Terrified, she wrote to Fried at the end of December 1919: "You want to go to Germany? How do you plan to live there? Many have left here for there because of the currency, and we are constantly hearing complaints and regrets – we should have stayed there in Switzerland, because life in Germany was intolerable [...] If you can live in a hotel with all your family members and you can pay for it, then you will be well fed and warm, but to have an apartment, and to manage the upkeep, this seems to me to be quite impossible according to everything that I have heard about the life in

---

159   Fried to Wehberg, June 2, 1919, in Nachlass Wehberg, vol. 59b, BA Koblenz.
160   Even in October 1919, Fritz Röttcher begins his report about the general assembly of the German Peace Society with a comment that the trip is "a difficult and possibly dangerous undertaking." "The train cars are unheated, and the connections are poor and erratic. The trains are so crowded that one fears for one's life, and the hotel rooms have no doubt already been taken." *Friedens-Warte* 21, no. 9/10 (October 1919): 170. In addition, there was no certainty that well-known pacifists such as Fried could be protected.

Germany [...] And you want to go there now in January, to freeze? You were very ill two years ago; what if it hits you again in such unsanitary circumstances?"[161]

But Fried had long since felt that he had no other choice; he simply could not afford to stay in Switzerland anymore. The war had also left its mark on the host country, not only because it led to an inner tug-of-war between German-speaking Switzerland and the rest of the country, but above all because Switzerland was dependent on imports to provide for its people. As in the warring countries, foodstuffs had to be rationed in Switzerland from 1917 on, and in 1918 every sixth Swiss already lived below the subsistence level. The steadily rising prices also affected the printing cost of the *Friedens-Warte*, an expense that Fried had been unable to pay for some time because he could not rely on his devalued Austrian savings.

---

161 Elsbeth Friedrichs to Fried, December 27, 1919, in Nachlass Fried, Box 88. Elsbeth Friedrichs' fears were to be realized in the following winter.

CHAPTER 5

Everywhere a Foreigner

1   Back to Vienna, via Munich

With a recommendation from Dr. Adolf Müller, the German ambassador in Berne, Fried traveled to Germany in early February 1920 to re-establish the *Friedens-Warte*. From Munich he made his way via Berlin to Leipzig, where he sought to negotiate a contract with the publishing house Neuer Geist to take over the publication of his journal. But when the publisher hesitated, his attention turned to Munich. There the situation seemed more favorable, but his request to immigrate was submitted in unsettled times: "The government in Bavaria seemed prepared to extend a favorable [...] opinion on the application. But as a result of the Kapp Putsch, the government resigned, and the new government pursued a strict policy against non-native Bavarians."[1]

Despite the resignation of the social-democratic government on March 14 and the seizure of power by the right-wing monarchist Gustav von Kahr, the chief executive of the district of Upper Bavaria, the old government coalition nevertheless continued to rule but without the Social Democrats. Within a very short time, von Kahr made Bavaria a "haven for the growing nationalistic forces," a "locus of order in the Reich."[2] As a result, Fried no longer had any hope of feeling welcome in Bavaria.

During these weeks, Fried was often plagued by doubts about whether he should stay in Germany given the local political and economic conditions or whether he should really return to Switzerland. When he expressed his fears to his secretary, Mundy Schwalb,[3] she offered him these sympathetic words of consolation: "As if home were simply the stones of the streets, which certainly remained the same. Home is the inexpressible feeling that gently embraces us whenever we come home. That is now gone. Everywhere. We have become foreigners everywhere. And we are most foreign where we were once most at home."[4]

---

1   *Friedens-Warte* 22, no. 3 (June 3, 1920): 95. See the article "Meine Ausweisung aus München."
2   Kraus, *Geschichte Bayerns*, 672.
3   Cf. the numerous letters that Mundy Schwalb wrote in response in February 1920, in Nachlass Fried, Box 91.
4   Mundy Schwalb to Fried, February 17, 1920, in Nachlass Fried, Box 91.

Despite his many doubts, Fried decided at the end of February to have his office moved to Munich. As his two secretaries traveled to Munich, he once again went to Berlin. Obliging yet skeptical, Mundy Schwalb remarked: "So you merrily go on to Berlin, while your wife stays behind in Munich, if she is not deported? We'll come to Munich next week, and then in about eight days we'll be asked to leave the city, and then go where?"[5] Nevertheless, following a few days delay at the beginning of March, Mundy arrived in Munich. Like Fried, she too was shocked by the economic situation: "We like the city. But food is expensive, and the people are malnourished! I don't see how one can possibly live here."[6] Like her sister, Mundy Schwalb also did not expect to be allowed to move there at this time. "I boldly look ahead, but I do not know where to go."[7]

In fact, at the end of March 1920, Fried's first petition was indeed rejected by the Munich Police Department. At the same time, he was requested to leave Munich by April 1, but Fried had already left Munich! After traveling across Germany, he went to Constance, where he temporarily left his wife and secretaries at the Hotel Hecht to return to Berne for a short time. While Mundy Schwalb tried in vain to stop the arrival of the Fried's luggage in Lindau, which had been sent from Berne to Munich at the beginning of March, Fried was looking for a new, temporary place to stay. Again Elsbeth Friedrichs tried to keep him in Switzerland: "Now, besides your bad experiences and the misery you experienced in Germany during this past month, you've also lost so much money, and now you are burning through money again in Berne. And so you are desperate. Yes, I do think that you have reason to feel that way. But you should seriously consider taking your family to a less expensive town in Switzerland where you could live simply and economically."[8]

But Fried wanted to return to Germany. He still hoped that the appeal filed by his attorney in Munich could be successful. His future remained in doubt until early May when he was informed by his lawyer that the government of Upper Bavaria upheld the earlier decision by the administration. At the same time, he made one final attempt and lodged a complaint with the Bavarian State Ministry of the Interior. His lawyer pointed out in his argument that the police had mistakenly presumed that many people would be accompanying Fried but that Fried did not intend to bring any staff or family except his wife and two secretaries. Above all, he emphasized Fried's international significance: "Dr. Fried enjoys a great international reputation as a politician and

---

5 Mundy Schwalb to Fried, February 24, 1920, in Nachlass Fried, Box 91.
6 Mundy Schwalb to Fried, March 11, 1920, in Nachlass Fried, Box 91.
7 Ibid.
8 Elsbeth Friedrichs to Fried, March 26, 1920, in Nachlass Fried, Box 88.

scholar; he is a reputable journalist. It would therefore be, as I have already explained, a serious political mistake to make it impossible for him to work in Germany. This would not easily be understood, both by those inside and outside of Germany [...]."[9]

The final decision did not come quickly. Even before it was issued, a short notice in the *Münchener Post* on June 12, which dealt with Fried's expulsion from Munich, unleashed a worldwide response in the press. The *Berliner Tagblatt* reported: "If Fried, who is known and respected throughout the civilized world, should really be expelled, that would only show once again that reactionary forces and stupidity are synonymous. The 'victors' of November 6 apparently want to show the world what it should expect of them [...]."[10]

Fried himself commented in the *Friedens-Warte* on the press releases and on the dementi by the Munich Police Department. Contrary to the opinion of his lawyer that the rejection of his application to immigrate was not politically motivated, "but rather resulted from the application of known regulations,"[11] Fried, like many other commentators, assumed the decision was political: "Well, whoever has convictions and seeks to defend them in today's Bavaria will be punished by having his residence permit revoked 'in perpetuity' and ordered to leave by next Thursday if these beliefs don't suit the ruling regime. Long live democracy!"[12]

After the rejection, however, Fried did decide to return to Vienna, his hometown. He wrote to Georg Arnhold: "After I had to give up my residence in Switzerland for lack of money, I wandered around Germany for four months without finding a place to live. I was indeed expelled from Munich, despite the denials of the police. [...] At Lake Constance I had only a limited permit for a few weeks. That's how I finally landed in Vienna."[13]

Nevertheless, Fried hoped that it would ultimately be only a temporary stay. The newspaper of the Vienna Freemasons included a report about a meeting of the Viennese Grand Lodge in May: "The ceremonial address was delivered by the Nobel Prize recipient Dr. Alfred Hermann Fried who has returned to Vienna for a short stay following some time abroad."[14]

The lack of alternatives, however, forced Fried to stay in his native city for the time being, which at least had the advantage that it could not expel him.

---

9 Rheinstrom to Fried, copy of a complaint filed with the Bavarian State Ministry of the Interior, May 3, 1920, in Nachlass Fried, Box 90.
10 *Berliner Tageblatt*, no. 274, 13 June 1920.
11 Rheinstrom to Fried, 13 July 1920, in Nachlass Fried, Box 90.
12 "Nochmals meine Ausweisung aus München," in *Friedens-Warte* 22, no. 3 (July 1920): 125.
13 Fried to Georg Arnhold, undated [May/June 1920], in Nachlass Fried, Box 87.
14 *Wiener Freimaurer-Zeitung* 2, no. 6 (June 1920): 4f.

He remarked to David Starr Jordan in California: "I have been back in Austria since May. I do so of necessity, not of my own desire. The worthlessness of our currency has made it impossible for me to live in Switzerland. But here in Vienna, as nowhere else, I can find an apartment. Some rooms in a school building were temporarily made available to me, but as soon as the school opens in January, I'll have to move again. Where to, I don't know. [...] There are some things in this ignoble life that you just have to put up with."[15] At the same time, he outlined the dangerous political situation that had emerged with the victory of the reactionaries in Austria, "which, together with the barbaric forces of General Horty[16] in Hungary, could restore the monarchy and, with it, the full measure of its reactionary power." And with resignation he added, "Things look bad all over the world."

Only a few of Vienna's citizens welcomed his return as joyfully as did Arthur Schnitzler, who wrote to Fried in June that he hoped there would be no more six-year breaks in their relationship and that they would now see each other more often.[17] Fried was also cordially received by the members of his lodge. After the Republic of Austria was founded in 1918 and the Free Masons were once again permitted to assemble, the former border lodges joined forces to form the Grand Lodge of Vienna. This strengthened the ties to pacifism to an even greater extent than had been the case earlier with the border lodges: "The Grand Lodge of Vienna has joined the peace society, the parent organization of all the associations that strive for equality, and has made a founder's contribution; in so doing, it acknowledges the work and support of this exemplary cultural institution, whose leader today, the successor of the famous founder and longtime first president, Bertha Suttner [sic], is Brother Alfred Hermann Fried, her confidant and loyal collaborator."[18]

At this time, the president of the Austrian Peace Society was in need of any assistance he could get. Only a few of the society's members were part of the circle around the Freemasons – Heinrich Glücksmann, Karl Barolin, and Paul Kammerer – who were now members of the executive board of the Austrian Peace Society, and Rudolf Goldscheid, who had worked with the *Bund Neues Vaterland* (Federation for a New Fatherland) during the war. Ever so gradually the small group managed to bring society back to life.

---

15   Fried to David Starr Jordan, undated, in Nachlass Fried, Box 88. The following quotation is also taken from this source.
16   Translators' note: Fried means Admiral Miklós Horthy.
17   Arthur Schnitzler to Fried, June 12, 1920, in Nachlass Fried, Box 90.
18   *Wiener Freimaurer-Zeitung* 1, no. 8 (August 1919): 17.

After a few weeks in the hotel, Fried probably did not move into the school rooms mentioned in his letter to Jordan because he had found accommodations on the outskirts of Vienna in a garden house at Kaasgraben 6, where he could remain until year's end. The house was actually intended for the women of the peace movement.[19] Nevertheless, he remained discontent, lamenting the absence of his library, "which is stored in 46 boxes in Vienna, Berne, and Constance," the lack of a telephone, and the lack of postal services.

Like so many emigrants, Fried no longer felt at home in Vienna. Although one can safely assume that among the Viennese pacifists and Freemasons there must have been some who were in essential agreement with him, he nevertheless wrote to René Schickele that he now lived in an intellectual vacuum: "In innermost Africa one could not be more isolated." There was no one with whom he could discuss his problems, "no trace of a group of like-minded people such as we had in Berne." In the summer of 1920, Fried also wrote to Otto Lehmann-Russbüldt in Berlin that he was only in Vienna because he could not be expelled from there: "But, with all kindness, the poor Austrians are losers, who live their daily lives unconsciously and with a caricatured worldview, so that I am without like-minded colleagues; everything that is done here is only 'self-promotion,' with a yearning to see one's name in the newspaper."[20] He was therefore happy to accept a proposal by Lehman-Russbüldt who wanted to petition the government in the name of all the peace organizations to have Fried sent to Geneva as a special representative, permanent contact person, and observer to the League of Nations.[21] In August, Lehmann-Russbüldt reported that thus far "only one step has been taken, and one has to wait and see if it will be successful."[22] But that was the end of the exchange, so that this hope too was dashed.

Separated from others by virtue of his emigration, Fried felt one particular loss very deeply: Mundy Schwalb and her sister did not follow the Frieds to Vienna, but returned to Switzerland from Lake Constance in August. To Schickele he lamented, "If for years you've been attuned to a person who knows the whole range of your interests, with whom you could talk about all kinds of things, events, and people, and then when you suddenly find yourself alone, because my good wife was never concerned about such things, that's

---

19 Fried to René Schickele, carbon copy without date [ca. May/June 1920], in Nachlass Fried, Box 91a. Fried writes that Frau Hertzka from the Frauen-Friedensbewegung (Womens Peace Movement) made four rooms available to him for the summer, which he was even able to furnish with his own furniture.
20 Fried to Lehmann-Russbüldt, July 9, 1920, in Nachlass Fried, Box 89.
21 Cf. Lehmann-Russbüldt, July 3, 1920, in Nachlass Fried, Box 89.
22 Lehmann-Russbüldt, August 2, 1920, in Nachlass Fried, Box 89.

just terrible. Incidentally, I also miss the clerical help, which is no small thing when it comes to my correspondence and all of my projects. Only a woman is capable of behaving like that! A man could never do that, abandon someone suddenly and dispassionately.[23]

Even when he was able to persuade the Schwalb sisters to stay in Vienna for a while in the summer, he was not content. He wrote to Schickele: "Schwalb's presence here is good for me; I almost think that I would not be able to work at all without her, but she has made up her mind not to stay and to return to Switzerland, which I can hardly begrudge her. Then I'll be sitting here again in the most abysmal isolation possible. Terrible."[24]

In point of fact, Mundy Schwalb and her sister Irene did go back to Switzerland in August; again and again, they tried to persuade Fried to join them there.[25] Fried, on the other hand, was trying to bring Annette Kolb and René Schickele, his friends from Berne, to Vienna to counter the feeling of rootlessness. He wrote longingly to Schickele: "We could re-imagine the old days in Berne here, and perhaps make plans for a future home somewhere, somehow."[26]

Even before the planned departure of the Schwalb sisters, Fried was struck by a new blow: on August 8, his mother, Berta Fried-Engel, died at the age of 77 in Bernburg. The death of his sprightly mother, who at the beginning of May had demanded a quick visit from her son, came as a surprise to Fried. Despite the spatial distance, the two had always been close.

Fried attended the funeral in Bernburg,[27] but contrary to his usual custom he did not combine this trip with a visit to other German cities. Instead, he returned to Germany a month later, this time to Braunschweig, where from the September 30 to October 3 the ninth German pacifist convention was being held. It would be the last Peace Congress that Fried would personally attend. In his report he emphasized the great interest and dedication of the participants from twelve different pacifist organizations in Germany, who, unlike in the past, no longer passively approved all the decisions of the executive board but actively supported their ideas. "Passive indifference no longer rules the day. A radical view prevails there, one that is averse to any compromise. How logical and how gratifying this is! Nothing would be more inappropriate after

---

23 Fried to René Schickele, carbon copy without date [ca. May/June 1920], in Nachlass Fried, Box 91a.
24 Fried to René Schickele, August 3, 1920, in Nachlass Fried, Box 91a.
25 Cf. the letters of Mundy Schwalb to Fried in 1920 and January 1921, in Nachlass Fried, Box 91a.
26 Fried to René Schickele, August 3, 1920, in Nachlass Fried, Box 91a.
27 The grave of Bertha Fried-Engels has been preserved, even today, at the Jewish cemetery in Bernburg.

the frightening experience of the World War, after the terrible collapse of the world, than to conform to others' opinions, to strike a balance, and to seek reconciliation, and thus to want to employ the methods of the pre-August peace movement."[28]

Fried wholeheartedly welcomed this fresh start, even though he himself—as Bertha von Suttner had once criticized him—now disapproved of the sometimes rather coarse tone, and he emphasized that the power of the thought was sufficient to implement an idea. According to von Suttner, the "use of outrageous language" was unnecessary. However, the venue and the way the congress unfolded did not find his full approval; he criticized the selection of Braunschweig and the complete absence of the international press. He also complained about the rigidity of the program: "Quiddes' capacity for work is admirable. He's focused on the congress from seven in the morning until two at night. Not everyone can do that. Besides, the most important thing is not to spend hours on end scuffling about the wording of a resolution like a pack of wolves for a lamb. Some interpersonal communication is also required. We should not miss this opportunity that brings together a few hundred fellow pacifists from all parts of the country!" Fried, who experienced isolation in Vienna, probably felt this shortcoming far more than did the other pacifists.

On October 1, he gave a speech in front of 1,500 people at the general assembly and, as so often, called for "the German acknowledgement of its explicit guilt in causing the war." While he believed that he saw only weak opposition in the reaction of the audience, the local press reacted far more aggressively. The question of guilt for the war still remained one of the most contentious issues in Germany, and both a majority of the population and also the moderate pacifists continued to reject an acknowledgement of guilt.

Shortly after his return, Fried received more bad news. On September 30, his former Swiss publisher Orell Füssli sent him an account statement showing a deficit of 4,150 Swiss francs for the production of the *Friedens-Warte* and requested that he pay at least part of the amount. For the almost penniless Fried this was an impossibility. "The sum that you demand of me today, given the present state of our Austrian currency, exceeds the dizzying amount of more than a third of a million. I must confess to you, quite frankly, that as a freelance writer I am unable to pay this sum, and I am certain that I will never be able to do so."[29]

---

28   *Friedens-Warte* 22, no. 8/9 [!] (October/November 1920): 218. The following quotation is also taken from this source.

29   Fried to the supervisory board of the Art Institute Orell Füssli, November 25, 1920, in Nachlass Fried, Box 90. The following quotation is also taken from this source.

He further wrote that he had paid the publisher almost 100,000 francs between 1915 and 1919 for the production and distribution of the journal and that he was now appealing to the better judgment of the supervisory board to ask that the small deficit, "for me of catastrophic impact," be written off permanently. At the same time, Fried mentioned the 779 complete issues of the journal from the war years that were still in storage and that represented a value that was not to be underestimated, since in England and the USA "several hundred libraries and scholars had ordered the *Friedens-Warte* for years before the war and will likely want to own the volumes that appeared during the war."

An answer to Fried's response is not extant, but an ad by the publisher, which appeared in the December 1919 issue of the *Friedens-Warte* and advertised the issues from the war years, indicates that there had been attempts to sell at least some of the inventory. It is possible that the publisher actually dropped his remaining claims, since there was little chance of satisfaction anyway. But it is also possible that his demands were part of the mountain of debt that Therese Fried later inherited from her husband.

2 Final Works and Plans

To keep himself afloat financially, Fried worked himself to exhaustion. There were of course the countless newspaper articles he produced, but he also made plans for new, large-scale projects that he would tackle as soon as his archive was available again.

In January 1920, as he was staying in Berne, Fried explained to David Starr Jordan, his American patron: "First of all, I am writing a book in which I describe the last thirty years of the peace movement in Germany and its campaign against the German government. It is a historical account, based on my own experiences in this thirty-year struggle. I am in possession of Bertha von Suttner's diaries from 1900 to shortly before her death in 1914. I have these from her estate. They include very interesting, mostly aphoristic entries about political events. [...] From this fifteen-year record I need only make excerpts and add some explanatory remarks. [...] As my third major project, I have in mind an edition of my collected writings on the peace question, most of which are scattered in smaller leaflets and in thousands of newspaper articles, but which, collectively, would offer an encyclopedia of the science of pacifism and of pacifist-political criticism."[30]

---

30   Fried to David Starr Jordan, January 22, 1920, in Nachlass Fried, Box 90.

Fried also had in mind a new edition of his handbook, but he did not really believe he could start the work without access to his library and archive. While he was in Vienna, he tried to plan all three projects in more detail, even as he was looking for possible publishers. But, under such adverse conditions, the work did not progress very well.

A hand-written notebook,[31] preserved in his papers, indicates the contours of the conceptual framework of his autobiography "Dreißig Jahre Pazifismus" (Thirty Years of Pacifism), which, though he had already found a publisher,[32] did not get beyond a first, rough outline, and only the first chapter would be completed by the time of his death. At the same time, he tried to sell his archive and the estate of Bertha von Suttner; in an offer that is preserved only in a fragment, he imagined that he could get ten to fifteen thousand dollars for both together: "This sum would enable me to finally find a place to live and be able to devote myself to my work without any financial worries. Since I can't find an apartment, I would like to be able to buy a small house, preferably in Switzerland. There I would be able to unpack and catalog the archive." This project too was one that Fried was not able to realize in his lifetime.[33] And so he remained in his summer apartment in the Kaasgraben into the winter and devoted himself to his writing and to rebuilding the Austrian Peace Society.

Bertha von Suttner continued to be a major topic for Fried. In addition to his efforts to secure permission to publish her diary, he was also the driving force behind the committee within the Austrian Peace Society to establish a Suttner Memorial. The plans included a dignified burial of the Suttner urn in an honorary grave in Gotha and the erection of a monument designed by the

---

[31] The handwritten notebook, which contains roughly 20 pages of unordered notes, is located in Nachlass Fried, Box 9, file 180. The planned structure of the work was reconstructed from these notes. Similarly, the following quotations are transcriptions from this notebook.

[32] By October 23, 1919 Fried had already entered into a contract with the publisher Neuer Geist Verlag in Leipzig. The contract granted the publisher the sole rights for a planned autobiography. As remuneration, fifteen percent of the retail price along with an advance of 10,000 marks was agreed upon. The advance was to be paid in monthly installments of 1,000 marks beginning in January 1920. The work was to comprise 230,000 to 340,000 characters and the first ten printed sheets were to be completed by June 1920; the rest was to be submitted by the end of the year. Since Fried was unable to adhere to this timeline, the contract was voided in July 1920. Cf. the contract with the publisher of October 23, 1919 in Nachlass Fried, Box 89 (Neuer Geist Verlag).

[33] Fried's handwritten offer, undated, in Nachlass Fried, Box 92. Fried thought that he could guarantee the sale by taking a down payment; that way he could have access to his archive and the Nachlass until his death, and he would then be able organize the files for the new owner.

Viennese sculptor Hugo Taglang,[34] who had already made the death mask of the deceased and would also later make Fried's.[35]

However, Fried expended most of his energy in the final months of 1920 on his increasingly desperate search for a new place to live. Although it was quite certain that he could remain in his residence only until the end of the year, there was still no prospect of a new home. Desperately, he turned to acquaintances and friends for help, including the editor of the *Wiener Freimaurer-Zeitung* newspaper, Heinrich Glücksmann, who made a final attempt in December to describe Fried's situation to the Freemason circles beyond his own lodge, and, under the headline "Ein berühmter Bruder – Obdachlos" (A Famous Brother – Homeless), published a letter by Fried in his journal. Fried wrote: "I came to Vienna in May, hoping to permanently settle here. A lot of promises were made to me, but so far none has been kept."[36] He further wrote that, before he was forced to leave Vienna in search of a new home elsewhere, he wanted to turn once more to the Masonic brothers and ask "if perhaps through the intervention of some dear brothers I could find a place to live and space to work."

But this time, apparently, even the brothers could not help. By December 21, 1920, there was still no new home for Fried on the horizon. There is a personal request with this date on it; it is presumably directed to Dr. Wengraf, the president of "Concordia," an association of journalists and writers. Fried concluded the petition with the words: "If you would appeal to the public for me, it may still be possible to find someone who has more living space than he needs and would be willing to take me in, or to interest a government agency that might help me."[37]

The specter of homelessness drew ever nearer. Two days later, on December 23, Fried fell ill with pneumonia but still continued to work. Shortly thereafter, the appeal that he had hoped the writer's union would make was published in the press. Under the headline "Ein obdachloser Schriftsteller" (A Homeless Writer),[38] the president, "dutifully representing the interests of writers," called upon those who owned houses and villas to provide Fried with a place to live and work: "One may or may not share the political views of this tireless apostle

---

34   Cf. *Wiener Freimaurer-Zeitung* 2, no. 9/12 (December 1920): 14.
35   Fried's death mask is located today in the Historisches Museum of the city of Vienna.
36   *Wiener Freimaurer-Zeitung* 2, no. 9/12 (December 1920): 12.
37   Fried to "Herr Präsident," carbon copy of a letter of December 21, 1920, in Nachlass Fried, Box 20, file 341.
38   Appeal of the association of journalists and writers, "Concordia," undated. Excerpt from a newspaper, in Nachlass Fried, Box 20. The following quotations are taken from this newspaper article.

of peace, but everyone would find it lamentable if a writer of international renown had to leave Vienna and move abroad because he could not find a place to live in his own country."

Unlike the call of the Freemasons, this appeal was not without resonance. When the news of the imminent homelessness of the Nobel Prize laureate reached Berne and Paris,[39] Fried received a last-minute offer at the end of December to live in a residence on Praterstraße, one of the major streets in Leopoldstadt, not far from the Weintraub School, which he had attended during his final year of primary school. Fried was not exactly thrilled about this situation, as it was coupled with some unpleasant memories.[40] Mundy Schwalb was now working for the Swiss consulate in Berne but still felt like Fried's secretary. Deeply troubled by the illness of her friend, she tried to console him: "Praterstraße is not as bad as Mariahilferstraße or Gumpendorferstraße, for example. When you're well again, you'll see that it will all work out."[41]

However, these words of encouragement ring somewhat hollow, for only a few days earlier, on first hearing of the apartment on Praterstraße, she had drafted various plans for the return of Fried to Switzerland. She had urged him to go there, as Elsbeth Friedrichs had done a year before: "If you feel that Lammasch is right and that you can no longer live in Vienna after your time in Switzerland, then just take the leap and come back here. You'll see, it will work out. It may not be luxurious, but it'll work [...] And since we only live once, why should it be somewhere where we don't feel right?"[42] And she added cheerfully: "Where does the path lead from the Kaasgraben, you ask? To life, Alfred Fried, just to life."

But in the next letter the cheerful tone gave way to a serious concern. Fried's recovery was the only thing that really mattered: "We are so upset about your illness that I don't know what to say. I telegraphed you today, so I hope I'll know

---

39 Cf. the article "Un 'prix Nobel' sans logis" in the *Journal Paris* of December 29, 1920. Here one reads: "Vienne, 28 décembre. La crise des logements continue à sévir à Vienne avec la méme intensité. Le club des journalistes, 'La Concordia,' cherche actuellement pour le Fr. Fried, lauréat du prix Nobel." Cf. also "Ein obdachloser Friedensfreund" in the *Berner Nachrichten* of January 4, 1921. Both are in Nachlass Fried, Box 20.

40 Just as in 1913 he had followed the path of his family toward upward mobility, either coincidentally or intentionally, by taking an apartment in the Bastiengasse, so now at the end of his life, as he returns to Leopoldstadt, which had marked a moment of permanent failure for his parents, he now finds a parallel, which likely did not escape his notice.

41 Mundy Schwalb to Fried, January 10, 1921, in Nachlass Fried, Box 91.

42 Mundy Schwalb to Fried, January 6, 1921, in Nachlass Fried, Box 91. The following quote is also from this source.

more tomorrow, and I want to ask you – before you are no longer able to – to send me a telegraph every other day. [...] It is not at all kind of you, Alfred H., to cause us such worry. In general, I have noticed that in the last year you've reacted to unpleasant experiences with fever and illness. You are becoming terribly feminine."[43]

Again and again, Mundy Schwalb tried to cheer Fried up, writing that all he had to do was to want to get better, then everything would be fine, and "if there's no other way, we'll come, Alfred H. So, do your duty!" But Fried's already long-weakened resilience finally collapsed. On January 14, he was transferred to Rudolf Hospital. At the end of the month, Therese Fried wrote to Wehberg: "Unfortunately, for the foreseeable future, you cannot expect a response from my husband to the letter we received from you today. He has been suffering since the beginning of the year from typhoid bronchitis and an inflammation of the lungs. There were many worrisome days – he's doing a little better now – but the doctors figure that he will be ill for at least two more months, and then he'll immediately have to go somewhere to recover. He will, therefore, be unable to work for a long time. In the meantime I have moved into a new home – having a seriously ill person to deal with and having to move at the same time – given the conditions in Vienna – is enough to make you lose your mind. My husband is now in Rudolf Hospital and is receiving good medical care. Yours, R. Fried."[44]

Fried never set foot in his new apartment at Praterstrasse 25a. His condition continued to worsen until the beginning of February, as Therese informed Wehberg. On February 9, she wrote to him regarding his offer to carry on with the *Friedens-Warte* for the time being: "My husband's condition is still very worrying – and according to the attending physician he has not improved at all – to the contrary, he has physically deteriorated quite a bit – he comes down with a fever in the evening and he eats nothing at all. His mind is also affected. It is not possible for me to extend to him your kind offer at this time, because he hardly understands the content of a simple postcard – when his sister asks how he feels."[45]

Annette Kolb in Badenweiler was also extremely concerned. She wrote to Therese that she and Schickele were "deeply upset" about the crisis: "This is all we can think about. You know how much I love and respect Fried, this splendid

---

43 Mundy Schwalb to Fried, January 10, 1921, in Nachlass Fried, Box 91. The following quote is also from this source.
44 Therese Fried to Wehberg, January 28, 1921, in Nachlass Wehberg, vol. 59b, BA Koblenz.
45 Therese Fried to Wehberg, February 9, 1921, in Nachlass Wehberg, vol. 59b, BA Koblenz.

and so unique man." At the same time she asked for constant updates, as did Mundy Schwalb in Berne.

The ongoing correspondence reflects the course of his illness. While an improvement seems to have occurred at the end of March, there was another relapse in early April. Sometime during the month of March, a worried Mundy Schwalb temporarily returned to Vienna to assist Therese in caring for Fried. In mid-April, he was doing much better, and he was making plans for the future again. On April 13, Mundy Schwalb wrote to Wehberg: "Dr. Fried asks that you set aside for the FW [*Friedens-Warte*] the financial contribution that was promised to him. Two weeks ago, he suffered a relapse, but just recently he has shown greater interest in his surroundings and in the world outside, and, it is our hope that he has taken a turn for the better and that his health will also be served by it. He read your letter and was very pleased with your kind words of sympathy."[46]

At the end of April, the illness finally seemed to have been overcome. Therese later wrote to David Starr Jordan at Stanford,[47] "Just the last weeks he was so full of projects, so happy to begin to work again."[48] And she did not forget to thank him for the package of food, which Fried was pleased to receive just a few days before his death. Mundy Schwalb also later wrote that Fried had recently shown greater zest for life "in his desires, his cheerful disposition, yes, even euphoric ecstasy."[49] But it was only one final surge of life. On Wednesday, May 4, at half past nine in the evening, Fried died, rather unexpectedly, of a pulmonary hemorrhage, much to the shock of those around him.

Therese remained alone in the new apartment, where she would spend three and a half decades until her own death. She was only 52 years old. What she felt, she tried to express in the aforementioned letter to David Starr Jordan:[50] "Dear Mr Jordan, all his friends tell me what the movement and the world lost with him. I lost more: the containing of my live and now it seems to me that I have nothing more to do there."[51]

Since Fried had no children, Therese was the sole heir to his estate, which in addition to Fried's writings and those of Bertha von Suttner, as well as the archive and the library, included, above all, massive debt. Emil Frankl's application to the Leopoldstadt District Court[52] "for the transfer of the passive estate

---

46 Therese Fried to Wehberg, April 13, 1921, in Nachlass Wehberg, vol. 59b, BA Koblenz.
47 Therese Fried to David Starr Jordan, June 9, 1921, in Nachlass Fried, Box 25, file 366.
48 Translator's footnote: this sentence was in English in the original.
49 On the following issue, see Mundy Schwalb in Goldscheid, *Gedenkblätter*, 68.
50 Translator's footnote: the following sentence was in English in the original.
51 Therese Fried to David Starr Jordan, June 9, 1921, in Nachlass Fried, Box 25, file 366.
52 Probate court records for Fried, Wiener Stadt- und Landesarchiv.

of Dr. Alfred Hermann Fried to the applicant as the deceased's widow and sole heir" of March 27 1923(!) revealed a debt in the amount of about 90,000,000 crowns, according to a detailed listing of the assets (mainly Austrian securities) and liabilities (which were assessed in Swiss francs).[53]

The couple had recorded the actual will with a notary in Vienna shortly after their wedding on February 5, 1909.[54] In particular, it stated that Therese's contribution to the marriage consisted of all the furnishings in the apartment at Widerhofergasse 5 and that they would remain in her sole possession even if they were divorced. In addition, the spouses had declared each other as their sole heirs. On July 5, 1918, Fried once again confirmed this agreement in Berne with a notary, but on the same day he wrote another, more private will with the title "Wünsche und Ratschläge an meine geliebte Frau für den Fall meines Ablebens"[55] (Some Requests and Advice to my Beloved Wife in the Case of my Passing), which was intended to give her some guidelines for the future. By 1921, some points were no longer relevant, but most of them were still applicable. Thus, Fried's absolute insistence on being cremated, for which "No expense should be spared," whereas the funeral should be simple, without religious ceremony and without great expense. "No speeches by rabbis. I die as a freethinker."

As early as 1911, Fried and Therese had become members of "Die Flamme" (The Flame), a newly founded Viennese Association of Friends of Cremation.[56] However, there was no crematorium in Vienna until 1923, so that the corpses had to be transported to another city. Therese did not choose Gotha, where Bertha von Suttner had been cremated, but Munich, which was closer, the city that had rejected Fried.

The main part of the will dealt with how Therese's financial future could best be secured. The will noted the value of his letter archive, which, together with the estate of Bertha von Suttner, he estimated to be worth "five to ten thousand dollars." Interest in the letters and the estate, he believed, would come mainly from the USA. His numerous newspaper and journal articles could be

---

53   Frankl notes, in addition, that Therese only inherited her husband's wedding ring, a signet ring, and a clock, since all his clothing was given to an epileptic, needy brother – it is certainly Leopold, who was living in Berlin, that is meant here.
54   A certified copy of this will can be found in the Wiener Stadt- und Landesarchiv along with an additional clause from Fried's probate file of 1918.
55   A copy of the will that Fried had written and signed on July 5, 1918 can be found in the appendix of this book. The original, held privately by Trude Simonsohn, was transferred to the Nachlass Fried.
56   The yearly-renewed membership cards bear the numbers 2111 (Alfred Hermann Fried) and 2112 (Therese Fried). See Nachlass Fried, Box 91a.

"published as a collection, a rich source of income, when the world will have more understanding for pacifist work." If things should still not work out, he wrote, Therese should appeal to the boards of Socrates and Concordia, but also to the organizations of the peace movement in all countries: "I dedicated my whole life to the peace movement, suffered and went hungry for it, and, when I'm no longer alive, I am counting on the fact they will ease the burden of the woman I loved most dearly and to whom I am grateful for the greatest happiness in my life." And a little further down one reads: "I counted for something in the world, one day my work will be preserved, so I can assume, they will certainly not forget the woman who was the dearest person to me on earth, and they will stand by her side." This was a wish that would be realized at least in its final part. Fried also required her to provide financial support for his brother Leopold in Berlin, if at all possible, as he had done. Leopold had been ill since 1915, but he had also suffered the loss of his wife Marie and lived in poor conditions in Berlin with their four children.

In the next paragraph, Fried summarized his relationship with Therese in a nutshell, and one is reminded of the passionate letters of 1903, when one reads: "I thank the good fortune that brought you to me. I can't say how much I love you, and I will love you until my last dying breath. [...] Yours, for all eternity, Alfred."

Although Fried's lawyer, Emil Frankl,[57] advised Therese in all legal and financial matters, it was Mundy Schwalb who took charge and sorted out what needed to be sorted out. On the very next day, she sent a telegram to Wehberg, which, together with the news of Fried's death, also informed him that he and Schücking, according to the testament, were to take over the editorial duties of the *Friedens-Warte*. Presumably, she was the one who informed the press.

3   Obituaries and Testimonials

Two days later, the news of Fried's death had already appeared in the newspapers both at home and abroad. The Viennese newspapers were the first to report it, on May 6, albeit with clearly different levels of information and commentary. One of the most informative articles appeared in the *Wiener Arbeiter-Zeitung*, which acknowledged Fried's *oeuvre* without reservation and

---

57   According to the information in the Totenbuch Theresienstadt, Dr. Emil Frankl and his wife Else were transported from Vienna to Theresienstadt in 1942. However, they never arrived. His fate is unknown. Cf. *Totenbuch Theresienstadt*, ed. Mary Steinhauser (Vienna, 1987), 32.

expressed its pride that "the well-known and outstanding pioneer of the idea of world peace [...] published many of his important essays in our newspaper during and after the war."[58] Fried's works, it was said, were no utopian treatises, but rather he had wanted to ground the idea of peace in the "soil of specific facts": "Alfred H. Fried devoted his whole life to a deeply moral idea, for which he fought bravely; and in the ranks of those who want to eradicate war—the final expression of barbarism in humanity—from the consciousness of humanity, he is at the top of the list. Now that humanity has learned to its horror, what war is, it will better remember him in gratitude and devotion."

The Marxist-oriented Viennese newspaper *Der Abend* (The Evening), which acknowledged Fried's "noble heart" and "his profound knowledge" in a detailed but far more general way, expressed a different view of him and thanked him for his commitment to pacifism at a time of great self-interest, but it then concluded: "Pacifism, as Fried understood it, had to fail. It was a pacifism of a highly genteel, overly refined bourgeoisie, but Marxism has long known that war is only the fever, the true disease is capitalism. [...] We would like to hope that he did not die recognizing the tragic contradiction between his noble desire for peace and the impossibility of achieving it."[59] The *Neue Freie Zeitung*[60] saw Fried still differently; it accentuated Fried's literary work and emphasized that "the very internationally-minded" Fried was esteemed far beyond Austria's borders not only as a pacifist and editor of the *Friedens-Warte* "but also as a friend and mentor."

On May 6, the *Berliner Tageblatt* was one of the first newspapers of the German Reich to report Fried's death.[61] The author responsible for the article, however, was far less knowledgeable about Fried and claimed that Fried received the Nobel Prize in 1910. While he stressed Fried's empathetic "relief activities to improve the situation of war prisoners" during his time in Berne, the article asserted that Fried's war diary, although it was "not free of some one-sidedness and inaccuracies," was nevertheless "an important contemporary document" and part of Fried's "legacy."

For Carl von Ossietzky of the *Berliner Volkszeitung*, Fried was "a true intellectual hero"[62] who had never contented himself with vague phrases, but whose

---

58   "Alfred H. Fried gestorben," in *Arbeiter-Zeitung*, Vienna, no. 123, May 6, 1921. The following citations are also taken from there. The following articles, which were cut out of newspapers, are located in Nachlass Fried, Box 11, file 235.
59   "Alfred Hermann Fried," in *Der Abend*, Vienna, no. 102, May 6, 1921.
60   "Alfred H. Fried gestorben," in *Neue Freie Presse*, Vienna, May 6, 1921.
61   "Alfred H. Fried gest.," in *Berliner Tageblatt*, no. 210, Edition B (104), May 6, 1921.
62   Carl v. Ossietzky, "Alfred H. Fried gest.," in *Berliner Volkszeitung*, evening edition, May 6, 1921.

efforts sought to eliminate the causes of war through his notion of scientific pacifism. Ossietzky even believed that Fried's name was "closely connected" with the realization of the First Hague Conference. While Ossietzky felt it was true that Fried's move to Switzerland and his criticism of German politics and Germany's management of the war had brought him enemies, "who will pursue him even beyond his grave," he also believed that Fried had never been an unpatriotic fellow but was, in fact, a true citizen of Europe. Even the *Welt am Montag* in Berlin remembered Fried: "Our readers will, incidentally, be particularly interested to learn that Fried worked for the *WaM* in the first years of its existence."[63]

Over the course of the next few days and weeks these first reports were followed by countless others, in which his friends and acquaintances spoke of him. While almost all emphasized his reliability and human goodness, and the majority described him as a rather withdrawn scholarly type, Rudolf Jeremias Kreutz saw in him the personality of a "leader": "Those who met this man, who has been taken from us too soon, were immediately struck by his outward appearance. The head of a dictator with the eyes of a dreamer – the leader. Anyone who knew Alfred H. Fried personally entered into the aura of a great person whose outward appearance remained in perfect harmony with his nature. In all things he had a personality that was imbued with the power of suggestion and was preordained to find success among the masses."[64]

In addition to these differing interpretations, totally new rumors about Fried surfaced. For example, in one article in the *Süddeutsche Presse* of May 13, by an author listed as Dr. M. A., entitled "Tragödie eines Menschenfreundes" (Tragedy of a Humanitarian),[65] Fried is said to have died in Rudolf Hospital, "not because he was ill, but because he was homeless." Thus, according to Dr. M. A., war, which had been Fried's archenemy, avenged itself on him. In addition, it was further reported that Fried had been brought to a Bavarian sanatorium, but the Kahr government had refused him entry.

On May 18, Fried's body was transported to the Munich crematorium. The *Münchener Post* announced a day before: "The funeral service for the pacifist Dr. Fried, who is being transported from Vienna to Munich for cremation, will take place at the Ostfriedhof on Wednesday morning at 11 o'clock. Supporters and like-minded friends are invited to attend the service."[66] Two days later, the

---

63   "Alfred H. Fried gest.," in *Die Welt am Montag*, Berlin, May 9, 1921.
64   Rudolf Jeremias Kreutz, "Zum Gedächtnis Alfred H. Frieds," in *Prager Tageblatt*, no. 109, May 11, 1921.
65   "Tragödie eines Menschenfreunds," *Süddeutsche Presse*, no. 82, May 13, 1921.
66   *Münchener Post*, May 17, 1921.

same newspaper reported: "Simple and unpretentious, Prof.[!] Fried, the intellectual leader of German pacifism, was accompanied to his final resting place by a small gathering of friends and supporters. Prof. Quidde gave a eulogy, in which he praised Fried's intellectual leadership and [...] gave a vivid portrait of the deceased as a person and politician. Following Quidde, there were talks by representatives from *Frauenliga für Frieden und Freiheit* (the Women's League for Peace and Freedom), from the cartel of pacifist organizations, from the pacifist student group, from the *Bund Neues Vaterland* (Federation of the New Fatherland), and by Karl Gareis, a representative of the *Unabhängige Sozialdemokratische Partei* (Independent Social-Democratic Party). Army Captain Schützinger, ret., delivered a eulogy to the deceased on behalf of the *Friedensbund der Kriegsteilnehmer* (Peace Association of War Veterans) and of the *Republikanischer Reichsbund* (Republican Reichsbund). [...] Organ music concluded the simple, impressive ceremony."[67] However, there were other commentaries on Fried's funeral service. The Berlin newspaper *Freiheit* complained on May 20[68] that "the entire 'intellectual' class of Munich was conspicuous by its absence" and only a small group of 20 people gave Fried his final escort.

A month later, Fried's life would also be commemorated in Vienna. On July 9, at the beginning of a congress of the International Women's League for Peace and Freedom, the Austrian Peace Society co-organized a ceremonial commemoration for Fried and Bertha von Suttner. According to the *Wiener Freimaurer-Zeitung*,[69] the event was well attended and included speeches by both domestic and foreign pacifists. Unfortunately, the newspaper did not provide names. Only excerpts of the commemorative speech of the Free Mason Dr. Franz Jäger have been preserved.[70] In his speech he described Fried's essential personality, which subsequently enabled his future development, "one might almost say, the phenomenon A. H. Fried": "The essence of his being was kindness and simple, natural goodness. He also possessed an honesty of character and spirit as well as a rare clarity of thought." He added that Fried, to his very death, was faithful to his convictions and remained unvanquished in mind and spirit, even though his body had succumbed to "the conditions of the postwar period." Jäger ended his speech with a vow: "Brother A. H. Fried! Your body no longer dwells among us, but your spirit hovers over us and—no matter how

---

67 "Einäscherungsfeier des Prof. Alfred H. Fried," in *Münchener Post*, May 19, 1921.
68 "Alfred Frieds Beisetzung in München," in *Die Freiheit*, Berlin, May 20, 1921. Newspaper cut-out in Nachlass Fried, Box 11, file 235.
69 *Wiener Freimaurer-Zeitung* 3, no. 3, (September 1921): 12.
70 *Wiener Freimaurer-Zeitung* 3, no. 4, (December 1921): 2.

one thinks about the immortality of the soul—your soul remains immortal in us. And so we pledge to you that we shall use all our powers to continue your work and, above all, to educate those who follow us as we keep your interests in mind. This is the monument, more durable than iron ore, which the lodge "Socrates" has built for you now and forever in the hearts of its brothers."

While the brothers erected a memorial in their hearts to Fried, Therese, together with Mundy Schwalb and a few friends, planned a memorial edition of the *Friedens-Warte*. By May 17, 1921, Fried's lawyer, Emil Frankl, had appealed to the owner of the publishing house Neuer Geist to continue the journal "the only thing that remains of the life's work of our dear friend." His primary aim was to create "for [Fried's] widow, who has been left behind in rather bad circumstances – the estate is heavily indebted – [. . .] a permanent, albeit at first very modest, source of income."[71] When the publisher expressed his general agreement with the plan, despite some reservations, Therese wrote a circular letter in May to her husband's most important friends and like-minded colleagues, in which she told them that a commemorative edition was planned: "The most important fighters of the movement and all of Alfred Fried's colleagues should be united in expressing what had led them to follow this common path. I hope that you too will be a willing contributor."[72] She concluded with a request for an immediate response, informed them that no article should exceed two columns, and that all contributions needed to be received no later than June 20.

It is not known how many pacifists Therese sent the appeal to; a note in pencil on the margin of the draft letter – "70 pieces, K 170" – suggests, however, that she had 70 addresses. This is probably accurate since 57 letters were actually written. When the memorial edition appeared in the spring of 1922, after several delays,[73] it contained, in addition to a biographical sketch written by Elsbeth Friedrich, articles by pacifists of various countries, including Dutch, Swiss, Norwegians, Swedes and Danes as well as four Frenchmen,[74] six Englishmen[75] and three Americans.[76] The small number of contributors was probably due to the quick turn-around time of the initial deadline, which

---

71 Emil Frankl to Der Neue Geist Verlag, May 17, 1921, in Nachlass Fried, Box 25, file 366.
72 Draft of a letter of May 31,1921, in Nachlass Fried, Box 25, file 366.
73 The first issue appeared toward the end of 1920, while Fried was still alive; it was printed separately from the fourth volume of his *Kriegs-Tagebuch* under the title Alfred H. Fried, *Mein Kampf gegen Versailles und St. Germain* (Leipzig, 1920).
74 Lucien Le Foyer, Charles Richet, Romain Rolland, Theodore Ruyssen.
75 Norman Angell, H. N. Brailsford, Charles Roden Buxton, Joseph King, Lord Weardale, Israel Zangwill.
76 Fannie Fern Andrews, David Starr Jordan, Lucia Ames Mead.

meant that "some letters were shorter than they otherwise would have been, and that some devoted comrades were not included in the volume at all."[77] There was even a Belgian among the authors, but it was not Henri La Fontaine, whose name was missing; Otfried Nippold, Hellmut von Gerlach, Eduard de Neufville and Margarethe Selenka, all of whom had certainly received the circular letter, did not contribute. The Belgian was the painter Paul Colin, who, in a retrospective, praised Fried's conduct in the World War, which other pacifists in Belgium had so often criticized. Colin emphasized: "But while his French and Belgian friends castigated him in order to lose themselves in warfare, Fried countered the general madness with his passion, however powerless it was."[78]

The majority of the articles (28) came from Germany and Austria, including recollections by long-time friends and colleagues such as Georg Arnhold, Eduard Bernstein, Richard Grelling, Adolf Heilberg, Ludwig Quidde, Hans Wehberg, Mundy Schwalb, and Walther Schücking, as well as other friends and acquaintances of the emigration period, like Ernst Bloch,[79] Annette Kolb, and René Schickele. Taken together, they painted a vivid, multi-faceted image of the deceased, although some authors used the space to speak more of themselves than to express their appreciation of Fried.

Therese Fried did not contribute to the commemorative book, but Mundy Schwalb reported on the last decade of the life of her employer. Elsbeth Friedrichs offered, as an introduction, a brief biography of the deceased and, in an additional contribution, his relationship to Bertha von Suttner.[80] She wrote a particularly moving tribute at the conclusion of her piece: "Whoever was personally close to Fried, has indeed lost a lot. He was a completely loyal and reliable friend. In addition to being a good thinker, he was a real human being! That says it all."[81]

---

77 Goldscheid, *Gedenkblätter*, 3.
78 Paul Colin in Goldscheid, *Gedenkblätter*, 18.
79 It is rather astonishing that Ernst Bloch, who, when he was in Switzerland, could not be counted among Fried's closest friends and indeed frequently attacked him, offered in hindsight a totally different judgment of him. About his time in Berne, Bloch now writes (similar to what Annette Kolb had written): "There was always a harmonious atmosphere around Fried; his little room in Berne was more than just a friendly refuge, one felt as if one had landed on an island, it was the essence of propriety. Fried appeared to be a perfectly secure human being, unflappable about all the speculation and all the intrigue that surrounded him, that sounded him out, that sought its own advantage." Ernst Bloch in Goldscheid, *Gedenkblätter*, 16.
80 Elsbeth Friedrichs in Goldscheid, *Gedenkblätter*, 25ff.
81 Ibid, 10.

And she promised to have a more detailed biography of Fried in a subsequent volume. In fact, Elsbeth Friedrichs, who settled permanently in Locarno after the war, fulfilled her promise and shortly thereafter wrote a biography of Fried for the general public, for which, however, according to a later statement by Wehberg, she could not find a publisher.[82] The manuscript has since disappeared. Despite an intensive search, no literary estate of Elsbeth Friedrichs, who died in 1930, could be located.

At the beginning of 1925, the *Friedens-Warte*, which at that time appeared in Berlin under the direction of Hans Wehberg, published a small segment of Fried's autobiography, which he had written in the second half of 1920, entitled *Jugenderinnerungen* (Memories of my Youth).[83]

In the same year, on December 5, 1925, the ashes of Alfred Hermann Fried were placed in an honorary vault in the arcade of the newly erected crematorium in Vienna during a solemn ceremony. Inscribed on the marble plaque are the words: "To the great pioneer of the Peace Movement." Laurel wreaths were laid in front of the plaque; their ribbons bore several inscriptions in golden letters: "To the founder and great pioneer of the German Peace Society." – "To the leader of international pacifism from The German Peace Cartel." – "To the founder of scientific internationalism from The Austrian Peace Society."[84]

On the tenth anniversary of Fried's death in 1931, the *Friedens-Warte* reported on another tribute in Vienna: Next to the Bertha-von-Suttner-Platz, which had already existed for some time, there was to be a street named for Fried, Alfred-Hermann-Fried-Straße.[85] This information is only partially correct. In fact, not a street but one of the numerous squares in the 10th district of Vienna, "Favoriten," was named for Fried (Friedplatz), but only temporarily, because in 1938 the name was changed to Engländerplatz.[86]

---

82   Cf. *Friedens-Warte* 30, 230. Elsbeth Friedrichs increasingly withdrew from the peace movement in her later years and dedicated herself to the studies on sight that the American physician William Bates carried out; this then resulted in her establishing an institute in Locarno.

83   Alfred H. Fried, *Jugenderinnerungen* (Berlin, 1925).

84   On Fried's funeral, see the article by Professor Karl Brockhausen, "Ein Ehrengrab für den Friedensapostel Alfred H. Fried. Anlässlich der Enthüllung am Samstag," in *Neue Freie Presse*, Vienna, December 6, 1925. As a separate publication, in Nachlass Fried, Box 11, file 235. Excerpts of the article also appeared in *Friedens-Warte* 26, no. 2 (February 1926): 51ff.

85   Cf. *Friedens-Warte* 31 (1931): 21.

86   According to written documentation provided by Dr. Brigitta Psarakis of the Wiener Stadt- und Landesarchiv.

CHAPTER 6

Survivors and Successors

1 Therese Fried

After Fried's death, Therese initially lived alone in the apartment on Praterstraße. Later, Fried's brother Otto[1] and his wife Marie left Berlin to live with her. Mundy Schwalb went back to Switzerland. Therese stayed in contact with Fried's family: with Pauline's son Gordon Wyon in England, with Leopold's four children (Leopold committed suicide in 1923)[2] in Berlin, and especially with Sidonie and Fried's favorite nephew, Berthold, whom she sought, through her connections, to promote as Fried's protégé. In 1934, she advised him to send his doctoral thesis, which he had completed in law under the most trying circumstances, to Hans Wehberg in Geneva, to Prof. Friedrich Harty in Vienna, and to Mundy Schwalb, who was living in London at the time; she also provided him with their respective addresses.

Nothing else is known about her other activities in these years, not even the extent to which she was active in the Austrian Peace Society in the 1920s and 1930s[3] although she did remain a member. It seems that Therese stayed out of the limelight after the death of her husband, living on her memories, and did not actively participate in pacifist activities. This was a decision that may have saved her from personal attacks after 1938.

Financial hardship soon forced Therese to sell off her husband's extensive library. Interested parties included the Hoover War Library[4] of Stanford University in California. The library was established in 1919 by Herbert Clark Hoover, who was to become the 31st president of the United States. It had already acquired numerous works from the World War I period, including books, newspapers, pamphlets, correspondence, diaries, and publicity and promotional materials.[5] In the December 1924 issue of the *Friedens-Warte*, Hans Wehberg

---

1 Cf. Nachlass Fried, Box 88.
2 Cf. the files of the Jüdischer Friedhof Weißensee, Berlin.
3 According to information provided by Ernst Pecha, a member of the newly formed Austrian Peace Society, the documents that were retained by the Austrian Peace Society were destroyed by the last secretary in a fit of mental confusion. (In written documentation to this author [Schönemann-Behrens] on November 10, 2000, Prof. Ernst Schwarcz, a former member of the executive board of the Austrian Peace Society, confirmed this view.)
4 Today: Hoover Institution on War, Revolution and Peace.
5 Cf. the report by John Mez in *Friedens-Warte* 27 (1927): 371.

reported on the sale: "What was ardently collected in the pursuit of peace for more than thirty years, and what served him as armor in his dedicated enthusiasm for the idea of peace, remains a cohesive whole and will not be scattered to the winds."[6] Wehberg then expressed the hope that (at least) America would recognize "Fried's great importance and memorialize him."

By contrast, Therese did not easily let go of the estate of her husband or that of Bertha von Suttner. Only after she kept both estates in her apartment for ten years, was she ready to part with them, keeping her husband's works, some photos, and some personal documents that were important to her.[7]

Presumably on the recommendation of Wehberg, who had been teaching at the Institut de hautes études internationales in Geneva since 1928, she decided to write to T. B. Sevensma, the director of the library of the League of Nations in Geneva, who was in the process of informally establishing a peace museum in which he wanted to preserve historical documents of the peace movement for later generations.[8]

The letter was received with great interest in Geneva. Sevensma traveled to Vienna in person and later reported to his supervisor that he had found a remarkably complete collection. Before entering into actual negotiations for the sale, he commissioned an evaluation of the two literary estates by the director of the Vienna State Archives, Professor Bittner. In mid-May 1931, Professor Bittner estimated the total value of the estates to be 14,000 shillings, about 10,000 Swiss francs.[9]

This was a very buyer-friendly valuation because, as one of Bittner's co-workers explained to Sevensma, "the price was set rather low; we started from a price that was normally set for the purchase of autographed materials and not for the sale of such items."[10] So Bertha von Suttner's letters were valued at a price of 3 marks each, instead of the customary 8 marks, and the letters to her or to Fried were valued at one mark each with a few exceptions. Sevensma wrote: "These estates constituted an important and complete source of three decades of the history of the peace movement, and that was not included in the pricing."[11]

---

6   *Friedens-Warte* 24, no. 12 (December 1924): 333f. The following quotation is taken from the same source.
7   After Therese's death these documents were given to Berthold Simonsohn and his wife Trude, where they remained until 2001. In the course of work on this book, the material was transferred to Fried's Nachlass.
8   Cf. Wehberg, "Alfred H. Frieds Todestag," in *Friedens-Warte* 31 (1931): 130.
9   Bittner, who worked at the Archivamt in Vienna, to Sevensma, May 15, 1931.
10 Dr. Wilhelm, who worked at the Archivamt in Vienna, to Sevensma, June 6, 1931.
11 Ibid.

Therese and her lawyer Emil Frankl were not enthusiastic about the low valuation and tried to get a higher appraisal—but to no avail. Sevensma, who himself did not yet have permission from his superiors to make the purchase, was no more inclined to accept a higher price than he was to grant Frankl, on behalf of Hans Wehberg, the rights to an advance copy of important letters and documents. Instead, he urged that they accelerate the deal and questioned whether the League of Nations would make the purchase if there were further delays. Frankl had to give in. On June 25, 1931, he agreed to the sale for 10,000 Swiss francs. After some back and forth, the purchase was now also unanimously accepted in Geneva, and Sevensma was commissioned to negotiate with the Austrian ambassador for a possible waiver of the 10% export tax.

In 1931, the export of archival material from Austria was prohibited by law; it was only possible if a formal permit had been granted by the Archives Office. This linked the authorization to two conditions that were readily acceptable in Geneva: "1. the estate of Alfred Fried, including the parts of the inheritance of Bertha von Suttner and of Carneri, may be consulted at any time by Austrian researchers in Geneva, or, as the case may be, any portions of this estate, intended for use by the Austrian scholars, may be sent at their expense to private archives, court archives, and the state archive and be borrowed free of charge;[12] 2. a copy of the inventory, once it has been finalized, is to be sent to the private archive, the court archive, and the state archive free of charge."[13] With this agreement, the literary legacy of Fried and Bertha von Suttner finally became the property of the library of the League of Nations.

As the estate was carefully packed into boxes, Fried's express wish remained unfulfilled, namely, that Mundy Schwalb or Hans Wehberg review the materials since "Family letters, bills, and other materials not of general interest are best destroyed."[14] But this review was not undertaken. Even today, Fried's estate in Geneva contains family letters, bills, calculations, diaries, and handwritten notes in pencil, in addition to manuscripts, periodicals, and worldwide correspondence. Even Fried's unique menu card collection, which fills a whole box, is preserved *in toto*. Fried had begun the collection in 1895, probably as he

---

12 This arrangement, which is still in effect today, enabled Brigitte Hamann to have parts of the Nachlass of Suttner/Fried sent to Vienna to complete her work on the biography of Bertha von Suttner. Without this cooperative arrangement, that would not have been possible.

13 Bittner, Archivamt Wien, to Sevensma, May 15, 1931, in Verwaltungs-Akte 29570, VB Archiv. These guidelines still apply. Since, even today, a list of the inventory is only available on index cards, there is still no copy in Vienna. In working on this project, however, the author was able to capture the data electronically.

14 Fried, "Ratschläge und Wünsche."

recalled the times when he was hungry as a child; he continued it until 1913. In addition, he collected cards from important banquets that he had attended, at which he had requested autographs of the most important participants.[15]

The press and the general public were largely unaware that Fried's papers had been exported from Austria. Only an article on the third page of the *Prager Tagblatt* of November 12, 1931 mentioned it. In hindsight, the subsequent historical events make clear that it was fortunate that the estate had been taken to Switzerland when it was, thus escaping both destruction by the National Socialists and the turmoil of the war and the post-war period.

After Austria's annexation in 1938, Therese, as a non-Jew with unblemished Aryan documentation, was not harassed.[16] Even Fried's brother Otto, who was protected as a veteran of the World War and through his marriage to Marie, a Catholic, was initially left alone, although he later would have to leave their common apartment and move into an assigned residence. After the war, weak and ill, he returned to the apartment on Praterstraße where he died a few months later at the end of November 1945.

Fried's youngest sister, Sidonie, who was living in Bernburg, had it far worse: she suffered discrimination in increasing degrees, which she then detailed in cautiously formulated letters to Therese, [17] before she was ultimately deported to Theresienstadt along with her children, Inge and Berthold.[18] While Sidonie died there on August 6, 1944 at the age of 64, Berthold Simonsohn was deported to Auschwitz with his wife Trude, a woman from Olomouc in Moravia, whom he had met in Theresienstadt.[19] Miraculously, both survived the extermination camp and were reunited at an agreed upon meeting place in Theresienstadt after the war.[20]

Leopold's children also survived the war and the persecution; they later lived in Hamburg and Berlin. Trude and Berthold Simonsohn traveled to Frankfurt via Hamburg after a stay in Switzerland. Only Pauline's fate could not

---

15   Nachlass Box 12b; see also Dr. Fried's "Esschronik" in *Prager Tagblatt* no. 120 (May 25, 1921): 3.
16   Nachlass Fried, Box 92.
17   These letters, along with several hundred more from between 1935 and 1955, present a unique perspective on the history of the period and could be the basis of a separate research project. (In the course of my work on this project, the letters were found among the personal articles of Trude Simonsohn in an abandoned suitcase in her basement.) The finding comprises mainly correspondence with largely Jewish relatives and friends in Germany, Austria, Israel, and South America.
18   The older son, Karl, had already been deported from Germany.
19   Inge Simonsohn wound up in Davos, Switzerland, by virtue of a deportation train that had been redirected by Himmler. From there, she tried to get information about the fate of her other family members.
20   For a more detailed account, see the memoir of Trude Simonsohn in *Jüdisches Leben in Deutschland. Siebzehn Gespräche*, ed. Ingrid Wiltmann (Frankfurt a. M., 1999), 100ff.

be learned. Later family correspondence makes clear that Pauline had already died by 1945 and had been buried in Vienna. Her son, Gordon Wyon, who was living in England, maintained contact with Therese and other family members throughout the war and beyond.

After the war, Therese, as Fried's widow, was once again in the spotlight for a short time: those who sought to re-establish the Austrian Peace Society planned a commemoration of Bertha von Suttner at which Fried was also to be recognized. Egon Kieffer emphasized Fried's engagement for peace in a lengthy newspaper article in 1946: "A short quarter of a century after his death, the world stands at the end of an even greater collapse, caused by the destructive forces of exaggerated nationalism. At such a time, it is good to remember the very realistic and constructive ideas for peace that this energetic and scholarly promoter of peace among nations had championed."[21]

Therese attended the first sessions and wrote to her nephew Berthold Simonsohn at the beginning of February 1946: "The Austrian Peace Society is to be resurrected – yesterday was the first preliminary meeting. I had registered as an old new member – and was greatly honored as the wife of Alfred Fried. It will take some time for everything to be reorganized – in fact, there shouldn't be a need for peace societies at all – the idea has already outgrown this lower level of organization."[22]

Therese's pride in the acknowledgments that she received both at this time and in subsequent years as the widow of "Fried the Pacifist" is unmistakable.[23] She became an honorary member of the Austrian Peace Society and was also invited to become a guest of honor in the reestablishment of the League for Human Rights.[24]

In 1948, Fried's life and work became the subject of a 20-minute radio broadcast; the manuscript of the production can be found in his papers. Here, too, the selected excerpts from his work indicate his commitment to mutual understanding among peoples, and especially his steadfastness during the war: "Fried is a model for our time and for all time because he showed us how to defend one's viewpoint against the delusions of the world."

---

21 Egon Kieffer, "Rufer zum Weltfrieden. Alfred Hermann Fried und sein Werk. Excerpt of a newspaper article (1946) in the private collection of Trude Simonsohn, now in Nachlass Fried.

22 Therese Fried to Berthold Simonsohn, February 6, 1946. Private collection of Trude Simonsohn.

23 This recognition also brought some welcome material benefit to Therese: the Austrian Peace Society was able to arrange for an increase in Therese's social security payment. See Therese Fried to Berthold Simonsohn, January 3, 1947. Private collection of Trude Simonsohn.

24 Therese Fried to Berthold Simonsohn, May 15, 1946. Private collection of Trude Simonsohn.

In February 1949, the Josef-Meise-Strasse in the 21st district of Donaufeld in Vienna, on the Danube Island, was renamed to Friedstraße, and it is still called that today.[25] But the name of the street was not entirely unambiguous; it could also evoke the memory of another great son of the city, the poet Erich Fried,[26] and thus could suggest that in the minds of the citizens the street may have nothing to do with Alfred H. Fried. How else to explain that the Executive Committee of the Wiener Weltbürger (Viennese World Citizens) sent an urgent petition to the mayor of the city of Vienna in 1956 recommending that they should finally compensate for the error and erect a memorial or name a square or a street for Fried.[27]

In the summer of 1950, Therese was the recipient of two honors: on the 10th and 11th of June 1950, the first Austrian Peace Congress was held in the large hall of the Konzerthaus in Vienna; it was attended by 2,100 delegates from all over Austria and from numerous foreign countries. The congress marked the first high point of the peace movement, which had been growing in Austria since 1948, and at the same time it provided strong support for the Stockholm appeal to ban nuclear weapons.[28] Therese reported enthusiastically to her nephew: "**We – and that includes me** – participated in the **large, really huge** peace congress on the 10th and 11th of June. I had made up my mind that I had to be there—in spite of my ailments—and I did it, with lots of support. [...] So I persevered for two days in a row – and I was very proud, I felt Alfred would feel that I was there in his place."[29]

Therese was given a ticket by a "prominent person" to be a distinguished guest, and so she was provided with a car to take her back and forth to the meeting venue. "I had a place of honor among the delegates, and many speeches and newspapers mentioned that the widow of Dr. Alfred Fried was in attendance, and so I had to shake a lot of hands and sign autographs." The

---

25 Written response from Dr. B. Psarakis, Wiener Stadt- und Landesarchiv.
26 Erich Fried, who was born into a well-off Jewish family two days after the death of Alfred Hermann Fried, was not related to him. In 1938, Erich Fried emigrated to London after his father died during an interrogation by the Gestapo. He then became known as a pacifist writer and poet who was critical of the times, especially of the Vietnam War. This has led to some confusion between the two men, for example on the internet. Some poems by Erich Fried, for instance the poem "Antwort," have been incorrectly attributed to Alfred H. Fried. See E. Jessen, *Erich Fried, eine Chronik. Leben und Werk*, 1998, and G. Lampe, *Erich Fried. Biographie und Werk eines "deutschen Dichters,"* 2nd ed., 1998.
27 See Dr. Stefan Matzenberger, "Ein österreichischer Nobelpreisträger," in *Demokratie, Friedensgesinnung, Völkerverständigung. Mitteilungen für Lehrer und Erzieher*, Vienna (May 1957), 4ff.
28 Appeal of the Permanent Committee of the World Peace Congress in March 1950.
29 Therese Fried to Berthold Simonsohn, June 13, 1950. Private collection of Trude Simonsohn.

81-year-old offered a detailed description of the events to her nephew, whom she still saw as a possible successor to her husband, especially of the overwhelming impression that the delegations of young people and the public closing ceremony at Rathausplatz (City Hall Square) had made on her: "[...] It was as if a million people were all vowing at once: 'Never again war'."

The second major event took place just about a month later: the opening of the Suttner-Fried memorial exhibition in Vienna's Historical Museum, a special exhibition with the official title "Bertha von Suttner und die Anfänge der österreichischen Friedensbewegung" (Bertha von Suttner and the Origins of the Austrian Peace Movement). Once again, Therese Fried proudly reported to her nephew: "After the great peace congress in June, yesterday there was a second major honor for our dearly departed Alfred. – It may well be the last one that I get to experience. Once again, I was picked up and brought back home by a car sent from City Hall. To my surprise, as a gift, a large picture entitled 'Dr. Alfred H. Fried in his Study,' modeled on a small photograph, hung in the hall – of course, I was very pleased by this. I felt like an **opera diva** whom everyone wanted to meet."[30]

In fact, the two events in 1950 are probably the last in which the ageing woman participated, since she was suffering from painful vascular sclerosis, cataracts, and severe hypertension. Although she was still listed as a member of the Executive Committee of the Austrian Peace Council in 1954, Therese had already become more of a symbolic figure than an active member, as is clear from the congratulatory letter on her 85th birthday: "We have often regretted in the past few years that we have not been able to meet with you more often, my dear Mrs. Fried. However, we have been kept up to date by Frau Dr. Glück about the state of your health, such that in the course of our work we always kept in mind one thing: even if Mrs. Therese Fried, the widow of the great pioneer of peace, Alfred H. Fried, is not physically with us, we know that in spirit she is supportive of all our endeavors to serve the preservation of peace."[31]

Up to the very end, despite the fact that she found writing and walking increasingly difficult, Therese kept in touch with the few surviving old pacifist friends and acquaintances, such as Hans Wehberg, Mundy Schwalb, Annette Kolb and Rudolf Suttner, the last nephew of Bertha von Suttner. And for the younger generation of pacifists, she also served as a contact person for and a mediator of her husband's ideas. How a group of young pacifists described a visit to Therese in November of 1954 is still impressive today;[32] they contrasted

---

30 Therese Fried to Berthold Simonsohn, July 7, 1950. Private collection of Trude Simonsohn.
31 Austrian Peace Council to Therese Fried, February 20, 1954, in Nachlass Fried, Box 92.
32 See "Ein Besuch bei Alfred H. Fried," in *Friedenszeitung Wien* (November 7 1954), in Nachlass Fried, Box 92. The following quotation is also taken from this source.

the poverty, in which Therese was living – "in these rooms, unfortunately, the most basic needs often remain unfulfilled" – with her unaltered interest in the world, her youthful heart, and "the warmth of her most vibrant humanity." Above all, she impressed the adolescents with her unwavering belief that "our ideas will become reality," and she promoted, apparently quite successfully, the reading of her husband's works, which she kept next to his photos in a bookcase in the apartment.

Following a mild stroke a few years earlier, Therese suffered a severe stroke at the beginning of April 1957 and died a week later, on April 11, in Lainz hospital. Not only did the newspapers in Vienna[33] find her death newsworthy, in Oldham (England), her nephew Gordon Wyon learned the news of her death from a newspaper, as he angrily let his relatives know.[34] Like her husband, Therese also wanted to be cremated, and on April 19 her remains were placed in the Fried honorary grave.

Her sister-in-law Marie gave some valuable pieces of her estate, such as the official document of the Nobel Prize, Fried's death mask, and some photos, to the Historical Museum in Vienna, while the Austrian Peace Society received Fried's books. After Marie's death, the remaining documents were passed on to Berthold and Trude Simonsohn in Frankfurt, and, for the most part, they are now part of Fried's estate in Geneva.

2   Fried and German Pacifism after 1921

Even during the war, pacifism in Germany had undergone noticeable changes.[35] In his book on pacifism of the Weimar period,[36] Reinhold Lütgemeier-Davin

---

[33]   Her death was also reported in *Neues Österreich. Organ der demokratischen Einigung* 13 (no. 88), no. 3637, Saturday, April 13, 1957, 5; *Arbeiter-Zeitung*, Vienna, no. 89, Sunday, April 14, 1957, 4; *Die Presse*, Vienna, no. 2575, Sunday, April 14, 1957, 11; *Volksstimme. Zentralorgan der Kommunistischen Partei Österreichs*, Vienna, no. 89, Sunday, April 14, 1957, 2. Private collection of Trude Simonsohn, now in Nachlass Fried.

[34]   Telegram from Gordon Wyon to Marie Fried on April 17, 1957: "Deeply saddened about the newspaper report on the death of our aunt. Incomprehensible that we were not notified. Request clarification and update." Private collection Trude Simonsohn, now in Nachlass Fried.

[35]   On the history of German pacifism in World War I, see, in particular, Wilfried Eisenbeiß, *Die bürgerliche Friedensbewegung in Deutschland während des Ersten Weltkrieges. Organisation, Selbstverständnis und politische Praxis 1913/14–1919* (Frankfurt, 1980), but also the relevant chapters in Holl, *Pazifismus in Deutschland*, 103ff and Riesenberger, *Friedensbewegung*, 98ff.

[36]   Cf. Reinhold Lütgemeier-Davin, *Pazifismus zwischen Kooperation und Konfrontation in der Weimarer Republik* (Cologne, 1982).

cites twenty-five organizations, in addition to those that already existed, that were dedicated to pacifist agitation either exclusively or partially. The "Deutsche Liga für Völkerbund" (German League for a League of Nations) formed the right wing, and the "Gruppe Revolutionärer Pazifisten" (Group of Revolutionary Pacifists) comprised the left wing of the spectrum. Among all these groups, many of which were quite small, the German Peace Society, whose membership rose from 5,000 during the war to about 30,000 in 1926, was still the largest pacifist organization, but it too was soon embroiled in ever more heated controversies, especially between the left-wing intellectuals and those members who were part of the generation that had fought at the front.

At the time, the radical pacifists could be found mainly in the "Westdeutsche Landesverband." It was headed by Fritz Küster, had a large membership, and supported the journal *Das andere Deutschland* (The Other Germany). As early as 1926, they gained the upper hand within the German Peace Society. Along with their willingness to engage in active agitation, by 1929, they finally succeeded in fully ousting the bourgeois-democratic forces around Ludwig Quidde from the leadership of the German Peace Society by virtue of their clear and uncompromising positions on the question of the culpability for the war, rearmament, expropriation of the princes, and the Treaty of Versailles. As chairman, Küster tried to transform the German Peace Society into a well-organized cohesive combat unit against the growing radical right wing of the Weimar Republic, but such a tact ended the cooperation with the SPD and increased its isolation within the rest of the pacifist camp. Ultimately, because of the segregation of the pacifist groups and their ever-shrinking popular support, they were easily crushed by the National Socialists in 1933.

In the months leading up to his death, Fried had had little time to deal with the new currents within the peace movement and to adapt his theory of pacifism to the changed conditions. As a result, it is not surprising that his causal/organizational pacifism faded into obscurity, since it was less forward looking. This was the pacifism that the internationalists Schücking and Wehberg had embodied and further developed in the 1920s, and it thus became ever more centered on the League of Nations. Later researchers then combined this pacifism with the democratic pacifism of Quidde and other similar currents into what they called "moderate pacifism," which finally succumbed in the factional struggle for the future direction of the anti-militarist movement to a "radical pacifism." Even after World War II, it failed to catch hold.

The position that Fried would have taken in the movement, had he not died in 1921, remains unclear. The fundamental structure of his thinking, namely the integration of new developments and ideas into his own train of thought, would undoubtedly have led to a revision of his only provisional theories. Since he had already taken up a position on the left of the German Peace Movement before the war and had made clear his differences with the moderate pacifists, such as Ludwig Quidde and the internationalists Schücking and Wehberg vis-a-vis the Germany's guilt for the war both during and after the war, it is quite probable that he would have ultimately taken a position midway between organizational and radical pacifism, perhaps also giving his own "scientific" ("ursächlich") pacifism a new, expanded orientation. In his comments about the Congress of Pacifism in Braunschweig, he had already said that the ascendancy of a radical, non-compromising attitude was logical and gratifying, and that the methods of the "pre-August peace movement," i.e., accommodation and compromise, had resulted in the loss of their *raison d'être,* as in the case of the failed "Verband für internationale Verständigung" (Union for International Understanding), which "had been founded for tactical reasons but which today can no longer justify its existence."[37]

In order to have an approximate idea of what Fried's positions were shortly before his death, it is worth taking a look at some of his last articles in the *Friedens-Warte*. Here he dealt with the two central themes of the peace movement at the time: the development of the League of Nations and the radical pacifism of Kurt Hiller. In "Die Enttäuschung von Genf"[38] (The Geneva Disappointment), Fried clearly backed away from his previous hopes for the League of Nations and stated that even the minimal expectations of the pacifists had not been met. Instead of a radical and necessary fresh start, he noted that the old mechanisms of secret diplomacy in support of the selfish interests of nation states had continued. Disarmament was blocked; article 18, which prohibited the secret negotiation of treaties, was circumvented; the international court, while permanent, was not mandatory; and that the whole of the League of Nations, through the appointment of delegates as representatives of their respective governments, was not a league of nations (Völker-Bund) at all, but a league of governments that was often paralyzed by the necessity of unanimous decisions. In addition, the League was hardly viable because of the absence of the United States. In contrast to Wehberg and other representatives of the version of pacifism that was later described as "moderate" or "organizational,"[39] Fried's criticism shows that he was not hopeful that the League of Nations could be gradually developed and improved: "Today there is no longer time for

---

37   Fried, "Braunschweig. Eindrücke vom IX. deutschen Pazifistenkongress," *Friedens-Warte* 22, no. 8/9 (October/November 1920): 218.
38   Fried, "Die Enttäuschung von Genf," *Friedens-Warte* 22, no. 11/12 (December 1920): 289–293.
39   Cf. Scheer, *Deutsche Friedensgesellschaft*, 372.

gradualism, for stating our wishes for the future, for hopes and promises. We can no longer be content with the complaisant contemplation of embryonic ideas, no matter how promising they may be."[40] At the present time, according to Fried, only a complete break with tradition could offer a solution, and the League of Nations did not offer such a break.

Fried's position on the anti-militarist demand for the possibility of conscientious objection was laid out in his article "Kurt Hillers Neuer Pazifismus: Kriegsdienstverweigerung oder Kriegsvorbeugung" (Kurt Hiller's New Pacifism: Conscientious Objection or the Prevention of War).[41] In this article he first made clear that the demand for the inviolability of human life, which this new pacifist direction asserted, had been an integral part of the peace movement for decades.

However, he simultaneously emphasized that anti-militarism, "[which is] deeply rooted in the terrible conditions that Prussian militarism has brought about," was more than justified. He even claimed: "Every convinced pacifist today must be an anti-militarist." Anti-militarism was accordingly only one aspect of pacifist activity, and it would not be able to prevent a new war by itself; such prevention was ultimately only possible "through a transformation of the minds, through a revolution of human thinking." Fried considered it a mistake to use conscientious objection as a means to prevent war, since it could only be effective if all those who opposed war were in the majority. Looking ahead, he added this warning: "If they are not [in the majority], then they sacrifice, certainly heroically, their own lives (but that's not what matters now), and they place the others, who did not dare to follow them, in the hands of the merciless war makers, who will have grown stronger as a result of the terror they employed." In order to prevent the "movement against murder" from becoming a "temptation to murder," one must strive not only to oppose war for reasons of conscience, but to "render impossible the demand for the military service."

Fried also addressed the possible reintroduction of mandatory military service in Germany by first criticizing Hiller's identification of mandatory military service with a compulsory national service. He emphasized that the general conscription of earlier times should be completely rejected as undignified slavery or "war bondage," but not necessarily as a form of military service: "It does not seem possible to me today to reject a mandatory national service

---

40 Fried, "Die Enttäuschung von Genf," *Friedens-Warte* 22, no. 11/12 (December 1920): 289.
41 *Friedens-Warte* 22, no. 11/12 (December 1920): 293–296. The following quotation is also taken from this source.

that is under a democratically led militia, that guarantees the human rights of its recruits, and that is deployed only for defensive purposes."

Under these conditions, Fried claimed, compulsory military service was not murder, but the prevention of murder, and it was indeed necessary for a "just defense." Unlike Hiller and many other anti-militarists, Fried certainly saw that a case could be made for a just defense, and he cited the Belgian struggle against the German occupiers as an example.

Despite his predominantly negative view of Hiller's proposals, Fried had a sympathetic opinion of Hiller the person, whom he knew from his work with the journal "Weiße Blätter" during the World War and from his attempt to found a "political council of intellectual workers" in November 1918. In January 1920, Fried wrote: "But I really want to count on your cooperation. You could present your ideas, which I find attractive, as often as you like in *Friedens-Warte,* and you may do so in your own style, which I also like."[42]

No matter where he would have stood in the pacifist camp at the end of the Weimar Republic, the "pacifist Jew" Fried would undoubtedly have been subject to Nazi persecution and hatred.[43] Even twelve years after his death, the Nazis still remembered this pacifist leader, burned his books and reviled his memory, which confirmed what Carl von Ossietzky had written in an obituary, namely, that his opponents would continue to pursue Fried beyond the grave.

Unlike in Austria, where he was remembered at least for his relationship with Bertha von Suttner, Fried had no place in the consciousness of the German Peace Society after the war. Most of his former, younger comrades were dead or living abroad. Moreover, there was the specific situation of the post-1945 peace movement, which, after more than a decade of the complete destruction of its organization and the persecution of its members, was not really able to build on the Weimar period. In addition, the political situation in the modern world made a return to the "pacifism of prominent individuals" of the German Empire seem less meaningful, for it was a world in which soon two highly armed power blocs, whose frontline ran directly through Germany and filled it with new weapons of mass destruction that threatened the existence of all life, no longer seemed to offer pacifists an opportunity for engagement.

Today, however, more than a hundred years after the Nobel Peace Prize was awarded to Alfred H. Fried, a constructive evaluation of his ideas for the modern age seems possible, and a rediscovery of strong pacifist personalities as models for future generations is important and meaningful.

---

42   Fried to Hiller, January 22, 1920, in Nachlass Fried, Box 88.
43   Cf. Riesenberger, *Friedensbewegung*, 246.

CHAPTER 7

Die Friedens-Warte

The journal *Die Friedens-Warte*, which Alfred H. Fried founded in the summer of 1899 at the time of the first Hague Conference and subsequently published for 22 years, was intended to give modern pacifism a platform and the various factions within the peace movement a forum for discussion. It is likely the most significant part of his oeuvres.[1] Fried himself saw it as his most important legacy and left a note in his will that it should be continued, with the title page permanently bearing the notation: "Founded by Alfred H. Fried at the time of the first Hague Conference." More than any other of his works, the *Friedens-Warte* demonstrates the interconnection between Fried's life and thought, and the journal reflects both the changes in his personal circumstances and in his view of pacifism.

1 The First Years 1899–1904

In December 1904, Fried explained the origins of the journal: "In retrospect, the plan for the *Friedens-Warte* first surfaced during those days in The Hague where we, friends of peace, were full of expectation and confident of victory, and where we paid attention to the events that took place in the secluded house behind the bushes that was sealed off from ordinary souls, where that memorable side-congress of pacifists took place, one that was never officially convened but was simultaneously both one of the most interesting and most important meetings. It was at that time, in the salon of Bertha von Suttner in the *Zentral-Hotel*, on whose roof the white flag fluttered in the wind, in whose room the preeminent representatives of pacifism flocked around the famous peace pioneer – Bloch, Stead, Novicov, Moscheles, Darby, Trueblood, Lafontaine, Türr, Richet, Selenka and many others – and where journalists from all different countries met and the delegates of all governments were stirred by the numerous ideas that influenced the work they did there; it was at that time, a consecrated place so to speak, that the plan for the *Friedens-Warte* first took hold."[2]

---

1 On the history of the *Friedens-Warte*, see also the essay by Daniel Porsch, "Die *Friedens-Warte* zwischen Friedensbewegung und Wissenschaft," *Friedens-Warte* 74, no. ½ (1999): 39ff.
2 *Friedens-Warte* 6, no. 12 (December 1904): 225.

The conference at The Hague did indeed bring pacifism into a new phase, one in which its ideas not only found some resonance in politics but were also discussed by broad sections of the population. Thus, a new, politically oriented peace journal, which could appear as a weekly and which could address a broader segment of the population, was conceivable for Germany. The flawed or even false representation of the events at The Hague, which the pacifists had lamented, and the increasingly frequent attacks on pacifist ideas in the daily press seemed to demand a journal that could quickly and forcefully take an opposing stance. Some early supporters and a small amount of start-up capital were quickly found.[3]

When Fried returned to Berlin on June 2, he immediately set to work and was able to publish the first issue of a weekly journal bearing the subtitle *Wochenschrift für internationale Verständigung* (Weekly Magazine for International Understanding) on July 1, 1899 (even while the conference was still in progress).[4] Fried was still influenced by what he had experienced: "The peace movement has entered a new phase; based on facts, it has taken on a new structure after numerous changes, and it will now assume an important role in the political life of the nations of the world."[5]

After he assured the readers of the journal's factual foundation and of its mission to uncover the important commonalities that unite the differing nations, he continued: "This journal will allow the friends of peace, for the first time, to have a forum where they will be able to keep abreast of the developments of the movement more quickly and in a more contemporary manner than had been possible in the previous monthly publications. That it actually meets a need can best be judged by those who are in the movement and who have felt dismay at the lack of such a journal to help them sort out the vast amount of material and the numerous events of recent years." At the same time, Fried made clear that he was definitely seeking a leading role in the movement through the establishment of the journal: "Furthermore, it will take a position on contemporary events, from the perspective of the *Friedens-Warte*, note the progress of the movement, and strive to pursue the path, with the help of the most outstanding supporters of peace, that leads to the well-being of humanity and to that of the individual nations." Fried has thus staked out the framework of the journal. As noted in the masthead, the journal was to be published every Saturday evening at a cost 1.50 marks each quarter. But already in the next issue, on July 10, Fried changed the day of publication to Monday.

---

[3] See *Friedens-Warte* 3, no. 1/2 (January 14, 1901): 1.
[4] Karl Ferdinand Reichel states the date as August 28, 1899 and incorrectly cites the subtitle as "Monatsschrift." Cf. Karl Ferdinand Reichel, *Die pazifistische Presse* (Würzburg, 1938), 7.
[5] *Friedens-Warte* 1, no. 1 (July 1899): 1. The following quotation is also taken from this source.

FIGURE 1
The Changing Face of Die Friedens-Warte

The new journal initially consisted of eight pages and within its first six months included established columns, although they did not appear in each issue. In most cases, a larger editorial was followed by a column entitled "Aus der Zeit" (Our Times), which contained information on general political themes as well as on issues related to pacifism. Next came a column entitled "Aus der Bewegung" (Our Movement), which included articles on the meetings and conferences of peace societies or of the IPU (Inter-Parliamentary Union).[6] What did not fit into either category could be found under "Vermischtes" (Miscellaneous). The section "Literatur und Presse" (Literature and the Press) included book reviews and references to articles in other journals.

---

6 The boundaries were initially fluid. The announcement of the general assembly of the Austrian friends of peace is to be found in issue 22, page 144 under the rubric "Aus der Zeit," while the report about the assembly is located in issue 24, page 155 under the rubric "Aus der Bewegung."

The final section consisted of the "Briefkasten" (Readers' Questions), in which Fried responded to questions whose authors were often only indicated by their initials. This section also included a few smaller advertisements – if there were any. The "most outstanding peacemakers," for whose help he had earlier pleaded, were only infrequently represented. Most of the articles were written by Fried himself, and more than once, when he was on the road or doing other things, the periodical consisted of only four pages instead of eight.[7] Nevertheless, at the end of the year, he gave an overall positive assessment: "A half-year is now behind us, a period full of strife and tribulations, but also full of satisfaction and success; the little journal has quickly established itself among the friends of peace. [...] Moreover, we have not given up hope that [...] a more significant journal may one day emerge from this small endeavor."[8]

At the same time, in December 1899, the journal *Die Waffen nieder!* ceased publication. With its demise, many of its earlier readers inevitably switched to *Die Friedens-Warte*, which for financial reasons now consisted of only four pages. Some of the authors who had written for *Die Waffen nieder!* offered their support to the new journal, as Fried had hoped. On January 8, 1900, Fried triumphantly wrote on the front page of the second issue: "It is true that *Die Friedens-Warte* has only been in existence for half a year, but it has already become the leading journal of the movement. This is the result not only of the increasing interest of readers and the growing number of subscribers, but, first and foremost, it is the result of the outstanding collaborators who have supported it."[9]

As early as July 1900, when the *Friedens-Warte* celebrated its first anniversary, Fried no longer sounded so optimistic when he thanked the "few supporters of the project" and said that the journal's future existence "is still uncertain." At the same time, he asked for the support of "the many people who have shown indifference to the journal." Fried now also assessed its overall impact more modestly and observed that "after all, it has achieved something."[10]

In October, he proudly noted the first donation to his paper: one English pound sterling that Felix Moscheles had given him when they met at the Peace Congress in Paris. Although he received a few more donations, the total amount was far from sufficient. At the end of the second year, he claimed: "Today the last issue of the second year of this weekly is being sent out; whether it's going

---

7 In 1899, this applied to issues 5, 11, 18, 22, 23, 25, and 26.
8 *Friedens-Warte* 1, no. 26 (December 25, 1899): 164. The following quotation is also taken from this source.
9 *Friedens-Warte* 2, no. 2 (January 8, 1900): 5.
10 *Friedens-Warte* 2, no. 26 (July 2, 1900): 101.

to be the final issue of the journal has yet to be determined. The previous backers and supporters of the journal have not yet shared their decision with me whether they want me to continue in 1901."[11]

In the first issue of the third year, Fried explained the financial situation of the journal in greater detail. "Friends of our idea,"[12] he wrote, had provided him with a fund that covered the deficit of the first two years, but that fund was now exhausted. Other promised payments had not yet arrived. Fried was – once again – broke. Nevertheless, on January 14, 1901, he published a double number, a *"ballon d'essaie,"* as he himself wrote, which was intended to entice paying subscribers and supportive friends. It was noted that money did not need to be sent in at the present time, but that potential contributors only had to tell him to what extent they were prepared to support the journal: "If the promised support is sufficient, the amounts will occasionally be requested; if they are not enough, then the editor would still like to pass on his regards to his friends at this point."[13] This time the appeal was more successful. Within a few days, 181 marks were donated, which Fried earmarked "for the *Friedens-Warte* fund." Although the amount was by no means sufficient, he still felt encouraged to continue. For the next few issues, he announced that, until further notice, he would be issuing the journal at 14-day intervals as double-editions for financial reasons. In spite of the ongoing precarious financial situation, Fried was again optimistic: "My plans for the *Friedens-Warte* have not yet been exhausted. I hope that I will one day be able to produce a significant weekly journal in a large format and that perhaps a political daily newspaper will grow from the movement's small journal. It won't be for lack of trying on my part if it doesn't happen."[14]

For the moment, however, each individual donation was treasured. By mid-May, about 430 marks had been received,[15] but only 100 marks came in for the rest of year. That was not nearly enough; according to his own calculations, Fried needed 1,600 marks just for a biweekly publication.[16] Again it was feared that the journal would have to shut down—but once more willing donors were

---

11   *Friedens-Warte* 2, no. 50/51: 204.
12   Only the support of Jan Bloch is known for sure, that of Felix Moscheles is probable.
13   *Friedens-Warte* 3, no. 1/2 (January 14, 1901): 2.
14   *Friedens-Warte* 3, no. 3/4 (January 28, 1901): 9. This plan allegedly goes back to Bertha von Suttner who had written in the conclusion of her *Revue*: "The struggle for peace, as it has developed today [...], must really have a major daily newspaper in every country in order to have an effective and creditable journal." *Die Waffen nieder!* 8 (December 1899): 439.
15   *Friedens-Warte* 2, no. 17/18 (May 13, 1901). At this time, Fried specifies that the total amount of money donated was 429.46 marks.
16   Cf. *Friedens-Warte* 3, no. 39/40 (December 23, 1901): 153.

found. The first issue of the fourth year (1902) noted that 26 donors contributed a total of 321 marks, but it mentioned only a few new names. The next issue showed an increase of another 217 marks, mainly from larger donations by Heinrich von Bloch, the son of the late Jan Bloch, and by Felix Moscheles. But then the donations fell off again. Nevertheless, Fried seemed to be a little better off at the end of the year, because he planned some aesthetic improvements—of course, only after the "not insignificant bill for the printer" in 1902 was settled.[17] "Then I would like to be able to increase the circulation of next year's journal; if possible, each issue would be stapled to a colored cover, in order to give it a more pleasing appearance. Of course, that would almost double the cost. But the budget is so ridiculously low that even if it were doubled, it still wouldn't be very large."[18]

This comment clearly shows an aspect of Fried's character that he would also display later, much to the dismay of those who sought to consolidate the journal's finances. Fried was not an astute businessman; instead of waiting for his financial situation to improve, he took advantage of every opportunity to put his plans into action. Despite the financial difficulties of the journal, he continued to provide free access to those who could not afford the subscription.[19]

By March 1903, the journal was appearing punctually each month, once in the middle and again at the end. But then the impact of Fried's marital drama – his separation from Martha and the exile of Therese to Vienna – took its toll. From April to June, the journal appeared only at the end of the month and comprised only twelve pages, instead of the sixteen pages that one would expect of a double issue.

Few of his readers would suspect that Fried was constantly shuttling between Berlin and Vienna, where he was looking for a place to stay with his lover Therese Frankl. In the June issue, he listed his full address as only Berlin-Schöneberg for the first time, without giving any further details. He still felt more at home in Berlin than in Vienna, and he hoped for a speedy return to the capital of the Reich. It was not until 1906, after he had been living in Vienna for some time, that the journal contained the notice: "Self-published by Alfred H. Fried (currently Vienna IX/4)." This information, however, did not appear in the altered masthead but only at the bottom of the last page of the issue.

---

17   Fried gives more precise numbers in the letters to the editor in the edition of January 15, 1903. Accordingly, the revenues for the *Friedens-Warte* for the year 1902 amounted to 2,200.88 marks and the expenses were 2932.59 marks. See *Friedens-Warte* 5, no. 1 (January 15, 1918): 8.
18   *Friedens-Warte* 4, no. 24 (December 21, 1902): 185.
19   See *Friedens-Warte* 5, no. 4 (February 28, 1903): 132.

At the end of September 1903, the journal was once again suddenly published monthly. In the December issue, Fried let his readers know that he intended to publish the *Friedens-Warte* in the coming year with a minimum of 40 print columns (20 pages) plus a cover; moreover, it would be published only once a month: "It is my intention, for the foreseeable future, to make the *Friedens-Warte* a leading journal of political pacifism; I want it to become a suitable vehicle to champion the worthy idea of peace in Germany, to create a platform on which international events can be interrogated from the pacifist standpoint, and where the leading voices of international pacifism can present their views. I have refrained from publishing the *Friedens-Warte* in biweekly intervals, since today's movement has become so vast that even a biweekly organ can no longer keep up with it [...] at the same time I shall endeavor to live up to the demand to gradually let the journal take on the form of a review and to continue to expand it."[20]

This decision marked a completely new direction for Fried. It is likely that a variety of considerations played a role in it: the lack of financial support by the German pacifists, who dashed any plans for a daily newspaper; the cost of a biweekly publication that could no longer guarantee reports on current events; the hope that a new, more impressive outward appearance could secure foreign collaborators; and, not least, the influence of Bertha von Suttner, who during these months was debating whether the *Friedens-Warte* should be declared the new journal of the Austrian Peace Society.

2   Consolidation Phase 1904–1909

What is certain is that the *Friedens-Warte*, in the middle of January 1904, was innovative, and not only in its appearance. The journal, which was now consistently almost twenty pages long, regularly published news of the Austrian Peace Society in its own independent column (and noted in the subtitle) on the final page of each issue. Since the Austrian Peace Society covered most of the additional costs from its own budget,[21] the journal gained a new financial pillar and, at the same time, broader distribution in Austria. In the long run, this led to Fried's acquiring a group of more or less permanent advertisers, some of whom had no direct connection to pacifism.

---

20   *Friedens-Warte* 5, no. 23/24 (December 15, 1903): 192.
21   See the report submitted to the executive board at the meeting of the Austrian Peace Society on January 4, 1904, page 20. It is noted there that one hopes "to cover the considerable expenses" by asking the members who pay the minimal dues of two crowns to raise their contribution by a crown.

Another positive development in the same direction was that Fried, in the spring of 1904, was able to make his journal "the official publication of the International Museum of War and Peace in Lucerne," a foundation of the late Jan Bloch. Except for the publication of an index to Bloch's monumental work *Der Krieg* (The War), which Fried created and published in the *Friedens-Warte* in May 1905, the "official publication" remained largely unused by the museum, but it did allow further funds to flow from the Bloch Foundation.[22] In addition to Berlin, the places of publication now included Vienna and Leipzig. But Fried still stated his own residence as Berlin-Schöneberg and also called himself the editor responsible for the German Empire, while he appointed Vinzens Jerabek in Vienna the editor for Austria-Hungary.

The secretive back and forth between Berlin and Vienna led to some complications: on occasion, money was sent to Fried's address in Berlin, which, due to his long absence, was disadvantageous; but, above all, the dispute over the amount of the financial support he was expected to pay for his family along with the Holländer family's attempts to garnish his wages complicated matters. He had to ask his readers in January 1904 to refrain from sending their subscription fees and donations to him directly, but rather to the printer Pass & Garleb in Berlin.

In terms of content, the most prominent topic in 1904 was the Russo-Japanese War. Interestingly, in March 1904 Fried also began an ongoing report of his impressions of the "distant" war, which he called "Kriegsbriefe eines Pazifisten" (War Letters of a Pacifist). He continued these letters until October 1904,[23] which may be seen as an early prelude to his subsequent famous World War I *Kriegs-Tagebücher* (War Diaries), fragments of which would appear during the war in the *Friedens-Warte*.

When the monthly publication was regularized and greater space in the journal became available, Fried was able to engage his first steady contributors, something that he had long hoped for. Among the contributors were Anna B. Eckstein[24] from Boston, an officer of the American Peace Society, and Richard Reuter, an important leader of the German Peace Society. But when Reuter died in December 1904,[25] Fried was only able to publish the writings held in his estate. From 1905 on, Bertha von Suttner was also a permanent contributor

---

22   In addition, the museum agreed to cover the cost of publication of the *Friedens-Warte*. See Fried's note in January 1906 referring to a donation of 100 marks. *Friedens-Warte* 8, no. 1: 19.

23   *Friedens-Warte* 4, no. 3: 45–48; *Friedens-*Warte, no. 4: 69–71; no. 5: 93–95; no. 6: 106–108; no. 7: 133–134; no. 8: 152–155; no. 9: 169–171; no. 10: 190–191.

24   On Anna B. Eckstein, see Fried, *Handbuch*, (1913), 343.

25   See the obituary by Fried in *Friedens-Warte* 7, no. 1 (January 1905): 10.

to the journal. Her "Zeitschau" (Reflections on the Times) was now published every month until her death in 1914 under the title "Randglossen zur Zeitgeschichte" (Commentaries on Contemporary History), which appeared after the peace-specific articles.

In his lead article "System des revolutionären Pacifismus" [sic] (System of Revolutionary Pacifism) of August 1905, Fried also clearly delineated the programmatic direction of the journal by distinguishing his pacifism from any form of "reform pacifism." He defined true pacifism as the only kind of pacifism that combatted the deeper causes of war, i.e., inter-state anarchy; the aim of his pacifism was the promotion and continued development of an inter-governmental organization. Fried underscored the content of this direction in 1906 with a logo. He quite deliberately chose a symbol that was unusual for the peace movement: interlocking gears above the motto "Organize the World." What he wanted to express with this new symbol was then explained to his readers in the January issue: "The *Friedens-Warte* will henceforth appear with an image on the cover. – Finding the right emblem was not easy. We had to avoid traditional symbolism. No olive branches, no doves, no angels, no white flags, no broken swords, no plowshares! [...] A series of interlocking gears seemed to be the right symbol to us. It demonstrates collaboration toward a common goal; it shows the interrelationship between the part and the whole: the peaceful, yet certain impact through organization. The symbol shows the hegemony of the spirit over matter, the power of order through spirit, the victory of human ingenuity over animalistic instinct. And that is precisely the essence of the pacifism that is represented in these pages, 'revolutionary' pacifism [...]."[26]

The attempt to achieve a new, sharper profile was successful. Over the next few years, the number of articles not written by Fried skyrocketed. Often there were articles by Eugen Schlief alongside texts by Novicow, Frédéric Passy and Otto Umfrid. In the context of the second Hague Conference in 1907, the names Otfried Nippold and the Russian internationalist Friedrich Martens can also be found under individual articles, albeit mostly as reprints. On the other hand, the Königsberg journalist Oskar Schwonder,[27] who published numerous articles under the name of Carl Ludwig Siemering, became a permanent contributor. It is unlikely that he received a fee, because the journal still ran a deficit.

In 1909, the journal appeared with a new subtitle for the first time. Instead of a *Zeitschrift für internationale Verständigung* (Journal for International Understanding), Fried now published his *Zeitschrift für zwischenstaatliche Organisation* (Journal for International Organization), which was more in keeping with

---

26 *Friedens-Warte* 8, no. 1 (January 1906): 2.
27 On Oskar Schwonder, see Fried, *Handbuch*, (1913), 405f.

the direction the journal had been taking for years. The number of reports on international legal issues increased, but Fried was careful to give enough space to the peace societies and their representatives. Bertha von Suttner remained a stalwart contributor with her own column, and Otto Umfrid, who had served as President of the German Peace Society since 1900, frequently contributed his thoughts, as did representatives of the peace societies from other countries. At the same time, Fried reported in detail about the World Peace Congresses, meetings of the Berne Peace Bureau, the first German peace congresses (which had met every year since 1908), meetings of the IPU, etc. He also informed his readers in the column "Aus der Bewegung" (From the Movement) of the milestone birthdays of leading pacifists, or he used the column to write the obituary of important pacifists. From 1909 on, Fried offered a general overview of pacifist developments via his own "Pazifistische Chronik" (Pacifist Chronicle), which chronologically listed events of importance to pacifism. Beginning around 1908, Fried expanded the rubric "Literatur und Presse" (Literature and Press) to include international pacifist writing, such that individual journals were listed with their main articles. But the mere listing of the newspaper articles took on such a scale that in 1911 Fried began to assign them to particular subject areas such as "peace movement in general," "international politics," "international law," "miscellaneous international," and "economics."

3 Period of Growth, 1910–1914

Fried's ambition was to make the *Friedens-Warte* an internationally respected journal. By 1911, he managed to increase the length of the issues to 32 pages each month, and just a year later to 40 pages. Nor did he wait, as was usual for him, for the means to do so, but rather he counted on the fact that the necessary funds would materialize. At the same time, circulation was increased in part through an additional donation fund in the summer of 1910, which was the result of the efforts of Hans Wehberg, a new, very active co-worker and expert in international law.

The "Aufruf für die Sammlung zur Verbreitung der *Friedens-Warte*" (Appeal for Funding to Disseminate the *Friedens-Warte*) that Hans Wehberg sent out with the intention of distributing copies of the journal, free of charge, to the reading halls of German and Austrian universities and technical colleges, included the signatures of eleven people in addition to Wehberg's own: Reichstag Deputy Dr. Bruno Ablaß, Councillor of the Mines Georg Gothein, Dr. Johannes Leonhart, M.D., Professor Richard Eickhoff, the professors of international law Christian Meurer, Karl Lamprecht, Paul Laband, Ludwig von

Bar, Walther Schücking and Emanuel Ritter von Ullmann.[28] By mid-January, more than 860 marks had been raised, which was more than the initiators had hoped. And this did not include a subsidy of 400 Norwegian kroner (about 443 marks) that the Nobel committee of Norway's Storthing approved for the *Friedens-Warte* on the condition that it also send the journal to the universities and colleges of the Scandinavian countries.[29] This official recognition of Fried's journal may have indirectly led to his receiving the Nobel Peace Prize a year later.

Many of the donors were experts in international law. However, the largest single donation (200 marks) came from the Councilor of Commerce Georg Arnhold of Dresden, whose bank managed the Wehberg Fund, the Publication Fund of the *Friedens-Warte,* and another fund. In 1908, Georg Arnhold, chairman of the Dresden branch of the German Peace Society and one of Fried's most important patrons,[30] had started a second fund for the journal, which was to be used for its final consolidation within three years. Eight people from the Peace Movement had signed guarantees of over 4,000 marks. At the same time, Fried and Arnhold succeeded in persuading the various peace societies, which together received some 1,500 copies of the journal, to double their annual subscription price from one to two marks. In return, Arnhold insisted that he be able to examine Fried's bookkeeping in detail, and he assigned one of his own staff to manage the journal's expenses and develop a suitable saving plan.

Although Fried too always cited consolidation as his clear goal, Arnhold's warnings and those of his co-worker Schulz usually fell on deaf ears. Schulz and Arnhold particularly emphasized Fried's need to secure more advertisers and follow a cost-oriented business model. The establishment of the fund that Wehberg had created (which was not intended to consolidate the journal but to ensure its greater dissemination) ultimately aroused Arnhold's distrust, especially since he had not been included in the planning. In July 1910, when he heard of the appeal from a third party, he wrote to Fried: "I must frankly confess that I am greatly disturbed that I was completely left out of the loop in this matter after I had gone to the trouble to support the *Friedens-Warte*[31] and continue to do so today."

---

28 The precise wording of the appeal and the complete list of the names of the signatories, as well as of the first donors, is to be found in *Friedens-Warte* 13, no. 1 (January 1911): 1f.
29 See the correspondence with the Nobel committee, in Nachlass Fried, Box 72.
30 Arnhold, who was a friend of Bertha von Suttner, financed the publication of the *Handbuch der Friedensbwegung* in 1905 as well as the subsequent edition in 1911/1913. He also made generous donations to some of Fried's other projects.
31 Arnhold to Fried, July 21, 1910, in Nachlass Fried, Box 47.

What Arnhold most feared at this time was that the two funding appeals would overlap and could thus irritate some donors—but also that Fried would be encouraged by the result to once again embark on new ventures. And in this regard he was right. Reassured by recent developments, Fried began to defend himself toward the end of 1910 against Schulz' repeated demands and cost-cutting plans, and he denied him further access to his books. Moreover, he decided to use a donation of about 800 marks—presumably from the USA—to expand the scope of the journal from 20 to 32 pages. Arnhold was not pleased with this new development, but he too was ultimately supportive of the Wehberg Fund, because the bold concept seemed to work. The *Friedens-Warte* had attracted attention especially in an economically strong America. According to the Carnegie Foundation's annual report of 1911: "It is, on the whole, the most substantial and effective of the publications devoted to peace and arbitration."[32] And the report emphasized that some 2,000 copies of the journal were read not only in Germany and Austria, but also in the Balkan provinces, Italy, Belgium, Holland and even Russia.

When Fried demanded the final installment of the consolidation funds from Arnhold in the autumn of 1911 in order to be able to expand the scope of the journal even further—while also expressing his opposition to further interference by Mr. Schulz in his project—an open dispute ensued. On November 7, 1911, Arnhold personally addressed Fried: "In response to your esteemed letter, I would not like to see things turned upside down. It was not a question of administering a fund that was made available to you for three years, but rather I had approached a number of people with a request for funding so that the *Friedens-Warte* could gradually be placed on secure financial footing – I was looking at a three-year window. You seem to have been in agreement with this plan only to the extent that it procured greater funding, but shortly thereafter you changed your tune."[33]

Arnhold was particularly annoyed at how Fried managed money, unreasonably in his view. He mentioned as an example the edition of Bertha von Suttner's novel *Der Menschheit Hochgedanken* (*When Thoughts Will Soar: A Romance of the Immediate Future*) that was published by the Verlag der Friedens-Warte. "I am certainly pleased with the publication of the Suttner novel, but it goes against sound business principles for the Verlag der Friedens-Warte or you to have taken on a risk that you really could not afford to." He himself, as Arnhold writes, had to provide financial assistance to Bertha von Suttner's

---

32   Carnegie Endowment for International Peace. *Year Book for 1911* (Washington, D.C. 1912), 57.
33   Arnhold to Fried, November 7, 1911, in Nachlass Fried, Box 47. The following quotation is also taken from this source.

former publisher, Mr. Pierson, since the latter had incurred huge losses by publishing Suttner's entire writings and then had to personally ask him (Arnhold), as a friend of the baroness, for his support.

Fried felt hurt,[34] claiming that he assumed that the journal had been on secure financial footing since the end of 1910 and that the reorganization period—including the external controls—had thus ended. Moreover, he argued that he had not changed "his tune" but was simply opposed to "the bureaucratic proposals of Mr. Schulz." Fried also did not let Arnhold's accusation concerning the Suttner novel stand. After all, in Germany, not a single publisher had agreed to accept the novel, and he had therefore considered it his duty to "obtain satisfaction for the woman whose feelings were seriously hurt." However, Fried did not deny the accusation of having violated sound business principles: "But if I were only to be guided by commercial considerations, I would have turned to promoting the naval fleet 20 years ago instead of trying to advance the prospect for peace."

Despite Arnhold's fears, the situation improved significantly a little later since, beginning in January 1912, the Carnegie Foundation awarded the *Friedens-Warte* a yearly subsidy of $6,800 thus enabling Fried to increase the circulation to 4,000 copies; these were to be placed in libraries and reading rooms. Nevertheless, a dispute arose when Fried informed Arnhold of the support that he had obtained from the Carnegie Foundation and then demanded that the funds still in the consolidation fund be used to cover deficits from the previous year. For his part, Arnhold wanted to return the funds to the donors.[35] When Fried objected, arguing that he had to account for the new funds in January 1912 and thus urgently needed a clean balance sheet, Arnhold finally gave up in exasperation. On January 17, he wrote to Fried that he had just transferred the remainder of the money to Pass & Garleb.[36] Fried had triumphed. Without debt and with support from the Carnegie Foundation, he could finally expand the journal, beginning in 1912. From January on, it appeared monthly as a forty-page journal with a circulation of 6,000 copies. The growing reputation of the journal and its editor, who had just received the Nobel Prize, and probably the fact that Fried could now pay the contributors for their articles, quickly led to a significant increase in the number of authors.

Fried only wrote one or two specialized articles per month, almost always the lead editorial. Moreover, in the volume of 1912, there were articles by Eduard Bernstein, Ludwig Quidde, David Starr Jordan, Richard Gädke, Ellen Key,

---

34 Fried to Arnhold, November 9, 1911, in Nachlass Fried, Box 47.
35 Arnhold to Fried, January 10, 1912, in Nachlass Fried, Box 47.
36 Arnhold to Fried, January 17, 1912, in Nachlass Fried, Box 47.

Paolo Baccari, Norman Angell, Elsbeth Friedrichs, T.E. Burton, Hermann Fernau, Jong van Beek en Donk, Rudolf Kraus, Rudolf Goldscheid, Ludwig von Bar, Robert Piloty, Wilhelm Lamszus, Edouard de Neufville, besides the familiar names. The section entitled "Mitteilungen der Friedensgesellschaften" (Communications of the Peace Societies) was also expanded. From 1911 on, notices from Sweden, the United Kingdom, and the United States were also included there.

Above all else, it was important to Fried that his journal be distributed to the influential educated middle class, i.e., academics, parliamentarians and journalists, in order to have the greatest impact on public opinion through these multipliers.[37] He tried to compensate for the still relatively small number of copies (6,000) by placing them in libraries and reading rooms where one could assume that one copy would be read several times—a thoroughly promising tactic, if one, like Fried, were focused on the long-term effects and not on immediate success. In March 1912, he wrote to Wehberg with satisfaction: "The dissemination of F. W. is now excellently organized. It is received by all of the members of Austrian and German parliaments, 490 university professors, and by prominent people in America and England, as well as by all the diplomats in the European capitals, etc."[38] Of course, the subscriptions did not mean that the journal was having the desired effect, but Fried was quite proud of the success he had achieved. By the summer of 1914, his journal had steadily gained in respect and in distribution.

4 War Censorship and the Path into Exile

The death of Bertha von Suttner on June 21, 1914 brought about the first unplanned change to the *Friedens-Warte*. In July, a special edition appeared in her honor. On 20 of the 40 pages, her friends, like Hedwig Pötting, Carl Hauptmann, Edwin Mead, Wilhelm Ostwald, Ellen Key, Walther Schücking, Baron d'Estourelles de Constant, and Fried all wrote commemorative texts about her. Amid all the grief, one international event almost went unnoticed. Under "miscellaneous" in the column "Aus der Zeit" (Our Times), a short article appeared

---

37 Report of the Carnegie-Foundation in 1912: "Beginning of January 1, 1912, the number of pages of each issue was increased from 32 to 40, and 4,076 new addresses, including students, teachers, university professors, organizations of students and teachers, societies of lawyers, editors, diplomats, members of the Reichstag and of the Austrian Parliament, libraries, reading rooms, newspapers and periodicals." Carnegie Endowment for International Peace, *Year Book for 1912* (Washington, D.C. 1913), 66.
38 Fried to Wehberg, March 18, 1912, in Nachlass Wehberg, vol. 59a, BA Koblenz.

under the headline: "The Bloody Deed of Sarajevo." The article did not seem to portend any increased danger of war. Instead, the journal concluded with a four-page spread on the 21st World Peace Congress. Fried, as the main organizer of the congress, was still in the midst of the labor-intensive preparations and was probably paying less attention to politics than usual in this crucial month.

The outbreak of war had an immediate impact on the publication of *Die Friedens-Warte*. The great distance between the publisher in Vienna and the printer in Berlin became an obstacle. Fried was unable to publish the August issue, which he had finalized before the war broke out, since he did not receive the proofs until the end of the month, and their content was by that time completely outdated.[39] Initially disappointed, he decided to temporarily discontinue the journal. "What's the purpose of the *Friedens-Warte* now? The theory is over. To criticize the events would now be highly inappropriate. There will be time for that later. In the given situation one simply cannot be up to date. The best thing to do is to discontinue its publication. When the moment is right, I'll be able to bring out an issue."[40]

But Fried's depression did not last long. He soon started to compile a new edition of the journal; it appeared as a double issue (August/September) on October 3, 1914, but it consisted of only 40 pages. Fried justified his change of heart: "There was a great demand for it, and it also seemed necessary to give some direction to the many pacifists whose outlook on life had been totally shaken as well as to those for whom the outbreak of the war offered an opportunity to join the pacifists. I wish I could distribute a million copies of the journal. It would find readers."[41] Fried wrote all the articles himself with the exception of a short article "Es war einmal" (Once Upon a Time) by Heinrich Lammasch, who offered an analysis of the possibilities of the further development of international law after the war, and two texts that had been submitted before the war. The main part of the new edition consisted of a new series of 16 pages, which Fried called "Aus meinem Kriegs-Tagebuch" (From my War Diary) and in which he now published the first "fragments" of August 7 to 27. These entries interpreted the recent events and subsequent developments from the pacifist point of view. But he also published the second anti-war flyer of the

---

39 Cf. "An unsere Leser," in *Friedens-Warte* 16, no. 8 (August/September 1914): 319.
40 Fried, *Kriegs-Tagebuch*, 1 (August 22, 1914), 139. These statements are not found in the excerpt of the *Kriegs-Tagebuch* (293f.) that was published in *Friedens-Warte* 16, no. 8 (August/September 1914).
41 Fried, *Kriegs-Tagebuch*, 1, 120 (3 October 1914).

German Peace Society of August 15, 1914, the resolution of the Austrian Peace Society, and the resolutions of English and American peace associations.

The journal was not put under duress until mid-November 1914 when the censor, presumably as a result of a critical article in the *Kölnische Zeitung*, grew interested in the *Friedens-Warte*. Under the title "A. H. Fried und der Weltkrieg" (A. H. Fried and the World War), Dr. W. Schoenborn, J.D., a professor (Privatdozent) in Heidelberg, pointed to the not-to-be-underestimated dangers for the image of Germany abroad that arose from the journal. According to Schoenborn, Fried was "a publicist of considerable influence" and "the *Friedens-Warte* is a publication of a decidedly international character. It has a relatively large readership abroad, to my knowledge, especially in the neutral states, where truthful accounts are of particular importance to Germany at the present time. This is also the case for Holland and the United States of America."[42] He continued that it was therefore impossible to ignore the war diary, which had been appearing in the *Friedens-Warte* since August-September, nor to count on the fact that it would find very few readers in Germany and Austria. "In this war, we have repeatedly learned, much to our detriment, that missiles shot from the pen are also capable of spreading poisonous gases. Artillery that hurls such missiles must be silenced." Schoenborn was not the only critic, and other journals soon joined the call.

The board of censors reacted swiftly. The regional High Command ordered a pre-censorship review of the November issue. Almost all of the issue was declared unfit for publication, although, as Fried complained, it contained reprints of articles from German newspapers that had already been published. At the beginning of December, the board, presumably at the urging the Social Democratic Reichstag Deputy Eduard Bernstein,[43] who had been in contact with Fried since 1911, was prepared to review the journal again, but they did not change their opinion. Thus, at the end of the year, a ten-page skeleton edition was published; it included, as an editorial, a letter from Marschall von Biberstein, a County Commissioner in Prussia, called "An die Völker germanischen Blutes" (To the People of Germanic Blood). He wrote in favor of the fusion of all "Germanic peoples," and thus clearly differed from Fried. The final section of the issue was made up of one page, like a leaflet, on which Fried presented the basic values of pacifism in twelve short statements and tried to defend them against defamation. Coincidentally or not, he used the exact

---

42   See W. Schoenborn, J.D. and university professor (Privatdozent), "A. H. Fried und der Weltkrieg," in *Kölnische Zeitung*, midday edition, November 17, 1914. The following quotation is also taken from this source.

43   Fried, *Kriegs-Tagebuch*, 1, 224.

same initial phrase with which the six propositions in the well-known "Aufruf an die Kulturwelt" (Call to the World of Culture) of October 4, 1914 had begun. Signed by 93 scholars, it had rejected all the accusations against Germany while stressing the special importance of German militarism for German culture.[44]

Once again, Fried considered relocating the *Friedens-Warte* to Switzerland,[45] where he had been living since mid-October, but he was concerned about the hassle and the expenses, which were once again a problem. In mid-November 1914, he wrote to Hans Wehberg from Berne: "I admit that the direction of the FW is now a bit muddled. That is the result of the current circumstances. But at least it is being published. For how long, I do not know, because, since July, we no longer have access to the funds from the endowment. I have already accumulated a debt of 9,000 marks. How this will turn out, I also don't know. In general, I'm fearful of the new direction there."[46] But Fried's fears were unfounded, and the Carnegie Endowment continued to support him. In 1915 and 1916, in addition to personal contributions, he received $6,000 from Carnegie in the first year, which was then reduced in the summer of 1916 to $4,500, for the maintenance of the journal.[47]

But difficulties with the censors continued, and the frequent delays in the postal service between Berlin and Berne caused Fried ever more problems. The first issue of the new edition appeared toward the end of February 1915 as a heavily reduced double issue. As compensation for the delay, Fried announced special future issues, the first of which was published in Zurich in March under the title *Blätter für zwischenstaatliche Organisation* (Journal for an International Organization). Innocent-looking flower decorations now adorned the front page instead of the gears. But the "Journal" was by no means harmless; it contained well-reasoned articles by Lammasch, Wehberg, Umfrid, and Nippold—as well as, once again, excerpts from the war diary that were not approved by the censor. On March 14, Fried noted: "The first issue of *Blätter für zwischenstaatliche Organisation* was published today. It contains only the kinds of articles that the censor in Berlin considered unsuitable for publication

---

44   Verbatim it reads: "*It is not true*, that the fight against our so-called militarism is not a fight against our culture, as our enemies hypocritically allege. Without our German militarism, German culture would have been eradicated a long time ago." Rolland, *Das Gewissen Europas*, vol. 1, 96ff. It is also to be found in Georg Fr. Nicolai, *Die Biologie des Krieges*, original version, first edition (Zurich, 1919), 7ff.
45   Cf. Fried, *Kriegs-Tagebuch*, I, 224.
46   Fried to Wehberg, November 18, 1914, in Nachlass Wehberg, vol. 59b, BA Koblenz.
47   Cf. Carnegie Endowment for International Peace, *Year Book for 1915*, 63 and *Year Book for 1916*, 54.

in the *Friedens-Warte*. Later on, this issue will form a splendid document of the way one should deal with censorship. It contains nothing that cannot now be said without offense and nothing that cannot be heard daily in Germany."[48] Further special issues appeared in April and May of 1915. Fried informed Wehberg at the beginning of April that he was "pleased to have received so much warm support for his *Blätter*, and less than two weeks later he emphasized once again the great positive response that the *Blätter* enjoyed.[49] On the other hand, the real *Friedens-Warte* was encountering ever greater obstacles in Berlin. The double issue of March/April comprised only 20 pages; after its publication was delayed, Fried finally decided to move the journal completely to Switzerland.

5   *Die Friedens-Warte* in Swiss Exile

The first issue of the *Friedens-Warte* to be published in Zurich appeared in June 1915. It retained all the previous sections of the journal,[50] consisted of 40 pages, and was to be published monthly. The special issues were now no longer necessary. What was left of them was the title and the flower decoration that had replaced the old gear logo.

By the spring of 1916, the journal was being published by the firm Orell Füssli in Zurich, by and large in the same format. It was still not banned in Germany, and so initially only a few individual issues, whose publication had been delayed, fell victim to the German board of censorship. Then, however, in January 1916, "Bismarcks Werk im Lichte der großdeutschen Kritik" (Bismarck's Oeuvres in Light of the Criticism vis-à-vis Greater Germany)[51] appeared in the *Friedens-Warte*. The article, written by Friedrich Wilhelm Foerster, caused a sensation in Germany and unleashed a storm of outrage in the nationalist press, which was directed not only at Foerster but also at the *Friedens-Warte*. In early April 1916, the *Friedens-Warte* was banned in Germany. The news reached Fried during a stay in Basel. On April 7, he noted: "At last! What I had long feared. Silenced! The denunciation by the *Kreuzzeitung* has been successful. I take some consolation in the fact that the dissemination of an idea can never

---

48   Fried, *Kriegs-Tagebuch*, I, 321.
49   Fried to Wehberg, April 19, 1915, in Nachlass Wehberg, vol. 59b, BA Koblenz.
50   This is true except for the column "Aus der Bewegung," which no longer served any function during the war since the peace societies had been banned and since information did not flow very freely.
51   F. W. Foerster, "Bismarcks Werke im Lichte der großdeutschen Kritik," in *Friedens-Warte* 18, no. 1 (January 1916): 1–9.

be halted by the prohibition of a publication."[52] Thus the permanent relocation of the *Friedens-Warte* to Switzerland was finally settled. In July, Fried also noted that the journal was banned in Austria-Hungary.[53]

Nevertheless, in order to be able to deliver the *Friedens-Warte* to its subscribers in Germany and Austria, the publisher had to come up with a plan: "The issues have been given covers that suggest a different content. For example, with the title *Zeitschrift für die Finanzpolitik Mitteleuropas* or *Archiv für soziale Fürsorge*, etc. [...] In this way it was possible to get the pacifist 'poison', albeit in small doses, into Germany."[54]

But it was more difficult to smuggle the journal into Austria; only via a detour through Holland was it possible, and only in extraordinary cases. Some copies apparently arrived in Austria via the aid of the Austro-Hungarian legation in Berne; they were then sent by embassy curriers to some well-known individuals.[55] It was even difficult to send them to the Entente states since here too Fried could see that there was "fear of the word 'peace' on the envelope and, above all, of the German text."[56]

Because of the continuing uncertainty, Fried introduced a check-in system in the summer of 1917. Each issue that was sent abroad was accompanied by a postcard, which the recipient was to send back immediately upon receipt; only then would subsequent issues be sent out. It is not known whether this system, which also ran the risk of exposing the recipients of the prohibited journal to postal censorship, was successful, but it did continue until the end of the war.

It became ever more difficult for Fried to know whether the journal reached its subscribers because he lacked the financial resources to ascertain that information. When America entered the war, the Carnegie Foundation canceled any further financial support, which for Fried meant that he had to finance the production largely from his own resources. Difficulties in the procurement of paper led to a significant increase in the cost of production, so that in 1917 he was only able to publish 10 issues of the journal rather than the usual 11. From 1916 on, these editions only consisted of 32 pages. Finally, at the beginning of the 20th year of publication, he also stopped the practice of providing free copies.

In spite of all this, the *Friedens-Warte* increasingly became the voice of and a forum for moderate pacifists and German emigrants, i.e, those whose views

---

52   Fried, *Kriegs-Tagebuch*, II, 253.
53   Cf. Fried, *Kriegs-Tagebuch*, II (July 27, 1916), 367.
54   *Friedens-Warte* 20, no. 11/12 (November/December 1918): 291.
55   Ibid, 292.
56   Ibid.

FIGURE 2
A Dozen Truths, which appeared on the back of Die Friedens-Warte of November/December 1914

did not or only partially coincided with the more radical, Entente-oriented direction of the circles around the *Freie Zeitung*. From the very beginning, the central issue was the necessity for and the possibility of a new, post-war order. First, with respect to foreign policy it focused on the formation of a sustainable peace treaty, and later, with America's entry into the war, it reflected a turn towards domestic political issues, in particular, the demand for a democratization of the German Reich. In an article in June 1918, titled "Die Pazidemokratie,"[57] Fried himself wrote that, in one regard, post-war pacifism must clearly be different from pre-war pacifism: "It must recognize that pacifism and democracy are not two distinct phenomena, but the same phenomenon, viewed from different perspectives. [...] There can be no pacifist foreign policy without domestic democracy in the states."[58]

---

57   *Friedens-Warte* 16, no. 6 (June 1918): 157–161.
58   Ibid, 160.

This attitude, to which he later added his demand that Germany unambiguously admit its culpability for the war, did not make him many friends in Germany. For example, the *Rheinische Zeitung* reported in an article "Dr. A. H. Fried und die Pazidemokraten"[59] (Dr. A. H. Fried and the Peace Democrats) that Fried abused Swiss hospitality, in the worst way, in order to give the Entente "poisonous weapons to be used in their intellectual campaign of aggression against Germany." The author further suggested that there was "only *one* way to deal with this political germ carrier, whose views are dangerous to humanity, this warmongering wolf in pacifist sheep's clothing." In spite of these threats, which did not bode well for Fried's return to Germany, Fried nevertheless believed that the anticipated increased interest in pacifism and a democratic renewal of Germany would take place after the war, and that pacifists like himself would then be needed in the vanguard.

6 The *Friedens-Warte* after the War, 1918–1919

Immediately after the war, Fried did everything within his power to have the ban on imports into Germany lifted: "At present I am in touch with various members of the new government in order to have the journal approved for publication in Germany."[60] He was already considering taking up permanent residence in Germany, but the rapidly changing political developments made him hesitant: "I am not yet clear about the future of the *Friedens-Warte*. I do not know if it will be published in Berlin or Vienna or in Zurich. At the moment, the situation is entirely uncertain."[61]

The situation was still uncertain as late as February 1919. Fried apologized for the delayed publication of the January issue saying that he still did not know where the *Friedens-Warte* would be published in the future.[62] As the year progressed, however, it became more and more apparent that rising production costs in Switzerland exceeded Fried's dwindling resources. The publisher, Orell Füssli, was now making persistent demands for payment,[63] amounts that Fried could not pay due to the decline in value of his assets in Austria and the lack

---

59 "Dr. A. H. Fried und die Pazidemokraten," *Rheinische Zeitung*, no. 676 (August 23, 1918). The following quotation is also taken from this source.
60 Fried to Wehberg, October 24, 1918, in Nachlass Wehberg, vol. 59b, BA Koblenz.
61 Fried to Wehberg, November 18, 1918, in Nachlass Wehberg, vol. 59b, BA Koblenz.
62 Fried to Wehberg, February 3, 1919, in Nachlass Wehberg, vol. 59b, BA Koblenz.
63 Cf. Nachlass Fried, Box 90 (Orell Füssli).

of a substantial income from subscribers in both Germany and Austria. In the beginning of June, he wrote to Wehberg: "I am quite touched by your desire to see the *Friedens-Warte* soon expand. Certainly it ought to be bigger and more comprehensive today, but the facts are such that I am not at all sure whether the next issues can be published at all."[64]

In the summer of 1919, Fried began to look for a possible publisher in Germany, especially since Orell Füssli had increased its prices by 5% in September.[65] His efforts were focused on the Neuer Geist publishing house of Dr. Peter Reinhold in Leipzig. However, Reinhold insisted on financial guarantees. In the last edition of the 21st year of the journal in 1919,[66] Fried appealed to both old and new sponsors for help. Once again, he emphasized the importance of the journal as a "tried and true activist journal in the German-speaking countries" and its accomplishments with respect to the further development of the theory of peace and dissemination of internationalism. The war, Fried contended, had devoured billions of marks, and so, given the apparent present surplus of money, this small sum could surely be raised.

In view of the political and economic situation in Germany, Fried's call for support, dated mid-November, seemed very optimistic. However, it may have been based on conversations that Fried had had when he attended the German Peace Society's General Assembly in Kassel at the end of October. There he would certainly have had the opportunity to speak with various representatives of German pacifism about his situation and perhaps find his first donors. He did not, however, raise the required sum in the initial months. Only a special grant of 2,000 crowns, approved by the Nobel Committee in December 1919, provided the necessary basis for a new beginning.[67] In February 1920, Fried, who in the meantime was looking for a place to live in Germany, met Reinhold in person to try to persuade him, in spite of everything, to publish the *Friedens-Warte*. But in view of the difficult situation, the publisher at first declined. When Fried wrote to Mundy Schwalb about it, she replied: "Of all the information your letter contained, I was most deeply affected by Reinhold's refusal to help. I certainly won't get discouraged, and I know that you will find another publisher, but Neuer Geist Verlag was very highly regarded, distinguished, enterprising and supportive. Well, that can't be changed. Too bad."[68]

---

64   Fried to Wehberg, June 2, 1919, in Nachlass Wehberg, vol. 59b, BA Koblenz.
65   Cf. Nachlass Fried, Box 90 (Orell Füssli).
66   *Friedens-Warte* 21, no. 9/10 (October/December 1919): 169.
67   Cf. the letter indicating the approval of a subsidy by the Nobel Committee, signed by Lovland/Moe of December 5, 1919, in Nachlass Fried, Box 89.
68   Mundy Schwalb to Fried, February 17, 1920, in Nachlass Fried, Box 91.

But after several more attempts, Fried managed to change the publisher's mind, so that the first issue of *Die Friedens-Warte,* published in Germany, was available at the beginning of May 1920. The 32-page issue, which was to cover the months of January to April, included, in addition to the lead article written by Fried, contributions by Friedrich Wilhelm Foerster, Theodore Ruyssen, Lilli Jannasch, Alexander Hohenlohe-Schillingsfürst, and an essay by Heinrich Lammasch (published posthumously), among others. Besides a focus on the Treaty of Versailles, it also reported on corruption in Germany and recommended several German journals with a pacifist tendency to its readers.

In "Die neuen Aufgaben" (The New Tasks), Fried attempted to define the new orientation of pacifism and thus also that of the *Friedens-Warte:* "The situation in Germany is no longer the same as it was before the war, and consequently the task of the pacifist has changed both inside and outside of the state."[69] On the domestic front, the new task, according to Fried, was to strengthen and support democracy and to inculcate the pacifist spirit in all the social strata; with respect to foreign policy, he sought the promotion of pacifist tendencies in the other nations with the goal of revising the Treaty of Versailles and improving the League of Nations: "Our tasks are unfortunately still enormous! If everyone understands that and does their duty, our goals can be achieved. We won't abandon the fight here. May there be enough fellow activists!"[70]

At least as far as the number of contributors is concerned, Fried got his wish in the next few months. If one looks at the list of contributors, one finds not only well-known seasoned campaigners but also a remarkable list of new names including Lilli Jannasch from the International Women's League for Peace and Freedom (IFFF), Otto Lehmann-Russbüldt, Rudolf Jeremias Kreutz, Oscar Stillich, Kurt Lenz, Georg Grosch, Rosa Mayreder, and Bertrand Russell. Overall, the interest seemed so great that the August edition of the *Friedens-Warte* comprised 48 pages and the December edition 60 pages. The October/November issue (8/9), which was supposed to be 48 pages, included a supplement in November in the form of a 32-page edition (issue 10). In addition to the Treaty of Versailles and the League of Nations, the journal addressed such topics as the development of pacifism in Germany and Europe—whereby Fried, as always, strove to give voice to the most varied versions of pacifism.

Fried himself had been living in temporary housing in an outer district of Vienna since 1920. He had thought to spend only the summer there, but he managed to extend his time until the end of the year. At that point, however, he would have to leave the small apartment for good, without knowing where

---

69 *Friedens-Warte* 22, no. 1 (January/April 1920): 1.
70 Ibid, 4.

he might stay. Only at the end of December, at the very last minute, was he able to move into a small apartment on Praterstraße, one of the main thoroughfares of Leopoldstadt. But before the scheduled move in January, Fried came down with a severe case of typhoid bronchitis, accompanied by pneumonia, and was transferred at the beginning of the new year to a hospital, which he would never leave.

The material for the January edition that Fried had requested from various authors by the end of December[71] could not be used since his colleagues were waiting for him to recover. In the uncertain state between phases of apparent recuperation and severe relapse, those close to Fried were hesitant to hand over the editorial duties to someone else. Toward the end of April, when Fried had shown a marked improvement and was occasionally working from his sickbed, he himself assigned someone to represent him for the long overdue first double number. It was not, however, Hans Wehberg, but Fried's longtime associate and co-worker Dr. Johann Mez, who had just relocated from the USA to the University of Freiburg. Perhaps the friendship between David Starr Jordan, Fried's American benefactor, and John Mez played a role,[72] and Fried hoped to secure the journal financially by linking it to the United States. But while Mez was assembling the material for the first issue of 1921,[73] Fried died on May 4, 1921 from a pulmonary hemorrhage.

7   The Conflict over Succession, 1921–1924

Fried's death changed things substantially for the *Friedens-Warte*. Both John Mez and Hans Wehberg felt that they were Fried's legitimate heirs: Mez, since Fried had entrusted him with the last edition, and Wehberg on the basis of his long-standing relationship with Fried and since Fried had already approached him about being his successor. In 1918, Fried had also written in his will that Wehberg and Schücking should discuss the continuation of the journal after his death.[74] In addition, the day after Fried's death, Mundy Schwalb sent

---

[71]   In the Wehberg Nachlass, there is another of Fried's postcards, dated December 29, 1920, in which he asks Wehberg for "a factual article dealing with the rearmament problem in the Geneva assembly." It was to be published in the January issue of the *Friedens-Warte*. See Nachlass Wehberg, vol. 59b, BA Koblenz.

[72]   Cf. the article by Mez written on the occasion of David Starr Jordan's eightieth birthday for the *Friedens-Warte* 31 (1918): 142.

[73]   "Dr. Fried has requested that I take over the editorial duties of this issue of 64 pages, a double issue." Mez to Wehberg, in Nachlass Wehberg, vol. 59b, BA Koblenz.

[74]   Fried, *Ratschläge und Wünsche*.

Wehberg a telegram indicating that he, together with Schücking, should take over the editorial duties of the journal.

Even Otfried Nippold, who at that time was the President of the Supreme Court of the Saar region, wrote to Wehberg to inform him that he (Wehberg) "should take over the publication as Fried's successor."[75] Two days after Fried's death, Wehberg made inquiries of the Neuer Geist Verlag, the publisher of the *Friedens-Warte,* about how to proceed, and Mez, for his part, showed up in Leipzig in person ten days after that. But the publisher had far more to worry about at the moment. He was no longer willing to continue publishing the journal at his own expense without subsidies. In a letter to Wehberg, he wrote: "[...] we must first of all make the continuation of the *Friedens-Warte* contingent on a subsidy; even Dr. Fried's name and influence were unable to balance the revenue and the expenditures of the journal. We suffered a loss of about 15,000 marks on volume 22 of the journal, the first year that we published it."[76]

Furthermore, Paetzel noted that he was not willing to publish the first issue of volume 23, although the material had already been prepared, until a final solution to the problem could be found. On his contentious claim that he would only publish the journal once financing had been secured, Paetzel wrote: "According to the contract, which we agreed to with Dr. Fried in March of the previous year, we have the right to name the new editor subject to the consent of a majority of a committee consisting of you, Prof. Schücking, and a person to be determined by the German Peace Society. We would be very pleased if, in accordance with the above requirement, consideration could be given to Dr. Mez, who *pace* Fried's final explicit instructions, was named to oversee the publication of the next issues of the journal, as long as his (Fried's) disability was still ongoing."[77]

On May 25, Wehberg replied that Fried had designated him as his successor ten years earlier;[78] he further stated that "it has always been my wish to put the publication of a journal at the center of my activity." But Wehberg remained vague on the question of a subsidy. Due to the dismal financial situation of the German Peace Society, he believed it was impossible to have the *Friedens-Warte,* as the publisher had proposed, become the primary publication of the society with a guaranteed number of subscribers. But he did promise to seek subsidies

---

75 Nippold to Wehberg, May 15, 1921, in Nachlass Wehberg, vol. 67, BA Koblenz.
76 K. Paetzel, Der Neue Geist Verlag an Wehberg, May 18, 1921, in Nachlass Wehberg, vol. 59b, BA Koblenz.
77 Ibid.
78 All of the following quotations are taken from Hans Wehberg to Der Neue Geist Verlag, May 25, 1921, in Nachlass Wehberg, vol. 59b, BA Koblenz.

from third parties. At the same time, however, he urged that the publication of the journal not be delayed any longer.

Since the German Peace Society rejected the *Friedens-Warte* as its publication for financial reasons,[79] and there was little hope that new sponsors could be found in Germany, a request to the Carnegie Foundation for funding seemed to be their only hope. As a result, the publisher declared himself ready to publish only a commemorative issue in Fried's honor until a decision was reached on the request of the Carnegie Foundation.

At some point in November 1921, agreement was finally reached that a "five-man council" could act as editor;[80] it would consist of Rudolf Goldscheid and Friedrich Hertz from Vienna, Ludwig Quidde, Hans Wehberg and Walther Schücking. An official suggestion by Ludwig Quidde to include Helene Stöcker as a representative of left-wing pacifism in order to integrate all the different strands of pacifism was rigorously opposed by Walther Schücking and finally dropped in spite of fierce protest from the left.[81] When the members of the council were finally agreed upon, Schücking submitted a request to the Carnegie Endowment for International Peace in Washington for a subsidy on December 3, on behalf of the publishing committee, asking for an annual subsidy of about $500.

While they waited for an answer, the promised commemorative edition for Fried appeared in the Neuer Geist Verlag in January 1922.[82] Rudolf Goldscheid served as editor along with Therese Fried and Mundy Schwalb. This "commemorative collection" also announced the revival of the *Friedens-Warte* for the spring of 1922.

The publisher was satisfied with Rudolf Goldscheid as editor in chief since he was someone who had taken Fried's place in the International Peace Bureau and also in the Austrian Peace Society. He was also a personal friend of Therese Fried and intellectually comparable to Fried. The first issue of the *Friedens-Warte*, published under the direction of someone other than Alfred

---

79 Since January 1920, the German Peace Society had its own publication, called "Mitteilungen der deutschen Friedensgesellschaft," which was distributed to its members at no cost.
80 Walter Schücking to the Carnegie Endowment for International Peace, December 3, 1921, in Nachlass Wehberg, vol. 59b, BA Koblenz.
81 Cf. Helene Stöcker to Ludwig Quidde, October 22, 1921; Helene Stöcker to the board members of the German Peace Society, November 3, 1921. Both documents are located in Nachlass Wehberg, vol. 59b, BA Koblenz.
82 *Alfred H. Fried, geb. 11. Nov. 1864, und gest. 4. Mai 1921. Eine Sammlung von Gedenkblättern in Gemeinschaft mit Therese Fried und Mundy Schwalb*, ed. Rudolf Goldscheid. Leipzig 1922. Einzelschriften zu *Friedens-Warte,* issue 2.

H. Fried, appeared as a 64-page double issue in February 1923.[83] After a short appreciation of Fried, Goldscheid declared his intention to maintain the previous direction of the journal: "The new editors can promise only one thing, that they will honestly endeavor to continue the *Friedens-Warte* in Fried's spirit, animated by a strict adherence to objectivity, both externally and internally, and will always allow all strands of pacifism to speak freely."[84]

In the next few months, there was a wide range of contributors, such as Romain Rolland, Hellmut von Gerlach, Freiherr von Schoenaich and, from June 1923, also John Mez, who among other things worked to establish university chairs for peace science,[85] and who continued the discussion with Kurt Hiller entirely along the lines pursued by Fried.[86]

The layout of the journal, which usually appeared as a double issue throughout the year, was essentially the same as in the past. Instead of the column "Aus der Bewegung" (From the Movement), however, there was now "Dokumente der Friedensbewegung" (Documents of the Peace Movement), in which decisions, speeches, appeals, contracts, and announcements were printed verbatim. In addition, Goldscheid, who also wrote the lead article, changed the column that Bertha von Suttner had written, "Randglossen zur Zeitgeschichte" (Commentaries on Contemporary History), to his own column "Politische Glossen" (Political Marginalia).

If one is to believe the publisher and the editors, the number of subscribers also grew as had been hoped. Only the rapid devaluation of the currency presented a problem for the publisher. For example, the price of publishing a single issue rose from 400 marks in February 1923 to 1,500 marks in May and then to 150 billion marks in October, thereby requiring a complicated and steady system of differential payments from the subscribers, even as it was virtually impossible for the publisher to make a sensible cost calculation. Only the introduction of the gold mark in November 1923 stabilized the situation again.[87]

Despite all the success, however, there were significant problems in the following year. The first issue of the new year did not appear until Easter 1924; it was a 100-page, three-month edition. The next issue, that of April to July, was published in August. It was also the last issue edited by Rudolf Goldscheid.

---

83   After a two-year break from 1921 to 1922, the numbers of the individual volumes were again in agreement with the years.
84   *Friedens-Warte* 23, no. 1 (January/February 1923): 1.
85   *Friedens-Warte* 23, no. 6 (June 1923): 196.
86   *Friedens-Warte* 23, no. 7/8 (July/August 1923): 242ff.
87   From now on, an individual issue cost 1 gold mark, later 1.20 or 1.50.

8 The *Friedens-Warte* under Hans Wehberg, 1924–1962

Goldscheid had offered Wehberg the position of editor in chief in April 1924, apparently after massive attacks on the journal.[88] In July, he then fully withdrew from the journal. In the ninth issue,[89] Wehberg explained to his readers that Goldscheid's departure was the result of his "having been overburdened with important research," and he praised him lavishly for his contributions. At the same time, however, he felt compelled to emphasize his own greater reliability: "The readers of the *Friedens-Warte* should feel assured that, when they receive issue 10/11 at the beginning of November, care will have been taken to provide a consistent, monthly publication of the journal and that there will be no further interruption in service. The *Friedens-Warte* will once again be a monthly journal."[90]

Although Rudolf Goldscheid formally remained on the editorial board, he would publish only one article by the end of 1927.[91] The column "Politische Glossen" (Political Marginalia) disappeared completely, and Wehberg now wrote the lead articles. In 1924, the editorial board was expanded to include Hellmut von Gerlach;[92] a year later, both Veit Valentin,[93] a historian, and Albert Falkenberg, a union leader and chairman of the German Peace Society-Berlin, were added.[94]

Wehberg's dominant leadership style on the editorial board can be seen in a letter of December 1925, in which he informed the co-editors that the

---

[88] Cf. Goldscheid to Wehberg, April 30, 1924, in Nachlass Wehberg, vol. 59b, BA Koblenz.
[89] Cf. "An die Leser der *Friedens-Warte*," *Friedens-Warte* 24, no. 8/9 (August/September 1924): 232f.
[90] Ibid., 233.
[91] Rudolf Goldscheid, "Der Ausbau des Paktes von Locarno und der Zusammenschluss Europas," *Friedens-Warte* 26, no. 9 (September 1926): 270ff.
[92] Gerlach was a correspondent for Germany with the Carnegie Peace Foundation and was, at this time, a member of the executive board of the German Peace Society. His views placed him somewhere between the left wing and the center. Around 1924 he was subjected to prosecution because of his campaign against the "Black Reichswehr." Cf. Donat/Hall, *Handbuch*, 156ff.
[93] Veit Valentin (1885–1947), historian, writer, and journalist, was on the political advisory board of the German League for Human Rights and a contributor to the *Weltbühne*, the *Vossische Zeitung*, and the *Frankfurter Zeitung*. Cf. Donat/Hall, *Handbuch*, 296 and *Friedens-Warte* 47, (1947): 274ff.
[94] Albert Falkenberg (1871–1945), a union leader and a politician in the Social Democratic Party, held several positions in the German Peace Society at the federal level and was the president of the Berlin group. Falkenberg was viewed as a go-between among the various segments within the German Peace Society. On Falkenberg, see Wehberg's commemorative article in *Friedens-Warte* 46, (1946): 151f and Donat/Holl, *Handbuch*, 108.

Friedens-Warte would be published by Hensel & Co beginning in January 1926, since the current publisher Schwetschke & Sohn did not want to continue without an annual subsidy of 1,000 marks. The letter also stated his intention to name Falkenberg and Valentin as members of the editorial board: "The two gentlemen have also tentatively agreed to accept an invitation. Both will work closely with the *Friedens-Warte*. If there is no immediate objection, then I will presume that the editors agree with this decision."[95]

Wehberg's leadership style was not always met with appreciation. In 1925, he was repeatedly at odds with Otto Lehmann-Russbüldt, who accused him of purposely ignoring the controversial issue of Germany's secret rearmament. To gain support for his objections, Lehman-Russbüldt wrote to all the editors of the journal, much to Wehberg's dismay.[96] Overall, however, Wehberg attempted to "continue the editorial work in the spirit of the man who made [the *Friedens-Warte*] [...] the leading monthly journal of pacifism."[97]

Wehberg maintained close contact with the movement and tried to keep the *Friedens-Warte* open to all strands of pacifism until the Nazis fully eradicated the peace movement in Germany in 1933. Thus not only discussions between representatives of the right wing and the left wing of the German Peace Society can be found in the journal, but also meetings and congress reports of various pacifist organizations: the Catholic Peace Movement, the German Peace Society, the International Women's League for Peace and Freedom, the German League for Human Rights, and the IPU. In addition, Wehberg included in the column "Aus der Zeit" (Our Times) the rubric "Persönliches" (Personal Matters), in which he reported on birthdays and special events in the lives of individual pacifists, much as Fried did, or he devoted heartfelt obituaries to them. Wehberg himself also regularly dedicated individual articles to Fried, reprinted Fried's articles and letters, and reported on other events related to him, such as the establishment of an honorary grave or the sale of his library and his estate [*Nachlass*].[98]

---

95   Wehberg, Carbon copy, "An die Herren Mitherausgeber der *Friedens-Warte* (December 29, 1925), in Nachlass Wehberg, vol. 59b, BA Koblenz.
96   At the end of a circular response letter, likewise addressed to all the editors on July 10, 1925, Wehberg emphasizes: "Apart from that, I would consider it proper if the editors would indicate to Mr. Lehmann-Russbüldt that in the future he would be better off consulting with me before he sends a circular letter to the editors. To send off a circular letter in opposition to the *Friedens-Warte* too hastily is certainly not in the best interest of the pacifist cause." Nachlass Wehberg, vol. 59b, BA Koblenz.
97   *Friedens-Warte* 24, no. 8/9 (August/September 1924): 233.
98   Cf. *Friedens-Warte* 25 (1925): 25f, 47ff, 211, 357; *Friedens-Warte* 26 (1926): 19ff; *Friedens-Warte* 31 (1931): 21, 129ff, 131ff, 321ff, 369.

The continuation of a close relationship with the peace movement was also motivated by finances: following a resolution of the General Assembly of the German Peace Society in 1923, each of its local groups was obliged to subscribe to at least five copies of the *Friedens-Warte*. Even the developments at the German Peace Day in Erfurt in October 1927 did not change that, although the dominant radical wing of pacifism, represented primarily by the strong state association of western Germany, wanted to force a reconsideration of which journals were to be supported. The matter was ultimately resolved when the assembly required each member to subscribe to one of three journals representing the various schools of pacifist thought – *Das andere Deutschland, Die Friedens-Warte,* and *Die Menschheit*. This resulted in a significant increase in subscriptions even in the short run.[99]

Although Wehberg himself and most of the editors personally belonged to the moderate wing of the peace movement and supported the League of Nations, he nevertheless tried, as Fried had done, to preserve the journal as a forum for discussions of all the strands of pacifism. Nevertheless, the journal gradually lost some of its appeal as the radical pacifists increased their power; they wanted to read articles that were critical of German domestic policies, such as those found in the *Das andere Deutschland*.

Wehberg himself had been living in Geneva since 1928, where he held an appointment as a professor at the Institut Universitaire de Hautes Études International. His increasing contact with people who supported internationalist views, his physical separation from Germany, and above all the fact that after 1933 there was no longer an organized peace movement in Germany all inevitably caused *Die Friedens-Warte* to ultimately become a professional journal in those years.[100] But Wehberg still continued to be interested in any news of the pacifists who remained in Germany.[101]

After the outbreak of the Second World War, he often drew historical comparisons with the First World War. He especially tried to analyze the impact of the mistakes of the peace treaty on the post-war development in order to avoid them a second time. In addition, he gave German emigrants the opportunity to make their voices heard in the *Friedens-Warte*. The extent to which Wehberg relied on Fried's model in this phase is also evident in the fact that he reprinted

---

99 Cf. Porsch, *Friedens-Warte*: 67f. At this time the *Friedens-Warte* had about 1,800 subscribers. By 1940, the number had decreased to about 1000.
100 This situation may also have been the reason that it was not banned in Germany until 1936. Cf. Porsch, *Friedens-Warte*, 71.
101 Thus, for example, he published an article on the death of pacifist newspapers in Germany in 1934. Cf. *Friedens-Warte* 34 (1934): 80–81.

Fried's article "Die Grundlagen der künftigen Völkerorganisation" (The Foundations of the Future Organization of Nations) in 1944, stressing that it was "still of great interest today" even though it was written 25 years earlier.[102]

After 1945 Wehberg largely committed himself to the establishment and growth of the United Nations, about which he commented extensively and critically. At the same time, he also tried to reconnect with the newly developing pacifist organizations in Germany. In 1946, the *Friedens-Warte* reported on massive demonstrations by both the German Peace Society and the individual state associations and on the attempts of the International Peace Institute to reorganize itself. In a special series it also commemorated the early champions of mutual understanding between nations as well as the scholars of international law who had been the victims of the National Socialism. It further published, seemingly after some exhaustive research, a list of the deceased pacifists as well as a list of the addresses of the pacifists of pre-war Germany who were still alive.[103] The *Friedens-Warte* was, however, unable to connect to the peace movement in Germany, which was now dominated by such issues as conscientious objection, the need for the prevention of rearmament in East and West Germany, and the nuclear arms buildup during the Cold War. It had shown little interest in issues of international law. Since, in Wehberg's opinion, *Die Friedens-Warte* was not merely a professional journal, nor did it aspire to be, it did not find sufficient interest among specialists and university libraries, and so it barely kept its head above water financially. Another reason was probably that in these years the scientific focus was shifting "from the previous historical and legal study of the cause of war to a perspective of peace and conflict research that more demonstrably emphasized the political aspects."[104]

By the time of Wehberg's death, the journal had an increasingly irregular publishing timetable. In its 56th year, 1961, Wehberg was only able to oversee the publication of the first two editions; the third issue of that year, the year in which he died, was compiled and published in 1962 by his co-editors. Among the editors at the time were eleven scholars from various nations, including the Germans Friedrich Siegmund-Schultze from Münster in Westphalia and Friedrich August Freiherr von der Heydte from Würzburg, who took over the editorial duties. However, the fourth and final issue of the 56th volume did not appear until 1966 in an issue commemorating Hans Wehberg. The journal was not published for eight years after that.

---

102   *Friedens-Warte* 44 (1944): 399.
103   *Friedens-Warte* 46, no. 3 (1946): 155ff. and no. 6, 392f.
104   Porsch, *Friedens-Warte*, 76.

9 A New Beginning in 1974

Volume 57 of the *Die Friedens-Warte* did not appear until 1974 when a student of Hans Wehberg, a publisher named Arno Spitz, managed to publish the edition and to secure a professor of international law, Jost Delbrück, Walther Schücking's successor at the Institute for International Law in Kiel, as the editor. When the Federal Republic of Germany entered the United Nations amid much discussion the year before, hopes were raised that there would be new interest in the journal. However, the new beginning was only modestly successful. The journal did not appear regularly, nor was it able to establish a solid readership.

It was only at the beginning of the 1990s with the reunification of Germany and its expanding international role that there was renewed interest in the *Friedens-Warte*. Since the beginning of 1996, the journal of some 100 pages has been published quarterly by a editorial committee consisting of Knut Ipsen (until 2006), a professor of international law from Bochum, Volker Rittberger, a political scientist from Tübingen, and Christian Tomuschat, a professor of international law and European law in Berlin. Each issue was devoted to a particular topic. The guidelines of the journal still centered on the promotion of world peace, on its role as a forum for debate (now purely scholarly), and on its international (and interdisciplinary) orientation. The journal now bears the subtitle *Journal of International Peace and Organization*; Fried is mentioned on the imprint page ("Impressum") as its founder, but not on the title page as he once desired.

Epilogue

Alfred Hermann Fried, the subject of this excellent biography by Dr. Petra Schönemann-Behrens, was a great pioneer both of peace research and of the international peace movement. He deserves to be better known – not only in Vienna where he was born but also throughout the German-speaking world. Moreover, Fried, as an early advocate of a European Union and a world organization in the two decades before World War I, is deserving of international recognition.

This book, which does full justice to Fried's complex personality and a life wholly dedicated to the pursuit of world peace, makes a significant contribution to his rediscovery today and pays him the tribute that is his due. The date of the publication of this biography, namely 2011, has been suitably chosen: exactly one hundred years ago, Fried was awarded the Nobel Peace Prize—the first man in Austria or Germany to have been so honored. It was not until 1926 that a German, Gustav Stresemann, the foreign minister at the time, received the same award.

It is regrettable that so many champions of peace (and also most of the Nobel Peace Prize laureates) are so little known and appreciated. This is primarily the result of the educational system and the curriculum; it is a direct consequence of the fact that schools in most Western societies do not embrace a curriculum specifically dedicated to peace, which would include the history of the peace idea and of the peace movement. Ideas and ideals such as peace and non-violence also play little role in the respective cultures of remembrance; peace is often still interpreted as armed peace, even in the nuclear age. It is hard to believe that many people still adhere to the catchphrase of the ancients – "Si vis pacem, para bellum" ("If you want peace, prepare for war") – even though it endangers the future of the whole world as never before.

This lack of attention to the issues surrounding peace, indeed one can say— the invisibility of peace—stands in stark contrast to the countless war and military memorials and other commemorations and symbols of the culture of war, for example, in the names of streets and squares, and in the existence of so many war and military museums. In contrast, there are very few peace museums, and most of them are modest and off the beaten path, except in Japan. This results in the loss of a great opportunity to nurture the study of peace outside of the schools for the public at large. A visit to a museum or to an exhibition can be a life-changing experience, especially for adolescents, just as it was for Fried when, as a 17-year-old, he visited an exhibition of the paintings of the Russian artist Vasily Vereshchagin in 1881.

It is also significant that it took Fried, then living in Berlin, ten more years before he discovered that he was in fact not alone as a pacifist and that there even existed a peace society in Austria. During these years he had nurtured his pacifist views in private and had no idea of the activities of those who held similar views. Later, he wrote: "As someone who was interested in all aspects of public life, I never came across any information about the ideas and activities of people who wanted to get rid of war. I never heard anything about pacifist legislative initiatives in parliaments, about the (peace) associations and congresses."

Unfortunately, Fried's experience is still a common one. Even today, peace, pacifism, non-violence, and activities, movements, and organizations related to them are barely covered by the media, while reports and images of confrontation and violence are frequent. This is where peace museums could play a huge role, especially because in schools and in history books, those positive, hopeful, and inspiring perspectives, which are so important to the development of young minds, are neglected. Can it really be a coincidence that societies that are still largely dominated by war and violence are also characterized by an absence of means which could make significant contributions to reducing and ending the use of armed force?

Fried himself paid close attention to the International War and Peace Museum, founded in Lucerne in 1902 by the Russian-Polish State Councilor Jan Bloch, as he had to its predecessor, an exhibition that Bloch had organized for the Paris World's Fair in 1900 in collaboration with the International Peace Bureau in Berne. After years of research, Bloch published a six-volume treatise in 1898 on the war of the future in St. Petersburg. Basing his work on rigorous scientific and empirical facts, he concluded that a future war between the major powers would destroy Europe like never before and should therefore be avoided at all costs. On the occasion of the ceremonial inauguration of the museum in Lucerne, to which he was invited as a close friend and colleague of the founder, Fried published a long essay in the *Friedens-Warte*. Among other things, he wrote: "With the establishment of this museum, Bloch has created a kind of object lesson for his theory. He tended to accept, correctly, the notion that the visual image towers above the written word, that the masses are more easily moved by the tangible presentation of things than by the most beautiful words: if J. Novicow [...] regards the lack of imagination as one of the chief mental obstacles to the pacification of Europe, Bloch sees in the museum the best means to remedy this deficiency." (June 30, 1902)

Fried took great satisfaction in the fact that the sensation created by the opening of the museum attracted greater public attention to the idea of peace. Numerous newspapers wrote about the museum and reported on the quantitative and qualitative progress that the peace movement had made. In the years leading up to the beginning of the World War in August 1914, the Bloch Museum had the same effect on many of its visitors that Fried had experienced as a young man during his visit to the Wiener Künstlerhaus: they became pacifists. Peace museums today—as well as peace education in general—should focus on two complementary theses: that war and all its related preparations are—for ecological, economic, ethical, humanitarian, rational, and international legal reasons—no longer acceptable. Just as important is the other side of the coin: world peace is possible and is actually a prerequisite for the survival of humanity! In both areas, the notion of a "lack of imagination," as put forward by the respected Russian sociologist and pacifist Jacques Novicow, is applicable. An important factor in explaining this lack of imagination with regard to war is the ever-present and ubiquitous censorship that obscures the true face of war: its costs and the devastation and losses it brings about. As a leading pacifist writer and publisher in the German-speaking world, Fried was often subject to censorship. During World War I, he had to flee to Switzerland. We only deceive ourselves if we believe that it is different today, even in democratic societies.

The name Alfred Hermann Fried surfaces quickly and inevitably whenever people study the ideas, developments, and achievements of those who faced the challenge of eliminating war through the creation of a political world order, one based on law and peace, in the late nineteenth century and the first two decades of the twentieth century. In countless publications, Fried expounded on his concepts and theories, and documented the data he collected on pacifism and internationalism, the European Union and Pan-America, the Peace Movement and Peace Science, and international law and world organization; in so doing, he was a pioneer in the field. As a long-time editor of the *Friedens-Warte*, for which he wrote countless articles (signed or anonymous), he created an unprecedented forum for discussion. Jorgen G. Lovland, chairman of the Oslo Nobel Committee, maintained that Fried had gradually made the *Friedens-Warte* "the best journal in the peace movement" (see the December 10, 1911 announcement of the award of the Nobel Prize for Fried).

Fried also broke new ground with an encyclopedic work, for which he was better skilled than anybody else. As he wrote in the foreword to the first edition (1905), he conceived his *Handbuch der Friedensbewegung* (Handbook of the Peace Movement) as a guide for "the outsider who wanted to inform himself about the movement [...] but also as a useful reference work for those followers and active supporters who sought to promote the peace movement." In particular, the greatly expanded second edition (1911–1913) is still rightly praised as a complete and reliable handbook of the peace movement of its time; a hundred years later, it still represents an extremely important treasure trove for peace historians. If he had produced nothing other than this one work (and if he had never received the Nobel Peace Prize and even if he had not had a close relationship with Bertha von Suttner), today's experts would still know his name. Evidence of this can be found in the splendid *Hermes Handlexikon: Die Friedensbewegung. Organisierter Pazifismus in Deutschland, Österreich und in der Schweiz* (Hermes Dictionary: The Peace Movement. Organized Pacifism in Germany, Austria, and Switzerland), which was edited in 1983, 70 years after Fried's handbook, by Helmut Donat and Karl Holl. In his introduction, Holl writes that their encyclopedia "follows the tradition of the great German-language handbooks of the peace movement, that of Alfred Hermann Fried, of Kurt Lenz and Walter Fabian, and of Franz Kobler."

Karl Holl, the doyen of peace historians in the German-speaking world, describes one aspect that links the older historical peace movement with the present one: "The certainty that one is standing on the shoulders of one's predecessors who steadfastly maintained their pacifist convictions despite the hostility or indifference that they encountered among their contemporaries may allow today's peace movement to be better equipped to withstand the temptations of despondency." (ibid.) Equally important is his comment: "Familiarity with the historical peace movement would show skeptics, e.g., how much suffering Europe would have been spared if the warnings of the pacifists had fallen on fewer deaf ears and if the practical initiatives and proposals of organized pacifism had found their way into official politics and diplomacy." (ibid.). Dieter Lattmann emphasizes the term "special expertise of the pacifists:" "Up to now, the fears of the pacifists, of the lovers of peace, have always been realized, sooner or later...[even so], their representatives were ridiculed, persecuted, and arrested." (p. 7). The aspiration and suffering of pacifists, as summarized by Holl and Lattmann in these quotes, apply, to the fullest extent, to Fried.

Fried's relevance today is also shown in another but related field in which he was a pioneer: peace journalism, an expression presumably coined by Fried. The role of the media in reporting and interpreting the news is fundamental in shaping public opinion, especially in matters of war and peace. Fried recognized this fact in an era when only the press, and in particular the daily newspaper, existed as a means of mass communication. Nearly a hundred years before the concept of peace journalism was rediscovered and before peace journalism was seen both as a part of "peace science" and as an important aspect of a culture of peace, Fried described himself explicitly as a peace journalist, for example in his book *Unter der weißen Fahne! Aus der Mappe eines Friedensjournalisten* (Under the White Flag! From the Portfolio of a Peace Journalist), published in 1901. (The revival of peace journalism today is largely due to Johan Galtung, "the most prominent protagonist of peace journalism of our time," writes Andreas Landl in *100 Jahre Friedensnobelpreis an Alfred Hermann Fried* (Nobel peace prize to Alfred Hermann Fried 100 years ago), ed. Willi Urbanek, Vienna, 2011, p. 89.) It is clear that the so-called "embedded journalism" is far removed from the goals of peace journalism.

Fried dedicated his book to Count Albert Apponyi, a Hungarian statesman and member of the Hague Arbitration Court. In 1900, Apponyi encouraged the establishment of the International Press Union for Peace and Arbitration at the 10th Interparliamentary Conference in Paris. For some time there had indeed been an association of journalists in Paris who were well disposed toward peace. Nine years later in 1909, an International Union of the Peace Press was created at Fried's suggestion in Brussels, after a relevant draft had been approved by the General Assembly of the International Peace Bureau in Berne. Fried's journalistic activities encompassed both peace movement journals as well as the general daily press. The great challenge of that time is no less acute today, namely, to gradually transform the mass media so that their reports on current events are infused with the perspectives of peace. In his book, Fried wrote: "The peace movement journals [...] do not spread the idea [of peace] but only cherish it where it is already present [...] It is outside, in the daily press, that the great chase to conquer the press has to take place" (p. 13). "The main task of peace journalism," said Fried, "will always have to be that in the columns of the press [...] current events are characterized and clarified from the perspective of the peace journalist. This is no easy task." (p. 15).

Presumably, in the years ahead, when the world recalls that World War I took place more than 100 years ago, Fried's name will become better known. This horrific war lasted more than four long and difficult years; it destroyed the world, especially Europe. How this came about, and how it would have been possible to prevent this calamity if the leading European powers had pursued more sensible policies, has been extensively documented in *Randglossen zur Zeitgeschichte* (Commentaries on Contemporary History), which Bertha von Suttner published monthly in the *Friedens-Warte* in the two decades leading up to the war. It is one of Fried's great merits that he collected, annotated and edited these extremely rich and important comments. In the introduction to the two-volume work that was published in 1917 when he was in exile in Switzerland, Fried wrote that the collection represented the fulfillment of two obligations: "First, to fulfill a deep desire of the deceased and to carry out a task that she gave me while she was still alive. Further, to honor the underappreciated work of this great woman, to create a memorial to her." (*Der Kampf um die Vermeidung des Weltkriegs. Randglossen aus zwei Jahrzehnten zu den*

Zeitereignissen vor der Katastrophe 1892–1900 und 1907–1914, Zurich, 1917) (The Struggle to Prevent the World War. Two Decades of Commentary on the Events before the Catastrophe 1892–1900 and 1907–1914, Zurich 1917).

On the title page of the first volume, Fried quoted one of von Suttner's central thoughts: "In an age of explosives, violence has taken on a shape that is self-defeating. And that means either the end of the human race or the end of violence. We hope for the latter." Bertha von Suttner's insights and comments often proved prophetic. According to Fried, the novelist had become a journalist and critic of her age (p. IV). "What Bertha von Suttner wrote from week to week and from month to month during this time, amounts now in its totality to a valuable history of this most critical era of humanity" (ibid.). He further wrote: "Later, when one examines what led up to that world calamity and attempts to research its causes, it will not be possible to ignore the critique of the time offered by a great mind who commented on the events from the perspective of a higher vantage point. Bertha von Suttner was not heard during her lifetime. She experienced the fate of all seers and benefactors of mankind." (p. V).

When Fried wrote this introduction at Christmas 1915, he was keeping a war diary (excerpts of which were published in the *Friedens-Warte*). In an advance notice at the end of the second volume, he wrote: "A continuation of the present work will be the full publication of my war diary." (p. 575). These works by Fried are also of particular significance because they are among the few diaries of a pacifist immigrant that were published.

As a specialist in the publishing industry and as a scholar, Fried also compiled detailed personal and subject indices for these books. For the *Randglossen* (Commentaries) there is also a detailed table of contents. Fried wrote in the introduction: "The index contains not only the names of events and of the most important people, but also makes it easier to find ideas thus making the book particularly suitable for reference purposes." (p. VIII). As further proof of his scholarly and pedagogical convictions, as well as of his desire to make historical data available for the present, one could also point to the subject indices that Fried created for the six-volume work *Der Krieg* (*The Future of War*) by Jan Bloch. As the most fervent student and staunchest supporter of Bloch in the German-speaking area, Fried clearly felt the large work required a subject index. This effort (along with Bloch's work) should also be given the attention it deserves in the coming years.

More than 25 years after she first thought about the project, the publication of Petra Schönemann-Behrens' biography of Alfred H. Fried is the finest appreciation that Fried and his admirers today could wish for. The author has written not only a standard biography of one of the most deserving Nobel Peace Prize honorees. She has gone far beyond that. An important part of her research project is to have produced a ca. 100-page digital index of Fried's correspondence based on the material in the League of Nations archives of the United Nations Library in Geneva (Fried-Suttner-Archive). This information had previously only been available on index cards written in pencil. In doing so, she has considerably facilitated access to this material for future researchers. Also for this work – very much in the spirit of Fried – she deserves the gratitude of all peace historians who deal with the time period in which Fried was active.

The disappointment expressed by the author in her introduction, namely that there was still no biography of this important and interesting peace activist (and Nobel Peace Prize laureate) more than a half-century after his death, was also a question for me when, almost 40 years ago, I first dealt with Fried as a pioneer of peace studies. The absence of a biography seemed all the more surprising since his industrious journalistic activities had left a rich source of material for a biographer—not to mention the fertile *Nachlass* (literary estate) in the Fried-Suttner archive. It is a testament to Petra Schönemann-Behrens' courage and perseverance that she did not shy away from this task. It seems that she has read everything that Fried ever wrote in his innumerable works and as editor of the *Friedens-Warte*. And not least, by making full use of the Fried-Suttner Archive (as well as other archives) and by discovering previously unknown archival records in private hands, she has succeeded in presenting the reader with an impressive biography.

My sincere thanks also go to the publisher Anne Rüffer for her willingness to publish this book in Römerhof Verlag. As a long-time admirer of Bertha von Suttner, she was also convinced that von Suttner's most important collaborator and friend, who had actively supported her for more than 20 years, deserved a biography, at last. In addition to Vienna, Berlin and Berne, Zurich was the fourth city in Fried's life. While he was living in exile in Switzerland during World War I, the *Friedens-Warte* was published uncensored, and he was closely associated with the *Neue Zürcher Zeitung*. Also various great works that Fried completed during this period were published in Zurich, and so too now is this biography. May it find many readers also outside of Switzerland, especially in Germany and Austria, readers who will be inspired by Fried's great commitment to peace to pursue their own efforts to create a more peaceful world.

Dr. Peter van den Dungen
Department of Peace Studies
University of Bradford
UK
General Coordinator, International Network of Museums for Peace

APPENDIX 1

To My Beloved Wife

If I should die during the war while I am in Switzerland, I still want to be cremated. No expense should be spared, in spite of the shortage of coal, to have the cremation take place somewhere in Switzerland. And if that is not possible, then attempts should be made to have the cremation take place in a nearby city in Germany or France. For advice in all matters relating to my estate and to any other urgent questions relating to my death, you should consult our friend Mr. Scherrer-Füllemann, a member of the National Council in Switzerland, or our friend Dr. Emil Frankl in Austria. With regard to my assets, you will have easy and direct access to the securities and cash in my bank account (currently the Swiss Eidgenössische Bank in Berne) since your signature has also been notarized. This pertains also to the assets that the Swiss bank has placed in the account with the bank in Vienna. You will find information about the present balances of our assets in the little account books that I have kept (overview of investments and the capital cash book). The complete furnishings, which are stored with Garde Meuble Lüftschütz in Vienna (the inventory is in a file marked number 5) have also been placed in your name.

During the war I have estimated that my approximate yearly income was 4,000 francs, and I have paid taxes on this amount. I have informed the tax office that my income was quite low during the war and that I have been living mainly off of my investments, which is in fact what I did. With regard to the assets that you control, which you can withdraw at any time, you will not need to provide the tax office with any information, I believe.

If I should die here, you will be best off to return to Vienna since you have friends and acquaintances there. You will be able to live there, modestly, from the inherited assets and the interest from the Concordia pension fund. You'll probably want to try to sell some of the furniture and use that money to set yourself up in a small apartment. I leave it to your discretion whether you want to live off the interest of our small estate or whether you want to purchase an annuity for the rest of your life. The latter would certainly be good once the conditions are more stable again.

If you should have difficulties, which I fervently hope won't be the case, you can turn to the executive board of the "Socrates" organization or to the "Concordia," and you can also appeal to the existing organizations of the peace movement in Austria, Germany or abroad. Specifically, you can appeal to the Carnegie Endowment in America. I have dedicated my whole life to the peace movement; I have suffered and gone hungry for it. I figure that they can unburden the life of my deeply beloved wife, whom I thank for all the happiness in my life. In my writings there is some valuable material. I am thinking of the letters that I will leave behind as well as the letters that I have from Bertha von Suttner. These should be evaluated by an expert. They include the letters and views of nearly all of the people who worked for peace in the last few decades. Even those who are not as well known should be included in the collection because they can complete the picture of our work on behalf of peace. This way a collection can be published that would be of value to a large library or to a rich collector. I'm not underestimating their value when I say the material could be worth five to ten thousand dollars. I say dollars because I think that you will most likely find interest and money in America. To sort through the materials, perhaps Mundy Schwalb or Dr. Hans Wehberg, who was once an assessor, would be the most suitable persons. Family letters, bills, and other miscellaneous material, which is not of general interest, should probably be destroyed, unless my sister Toni Simonsohn wants to keep some of it. Perhaps a valuable source of income can be derived from my writings, in particular from those pieces that appeared in the *Friedens-Warte* and in other journals, by publishing a collection of them, when the world has gained a little more understanding for the pacifist cause. I would suggest that Dr. Wehberg or Dr. Walter Schücking would be the most appropriate editor. I would also request you consult with others to determine whether *Die Friedens-Warte*, which I founded and kept alive, should be continued. It should permanently bear on the title page the notice "Founded by Alfred H. Fried during the time of the first Hague Conference."

My brother Poldi gets a monthly stipend from me. You can continue to pay this if it is not too hard on you. But, given the low level of income that I am leaving you, I can, unfortunately, not oblige you to do so. Other than that, I have no financial obligations and debts. With regard to the formalities of my funeral services, I have only one request: that it be simple and inexpensive. There is to be no sermon by a rabbi; I die as a free thinker. The urn with my ashes should be buried in Vienna if conditions allow. My will and other important records can be found in my document folder. And you, my dear child, I want to thank you most fervently and profoundly for everything, for all the goodness that you brought into my life. And it was indeed a lot. You have made me completely happy. I am grateful to the benevolent fate that let me find you. I love you beyond words and will love you to my dying breath. Do not drown yourself in sorrow at my passing. I fear dying but not being dead. And when dying has been overcome, then there is no longer any reason to mourn or to lament. Live in the memory of the happy years that were given to us, and try to enjoy the years that you still have, as best you can. Beware of those who flatter you or who are evil. Only trust the best people. I had some standing in the world; one day my work will certainly be preserved, and so I believe that people will similarly not forget about my wife, who was the dearest thing on earth to me. In friendship, they will stand by you. If my dear mother survives me, I know that you will stand by her as a good and loyal daughter. She has suffered a great deal in life and has had to put up with a lot. But if fate does not want her to be spared the pain of outliving her oldest son, then please console her as best you can and tell her how much I loved her.

I have written this myself on my typewriter on the fifth of July nineteen hundred eighteen (July 5, 1918) and sign it with my own hand.

Dr. Alfred H. Fried
Forever yours,
Alfred

APPENDIX 2

Program of Revolutionary Pacifism, 1908

A. Protection of the Organizational Process from Contemporary Obstructive Influence

Foundation: Development of national education
1. **Immunization of the masses against militaristic influence**
   Goal: destruction of national prejudices
   Means: Facilitation of personal contact between peoples
   a) *personal interaction*
      corporate visits abroad | impactful exchanges of employees in foreign countries | educational trips abroad | international conventions
   b) *professional interaction*
      international trade associations, central offices, trade journals | international expositions and specialized national exhibitions in foreign countries | international competitions, international auxiliary language, international correspondence, etc.
2. **Termination of the influence of bellicose, impassioned masses**
   Expansion of the international investigative commissions (obligatory, permanent and mobile) | Introduction of mandatory mediation and similar de-escalating measures

B. Support for the Organizational Process

Foundation: the development of technology
1. **Support of transportation in general**
   Expansion of travel possibilities | Increase, acceleration and reduction in cost of travel by land, sea and air | Removal of all trade barriers | Promotion of international cooperation | Development of the communication sector
2. **Development of international law**
   Adaptation of the law to the needs of international cooperation | Codification of the law | Development of civil and public international law | Expansion of arbitration | Weakening of the factors that lead to violence

3. **Transformation of politics**
Alignment of politics with the law | Support for the politics of solidarity and for an international administrative structure | Increase in the number of regularly scheduled conferences at the state level | Public disclosure of foreign policy and modernization of diplomacy

Bibliography

Below is a list of all the books and brochures that Fried published either as author or editor. It also includes those works to which Fried made a substantial contribution as an author. They are listed in chronological order by year of publication of the first edition. An overview of his translated works follows this list. Two works that are often incorrectly attributed to him are not included in the list: the farce "Pele-mele," which was published under Fried's name in Vienna in 1891, and the "Katechismus des Friedensgedankens," which appeared under the pseudonym Pacificus Winfried with the support of the Peace Bureau in Berne.

Books, Brochures, and Offprints by year of publication

1887   *Der kleine Büchmann.* A collection of the most common quotations and most well-known sayings in German, Latin, French, English and Italian. In alphabetical order. Ed. Alfred Hermann Fried. First and second edition. Leipzig, 1887.

1888   *Lexikon deutscher Zitate.* Ed. Alfred Hermann Fried. Leipzig.
Lexikon fremdsprachlicher Zitate. Ed. Alfred Hermann Fried. Leipzig, 1888.

1894   *Friedens-Katechismus.* A compendium of the theory of peace as an introduction to the peace movement. Dresden/Leipzig/Vienna, 1894. Second, improved and expanded edition. Dresden/Leipzig/Vienna, 1895. Third improved and expanded edition. Dresden/Leipzig/Vienna, 1896.

1895   *Elsass-Lothringen und der Krieg.* An essay on peace with a side-by-side French translation. Leipzig/Paris, 1895.

1896   *Dschingis-Khan mit Telegraphen.* (Pseud. Mannfred Herald Frei). First and second edition. Leipzig, 1896.

1898   *Das Tagebuch eines zum Tode Verurteilten.* With an introduction on the death penalty by Professor Dr. Ludwig Büchner. Berlin, 1898.

1899   *Was kann die Petersburger Friedens-Konferenz erreichen?* A proposal to attain the goals put forth by the Tsar. Dresden/Leipzig, 1899.

1900   *Die Haager Konferenz, ihre Bedeutung und ihre Ergebnisse.* Composed at the behest of the Berlin Committee for Rallies at the Peace Conference (Berliner Comité für Kundgebungen zur Friedenskonferenz). With a forward by Baron d'Estournelles de Constant. Berlin, 1900.
Kleine Anzeige: Soziale Streifbilder vom Jahrmarkt des Lebens. Berlin, 1900.

1901   *Unter der weißen Fahne! Aus der Mappe eines Friedensjournalisten. Gesammelte Artikel und Aufsätze.* Ed. Alfred Hermann Fried. Berlin, 1901.

1902   *Der Theaterdusel. Eine Streitschrift gegen die Überschätzung des Theaters.* Bamberg, undated [1902].

1903 *Lehrbuch der Internationalen Hilfsprache "Esperanto." Mit Wörterbuch in Esperanto-Deutsch und Deutsch-Esperanto.* First edition. Berlin, 1903. Second improved and expanded edition. Stuttgart, 1905. Fifth improved and expanded edition. Stuttgart, 1908.

Die Ausgestaltung der Friedensaktion in Deutschland. Offprint. Berlin, 1903.

Die hauptsächlichsten Missverständnisse über die Friedensbewegung. Separate publication from the "Türner." Vol. 5, no. 3. Berlin, 1903.

Die Grundlage der modernen Wirtschaft und der Krieg. Commissioned by the Bloch-Stiftung in Berne. Esslingen, undated [1903].

Die Lasten des bewaffneten Friedens und der Zukunftskrieg. Commissioned by the Bloch Foundation in Berne. Esslingen, undated [1903].

1904 *Weder Sedan noch Jena.* First edition. Berlin, undated, [1904]. Second edition. Berlin, 1905.

Der gegenwärtige Krieg und die Friedensbewegung. Lecture by Alfred H. Fried. Vienna, 1904.

Deutschland und Frankreich. Ein Wort über die Notwendigkeit und Möglichkeit einer deutsch-französischen Verständigung. Berlin, 1904.

Die moderne Schiedsgerichtsbewegung. Berlin, 1904.

1905 *Das Abrüstungs-Problem. Eine Untersuchung.* Berlin, 1905

Die *Friedensbewegung, was sie will, und was sie erreicht hat.* First edition. Leipzig, 1905. Second and third editions. Leipzig, 1907.

Kaiser werde modern! Berlin, 1905.

Sachregister zu Johann von Blochs "Der Krieg." Ed. Alfred H. Fried. [Separate publication taken from the *Friedens-Warte*, May 1905, 91ff.]. Internationales Friedensbüro, Berne, undated [1905].

Kriegsmache und Kriegsgeschrei in den Denkwürdigkeiten des Fürsten Chlodwig zu Hohenlohe-Schillingsfürst. Flyer, 1905.

Handbuch der Friedensbewegung. Vienna, Leipzig, 1905.

Annuaire de la vie internationale. Vol. I. Monaco: Institut International de la Paix, 1905.

1906 *Die Nobelstiftung. Ihre Einrichtungen und ihre Bestimmungen.* First edition and second edition. Leipzig, 1906.

Annuaire de la vie internationale. Vol. 2. Monaco: Institut International de la Paix, 1906.

1907 *Die moderne Friedensbewegung.* In *Natur und Geisteswelt*, Vol. 157. Leipzig, 1907.

Annuaire de la vie internationale. Vol. 3. Monaco: Institut International de la Paix, 1907.

1908 *Wien- Berlin. Ein Vergleich.* Vienna/Leipzig, undated [1908].

Die moderne Friedensbewegung in Deutschland und Frankreich. ("Kultur und Fortschritt," 143). Leipzig.

Internationalismus und Patriotismus. ("Kultur und Fortschritt," 160). Leipzig, 1908.

Die Grundlagen des revolutionären Pazifismus. First edition. Tübingen, 1908. Second expanded edition. Zurich, 1916, published under the title *Die Grundlagen des ursächlichen Pazifismus.* Translation: *Les bases du pacifisme. Le pacifisme réformiste et le pacifisme révolutionaire.* First edition. Paris: A. Pedone, 1909.

Verzeichnis von 1000 Zeitungs-Artikeln Alfred H. Frieds zur Friedensbewegung (bis März 1908). Berlin, 1908.

Bertha von Suttner. Berlin, 1908.

Das internationale Leben der Gegenwart. In *Natur und Geisteswelt.* Vol. 226. Leipzig, 1908.

Die zweite Haager Konferenz, ihre Arbeiten, ihre Ergebnisse und ihre Bedeutung. Leipzig, undated [1908].

1909 *Der kranke Krieg.* Collection of essays. Leipzig, 1909.

Der Weg zum Weltfrieden im Jahre 1909. Pazifistische Chronik. Berlin, 1909.

1910 *Pan-Amerika. Entwickelung, Umfang und Bedeutung der panamerikanischen Bewegung (1810 - 1910).* First edition. Berlin, 1910. Second expanded edition, 1918 under the title *Pan-Amerika. Entwicklung, Umfang und Bedeutung der zwischenstaatlichen Organisation in Amerika (1810–1916).*

Der Kaiser und der Weltfrieden. Berlin, 1910. Translation: *The German Emperor and the Peace of the World.* With a preface by Norman Angell. London/New York/Toronto, 1912.

Der Weg zum Weltfrieden im Jahre 1910. Pazifistische Chronik. Berlin/Vienna/Leipzig, 1910.

1911 *Le développement récent du pacifisme allemand.* Paris, 1911.

Handbuch der Friedensbewegung. Erster Teil. Grundlagen, Inhalt und Ziele der Friedensbewegung. Second completely revised and expanded edition. Berlin/Leipzig, 1911.

Der Weg zum Weltfrieden im Jahre 1911. Pazifistische Chronik. Berlin /Vienna/ Leipzig, 1911.

1912 *Kurzgefasste Darstellung der pan-amerikanischen Bewegung.* (Internationale Verständigung/Internationale Organisation, no. 4). First edition. Berlin/Leipzig, 1912. Second edition. Zurich, 1916.

Der Dreibund und die Friedensfrage. In *Der Dreibund.* Five essays by Alfred H. Fried, Gerhard Hildebrand, Timon, Prof. A. Ghisleri, Bernhard Stern. Leipzig, 1912.

Der Weg zum Weltfrieden im Jahre 1912. Pazifistische Chronik. Berlin/Vienna/Leipzig, 1912.

1913   *Handbuch der Friedensbewegung. Zweiter Teil: Geschichte, Umfang und Organisation der Friedensbewegung.* Second completely revised and expanded edition. Berlin/Leipzig, 1913.

Friedensbewegung und Presse. Berne, 1913. Translation: *La presse au service du pacifisme.* Berne, 1913. *The Peace Movement and the Press.* IFB: Berne, 1913.

Die panamerikanische Bewegung. Munich/Leipzig, 1913.

Der Weg zum Weltfrieden im Jahre 1913. Pazifistische Chronik. Berlin/Vienna/Leipzig, 1913

1914   *A Few Lessons Taught by the Balkan War.* New York, 1914.

Kurze Aufklärung über Wesen und Ziel des Pazifismus. Berlin/Leipzig, 1914. Translation: *A Brief Outline of the Nature and Aims of Pacifism.* New York, 1915.

1915   *Europäische Wiederherstellung.* Zurich, 1915.

1916   *Gedankenaustausch über die Beendigung des Krieges seitens deutscher und französischer Pazifisten.* With essays by Fr. Wilhelm Foerster, Alfred H. Fried, Ludwig Quidde, d'Estournelles de Constant, and Theodore Ruyssen. First edition. Zurich, 1916.

Die internationale Kooperation als Grundlage einer internationalen Rechtspflege. The Hague: M. Nijhoff, 1916. Translation: *International Cooperation.* Richardson, New Castle and Tyne, 1918.

Vom Weltkrieg zum Weltfrieden. Twenty Essays on War. Zurich, 1916.

Die Forderung des Pazifismus. Zurich, 1916.

1917   *Die Bestrebungen der Vereinigten Staaten für Ausbau und Festigung einer Zwischenstaatlichen Ordnung (1794–1917).* (Capita Selecta, no. 2). The Hague: Nederlandsche Anti-Oorlog Raad, 1917.

Zur Psychologie der Schuldbegründung. Zurich, 1917.

Bertha von Suttner: Der Kampf um die Vermeidung des Weltkriegs. Randglossen aus zwei Jahrzehnten zu den Zeitereignissen vor der Katastrophe (1892–1900 und 1907–1914). 2 Vols. Ed. Dr. Alfred H. Fried. Zurich, 1917.

1918   *Probleme der Friedenstechnik.* Essays. Leipzig, 1918.

Mein Kriegs-Tagebuch. Vol. 1. *Das erste Kriegsjahr (7. August 1914 bis 28. Juli 1915).* Zurich, 1918.

1919   *Auf hartem Grund. Offene Antwort auf den an mich gerichteten offenen Brief von Dr. jur. Hermann M. Popert im "Vortrupp" vom 1. Marz 1919* (Pfadweiser-Flugschrift, no. 1). Hamburg, 1919.

Der Völkerbund. Ein Sammelbuch. Edited and with an introduction by Alfred H. Fried. Leipzig/Vienna, 1919.

Mein Kriegs-Tagebuch. Vol. 2. *Das zweite Kriegsjahr (1. August 1915 bis 28. Juli 1916).* Zurich, 1919.

Mein Kriegs-Tagebuch. Vol. 3. *Das dritte Kriegsjahr (1. August 1916 bis 28. Juli 1917).* Zurich, 1919.

1920 *Mein Kampf gegen Versailles und St. Germain vom Nov. 1918 bis Juni 1919.* [Separate publication from volume 4 of the *Kriegs-Tagebuch*]. Leipzig, 1920.

Der Weltprotest gegen den Versailler Frieden. Collected, edited and introduced by Dr. Alfred H. Fried. Leipzig, 1920.

Mein Kriegs-Tagebuch. Vol. 4. *Das vierte Kriegsjahr und der Friede von Versailles (1. August 1917 bis 30. Juni 1919).* Zurich, 1920.

1925 "Jugenderinnerungen" [posthumous]. In *Der Völkerfriede*, a supplement to *FriedensWarte*, no. 1. Berlin, 1925.

Translations:

1896 Michel Revon, *Die Philosophie des Krieges.* Munich/Leipzig, 1896.

J. Novicow, *Der Krieg und seine angeblichen Wohltaten.* Leipzig, 1896. Second, improved edition. Zurich, 1915.

1897 Édouard Descamps, *Die Organisation eines internationalen Schiedsgerichtes. Eine Denkschrift an die Mächte.* Munich/Leipzig, undated [1897].

1899 J. Novicow, *Der ewige Krieg. Antwort auf die Schrift "Der ewige Friede" des Prof. Karl Fr. v. Stengel.* Berlin, 1899.

1900 Gaston Moch, *Die Armee der Demokratie.* Stuttgart, 1900.

Johann von Bloch, *Zur gegenwärtigen Lage in China. Eine politisch-wirtschaftliche Studie.* Berlin /Berne, 1900.

1901 J. Novicow, *Die Föderation Europas.* Berlin/Berne, 1901.

Johann von Bloch, *Die wahrscheinlichen politischen und wirtschaftlichen Folgen eines Zukunftskrieges zwischen Großmächten.* Berlin/Berne, 1901.

Jean Finot, *Die Philosophie der Langlebigkeit.* Berlin, 1901.

1903 Albert I., Prince of Monaco, *Eine Seemanns-Laufbahn.* Berlin, 1903; Berlin, undated, [1908].

1904 Paul Dubuisson, *Die Warenhausdiebinnen.* Leipzig, 1903. Second and third editions. Leipzig, 1904.

1905 D'Estournelles de Constant, *Rede über eine frz.-engl. Entente zur Beschränkung der maritimen Rüstungen.* Berlin, 1905.

Reymond Recouly, *Zehn Kriegsmonate in der Mandschurei. Eindrücke eines Augenzeugen.* Bremerhaven, 1905.

1907 D'Estournelles de Constant, *Bericht über die Beschränkung des Militärbudgets.* Berlin, 1907.

J. Novicow, *Die Gerechtigkeit und die Entfaltung des Lebens.* Berlin, 1907.

1909 Carnegie, Butler, Jefferson, *Amerika gegen die Rüstungen.* Berlin, 1909.

J. Novicow, *Das Problem des Elends.* Leipzig, 1909.

Sources and List of References
(NL refers to the "Nachlass" or estate papers)
(BA refers to the Bundesarchiv)

Unpublished Sources

Akademie der Künste, Berlin: Sammlung Carl-Hauptmann Archiv. Sign. 22.
Bibliothek des Haager Friedenspalastes. Den Haag: Y 3462 (17 Letters from A. H. Fried to Bertha von Suttner, 1892–1908).
Bibliothek des Nobelinstituts. Oslo: Redegjorelse for Nobels Fredspris IX-XI, 1909–1911. Candidate recommendations from the years 1909–1911 (Pfl/x) 1909–1911.
Bundesarchiv Berlin, Dept. Pressarchiv: R 8034-Reichslandbund/Band 133.
Bundesarchiv Koblenz: N 1001, NL Lujo Brentano, Vol. 18, N 1006; NL Georg Gothein, Vol. 20, 28, 54, N 1008; NL Alexander HohenloheSchillingsfürst, Vol. 65, 75, 76, 76a, N 1017; NL Hans Delbrück, Vol. 38, 48, 49, N 1136; NL Georg Jellinek, Vol. 8, N 1199; NL Hans Wehberg, Vol. 45, 59a/b, 65, 77. Small acquisitions: 311, 753, ZSg. 1 (DFG – German Peace Society), no. 29; ZSg. 103 (Lauterbach), Nr. 1298, 1333; ZSg. 2/140 (Pazifismus).
Hoover Institution Archive, Stanford: NL Fried, Box 3 (Correspondence with Oskar Fried, Heinrich Lammasch, Eduard Bernstein).
Internationales Institut fur Sozialgeschichte, Amsterdam: Otto Antrick 4, Eduard Bernstein G 315, Karl Kautsky C 425, DX 475/476.
Magistrat der Stadt Wien (Municipal authorities of the city of Vienna) Abt. 61: Certificates of origin (Heimatscheine) of the Fried and Engel families, Abt. 8: Registration records of the Fried and Engel families.
Münchner Stadtbibliothek, Literaturarchiv: NL Annette Kolb.
Politisches Archiv des Auswärtigen Amtes (Political archive of the Foreign Office), Berlin: R 65 (IA Europa Generalia, IAAa 37, Vol. 5), R 68 (IA Europa Generalia, IAAa 37, Vol. 8), R 74 (IA Europa Generalia, IAAa, 37, Vol. 14), R 78 (IA Europa Generalia, IAAa, 37, Vol.18), R 20341 (IA Weltkrieg, WK Nr. 1, Vol. 15), R 20343 (IA Weltkrieg, WK No.1, Bd .17), R 204 59 (IA Weltkrieg, WK No. 2 bound, Vol. 13), R 20460 (IA Weltkrieg, WK No. 2, bound Vol. 14), R 2576 (IA Deutschland, 175 secr., Vol. 1), R 2578 (IA Deutschland, 175 secr., Vol. 3).
Trude Simonsohn, Frankfurt: NL of Therese and Marie Fried, Family documents of the Fried and Simonsohn family (privately held), now kept in part with NL Fried, Völkerbundarchiv Geneva. Documents and records about the Simonsohn family are now located for the most part in NL Berthold Simonsohn, BA Koblenz.
Staatsbibliothek zu Berlin, Handschriftenabteilung (Manuscript department): K 161, NL Delbrück, K 31, NL von Harnack, collection of documents Darmstaedter.
Völkerbundarchiv Geneva: NL Fried (IPM/Fried/Suttner Papers, A.H. Fried): boxes 1–29: file 1–408: manuscripts, notes, documents, bills, etc. including, in boxes 26–28,

the correspondence with Bertha von Suttner; boxes 30–32: Fried's correspondence with the Holländer family; boxes 33–44: general correspondence of 1892–1903; boxes 45–86: general correspondence of 1903–1914; boxes 87–91: general correspondence of 1915–1921;boxes 92 (accessed July 2000): papers of Alfred and Therese Fried. NL Bertha von Suttner: (IPM/Fried/Suttner Papers, B. v. Suttner): box 2: diaries of 1907–1909, box 3: diaries of 1909–1911 und 1912–1914, box 19: Fried's letters to Bertha von Suttner. Administrative files on the League of Nations 29570.

Wiener Stadt- und Landesarchiv: Probate file of Alfred H. Fried, Collection of manuscripts I.N. 225.950 (mezzanine), Registration of the Jewish Community in Vienna.

Zentralbibliothek Zurich, Manuscript department: Ms Rascher 260.15.

Published Sources, Diaries, and Memoirs

Alg. Ned. Bond. "Vrede door Recht," published by Naar Weenen. XXI. Wereldcongres voor den Vrede, September 1914. No place of publication, undated.

Angell, Norman. *After All. The Autobiography of Norman Angell*. London 1951.

Angell, Norman. *Die falsche Rechnung. Was bringt der Krieg ein?* Berlin, undated.

Appelius, Stefan, ed. *Fritz Kuster. Der Frieden muss erkämpft werden. Aufsätze eines deutschen Pazifisten*. Oldenburg 1989.

Auslandstelle des Kriegspresseamts, ed. *Handbuch der Auslandpresse*. Berlin 1918.

Bender, Hans, ed. *Annette Kolb - Rene Schickele. Briefe im Exil 1933–1940*. Mainz 1987.

Benedikt, Heinrich. Die Friedensaktion der Meinlgruppe 1917/18. Die Bemühungen um einen Verständigungsfrieden nach Dokumenten, Aktenstücken und Briefen. Graz, Cologne 1962.

Benz, Wolfgang, ed. *Pazifismus in Deutschland. Dokumente zur Friedensbewegung 1890–1939*. Frankfurt a. M. 1988.

Benz, Wolfgang, ed. *Wilhelm Muehlon. Ein Fremder im eigenen Land. Erinnerungen und Tagebuchaufzeichnungen eines Krupp-Direktors 1908–1914*. Bremen 1989.

Brinker-Gabler, Gisela, ed. *Kämpferin für den Frieden: Bertha von Suttner. Lebenserinnerungen, Reden und Schriften. Eine Auswahl*. Frankfurt a. M. 1982.

Bund "Neues Vaterland." *Sollen wir annektieren? Kritische Denkschrift zur Eingabe der sechs großen wirtschaftlichen Verbände vom 20. Mai 1915*.

Carnegie, Andrew. *Geschichte meines Lebens*. Zurich 1993.

Christaller, P. "Die Geschichte der Esperanto-Bewegung 1887–1912." *Germana Esperantisto/Der Deutsche Esperantist*. Berlin, vol. 9, no. 6B (June 1912).

Fabian, Walter and Kurt Lenz, eds. *Die Friedensbewegung. Ein Handbuch der Weltfriedensströmungen der Gegenwart*. (Reprint of 1922 with a foreword by W. Fabian). Cologne 1985.

Fried, Alfred H. Bücher und Broschüren. See the list of references in the appendix and diverse newspaper articles.

Ganghofer, Ludwig: *Lebenslauf eines Optimisten*. Revised edition. Munich 1966.

Gerlach, Hellmut von. *Die große Zeit der Lüge. Der Erste Weltkrieg und die deutsche Mentalität (1871–1821*. Helmut Donat und Adolf Wild, eds. Bremen 1994.
Goldscheid, Rudolf: *Friedensbewegung und Menschenökonomie*. Berlin, Leipzig 1912.
Grosch, Georg. *Die Friedensorganisation der Staaten*. Second edition. Zurich undated.
Hohenlohe, Alexander von. *Aus meinem Leben*. Frankfurt a. M. 1925.
Jordan, David Starr. *Krieg und Mannheit*. Berlin, Leipzig 1912.
Jordan, David Starr. *The Days of a Man. Being Memories of a Naturalist, Teacher and Minor Prophet of Democracy*. 2 vols. Vol. 2: 1900–1921. New York 1922.
Kolb, Annette. *Die Last. Sechs Aufsätze*. Zurich 1918.
Kolb, Annette. *Zarastro-Westliche Tage*. Berlin 1921.
Lammasch, Heinrich. *Die Fortbildung des Völkerrechts durch die Haager Konferenz*. Stuttgart and Vienna 1900.
Lehmann-Russbüldt, Otto. *Der Kampf der Deutschen Liga für Menschenrechte, vormals Bund Neues Vaterland für den Weltfrieden (1914–1927)*. Berlin 1927.
Lenz, Kurt and Walter Fabian. *Die Friedensbewegung. Ein Handbuch der Weltfriedensströmungen der Gegenwart*. Berlin 1922.
Loewenthal, Eduard. *Mein Lebenswerk auf sozialpolitischem, neu-religiösem, philosophischem und naturwissenschaftlichem Gebiete. Memoiren*. Berlin 1910.
Meurer, Christian. *Die Haager Friedenskonferenz*. Vol. 1: *Das Friedensrecht der Haager Konferenz*. Munich 1905.
Moch, Gaston. *Die Armee der Demokratie*. Stuttgart 1900.
Nicolai, Georg Friedrich. *Die Biologie des Krieges. Erste Originalausgabe*, 2nd ed. Zurich 1919.
Nippold, Otfried. *Meine Erlebnisse in Deutschland vor dem Weltkriege (1909–1914)*. Berne 1918.
Nordau, Max. *Die konventionellen Lügen der Kulturmenschheit*. Leipzig, undated.
Novicow, J. *Der Krieg und seine angeblichen Wohltaten*. Leipzig 1896.
Novicow, J. *Die Föderation Europas*. Berlin and Berne 1901.
Pfeiffer-Belli, Wolfgang, ed. *Harry Graf Kessler. Tagebücher 1918–1937*. 4th ed. Frankfurt 1979.
Quidde, Ludwig. *Der deutsche Pazifismus während des Weltkrieges 1914–1918*. From his papers, edited by Karl Holl und Helmut Donat. Boppard 1979.
Revon, Michel. *Die Philosophie des Krieges*. Munich and Leipzig 1896.
Rolland, Romain. *Das Gewissen Europas. Tagebuch der Kriegsjahre 1914–1919*. 3 vols. Berlin, undated [1963].
Schlief, Eugen. *Der Frieden in Europa. Eine völkerrechtlich-politische Studie*. Leipzig 1892.
Schücking, Walther. *Der Dauerfriede. Kriegsaufsätze eines Pazifisten*. Leipzig 1917.
Schücking, Walther. *Der Weltfriedensbund und die Wiedergeburt des Völkerrechts*. Leipzig 1917.

Seber, Max. *Die Schicksalsstunde des Pazifismus.* Basel 1917.

Selenka, M. L., ed. *Die internationale Kundgebung der Frauen zur Friedens-Konferenz vom 15. Mai 1899.* Munich 1900.

Suttner, Bertha von. *Das Maschinenzeitalter. Zukunftsvorlesung über unsere Zeit von "Jemand."* Dresden 1889.

Suttner, Bertha von. *Der Kampf um die Vermeidung des Weltkriegs. Randglossen aus zwei Jahrzehnten zu den Zeitereignissen vor der Katastrophe (1892–1900 und 1907–1914).* 2 vols., edited by Alfred H. Fried. Zurich 1917.

Suttner, Bertha von. *Die Haager Friedenskonferenz. Tagebuchblätter.* Dresden 1900. (Reprint Dusseldorf 1982)

Suttner, Bertha von. *Memoiren.* Stuttgart und Leipzig 1909.

Suttner, Bertha von. *Stimmen und Gestalten.* Leipzig undated [1907].

Wehberg, Hans. *Als Pazifist im Weltkrieg.* Leipzig 1919.

Wehberg, Hans. *Die internationale Beschränkung der Rüstungen.* Stuttgart und Berlin 1919.

Wrede, Richard and Hans von Reinfels, eds. *Das geistige Berlin. Eine Enzyklopädie des geistigen Lebens Berlins.* Vol. 1. Berlin 1897.

Zweig, Stefan. *Die Welt von gestern. Erinnerungen eines Europäers.* Frankfurt 1955.

Newspapers

Annuaire de la vie internationale. Alfred H. Fried, ed. Vol. 1–3, Monaco 1905–1907. Second Series, Henri La Fontaine, Paul Otlet, Alfred H. Fried, eds. Vol. 1–2, 1908/09, 1910/11.

Der Zirkel. Heinrich Glücksmann, ed. Vol. 36–47. Vienna 1905/06 - 1916/17. Continued later as Wiener Freimaurer Zeitung.

Die Friedens-Warte. Alfred H. Fried, ed. Vol. 1–3 (July 1899-December 1901), Berlin; *Wochenschrift für internationale Verständigung*, Vols. 4–10 (January 1902–December 1908), Berlin; *Zeitschrift für internationale Verständigung*, Vols. 11–17 (January 1909-March/April 1915), Berlin; *Zeitschrift für zwischenstaatliche Organisation* (March-May 1915), Zurich; *Blätter für zwischenstaatliche Organisation.* Vols. 17–21 (June 1915-December 1919) Zurich; *Blätter für zwischenstaatliche Organisation*, Vol. 22 (1920), Leipzig; *Blätter für zwischenstaatliche Organisation* (Völkerbund), Rudolf Goldscheid, ed.: Vols. 23–24 (January 1923 – July 1924), Berlin; *Blätter für internationale Verständigung und zwischenstaatliche Organisation.* Founded by Alfred H. Fried. Hans Wehberg, ed.: Vols. 24–56 (August 1924–1961), Berlin, Schweidniz, Zurich, Basel; *Blätter für internationale Verständigung und zwischenstaatliche Organisation.*

Die Waffen nieder! Monatsschrift zur Förderung der Friedens-Bewegung. Bertha von Suttner, ed. Vols. 1 – 8, 1892–1899.

Friedensblätter. Organ der Deutschen Friedensgesellschaft. Berlin 1899 (3 editions), then published in Esslingen. Vols. 1–10, 1900–1909.

Monatliche Friedens-Korrespondenz. Published by the German Peace Society (Deutsche Friedens-Gesellschaft). Berlin. Vols. 3 - 6, Dresden 1896–1899.

Roseggers Heimgarten. Eine Monatsschrift. Hans Ludw. Rosegger, ed. Graz. Vols. 38–40,1914–1916.

Wiener Freimaurer-Zeitung. Published by the Grand Lodge of Vienna. Heinrich Glücksmann, ed. Vols.1–4, Vienna 1919–1922.

Biographical Literature on Alfred H. Fried

Abrams, Irwin. *The Nobel Peace Prize and the Laureates. An Illustrated Biographical History 1901–1987.* Boston 1988, pp. 71ff.

Dauber, Doris. *Alfred Hermann Fried und sein Pazifismus.* Diss. Leipzig 1924.

Friedrichs, Elsbeth. "Alfred H. Fried, der Pazifist." In *Neue Wege. Blätter für religiöse Arbeit.* Vol. ll. Basel 1917, pp. 416–429.

Friedrichs, Elsbeth. "Biographische Skizze." In Rudolf Goldscheid, ed. *Alfred H. Fried. Eine Sammlung von Gedenkblättern.* Leipzig 1922, pp. 5–10.

Goldscheid, Rudolf. *Alfred H. Fried. Eine Sammlung von Gedenkblättern in Gemeinschaft mit Therese Fried und Mundy Schwalb.* (edited by all three). Leipzig 1922.

Lovland, Jorgen G. "Presentation Alfred H. Fried, Biography and selected Bibliography." In *Frederick W. Haberman: Nobel Lectures: Peace 1901–1925.* Vol. 1. Amsterdam/London/New York 1972, pp. 238–242.

Renate Heuer, ed. *Lexikon deutsch-jüdischer Autoren, Archiv Bibliographica Judaica* Vol. 8. Munich 2000, pp. 3–19.

Reut-Nicolussi, Eduard. "Drei österreichische Rufer zum Frieden (Suttner, Fried, Lammasch)." In *Gemeinschaft des Geistes. Ein Symposium.* Vienna 1957, pp.121–155.

Riesenberger, Dieter. "Alfred Hermann Fried (1864–1921). Die Überwindung des Krieges durch zwischenstaatliche Organisation." In Christiane Rajewsky and Dieter Riesenberger, eds. *Wider den Krieg. Große Pazifisten von Immanuel Kant bis Heinrich Böll.* Munich 1987, pp. 54–60.

Stenke, Wolfgang. "Alfred Hermann Fried – 'ein Pazifist der Tat'." In Michael Neumann, ed.: *Der Friedens-Nobelpreis von 1901 bis heute.* Vol. 2.

Wehberg, Hans. "Alfred Fried." In *Deutsches Biographisches Jahrbuch.* Berlin 1914–1929. Vol. 3, pp. 105–106.

Wehberg, Hans. "Alfred H. Fried." In Hans Wehberg, ed. Die Führer der deutschen Friedensbewegung (1890 bis 1923). Leipzig 1923, pp. 19–23.

Wehberg, Hans. "Alfred Hermann Fried." In *Neue Deutsche Biographie.* Vol. 5. Berlin 1961, pp. 441–442.

Wolbe, Eugen. "Alfred H. Fried." In Herlitz/Kirschner, eds. *Jüdisches Lexikon.* Vol. 2. Berlin 1928, pp. 809–810.

Works Referenced

Acker, Detlev. *Walther Schücking (1875–1935)*. Münster 1970.

Appelius, Stefan. *Zur Geschichte des kämpferischen Pazifismus. Die programmatische Entwicklung der Deutschen Friedensgesellschaft 1929–1959*. Oldenburg 1988.

Ash, Mitchell G. and Christian H. Stifter, eds. *Wissenschaft, Politik und Öffentlichkeit. Von der Wiener Moderne bis zur Gegenwart*. Vienna 2002.

Bariéty, Jacques and Antonie Fleury, eds. *Friedens-Bewegung und -Anregungen in der internationalen Politik 1867–1928*. Berne 1987.

Barkeley, Richard. *Die deutsche Friedensbewegung 1870–1933*. Hamburg 1948.

Bauer, Josef. "Die österreichische Friedensbewegung." Diss., Vienna 1949.

Belke, Ingrid. "Die sozialreformerischen Ideen von Josef Popper-Lynkeus 1838–1921." Diss., Tübingen 1978.

Beller, Steven. *Wien und die Juden 1867–1938*. Vienna, Cologne, Weimar 1993.

Bentmann, Friedrich, ed. *Rene Schickele. Leben und Werk in Dokumenten*. Nuremberg, 1974.

Berlin um 1900. Ausstellung der Berlinischen Galerie in Verbindung mit der Akademie der Künste zu den Berliner Festwochen. Berlin 1984.

Bodendiek, Frank. *Walther Schückings Konzeption der internationalen Ordnung. Dogmatische Strukturen und ideengeschichtliche Bedeutung*. Berlin 2001.

Boll, Friedhelm. *Frieden ohne Revolution? Friedensstrategien der deutschen Sozialdemokratie vom Erfurter Programm 1891 bis zur Revolution 1918*. Bonn 1980.

Brink, Marianne. "Deutschlands Stellung zum Völkerbund in den Jahren 1918/1919–1922 unter besonderer Berücksichtigung der politischen Parteien und der paz. Vereinigungen." Diss., Berlin 1968.

Carnegie Endowment for International Peace, ed. *Year Book, no. 1–17*, Washington 1911–1928.

Chickering, Roger. "A Voice of Moderation in Imperial Germany. The 'Verband für internat. Verständigung', 1911–1914." *Journal of Contemporary History*. Vol. 8, no.1 (1973): 147–164.

Chickering, Roger. *Imperial Germany and a World Without War. The Peace Movement and German Society, 1892–1914*. Princeton 1975.

Cooper, Sandi E. ed. *Internationalism in Nineteenth-Century Europe: The Crisis of Ideas and Purpose*. New York 1976.

Cooper, Sandi E. "Liberal Internationalists before World War I." *Peace and Change* 1 (1973): 11–19.

Cooper, Sandi E. *Patriotic Pacifism. Waging War on War in Europe 1815–1914*. New York, Oxford 1991.

Csendes, Peter. *Geschichte Wiens*. Munich 1981.

Deubert, Holger. *Deutsch-französische Verständigung: Rene Schickele*. Munich 1993.
Dickmann, Fritz. *Friedensrecht und Friedenssicherung. Studien zum Friedensproblem in der neueren Geschichte*. Göttingen 1971.
Dietz, Alexander. *Franz Wirth und der Frankfurter Friedensverein. Zur Feier seines 25-jährigen Bestehens 1886–1911*. Frankfurt am Main 1911.
Dipper, Christof, Andreas Gestrich and Lutz Raphael, eds. *Krieg, Frieden und Demokratie. Festschrift für Martin Vogel zum 65. Geburtstag*. Frankfurt 2001.
Doerry, Martin. *Übergangsmenschen. Die Mentalität der Wilhelminer und die Krise des Kaiserreichs*. Weinheim and Munich 1986.
Donat, H. and J. P. Tammen, eds. *Friedenszeichen, Lebenszeichen*. Bremerhaven 1982.
Donat, Helmut and Karl Holl, eds. *Die Friedensbewegung. Organisierter Pazifismus in Deutschland, Österreich und in der Schweiz*. Düsseldorf 1983.
Dülffer, Jost and Karl Holl, eds. *Bereit zum Krieg. Kriegsmentalität im wilhelminischen Deutschland 1890–1914*. Göttingen 1986.
Dülffer, Jost and Gerd Krumeich, eds. *Der verlorene Frieden. Politik und Kriegskultur nach 1918*. Essen 2002.
Dülffer, Jost, Martin Kröger, Rolf-Harald Wippich, eds. *Vermiedene Kriege. Deeskalation von Konflikten der Großmächte zwischen Krimkrieg und Erstem Weltkrieg 1865–1914*. Munich 1997.
Dülffer, Jost. *Regeln gegen den Krieg? Die Haager Friedenskonferenzen von 1899 und 1907 in der internationalen Politik*. Berlin, Frankfurt, Vienna 1981.
Eyffinger, Arthur. *The 1899 Hague Peace Conference*. The Hague, London, Boston, undated.
Eisenbeiss, Wilfried. Die bürgerliche Friedensbewegung in Deutschland während des Ersten Weltkrieges: Organisation, Selbstverständnis und politische Praxis 1913/14–1919. Berne/Frankfurt am Main 1980.
Ermert, Karl, ed. *Surgery strike. Über Zusammenhänge von Sprache, Krieg und Frieden*. Loccum 1992.
Fischer, Fritz. *Griff nach der Weltmacht*. Kronberg 1977.
Fischer, Fritz. *Krieg der Illusionen. Die deutsche Politik von 1911–1914*. Düsseldorf 1969.
Fischer, Heinz-Dietrich. *Handbuch der politischen Presse in Deutschland 1480–1980*. Düsseldorf 1981.
Fischer-Baling, Eugen. "Der Untersuchungsausschuss für die Schuldfragen des ersten Weltkrieges." In *Aus Geschichte und Politik: Festschrift zum 70. Geburtstag von Ludwig Bergsträsser*, edited by Alfred Herrmann, 117–137. Düsseldorf 1954.
Foerster, Friedrich Wilhelm. *Erlebte Weltgeschichte 1869–1953. Memoiren*. Nuremberg 1953.
Fortuna, Ursula. *Der Völkerbundgedanke in Deutschland während des Ersten Weltkrieges*. Zurich 1974.

Fraenkel, Ernst. "Das deutsche Wilsonbild." *Jahrbuch für Amerikastudien* 5 (Heidelberg 1960): 66–120.

Fraenkel, Ernst. "Idee und Realität des Völkerbundes im deutschen politischen Denken." *VfZG* 16, no. 1 (1968): 1–14.

Fricke, Dieter, ed. *Die bürgerlichen Parteien in Deutschland. Handbuch der Geschichte der bürgerlichen Parteien und anderer bürgerlicher Interessenorganisationen vom Vormärz bis zum Jahre 1945*. 2 vols. Berlin 1968/70.

Fuchs, Albert. *Geistige Strömungen in Österreich 1867–1918*. First edition 1946. Vienna 1996.

Geiss, Imanuel. *Das Deutsche Reich und die Vorgeschichte des 1. Weltkriegs*. Munich and Vienna 1978.

Geyer, Michael. *Deutsche Rüstungspolitik 1860–1980*. Frankfurt 1984.

Gilg, Peter. *Die Erneuerung des demokratischen Denkens im Wilhelminischen Deutschland*. Wiesbaden 1965.

Gold, Hugo. *Geschichte der Juden in Wien. Ein Gedenkbuch*. Tel Aviv 1966.

Gollwitzer, Heinz. *Europabild und Europagedanke*, 2nd revised edition. Munich 1964.

Gollwitzer, Heinz: *Geschichte des weltpolitischen Denkens*. Vol 2: *Zeitalter des Imperialismus und der Weltkriege*. Göttingen 1982.

Grappin, Pierre. *Le Bund Neues Vaterland (1914–1916). Ses rapports avec Romain Rolland*. Lyon, Paris 1952.

Gross, Leo. *Pazifismus und Imperialismus. Eine kritische Untersuchung ihrer theoretischen Begründungen*. Leipzig, Vienna 1931.

Grossi, Verdiana. *Le Pacifisme Europeen 1889–1914*. Brussels 1994.

Grünewald, Guido, ed. *Nieder die Waffen! Hundert Jahre deutsche Friedensgesellschaft (1892–1992)*. Bremen 1992.

Grünewald, Guido. *Jahrgang 1892. Zur Geschichte der ältesten deutschen Friedensorganisation*. Velbert 1999.

Gülzow, Erwin. "Der Bund Neues Vaterland: Probleme der bürgerlich-paz. Demokratie im Ersten Weltkrieg." Diss., Berlin 1969.

Gumbel, Emil J. *Verräter verfallen der Ferne 1919–1929*. Berlin 1929.

Hagemann, Walter. "Die Europaidee bei Briand und CoudenhoveKalergi. Ein Vergleich." In *Aus Geschichte und Politik*, edited by Alfred Herrmann, 153–166. Düsseldorf 1954.

Hamann, Brigitte. *Bertha von Suttner. Ein Leben für den Frieden*. Munich 1986.

Hamann, Brigitte. *Hitlers Wien. Lehrjahre eines Diktators*. Munich, Zurich 1996.

Harth, Dietrich, Dietrich Schubert, Ronald Michael Schmidt, eds. *Pazifismus zwischen den Weltkriegen. Deutsche Schriftsteller und Künstler gegen Krieg und Militarismus 1918–1933*. Heidelberg 1985.

Heinemann, Gottfried, Wolf-Dietrich Schmied-Kowarzik, eds. *Sabotage des Schicksals*. Tübingen 1982.

Herz, Heinz. *Alleingang wider die Mächtigen. Ein Bild vom Leben und Kämpfen Moritz van Egidys*. Leipzig 1970.

Hiller, Kurt. *Pazifismus der Tat - Revolutionärer Pazifismus*. Berlin 1981.

Höhne, Günther. "Zur Stellung führender Pazifisten zum Versailler Vertrag." *Jenaer Beiträge zur Parteiengeschichte*, no. 26/27, Jena 1970.

Holl, Karl, Hans Kloft, Gerd Fesser. *Caligula-Wilhelm II. und der Cäsarenwahnsinn. Antikenrezeption und wilhelminische Politik am Beispiel des "Caligula" von Ludwig Quidde*. Bremen 2001.

Holl, Karl, Anne C. Kjelling, eds. *The Nobel Peace Prize and the Laureates. The Meaning and Acceptance of the Nobel Peace Prize in the Prize Winners Countries*. Frankfurt am Main 1994.

Holl, Karl. "Die Vereinigung Gleichgesinnter: Ein Berliner Kreis pazifistischer Intellektueller im 1. Weltkrieg." *Archiv für Kulturgeschichte*, 54 (1972): 364–384.

Holl, Karl. "Europapolitik im Vorfeld der deutschen Regierungspolitik. Zur Tätigkeit proeuropäischer Organisationen in der Weimarer Republik." *HZ*, 219 (1974): 33–94.

Holl, Karl. *Pazifismus in Deutschland*. Frankfurt am Main 1988.

Hoover Institution on War, Revolution, and Peace, ed. *Catalog of The Western Language Collection*, Volume 63, Special Collections, Boston 1969.

Hürten, Heinz. *Friedenssicherung und Abrüstung. Erfahrungen aus der Geschichte*. Graz, Vienna, Cologne 1983.

Johnston, William M. *Österreichische Kultur- und Geistesgeschichte. Gesellschaft und Ideen im Donauraum 1848 bis 1938*. Vienna, Cologne, Graz 1974.

Josephson, Harold, ed. *Biographical Dictionary of Modern Peace Leaders*. Westport and London 1985.

Kaut, Hubert (curator). *Bertha von Suttner und die Anfänge der Österreichischen Friedensbewegung. Katalog der Sonderausstellung des Historischen Museums der Stadt Wien und der österreichischen Friedensgesellschaft*. Vienna 1950.

Keil, Martha, ed. *Jüdisches Städtebild*. Vienna, Frankfurt am Main 1995.

Keiner, Peter K. *Bürgerlicher Pazifismus und "Neues Völkerrecht." Hans Wehberg (1885–1962)*. Freiburg 1976.

Kelly, Andrew. "Film as Antiwar Propaganda: Lay Down Your Arms (1914)." *Peace and Change* 16 (1991): 97–112.

Kempf, Beatrix. *Bertha von Suttner. Das Lebensbild einer großen Frau*. Vienna 1964.

Kobler, Franz, ed. *Gewalt und Gewaltlosigkeit. Handbuch des aktiven Pazifismus*. Zurich, Leipzig 1928.

Kohler, Fritz. "DFG seit 1892." In Dieter Fricke: *Die bürgerlichen Parteien in Deutschland. Handbuch der Geschichte der bürgerlichen Parteien*. 2 vols. Vol 1: 191–240, Leipzig 1968–70.

Korol, Martin. "Deutsches Präexil in der Schweiz 1916–1918." Diss., Bremen 1999.

Koszyk, Kurt. *Deutsche Presse im 19. Jahrhundert. Geschichte der deutschen Presse, Teil II*. 1966.
Koszyk, Kurt. *Deutsche Pressepolitik im 1.Weltkrieg*. Düsseldorf 1968.
Kraus, Andreas. *Geschichte Bayerns. Von den Anfängen bis zur Gegenwart*. Munich 1983.
Krock, Alfred. *Geschichte des Alldeutschen Verbandes 1890–1939*. Wiesbaden 1954.
Kuehl, Warren F., ed. *Biographical Dictionary of Internationalists*. Westport and London 1983.
Lang, Gustav A. *Kampfplatz der Meinungen*. Zurich 1968.
Laurence, Richard R. "The Viennese Press and the Peace Movement 1899–1914." *Michigan Academician* 13 (1980): 155–163.
Lebedev, Andrej Konstantinovich. *V.V. Vereshchagin*. Moscow 1988.
Lemp, Richard. *Annette Kolb. Leben und Werk einer Europäerin*. Mainz 1970.
Lennhoff, Eugen, Oskar Posner, Dieter A. Binder. *Internationales Freimaurer-Lexikon*, revised and expanded version of the 1932 edition, Munich 2000.
Lennhoff, Eugen. *Die Freimaurer*. Reprint of the 1929 edition. Vienna, Munich 1981.
Lichtblau, Albert. *Antisemitismus und soziale Spannung in Berlin und Wien 1867–1914*. Berlin 1994.
Liedtke, Marianne. *Die Entwicklung des Pazifismus von der 1. zur 2. Haager Konferenz*. Cologne 1953.
Lütgemeier-Davin, Reinhold. *Pazifismus zwischen Kooperation und Konfrontation. Das Deutsche Friedenskartell in der Weimarer Republik*. Cologne 1982.
Marki, Hans. *Berühmte Ruhestätten auf Wiener Friedhöfen*. Vol 1: *Zentralfriedhof und Krematorium*. Vienna 1961.
Mattenklott, Gert, ed. *Jüdisches Städtebild Berlin*. Frankfurt am Main 1997.
Mauch, Christof, Tobias Brenner. *Für eine Welt ohne Krieg. Otto Umfrid und die Anfänge der Friedensbewegung*. Schönaich 1987.
Mauermann, Helmut. *Das Internationale Friedensbüro 1892–1950*. Stuttgart 1990.
Mendelssohn, Peter de. *Zeitungsstadt Berlin. Menschen und Mächte in der Geschichte der deutschen Presse*. Expanded new edition. Frankfurt, Berlin, Vienna 1982.
Meulen, Jacob ter. *Der Gedanke der internationalen Organisation in seiner Entwicklung*. 2 vols. The Hague 1929–1940.
Neumann, Michael, ed. *Der Friedens-Nobelpreis von 1901 bis heute*. Vol. 2: *Der Friedens-Nobelpreis von 1905 bis 1916*. Zug 1988.
Niedhart, Gottfried and Dieter Riesenberger, eds. *Lernen aus dem Krieg? Deutsche Nachkriegszeiten 1918 und 1945*. Munich 1992.
Nielsen, Erika, ed. *Focus on Vienna 1900. Change and Continuity in Literature, Music, Art and Intellectual History*. Munich 1982.
Pasiersbsky, Fritz. *Krieg und Frieden in der Sprache. Eine sprachwissenschaftliche Textanalyse*. Frankfurt am Main 1983.

Pfeil, Alfred. *Der Völkerbund*. Darmstadt 1976.
Potter, Pitman B. "Origin of the Term International Organization." *The American Journal of International Law*. (Washington 1945): 803–806.
Rajewski, Christiane and Dieter Riesenberger, eds. *Wider den Krieg. Große Pazifisten von Kant bis Böll*. Munich 1987.
Raschke, Joachim. *Soziale Bewegungen. Ein historisch-systematischer Grundriss*. Frankfurt, New York 1985.
Reichel, Karl Ferdinand. *Die pazifistische Presse*. Würzburg 1938.
Rieger, Isolde. *Die wilhelminische Presse im Überblick 1888–1918*. Munich 1957.
Riesenberger, Dieter. *Geschichte der Friedensbewegung in Deutschland. Von den Anfängen bis 1933*. Göttingen 1985.
Riesenberger, Dieter. "Deutsche Emigration und Schweizer Neutralität im Ersten Weltkrieg." *Schweizerische Zeitschrift für Geschichte* 38 (Basel 1988): 127ff.
Rogge, Heinrich. *Nationale Friedenspolitik. Handbuch des Friedensproblems und seiner Wissenschaft*. Berlin 1934.
Rozenblit, Marsha L: *Die Juden Wiens 1867–1914. Assimilation und Identität*. Vienna, Cologne, Graz 1988.
Saur, Klaus Gerhard, ed. *Aus alten Börsenblättern*. Munich 1966.
Scheer, Friedrich-Karl. *Die Deutsche Friedensgesellschaft (1892–1933). Organisation, Ideologie, politische Ziele*. 2nd improved edition. Frankfurt am Main 1983.
Schlochauer, Hans-Jürgen. *Die Idee des ewigen Friedens*. Frankfurt am Main 1953.
Schmutzer, Ernst, ed. *Sprache des Friedens*. Jena 1990.
Schoeps, Hans-Joachim. *Zeitgeist im Wandel. Das Wilhelminische Zeitalter*. Stuttgart 1967.
Seubert, Holger. *Deutsch-französische Verständigung. Rene Schickele*. Munich 1993.
Skalnik, Kurt. *Dr. Karl Lueger. Der Mann zwischen den Zeiten*. Vienna, Munich 1954.
Smekal, Ferdinand G. *Österreichs Nobelpreisträger*. Vienna, Stuttgart, Zurich 1961.
Sösemann, Bernd. *Theodor Wolff. Der Chronist. Krieg, Revolution und Frieden im Tagebuch 1914–1919*. Munich 1997.
Spalt, K. H., ed. *Der weite Weg. Ein Handbuch über den Pazifismus*. Aachen 1946.
Starker, Gerda. "Die geschichtliche Entwicklung des deutschen Pazifismus seit 1900. Ein Beitrag zum Zusammenbruch Deutschlands im Weltkrieg." Diss., Heidelberg 1935.
Steffahn, Harald. *Bertha von Suttner*. Reinbek 1998.
Steinhauser, Mary / Dokumentationsarchiv des österreichischen Widerstandes, eds. *Totenbuch Theresienstadt*. Vienna 1987.
Stiewe, Dorothee. "Die bürgerliche deutsche Friedensbewegung als soziale Bewegung bis zum Ende des Ersten Weltkriegs." Diss., Freiburg 1972.

Stürmer, Michael. *Das Deutsche Reich 1870–1919*. Berlin 2002.
Suchy, Barbara. "The Verein zur Abwehr des Antisemitismus. I. From its Beginnings to the First World War." *LBI Year Book* 28 (1983): 205–238. II. "From the First World War to its Dissolution in 1933." *LBI Year Book* 30 (1985): 67–103.
Tetzlaff, Walter. *2000 Kurzbiographien bedeutender deutscher Juden des 20. Jahrhunderts*. Lindhorst 1982.
Thimme, Hans. *Weltkrieg ohne Waffen. Die Propaganda der Westmächte gegen Deutschland, ihre Wirkung und ihre Abwehr*. Stuttgart, Berlin 1932.
Toury, Jacob. *Die jüdische Presse im Österreichischen Kaiserreich*. Tübingen 1983.
Toury, Jacob. *Die politische Orientierung der Juden in Deutschland. Von Jena bis Weimar*. Tübingen 1966.
Toury, Jacob. *Traum und Wirklichkeit, Wien 1870–1930. Katalog zur Sonderausstellung des Historischen Museums der Stadt Wien*. Vienna 1985.
Uhlig, Ralph. *Die Interparlamentarische Union 1889–1914*. Stuttgart 1988.
Völkerbundarchiv Genf, ed. *Bertha von Suttner. Katalog zur Ausstellung*. Geneva 1993.
Vondung, Klaus, ed. *Das wilhelminische Bildungsbürgertum*. Göttingen 1976.
Wagner, Hermann. *Die Welthilfssprache Esperanto*. Stuttgart 1946.
Walther, Rudolf. "Friede und NichtKrieg. Ideologie, regulative Idee oder Realziel? Zur Geschichte des Pazifismus." *Frankfurter Rundschau* no. 98, 27 (April 2002): 21.
Wank, Solomon, ed. *Doves and Diplomats. Foreign Offices and Peace Movements in Europe and America in the Twentieth Century*. Westport, London 1978.
Wehberg, Hans. "Die deutsche Friedensbewegung 1870–1933." *Friedens-Warte* (1948): 247–251.
Wehberg, Hans. *Die Führer der deutschen Friedensbewegung (1890–1923)*. Leipzig 1923.
Wehberg, Hans. *Ideen und Projekte betr. die Vereinigten Staaten von Europa in den letzten 100 Jahren*. Bremen 1984. (Reprint from the issue 2/3 of the *Friedens-Warte*, 1941).
Wehberg, Hans. *Ludwig Quidde. Ein deutscher Demokrat und Vorkämpfer der Völkerverständigung*. Offenbach a. M. 1948.
Wehler, Hans-Ulrich. *Das Deutsche Kaiserreich 1871–1918*. Göttingen 1983.
Wette, Wolfram. *Militarismus und Pazifismus. Auseinandersetzung mit den deutschen Kriegen*. Bremen 1991.
Wieland, Lothar. "Diese Lebensauffassung ist undeutsch. Zur Bekämpfung und Verfolgung des Pazifismus in Deutschland von 1914 bis 1933." In *Friedenszeichen, Lebenszeichen*, edited by Donat/Tammen, 241–257. Bremerhaven 1982.
Wiener Beiträge zur Geschichte der Neuzeit. Vol. 11. Munich 1981.
Wild, Adolf. *Baron d'Estournelles de Constant (1852–1924)*. Hamburg 1973.
Wistrich, Robert S. *The Jews of Vienna in the Age of Franz Joseph*. Oxford 1990.

Young, Nigel. "Why Peace Movements Fail: An Historical and Social Overview." *Social Alternatives* 4 (1984): 9–16.
Zechlin, Egmont. "Die 'Zentralorganisation für einen dauernden Frieden' und die Mittelmächte. Ein Beitrag zur politischen Tätigkeit Rudolf Launs im ersten Weltkrieg." *Jahrbuch für internationales Recht* 11 (1962): 448–511.
Zechlin, Egmont. *Die deutsche Politik und die Juden im Ersten Weltkrieg*. Göttingen 1969.
Ziemann, Benjamin, ed. *Perspektiven der Historischen Friedensforschung*. Essen 2002.
Zirkel und Winkelmaß. *200 Jahre Große Landesloge der Freimaurer*. Vienna 1984.
Zuelzer, Wolf. *Der Fall Nicolai*. Frankfurt a. M. 1981.
Zweig, Stefan. *Die Welt von gestern. Erinnerungen eines Europäers*. Frankfurt am Main 1955.
Zweig, Stefan. *Die schlaflose Welt. Aufsätze und Vorträge aus den Jahren 1909–1941*. Frankfurt 1990.

Index

Adler, Moritz 65
Antrick, Otto 102, 109
Anzengruber, Ludwig 11, 12
Arnhold, Georg 55, 224, 241, 265ff.

Bajer, Fredrik 49, 159, 160, 165
Bar, Carl Ludwig von 125, 160, 265, 268
Barbusse, Henri 206
Barth, Theodor 37, 39, 42
Baumbach, Karl Dr. 37
Becher, Johannes R. 206
Benn, Gottfried 206
Bernstein, Eduard 204, 241, 267, 270
Bloch, Ernst 205f., 241
Bloch, Heinrich von 260
Bloch, Johann von (Jan Bloch) 69, 76f., 79, 84, 193, 255, 260, 262, 292
Boll, Ernst 54
Bölsche, Wilhelm 37
Borel, Jean 92ff.
Bousset, Hermann 59
Brahm, Otto 22
Brasch, Moritz 41
Bucher-Heller, Franz 189
Butler, Nicholas Murray 155f. 167f.

Calwer, Richard 45
Carl, René 201f.
Cassirer, Paul 22
Chiavacci, Vincenz 1

Decker, Fritz 127
Dorn, Alexander von 174
Ducommun, Elie 47, 143
Dumba, Konstantin 158
Dunant, Henry 70, 76, 118, 164

Egidy, Moritz von 40f., 54, 88
Eickhoff, Richard 152, 264
Eisner, Kurt 204, 213
Engel, Katharina 5
Engel, Moritz 1, 5, 10, 15, 23, 110
Estournelles de Constant, Paul Henri Benjamin Baron d' x, 77, 79, 81, 154ff.,
Eysinga, Jonkheer Willem 169
Feldhaus, Richard 123

Fernau, Hermann 197, 217
Fischer, Samuel 22
Foerster, Friedrich Wilhelm 198f., 217, 272, 277
Foerster, Wilhelm 40, 161
Fontaine, Henri La 125, 131, 161
Frank, Leonhard 206
Frankl, Emil, Dr. 144, 184, 187, 234, 236, 240, 245, 294
Frankl, Ludwig August 12
Frankl, Siegfried 2f., 9, 12, 18f., 57, 97f., 100f., 111
Frankl, Therese 4, 57f., 91, 97ff., 106f., 108f., 111, 124, 127, 140, 166f., 169, 174f., 180, 185, 187, 229, 233ff., 240f., 243ff., 260, 281
Fried, Berta neé Engel 1ff., 6, 10, 14, 85, 161, 227
Fried, Carl Theodor 2, 84, 100, 108
Fried, David Leopold 2, 14, 84, 92, 93, 100, 108, 109, 180, 210, 235, 236, 244, 246
Fried, Pauline 2, 6, 13, 14, 23, 84, 101f., 107f., 209, 243, 246f.
Fried, Sidonie 2, 5, 6, 84, 85, 180, 243, 246
Friedrichs, Elsbeth 170, 220, 223, 232, 240

Ganghofer, Ludwig Albert 1, 104, 180, 202
Gerlach, Hellmut von 241, 281, 282
Glücksmann, Heinrich 144, 202, 225, 231
Gnadenfeld, Gertrud 28, 45, 58
Gnadenfeld, Jacques 26ff.
Gobat, Albert 188
Goldscheid, Rudolf 146ff., 174, 225, 268, 280ff.
Goldstein, Arnold 110
Gothein, Georg 104, 187, 204, 264
Grelling Richard 27f., 41, 42f., 46, 48f., 50f., 56, 191f., 205, 206, 217, 241
Groller, Balduin 116, 176

Haberland, George 51, 53, 56,
Haeckel, Ernst 65
Harmening, E. Dr. 41
Hart, Heinrich und Julius 88f.
Hasenclever, Walter 206
Heilberg, Adolf 156, 241
Heimann, Moritz 30

Hein, Adolf 53
Hiller, Kurt 206, 208, 252ff., 281
Hirsch, Max Dr. 37, 39, 51, 53ff., 74
Hohenlohe-Schillingsfürst, Alexander Prinz of 206, 27
Holländer, Felix 57, 58f., 89
Holländer, Martha 57ff., 92, 96ff., 101, 110f., 260

Katscher, Leopold 65, 127, 196
Kerr, Alfred 22, 65
Kohler, Josef 42
Kolb, Annette 207f., 213, 219, 227, 233, 241, 249,
Kreutz, Rudolf Jeremias 238, 277

Lammasch, Heinrich 116, 140f., 158, 269, 271, 277
Land, Hans 29, 51f., 57
Landauer, Gustav 89
Langen, Martin Dr. 72f.
Latzko, Andreas 206f.
Lazare, Bernard 63
Lehmann-Russbüldt, Otto 226, 277, 283
Leroy-Beaulieu, Pierre Paul 84
Levysohn, Arthur Dr. 37
Liebknecht, Karl 212, 213
Liebknecht, Wilhelm 43, 65
Loewenthal, Eduard Dr. 36, 48, 50f.
Lueger, Karl Dr. 103ff., 142

Marr, Wilhelm 22
Mauthner, Fritz 37
Mayreder, Rosa 158, 277
Mehlisch, Adolf 127, 132
Meinl, Julius 158
Meurer, Christian 264
Meyer, Albert 195
Mez, John Dr. 185, 278ff.
Moch, Gaston 65, 90, 120, 124, 160f.
Moneta, Ernesto T. 159, 160, 162, 165
Moscheles, Felix 34, 77, 161, 255, 258, 260
Müller, Adolf Dr. 222

Neufville, Eduard de 127, 241, 268
Nicolai, Georg Friedrich x, 220
Niemeyer, Theodor 159
Nippold, Otfried 148ff., 162, 185, 187, 188, 192f., 241, 263, 194ff., 210, 238, 240, 271, 279

Nordau, Max 65
Novicow, Jacques 49, 50, 70, 84, 113, 123, 132, 146, 159, 160, 255, 263, 288f.

Oppenheim, L. 160f.
Otlet, Paul 125

Passy, Frederic 165, 263
Penzig, Rudolph Dr. 54
Perris, G. H. 132
Prudhommeaux, Jules 131

Quidde, Ludwig x, 40, 96, 123, 138, 139, 149, 152, 16ff., 189, 217, 220, 228, 239, 241, 251f., 267, 280

Reinhardt, Max 22
Reuter, Richard 49, 50, 77
Revon, Michel 75, 107
Richet, Charles 77, 255
Richter, Adolf 56, 96, 123, 161, 163
Rolland, Romain 187, 206f., 281
Rossler, Heinrich Dr. 52, 72
Ruyssen, Theodore 277

Schickele, René 207ff., 226f., 233, 241
Schlief, Eugen 39ff., 43, 123, 132
Schmidt, Adolf 90f.
Schnitzler, Arthur 116, 225
Schönaich-Carolath, Heinrich Prinz zu 37
Schücking, Walther 139f., 149ff., 154, 160ff., 185, 217, 236, 241, 251f., 265, 268, 278ff., 286, 295
Schwalb, Rosamunde (Mundy) 166, 174, 185ff., 222f., 226f., 232ff., 236, 240, 241, 243, 245, 249, 276, 278, 280, 295
Schwonder, Oskar 200, 263
Selenka, Margarethe Leonore 73, 123, 241, 255
Simonsohn, Alfred 85
Simonsohn, Berthold 243, 246
Simonsohn, Trude 246, 250
Spielhagen, Friedrich 37
Starr Jordan, David 225, 229, 248, 267, 278
Stead, William T. 74, 90, 127, 162, 255
Stein, Maximilian 46
Stöcker, Adolf 22
Stöcker, Helene 280
Stürgkh, Karl Graf von 199
Südekum, Albert 41, 45, 63f.

INDEX

Suttner, Arthur Gundaccar Baron von   44, 105
Suttner, Bertha Baroness of   ix, x, 31ff., 37ff., 48, 55, 63, 67, 69f., 72ff., 79, 82, 84, 85, 87, 98ff., 104f., 109, 111ff., 119, 126f., 141, 144, 160f., 165, 167, 174ff., 184, 188, 196, 225, 228ff., 234f., 239, 241f., 244f., 247, 249, 254f., 261f., 264ff., 268, 281, 290ff., 295
Suttner, Rudolf   249

Ten Kate, Jan   6, 108
Treitschke, Heinrich von   22, 182

Ude, Johannes   158
Umfrid, Otto   x, 56, 65, 72, 106, 123, 263, 264, 271

Vereshchagin, Vasily Vasilyevich   16, 76, 287

Wavrinsky, Eduard   159, 161
Wehberg, Hans   x, 139f., 148, 152ff., 161f., 163f., 167f., 177f., 185, 193, 199, 219, 233f., 236, 241ff., 249, 251f., 264ff., 268, 271, 276, 278f., 280, 282ff., 295
Wilson, Woodrow   119, 203f., 210f., 214ff.
Wirth, Franz   37, 47ff., 52
Wrede, Richard   85
Wyon, Gordon   209, 243, 247, 250
Wyon, Lionel   209ff.
Wyon, Reginald   101, 108, 209

Zamenhof, Ludwig Dr.   91ff., 93
Zweig, Stefan   206

Printed in the United States
by Baker & Taylor Publisher Services